Managing Strateg

Managing Strategic Design

Ray Holland

and

Busayawan Lam

First published 2014 by
PALGRAVE

Palgrave in the UK is an imprint of Macmillan Publishers Limited, registered in England, company number 785998, of 4 Crinan Street, London N1 9XW.

Palgrave Macmillan in the US is a division of St Martin's Press LLC, 175 Fifth Avenue, New York, NY 10010.

Palgrave is a global imprint of the above companies and is represented throughout the world.

Palgrave® and Macmillan® are registered trademarks in the United States, the United Kingdom, Europe and other countries.

ISBN 978–1–137–32594–5

This book is printed on paper suitable for recycling and made from fully managed and sustained forest sources. Logging, pulping and manufacturing processes are expected to conform to the environmental regulations of the country of origin.

A catalogue record for this book is available from the British Library.

A catalog record for this book is available from the Library of Congress.

Typeset by MPS Limited, Chennai, India.

Printed in China.

Contents

List of Figures

List of Tables

Acknowledgements

The authors wish to thank their close colleagues in Brunel Design, in particular the postgraduate design management team members John Boult, Dr Youngok Choi and Chris Holt (who first conceived the idea of the 4D model), for their immensely valuable development of design strategy thinking which informed this book. Thanks also to the many industry and consultancy collaborators who give support and bring the subject to life by sharing their experiences, in particular Nick Gray (Design Bridge), Les Wynn (Xerox) and Jim Stewart (Design Q). Also to our principal supporters overseas, Dr Paul Cheng (Taiwan), Professor Deuksoo Kim (Korea) and Professor Qiu Song and Teddy Ma (China).

We are grateful to the UK Design Council for allowing us to use/adapt their published tools.

A special thank you is due to the hundreds of masters and PhD researchers who shared their thinking with us. It was, and continues to be, a great learning environment.

Thank you to our editors, Jenny Hindley, Martin Drewe and Rachel Bridgewater, for steering us so skillfully through this new experience.

Part I

INTRODUCING STRATEGIC DESIGN

Managing strategic design begins with a revision of the way that managers view design. There remains a widespread misconception that design is only an artistic endeavour for the purpose of adding beauty of style to the engineered functions of products. This in turn relegates design to a lowly service function to be called upon when the business/marketing strategy is complete, usually by presenting the designers with a brief. Many higher level managers miss the opportunity to gain the benefits of designers' creativity by not including them in strategic planning processes, indeed designers are often dismissed as having nothing valuable to contribute.

There remain vestiges of the management "myth" that designers are somehow different, difficult to manage (at least in the established way) and should be kept at arm's length. However many of the world's most successful organizations treat design with high respect and have integrated design fully into their activities. They have long established the strategic management of manufacturing, marketing, human resources, finance, research and development (R&D) and information, now they are addressing the strategic management of design. The benefits accruing to organizations can be identified and the momentum for innovation increased.

First it is necessary to redefine design and establish its power to contribute to management throughout the organization. Hence, the first section of this chapter introduces the relationship between management and design, the meaning and nature of design strategy and establishes the fundamental principles of developing a design strategy.

Chapter 1 goes on to address the relationship of Big-D design, holistic design thinking, and small-d design, hands-on design. Their equality of importance is emphasized as contributors to a real, added-value, designed experience. Three levels of managing strategic design are established and their activities and interdependence are explored.

In Chapter 2, the underlying tenets of the management of design strategy are explained through the 4Ds of the strategic design framework. The 4Ds model has the intrinsic advantage of being recognizable to management as part of their established practice and will thus demonstrate that design can be effectively introduced, developed, monitored, controlled and ultimately integrated into any organization.

1

Chapter 1
STRATEGIC DESIGN

Strategic design refers to using design management to drive and implement corporate strategic goals. It creates vision and integrates and orchestrates collaboration across disciplines in order to deliver real value to all stakeholders through creative solutions to business, social and environmental problems. It evolved from recognition of the potential of strategic design to contribute to business performance management: "Design Management is the business side of design" claimed the Design Management Institute in 2010. But it is now acknowledged to have the potential to contribute to the management and performance of all kinds of organizations, encompassing the "totality of design activity, its administration and contribution to an organisation's performance" (BSI, 2008).

A well-developed design strategy can deliver performance and competitive advantages across the triple bottom line of the economic, social/cultural and environmental aims of an organization. It combines artistic and scientific thinking concurrently (right-brain and left-brain thinking) to generate synergy in identifying innovation opportunities, evaluating alternative new directions and ultimately guiding management decision making. Grounded in powerful underlying theoretical models, a design strategy can be developed to address a very wide range of contemporary issues by posing the question "How can my design strategy contribute to improving performance/wellbeing in...?" It should always lead to a pragmatic implementation plan and a clear identification of the principal users and beneficiaries.

Objectives for this chapter:

- To explain the meaning of design and strategy;
- To evaluate the principal contributions of design to strategic management;
- To plot the evolution of design into management of business;
- To identify the characteristics of tangible and intangible design;
- To introduce the emergence of Big-D design and its relationship to small-d design;
- To compare design thinking and strategic thinking and examine their relationship;
- To explore the potential of design to support and develop management strategy;
- To apply the principles of design management to three levels of the organization;
- To establish the inter-dependency and relationship of the three levels.

1.1 THE NATURE OF STRATEGIC DESIGN

1.1.1 The Meaning of Design and Strategy

Defining *design* is an almost insurmountable problem, but in order to manage design well it is necessary to attempt it. The first stage is to review the existing meanings associated with design, then to introduce or refine a new way of looking at it.

Managers still tend to think of design as an artistic skill. The term "designer" conjures up images of somewhat Bohemian young people with very individual dress and hair styles, possibly immature in their attitudes and sense of responsibility. These young (on the whole) designers study such subjects as graphic design, fashion design, interior and product design and frequently show little interest in management of organizations. Thus, the myriad definitions of design usually preclude any reference to the benefits to management.

Designers themselves usually think of design as a process or a way of thinking. Indeed designers are taught to use processes to support their creative thinking as steps to the achievement of, for example, new products or services. These new products/services are also called designs. Therefore design is both a process and an outcome.

A useful working definition of design was provided by HM Treasury in 2005 as "design links creativity and innovation. It shapes ideas to become practical and attractive propositions for users or customers" (HM Treasury, 2005). In other words, design is about transforming creativity into practical, desirable and, in many cases, profitable applications that can be managed effectively, acquired, used and/or consumed by target audiences.

So design has come to mean much more than simply the artistic aspect. It has grown to reflect its increasing influence on the performance management of organizations. Almost all designers are now introduced to the influence of their work on the management of organizations and in particular marketing, and advanced education programmes address the use of design as a strategic weapon in the highly competitive business and social environment.

The famous management writer Henry Mintzberg offered five characteristics of a strategy as: plan, ploy, patterns, position and perspective. The strategy begins with a *plan,* a consciously intended course of action indicating what to do and how to do it. The *ploy* is less tangible, indeed when considering the description "ruse or trick" it almost seems dishonest. But the ploy is central to design's contribution to a strategy as it seeks to gain advantage over competitors through creative ideas. Designers operate at the cutting edge of the ploy, constantly looking for new opportunities, incremental and step-change improvements. In a sense all good designers are malcontents who want constant improvement.

The third aspect of strategy is *patterns* of, for example, the processes or methods used by an organization; what Charles Handy calls "the way we do things around here." Managers will always recognize that organizations do some things better than others and this is an essential element of their strategy to win. The *position* refers to where you want to be, the aim of the strategy, for example "to capture 25% of the market," and here the relationship between the design and marketing functions becomes critical as feedback from consumers drives design concepts and development. Finally *perspective* relates to the organization's outlook on the world, its purpose for existence. Businesses exist to make profit but must be increasingly aware of their social and environmental responsibilities. Charities exist to support people in need, hospitals to treat sickness, etc. Thus the primary purpose is central to the strategy.

For design to be strategic, the process and outcomes must be purposeful and effective. Purposes could be business goals and objectives, governmental targets, or charitable and social causes. The recognition of the power of design to contribute strategically is still relatively new. As recently as the early 1990s it was still regarded as an adjunct to industrial design to support such areas as lifestyle research and futures forecasting. In recent years the benefits of strategic design have been identified to incorporate:

- conceiving and creating added-value products and services;
- building product/service differentiation and customer loyalty;
- designing and developing total brand experiences;
- acting as a catalyst, integrator and mediator between professional domains, both within the organization (e.g. marketing, manufacturing) and outside (e.g. supply chains, distributors);
- possessing a hard-to-imitate tacit knowledge resource;
- shaping and developing an organization's internal culture;
- exploring uncertainty and evaluating risk and potential, through prototyping and visualization;
- stimulating creativity and providing fresh perspectives for strategic management.

The challenge for management is to recognize the potential of design and create an integrated, coherent design policy that can positively impact on organizational performance.

Example: Joseph Joseph

Joseph Joseph is a design-led kitchenware company founded by twin brothers, Richard and Antony Joseph. They have made a good use of their expertise and experiences in design and business (Antony was trained as a product designer and Richard studied business). This combination has led to a successful use of strategic design – design and creative thinking is evidenced in all elements of their business ranging from an attractive brand to beautifully designed products. Strategic use of design (colourful, playful and practical) helps the brand and its products stand out in a highly competitive market.

For more information, visit: www.josephjoseph.com

1.1.2 The Evolution of Strategic Design

The 1980s

Strategic design is a relatively new phenomenon. It began in the 1980s as a role for managing design projects, emerging largely as a reaction to increasing complexity of new product development. Dumas and Whitfield (1989;

cited in Design Council, 2007) observed that the presence of a design manager made the design process easier to manage. The design manager was therefore a project manager working in the design environment.

During this period, design contributed primarily to businesses at the project level or the *operational* level, since the focus was on physical outcomes, e.g. new products or retail stores. Figure 1.1 below shows how design was used to enhance product and service development by improving the designs as "fit for purpose," generating ideas for enhancement and new offerings, designing and launching new products/services. Four well-known examples of good users of operational level design are shown.

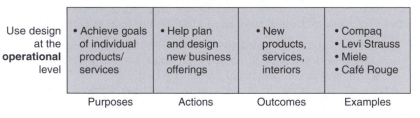

Use design at the **operational** level	• Achieve goals of individual products/ services	• Help plan and design new business offerings	• New products, services, interiors	• Compaq • Levi Strauss • Miele • Café Rouge
	Purposes	Actions	Outcomes	Examples

Figure 1.1   Design contributions at the operational level

Example: Cadbury

One company that made good use of design at the operational level at the early stage of design management evolution was Cadbury. Although design was not included as part of tactical and strategic plans, it was used to create distinctive identities of all product offerings. Interestingly, the "script" logo and the well-recognized corporate colour (Cadbury purple) were first introduced in 1920s. However, due to the lack of strategic and tactical thinking, both the logo and corporate colour were not effectively used across all product lines. Evidence of effective design management emerged in the 1980s and 90s, as all offerings became more coherent and the company displayed new creative practices, e.g. opening Cadbury World in 1990. This initiative has proven success, as it attracts over 500,000 visitors each year.

The Early1990s

It was mainly increased competition that drove design to the *tactical* level in the early 1990s. A number of needs were identified to address the problem. First companies wanted to increase their success rate for new product development projects as every failure was a serious economic burden. The established linear, sequential product development process was considered to be ineffective in the new environment and new processes were called for.

Getting different business functions working together well instead of contributing only to certain aspects of the design project was recognized as a key to management success. Until that time typically design was one step in the overall business project whereby, for example, the R&D team developed a new technology then passed it to a business planning team. The business planning team carried out a feasibility study and created a business plan, and then assigned design tasks to designers and engineering tasks to engineers. Designers and engineers developed different parts of the product independently and then passed technical drawings to the manufacturing team to develop suitable machinery tools and sort out manufacturing processes. Finally, marketers and the sales team came in to plan marketing activities and launch the product to the marketplace. Since all these aspects were developed independently, they were not very well integrated. This approach made the new product development process unnecessarily lengthy, and poor communication between the teams created further problems.

Cross-functional teams were perceived as a means to avoid or reduce downstream failures, to enhance the commitment of development teams, improve the speed to market and increase the chances of success (Walsh *et al.*, 1992). The concurrent engineering approach offered a way forward whereby all business functions are involved from the start right through to the end of the process, and became widely adopted. By starting the works of all parties concurrently, the speed to market may be increased.

For example, as soon as scientists come up with a new technology with strong potential, the business planning team will start checking the feasibility and preparing a business plan; designers, engineers and the manufacturing team will start working in collaboration on how best to develop an application of this technology; and the marketing and sales team will begin identifying suitable targets and planning marketing activities. This style of working can be compared to the approach of playing the sport rugby in which all the players are encouraged to work together and support each other. In rugby, the ball can only be passed backwards. Thus, it is in the best interest of all players not to fall too far behind their teammates. In this case, all business functions make sure that they keep up with each other. Extending the analogy further, the good manager may be likened to a good referee who, seeing any signs of conflict or blame, maintains the momentum and spirit of the game.

One important advantage of having all the functions working together is that any potential problems are likely to be flagged up and addressed early in the process. Further the collaborative process gave designers the chance to show what they could contribute to the strategic planning of new product development. Managers began to consider the possibility of design making a real contribution to achieving strategic success such as market growth.

This showed the way forward for some experts to examine the links between new product development and corporate tactical plans and objectives. Figure 1.2 shows the elevation of design to its use at tactical level. The principal differences are the recognition that design could help to achieve business goals and inform business plans. Four further examples of good users of tactical level design are shown.

However design had still to aspire to the strategic level. It was accepted that it could be used at the tactical level to gain advantages in a short term (e.g. promotional campaigns), but it had not been widely recognized as having a significant role in organizational strategy which emphasizes longer term development and survival, through such practices as brand positioning. Another analogy can be made to the sport football where the manager's

	Purposes	Actions	Outcomes	Examples
Use design at the **tactical** level	• Achieve goals of certain business activities	• Help plan and design for business activities	• New product lines, new business plans	• Dell • Calvin Klein • Electrolux • Costa Coffee
Use design at the **operational** level	• Achieve goals of individual products/ services	• Help plan and design new business offerings	• New products, services, interiors	• Compaq • Levi Strauss • Miele • Café Rouge

Figure 1.2 Design contributions at the tactical level

strategic plan is about the overall style of playing and how to nurture and get the best from talented players to achieve an agreed aim (e.g. winning the cup or finishing in the top five places in the league) whilst the tactical level is concerned with a game plan to win each match.

Example: Sony

An example of a company that made good use of design in the tactical level in the 1980s and 90s was Sony. Design was not included as part of Sony's visions and missions. However, product design was perceived by management and staff as the competitive advantage of the company. Design was exceptionally well used to develop Sony Walkman and PlayStation and thus achieve corporate objectives and business targets. The design team was valued, properly supported and given opportunities to engage with the top management to present their visions of the future, and thus indirectly but purposefully influence Sony's innovation plans.

The Late 1990s

By the late 1990s forward thinkers in academia and industry identified the role of design at *strategic* level for enhancing the organization's strategic goals through vision leadership. Whilst all professional managers may wish to aspire to the status of visionary leader, the design strategist combines business vision with a visual capability to imagine our futures: a visual interpretation of how our world will look and feel in the future. This capability is essential because ultimately designers deliver real experiences which change our world. Many eminent researchers lent support to the evolution of design as a strategic tool and leading companies such as those shown in Figure 1.3 began to recognize the opportunity. They agreed such principles as:

• Design has the power to improve strategic vision and leadership and nurture shared values throughout the organization;

- Managing design effectively can deliver tangible and intangible value to organizations;
- Design is the most effective way to build brands and communicate brand attributes consistently to the target market.

Design was finally infiltrating the boardroom. The design strategy was now about achieving aims, building and delivering brands, changing the culture to get management and staff to think forward, innovate and use the power of design thinking for organizational success.

Figure 1.3 shows what design offers at strategic level and a further four exemplary users.

The momentum for change was supported by such influential business schools as Harvard and Stanford which were among the first to introduce learning of strategic design management practices. Researchers Lester, Piore and Malek (1998) proposed a new concept of management called *interpretive management*, which derived from their observation of how designers and design managers deal with rapidly changing, unpredictable markets. They observed that the conventional ways of management or *analytical* approach where tasks must be clearly defined and assigned to different functions appropriately may no longer be suitable for all business activities and target markets. They pointed out that design managers' ability to interpret the new situation by constantly engaging with customers, engineers and experts, while adapting projects or tasks accordingly, is crucial to the success in the rapidly changing, unpredictable markets. Using the leader of a jazz combo as a metaphor they explained the flexible and adaptive style of design management, demonstrating ability to handle complexity and fast-moving demands.

	Purposes	Actions	Outcomes	Examples
Use design at the **strategic** level	• Achieve missions of a brand or an organization	• Help create visions and organization cultures	• New innovation directions, strategies	• Apple • Diesel • Dyson • Starbucks
Use design at the **tactical** level	• Achieve goals of certain business activities	• Help plan and design for business activities	• New product lines, new business plans	• Dell • Calvin Klein • Electrolux • Costa Coffee
Use design at the **operational** level	• Achieve goals of individual products/ services	• Help plan and design new business offerings	• New products, services, interiors	• Compaq • Levi Strauss • Miele • Café Rouge

Figure 1.3 Design contributions at the strategic level

Example: British Airways

A company that made good use of design at the strategic level in the late 1990s was British Airways. Design was effectively managed and used as strategic weapon to strengthen its world leader position, create unique identity and flying experience as well as differentiate itself from other leading airlines. Its progressive thinking was evidenced in many design-led initiatives. For example, the company introduced the world's first fully flat beds in First Class in 1995 and Business Class in 2000. These innovative practices have raised the standard in terms of travellers' experiences and fully flat beds have now become a common feature of all leading airlines.

1.1.3   Strategic Design for the Future

Strategic design has emerged as a powerful problem-solving tool for the challenges of the 21st-century conceptual economy. Whilst the former knowledge economy showed us how to exploit know-how, the conceptual economy demands creative ideas (Pink, 2006).

New platforms, such as crowdfunding (e.g. http://www.kickstarter.com) and peer-to-peer lending (e.g. http://uk.zopa.com), allow people to obtain financial support from their peers rather than financial institutions, making it easier to raise capital. Peer-to-peer lending practice has now been adopted as an effective way to tackle poverty in developing countries. Not-for-profit organizations, such as Kiva (www.kiva.org), provide a platform where people can lend money (minimum $25) to entrepreneurs in developing countries. This could help create new opportunities for people living in poverty. It is considered more effective than donating money, since, in most cases, lenders get their money back, which they can use to help more entrepreneurs in developing countries.

Crowdfunding is defined as "the practice of funding a project or venture by raising many small amounts of money from a large number of people, typically via the Internet" (Oxford Dictionary, 2013). For example, an innovator could post an idea on an online platform. People who are interested in the idea (or contributors) could offer financial support for the innovator. In this way, the capital could be raised without going to a bank. Nowadays, power has shifted from people with machines and know-how to people with ideas.

Example: Indiegogo

People can use the Indiegogo platform to raise money for all purposes – setting up a new business, raising funds for charities or getting financial support for all kinds of creative ideas (e.g. music, arts and products).

To be successful, design thinking is required throughout the whole process. Firstly, a fundraiser must create a compelling campaign to attract contributors. If the campaign fails to generate a "buzz" or significant interest and a sizable amount of money in the first day, the chance of becoming successful is low. This is because there are many campaigns fighting for contributors' attention – unmemorable campaigns will be forgotten in a matter of days! Secondly, a fundraiser also needs to come up with appealing incentives for contributors who support the campaign (e.g. shares in their business, a special edition of their products or interesting merchandises). Well-designed incentives could help convince contributors. Many successful campaigners use design thinking to start engaging potential contributors through various social media channels long before they launch the campaigns in order to guarantee success. For more information, visit: www. indiegogo.com.

Progressive managers have come to accept that innovation and creative thinking are essential for survival. Global connectivity means that organizations can rapidly access knowledge and production capabilities. Therefore, it is those people with design ideas that go beyond mere functionality and who are capable of engaging people emotionally that will thrive.

"Only one company can be the cheapest, everyone else must use design," claimed Rodney Fitch, chairman of Fitch & Co (cited in Creasey, 2006). The Design Council research showed effective users of design as 200% ahead of the FTSE 100 index companies (Rich, 2004). The Design Effectiveness Award, an annual award organized by the Design Business Association, has a plethora of examples of how all kinds of design ranging from packaging design to corporate identity design helped organizations achieve their goals, e.g. enter new markets or increase market share, and created a good return on investment. The evolution of the roles of design in business is summarized in Table 1.1. A more detailed account of the management of design at the three levels will be presented in subsequent chapters.

Table 1.1 Evolution of the roles of design in business

Era	Business challenges	Design contributions	Level
80s	Deliver integrated offerings Manage complex projects Better product	Product planning Design project management Design for quality	Operational
Early 90s	Improve time to market Increase product success rate Build cross-functional teams Enhance internal communication Understanding customers	Strategic planning for new product development process Design for communication Design for manufacturing User-centred design	Tactical
Late 90s	Keep up with rapid changes Handle unpredictable markets Encourage cross-cultural understanding	Design management Design research skills Design semantics	
2000s	Exploit globalization Ensure meaningful offerings Maintain uniqueness & authenticity Improve services	Design-led branding Design-led innovation Design-led business model Design of experiences...	Strategic
2010s	Embrace social responsibilities Adopt sustainable development Outsource services	Design for society Design for sustainability Design consultancy	

For the future, strategic design offers new opportunities in the public sector, such as using design to reduce crime, design for the elderly, design to protect the dignity of hospital patients and design for public transport and public spaces. Design-led branding has emerged as a very effective tool for delivering complete brand experiences which differentiate and add value. The old paradigm featured the designing of products including interiors, communication, architecture and information. New disciplines empha-size *purpose* such as design for sustainability and design for all. Consumers want to participate. They are no longer content to be passive. This leads to new practices, such as Open Design, where designers take a back seat and let people design for themselves. However, most people cannot cre-ate products/services themselves without support from designers. Thus, in the future designers will design not just products/services but tools to help people exercise their latent creativity, identifying and addressing their own needs. The trend may be expressed as *design for people* has changed to *design with people* and then *design by people*.

1.2 TANGIBLE DESIGN VS INTANGIBLE DESIGN

Tangible means that you can touch and feel something. All physical aspects of our designed world are tangible as is the work of artists and designers who are trained in craft and visual thinking to interpret ideas into reality. Every tangible aspect of our lives can be attributed to designers, some of whom are more talented than others.

By contrast, the word *intangible* means that you cannot see or touch it. However, everyone has intangible experiences which influence our percep-tions of the world around us. Thus, every tangible product has an intangible experience surrounding it. Even if the tangible product is impressive, it will not be successful if the experience is weak.

1.2.1 Big-D Design

Big-D design represents the holistic design thinking which seeks to iden-tify problems amenable to improvement by design. It is related to systems thinking in that it addresses how human activities are connected and the question of how to achieve deep understanding and insights into the needs of all systems players. It often employs tools of *soft systems thinking* to inter-pret complex situations, identify key stakeholders and explore their rela-tionships, and to identify the real needs or problems that designers are to address. This kind of design is what Gorb and Dumas (1987) describe as "silent design" which, in many cases, is carried out "by people who are not designers and are not aware that they are participating in design activity." Using a brand as an example, all the elements within the brand – product, campaigns, service, brand identities and user experiences – cannot be treated as separate entities because they are all interdependent. Thus, Big-D design is truly very big in that it starts at the highest level to see how these elements are connected and to identify design-led opportunities.

Design is often seen as a problem-solving tool, but it is first necessary to identify and visualize needs from complex and dynamic situations. You cannot touch Big-D, but it is a vital stage in formulating our real world experiences. It may be argued that the quality of Big-D design thinking is the key to managing organizational success. Leading organizations understand this and have invested well in promoting design management leadership and strategy development. The global economy has moved from providing commodities to producing goods, delivering services and offering experiences respectively. Now the focus of many businesses has shifted from products (tangible) to experiences (intangible).

Increasing environmental and ethical concern is also one of the key driving forces toward intangible offerings. The dematerialization trend, which promotes the reduction of materials, energy and wastes, means companies tend to offer upgrading services instead of pushing new products to the market. The need to re-think their offerings provides new opportunities for design to contribute at tactical and strategic levels (Big-D).

Example: Zipcar

Zipcar is car sharing service and is a fine example of Big-D intangible design. An opportunity was identified: people want to use a car, but do not need to own the car due to factors such as financial and/or environmental concerns. After registering to be a member, users can book a car online or via a telephone at any time of the day for hours, weeks or months. They can use their swipe cards to unlock a car, enter their pin number to release the key and then drive away. As every car has a designated parking space, users have no problem finding parking in big cities. Good service design ensures that every step is user-friendly and straightforward.

1.2.2   Small-d Design

Small-d design, on the other hand, is defined as the "hands-on" practical design activity of designers trained in such disciplines as product, interior, fashion, architecture, textiles and digital design. These designers produce the tangible designs which we use and experience every day. They are often very talented artistic and creative people who add to wellbeing and fulfilment in daily life. They usually have advanced drawing and/or craft skills and the visual capacity to add creative "magic" to any defined design brief.

Since every tangible design carries an intangible experience, it is essential that Big-D and small-d designers are equally valued and work together closely. Many poor designs, even unsafe products, can be attributed to a lack of Big-D design thinking.

Cognitive ergonomist guru Donald Norman (2004) recognized the importance of small-d designs as he explained that "aesthetically pleasing objects enable you to work better... attractive things make people feel good, which in turn make them think more creatively... making it easier for people to find solutions to the problems they encounter." He also pointed out good tangible design fulfils different levels of need – *visceral design* fulfils emotional needs for aesthetical appealing appearance; *behaviour design* fulfils practical requirements, such as functionality and usability; *reflective design* fulfils personal and spiritual needs by providing uplifting and inspirational experiences.

Example: Black & Decker

An example of small-d designs and good use of small-d design practice which helped a company to achieve attractive appearances and practical functions is Black & Decker power tools, which demonstrate high-quality small-d designs and operational design management processes. Black & Decker's products not only have distinctive looks and are easy to use, but also careful operational planning ensures that key components are shared across multiple products, increasing the design consistency and reducing production costs.

1.2.3   Interrelationships of Big-D and Small-d

While some experts argue that Big-D design thinking is more important than small-d design making, the practical design remains crucial since it is the making in the design studio/model-making environment, which brings the ideas into the real world. Without the making the designs remain as theoretical ideas and progress no further. Getting the right balance between Big-D design and small-d design is a key challenge to management and successful innovation. Marketers concentrate on being first to market but there are many examples of successful products which were not first to market, for example the iPod which was the first MP3 player to appeal to consumers emotions. The two types of design are interdependent. No Big-D design equates to no sense of vision and direction, no guidance to the designers and potential confusion among the stakeholders. No small-d design means no desirable practical outcome. A summary of Big-D and small-d reletionships is presented in Table 1.2 below.

Using a computer as a metaphor, Big-D design is like an operating system and small-d design is like an interface. People cannot access and will not appreciate a computer without an interface and the interface is as only good as its operating system.

Table 1.2   Relationships of Big-D and small-d design

	Big-D	**Small-d**
Function	Brain	Body
Outcomes	Strategic plans	Embodiment of the plans
Purposes	Guide design actions	Fulfil design goals
Nature	Long-term	Short-term
Characteristics	Visionary & meaningful	Desirable & practical
Impacts	Organizational level	Project execution
Aesthetics	Adding economic value	Artistic skills

Example: Remarkable Pencil Ltd

An example of a combination of Big-D and small-d designs is Remarkable Pencil, a company that has been acclaimed for its admirable values and principles. The company turns recycled materials like plastic cups, car tyres and so on, into stationery. The unique tangible designs, clean shapes, vibrant colours and witty graphic storytelling, e.g. "I used to be a car tyre," work interdependently to underpin the intangible concept in working practice. Without a compelling strategy and good storytelling, their business idea would not be so successful, as people find it hard to tell the difference between its products and those of their competitors.

1.2.4 Harnessing a Multidisciplinary Design Approach

It is tempting to separate the intangible and tangible stages and to consider Big-D and small-d designers as having different mindsets. However, the most successful organizations (such as IDEO) use a multidisciplinary approach, bringing together product designers, graphic designers, interaction designers, design strategists, psychologists, anthropologists and ergonomists according to the design project needs. This way, the tangible and intangible aspects of the designs are conceptualized and developed together.

For example, Philips Design under Chief Creative Director Stefano Marzano has developed an approach called *High Design*. Philips describes High Design as:

> an integrated approach, incorporating all of the traditional design skills, plus all of the new design-related skills needed to respond to the complexity and challenges of the present and the future. It is not a case of clever individuals or teams creating products in isolation, but of multidisciplinary organisations or networks creating 'relevant qualities' and 'cultural spheres'. We advocate the collaboration of designers, psychologists, ergonomists, sociologists, philosophers and anthropologists to understand people's needs and desires, in order to generate relevant designs which create value for people and ultimately make them happier.

This approach has helped Philips achieve products that are commercially successful, technologically advanced, desirable and easy to use (intuitive design).

Although Big-D design strategic thinking has great potential, if it is not understood and interpreted well by small-d designers, the benefits may be lost. Indeed, one of the principle challenges for management remains the building of good mutually respectful relationships between the design management thinkers and strategists and the hands-on designers.

1.3 DESIGN THINKING VS STRATEGIC THINKING

1.3.1 What is Design Thinking?

Managers who are not designers may find that learning to think like a designer can be challenging, especially for managers who are predominantly left-brain logical thinkers. Design thinking requires that the whole brain should be utilized.

Design thinking may be regarded as "thinking like a designer" and such thinking may embrace both Big-D and small-d design. Design thinking begins with Big-D design and essentially asks the question "How can we design a better way to ...?" developing a design strategy and practical solution in parallel using both left- and right-brain thinking. The outcome of this thinking is used by the small-d creative practical designers to turn into real tangible solutions which impact on our daily lives. Therefore, without small-d the design thinking remains theoretical, simply a set of ideas, it is the designers who bring it to life.

Design thinking is used to visualize the future and develop the design strategy. Science fiction writers try to look into the future too but the design strategist has to argue that the future vision has validity and value. The design strategist uses design thinking to generate vision, facts and analysis, but also needs to possess the ability to select and evaluate the critical elements which show direction signs for the future. It is essentially positive thinking based on a determination not to be daunted by current constraints, which may often be a lack of resources, a lack of political will and/ or a resistance to change.

Design thinking benefits from asking many questions, often questions that others are reluctant to ask, opening up the debate through exploring new directions. A good design thinker learns to collaborate but must also gain acceptance and credibility in dealing with and acting as a catalyst for a wide range of disciplines.

British standard BS 7000-10 defined design thinking as a "type of process or approach primarily centred around four aspects: customer focus and intimacy, experimentation, prototyping and emotional connectedness" (BSI, 2008). Designers will share with managers the customer focus but their approaches tend to be more emotional, in both following their own instincts and trying to deeply understand the emotions of others.

Brown (2008) described design thinking as a discipline to benefit business (and this may be extended to incorporate all organizations) by using designers' sensibility to match people's needs with what is technologically feasible and what a viable business strategy can convert into customer value and market opportunity. He also profiled the key characteristics of design thinkers as sensitive and empathetic, holistic and integrative, positive and optimistic, experimental and adventurous, catalysts and collaborators and creative and visionary. Good management practice seeks to embrace these characteristics but they may be regarded as natural aspects of the designer's personality. Thus the "design thinker" may potentially offer much added value. Table 1.3 below develops these ideas further into the "special" characteristics of design thinkers. The "behaviours" may be typically found in designers but are certainly not exclusive to designers. However it is important that design thinkers appreciate and respect design and fully support the design function. If they do not have this inherent or well-developed sense of what is "good" design they will not get the best from creative designers, indeed they may misdirect them and damage relationships.

Table 1.3   The added-value of design thinkers

Additional contribution of design thinkers	Behaviour of design thinkers
Understanding of the human condition	Develop intuition and insights into the changing world around them based on deep-seated caring about people.
Making connections	More likely to think holistically and make new connections between hitherto unconnected events, then subject them to closer scrutiny.
Attitude	Belief that design can find a solution to any problem
Risk and reward	Ready to take risks and demonstrate likely rewards
Co-operation	Challenging conventions and driving co-operation
A better world	A capacity to envision how a future world might look and feel and responsibility for the changes.

Brown (2008) further lends support to managers who directly manage the design process by identifying three "spaces": inspiration, ideation and implementation. First the inspiration is to recognize problematic situations and/or opportunities that motivate the search for design solution(s). Then follows the ideation process of generating, developing and testing ideas. Finally, the implementation turns ideas into reality and profitable outcomes. He uses the word *space* instead of *stage* to emphasize that these activities do not occur in a linear sequential order. The three activities may occur simultaneously. Moreover, the design process is considered to be iterative. Things could move forward and backward or go around in a circle. For example, while developing ideas, developers may check what is going on the market and revise the problem definition to reflect changing users' demands.

Thus design thinking is predominantly holistic, curious and imaginative, responsible, and positive about formulating and delivering design solutions. It challenges conventions and generates resistance from people with vested interests and those reluctant to change. Thus it requires great tact as well as personal conviction to communicate the benefits convincingly.

Effective design thinkers combine their creative capacity with the use of powerful thinking tools like *soft systems methodology* (SSM) which helps them to model and identify the key stakeholders, reconcile their needs and clearly define the problem to be solved. In the practice of design thinking, designers should be involved in using such tools from the outset in order to better understand the design environment and help direct and focus their solutions to the human needs identified.

1.3.2   What is Strategic Thinking?

Strategy is often referred to a careful plan of action designed to achieve long-term goals. Porter (2004) suggested that "the job of the strategist is to understand and cope with competition." Thus, the key is to identify what, when, where and how to compete effectively. If the competition is too narrowly defined, a company may miss a chance to exploit new opportunities and/or be unaware of new competitors/substitute products. It is also about differentiation and exploiting new opportunities. The business strategy seeks identify these opportunities, to discover what the company can do best and, in particular, to do it better than rivals. Managers devise a strategy for the organization as a whole and the subsets of the strategy will include such areas as marketing strategy, R&D strategy and design strategy.

The arena of strategic thinking is the established domain of managers who formulate the business strategy and regard design as a function which executes it. In such environments design is frequently treated as a low-level function and the organization does not recognize the power of design to contribute to performance. Whilst some elements of design thinking may be embedded within the strategic thinking, it is not recognized as a design-led creative process. It has evolved as a predominantly analytical process, deriving the strategy from hard facts and figures and trusted economic indicators.

Many management writers, both academic and renowned practitioners, regard strategic thinking as a key to survival and competitive advantage but do not include design or design thinking in their models or recommendations.

However, experts in strategic management such as Mintzberg (1994) point out that strategic thinking is about synthesis, using creativity and systems thinking to formulate visions or new ideas. It begins with systematic strategic planning analysis, breaking down corporate goals into several objectives, then planning how each objective can be achieved and developing the process. He argued that this is *strategic planning* not *strategic thinking*. Strategic planning is analysis and strategic thinking is synthesis.

Strategic planning is predominantly analytical, about breaking down goals into steps and expected outcomes, largely a left-brain exercise. By contrast strategic thinking is about synthesis which involves intuition and creativity. The outcome is less rigid and gives management a more integrated perspective of the organization, nor is the vision of direction precise. Such strategies often cannot be scheduled and executed in detail but are derived through messy processes of informal learning. To some managers a "messy" process may be an anathema as they may see it as high risk. But this open intuitive approach matches well with the designer's approach and could be regarded as more responsive and relevant to organizational responsiveness and flexibility in the current climate.

1.3.3 Parities between Design Thinking and Strategic Thinking

Design thinking and strategic thinking have much in common. Both are holistic, goal-oriented and creative. The business management field even describes strategic managers as "designers of organisations as systems for sustainable value creation and distribution" Sanchez (2006), thus showing that Big-D design can be seen as systems design. So it can be argued that progressive managers naturally embrace much of Big-D design into their thinking, using it as a way to promote designs that are both profitable and humanly satisfying.

Using Mintzberg's *5Ps of strategy* (see Section 1.1.1), it can be seen that:

1. Both design thinking and strategic thinking lead to a *plan*.
2. Design is arguably the more powerful tool to add the *ploy* because the ruse or trick is likely to come from good creative thinking.
3. Behaviour of people and organizations may also much benefit from design thinking as understanding *patterns* of human behaviour requires empathy and insights.
4. Both managers and designers are working to the same goals in establishing the best or most competitive *position* of the organization.
5. *Perspectives* or what may be alternatively described as the "outlook" of many organizations are changing in recent years. In the quest to be viewed as "responsible" organizations need help from design thinkers to design sustainable and value-added offerings.

Borja de Mozota (2006) determined how design thinking can be used in strategic management in four separate powerful ways. First she explained the power of design to differentiate, perhaps even make unique, the business offerings. Second she regards design as an integrator, using the power of design thinking to bring together all the business's assets and capabilities to form new capabilities and possible unique competitive advantages. Third she sees that design has power to transform the business by opening up new opportunities. Finally she argues that design has power to improve financial performance and return on investment. Examples of the successful application of these principles include:

- Alessi use design as a *differentiator*. All design elements of Alessi, ranging from the mechanism to the appearance, make their products stand out from the crowd. Alessi describes itself as "Italian Design Factory" and design is integrated into all elements of the company to create a clear value proposition.
- Apple use design as an *integrator*. Strategic design management underpins the integration and synergy of all assets (ranging from its technical capabilities to intimate customer relationships) to deliver a distinctive brand, compelling value proposition, appealing products and exceptional experience.
- Samsung's 'Le Fleur' editions shows how design can be used as a *transformer*. Electronic gadgets, such as mobile phones, are often perceived as "boys' toys" and, thus, little effort has been made to understand female targets and address their needs. Samsung recognized this as an opportunity and used design strategically to open up a new market and design a product range especially for female consumers. The range has helped Samsung to change the perception of female customers toward the brand and its products.
- Dulux's Perfect Painting Accessories range demonstrates how design can create a good business. Dulux, a leading paint company, spotted an opportunity to expand its range profitably, since there was no dominant brand in the painting accessory market. Due to insightful design research and clever product design, Dulux managed to gain 5% share of

the £160 million home decorating accessories market within 9 months of the initial launch without any support from advertisement and major marketing activities.

Whereas only two to three decades ago strategic thinking rarely considered input from designers, the integration of strategic thinking and design thinking is leading to new business and social models, organizational development and recognition of the value of creativity as a major resource and competitive weapon.

It is apparent that designers are learning the fundamental needs of managers in business and other organizations. In order to be successful in strategic management they need to:

- *Understand the issues associated with management decision making.* This means they need to become more outward looking. No longer should they regard their world as bounded by the design studio walls. They need to remind themselves they are "on duty" at all times gathering ideas to improve the world around them but aware of real world realities such as economic constraints.
- *Find their place where they can contribute the most value.* This means understanding "value" from the point of view of users. The designer cannot be a "prima donna" artist but must take a mature attitude to personal development.
- *Communicate their offerings in management language.* This point also begs the question as to how much of the designers' language is understood by management. Whilst designers are often accused of weakness in communicating with managers, more visual awareness among managers may greatly enhance the formulation of strategy. Some researchers, including Clark and Smith (2008), suggest that designers should avoid the use of the word "design" as it is open to too many potentially different interpretations, and instead use such terms as "innovation intelligence."

Designers can support strategic managers by:

- *Using their design research skills which have the potential to gain deep insights into target markets which helps to show where and how to be different from competitors.* This means a willingness to develop new skills beyond studio skills such as new methodologies to deal with complexity with increased confidence.
- *Applying "design thinking" to support managers in product planning and enhancing the product offer to meet consumer needs, wants and dreams.* Such design thinking needs to be part of every designer's armoury.
- *Through their user engagement, to identify and evaluate the priority "key activities" which must be successfully delivered with any product/service.* Designers need to develop a close understanding of users' changing requirements across cultures.
- *Use their Big–D design thinking to support the management in their systems design to link all aspects of the execution and delivering coherently, consistently to a high level of quality.* Enhancing the relationship between designers and managers and infusing management with more design ideas.

Case Study 1 Live/Work

Recently many design consultancies have realized that their success can be enhanced through design research, design thinking, developing new design processes and offering strategic design alternatives. Live/Work achieves synergy between design and strategic thinking. Using emergent techniques, such as participatory design, ethnographic research and customer journeys, they can identify the real needs and problems of their clients which may then be turned into design opportunities.

All the key characteristics of design thinking – user empathy, integrative approaches, multi-disciplinary collaboration and experimentation – are included in their approach. Most leading consultancies now see their methodology and their ability to contribute to strategic directions as a unique selling point (USP) that differentiates them from others.

Design thinking is used to underpin strategic thinking and vice versa. Design helps to develop strategy and strategy directs design effort. Clients want to engage in the process of coming up with creative solutions and new strategic design-led directions. They are keen to identify latent needs, open up new possibilities and overcome existing barriers to their survival and business success. Through a combination of design and strategic thinking, Live/Work seeks to deliver intuitive and engaging experiences for both private and public sector clients.

1.4 DESIGN MANAGEMENT

Whilst there is compelling evidence that design and management could be successfully integrated in practice (e.g. the Bauhaus Movement) they were traditionally seen as two unrelated academic fields. In 1989 Dumas and Mintzberg set the stage for new thinking and research about the relationship by pointing out that they share common characteristics and are mutually dependent:

> Management implies order, control and guidance of people, processes and activities. Design also implies order, control and guidance, but of things, artifacts and images. Neither process, however, is in itself one of order, control or guidance.

They saw "good" design as a symptom of good people, organization, strategy, cash flow, skills balance, attitude and motivation, thus implying that good strategic management leads to good design. They suggested design should not be managed in the same way as other resources but rather infused into the organization to get everyone thinking and using design, thereby building an appreciation of the value of design.

However many of the earliest definitions and proposed practices of design management concentrated on planning and managing design assets, so the management of design was largely confined to the management of design projects in a design studio. Many researchers began to explore the relationship and Cooper and Press (1995) suggested that design management is about setting agendas (e.g. goals and purposes) for design in an organization, making sure that design is an integral part of all levels of management, strategic, tactical and operational. Next, the management process, including planning, organization, implementation, monitoring and evaluation is applied to assure that design agendas are achieved.

Borja de Mozota's (2003) comparison helped to reveal the potential of design to encompass the needs for building an organizational structure and culture where design can flourish and contribute to key business functions, e.g. finance, human resources, marketing and business development. She also pointed out that both disciplines rely on decision-making processes.

The emergent links between design and management thinking show them to be evolving as complementary as summarized in Table 1.4.

To reflect the current thinking about the meaning of design management, the definition of design management should be regarded as "a catalyst to promote and develop the permeation of design throughout an organization, to get everyone concerned with design." This means that managers whose responsibilities touch design do not merely accept but become part of it. Design thus becomes a way of life for the organization. This also means that design is no longer the sole preserve of the designers. Some aspects of the convergence of disciplines around design generate new methodologies and processes but first and foremost it is a way of thinking to constantly feed the organization with new ideas and possibilities.

Table 1.4 Convergence of design and management thinking

Design see themselves	Management see themselves
Addressing problems – organizational, global, social	Identifying opportunities
Aesthetic open and creative	Innovators delivering value-added solutions
Holistic thinkers	Environmental scanners
Promoting harmony	Developing structures for effective operations
One world reaching out	Acquiring understanding of cultures

1.4.1 Three Levels of Design Management

Three fundamental levels of design management have been identified as strategic (top) level, tactical (middle) level and operational (bottom) level.

- *Strategic level*: This is where design operates at the top of the organization. It has an impact on the organization's direction and becomes a valuable resource for survival and competitive advantage. Here the design strategy focuses on design vision and the impact of the organization on its environment. It is a design-thinking level, as distinct from practical design, but it has the power and responsibility for making a major contribution to organizational success. It generates and evaluates alternative design directions and risks to support strategic management decision making.
- *Tactical level*: The tactical (alternatively called business or functional) level of design management supports objectives set by the organization. It is the method by which the organization delivers its offerings. At this

level design may also be used to explore new opportunities. Design is seen as a function supporting successful management by encouraging and integrating activities across departments.

- *Operational level*: This level is essentially the execution of design projects. The emphasis is on the efficiency and effectiveness of the design management process. Some operational level design projects will be contracted out to design firms. This is where the practical design takes place in an effort to add value and improve experiences.

1.4.2 Top Level: Design as Core Values

To be effective at the top strategic level, design must be embraced for its ability to add real value, change visions and generate new thinking about the organization as a system and what it offers. It needs the support of the senior management, ideally the CEO if it is to become a mainstream contributor to performance. The design leader sets the vision for the effective use of design in the organization. The strategic design vision is developed through good design research and challenging creative thinking which enables design to establish itself as a key activity and in turn delivers actions to deliver pragmatic design solutions.

Table 1.5 shows the main issues for attention and the consequent actions.

The planning stage presents the best opportunity to show clear intentions by linking the design strategy closely with the business strategy and the marketing strategy. If design is presented as the servant of the marketing strategy instead of its equal, this will inhibit the influence of design on future performance. However, as with all key functions, design must be expected to have targets set by management to facilitate review.

At the organizing stage the methods for building a strong design environment and infusing design thinking throughout the organization are invoked. Allocating budgets is always challenging and design may have to fight hard for a share of the resources available, especially as the benefits have not yet been delivered.

Table 1.5 Issues for attention at strategic level

Stage	Activities
Planning	Ensure design is recognized as an important resource
	Link design closely to business strategy and other key functions
Organization	Build a supportive environment for design
	Select and appoint able design leaders
	Establish training and education programmes in design and design thinking for everyone in the organization
	Allocate adequate budgets
Implementation	Clarify designers' roles and status in the organization
	Set criteria for review of design effectiveness
Review	Check performance thoroughly and often, learn from mistakes and revise

Implementing a design strategy means clarifying what is the role of design, enhancing its status and encouraging cooperation. Everyone in the organization should be told how the effectiveness of design will be judged.

Finally the review should be used to complete the circle of planning and control. Design may often be regarded as intangible and difficult to evaluate and control but should be subjected to the same high degree of rigour as all other functions.

To summarize, successful organizations embrace design fully, incorporating it into their mission statements, brand values, corporate philosophies and organizational cultures. Indeed design thinking is embedded in everything they do. Design strategies are treated as equally important to other strategies, such as marketing and manufacture.

Example: Dyson

Dyson is an excellent example of how design can be infused into an organization. All key staff in all functions, ranging from R&D to brand communication, understand and use design effectively. Design is truly a way of life in the organization. The brand and its experience reflect the ethos of the company: "new thinking to solve everyday problems."

1.4.3   Middle Level: Design as Business Tools

At the middle level organizations begin to ask the question "How do we use design to enhance performance?" Design may be used to create many new opportunities including products/services, developing new markets, protecting established markets, improving brand experiences, diversification and strengthening the organization for mergers and acquisition. Agenda and actions for the middle level can be summarized as shown in Table 1.6.

The planning change at tactical level should begin by ensuring that the relationship and alignment of design and organizational objectives is clear and, if there is any doubt, managers should refer the questions back to the strategic level for further clarification. In the event that there is any

Table 1.6   Issues for attention at the tactical level

Stage	Activities
Planning	Check the alignment of design and organizational objectives
	Formulate agreed standards for design and ensure they promote legal and corporate social responsibility
	Integrate design with other functions
	Prepare administrative procedures for design proposals and project monitoring
Organization	Select a suitable design leader
	Negotiate and agree sufficient resources and budgets
	Train staff in design thinking and cross-functional teamwork
	Establish approved suppliers/consultants
Implementation	Develop clear procedural guidelines and supporting documentation and reporting system
Review	Monitor and evaluate performance of design against agreed targets

weakness in the vital "bridge" from strategic to tactical, every further activity may be prone to misinterpretation and confusion. Design must then be subjected to a set of standards and expectations. In this respect it is managed in the same manner as all other organizational resources. Integrating design across other functions usually begins with marketing and is a particularly challenging step in organizations that have boundaries between functions and managers intent on defending them.

The organization stage offers help with cross-functional collaboration through training. A suitable design leader must be chosen and the required characteristics will be discussed in subsequent chapters. In all cases, the design leader must be a good communicator across the functions. The leader will negotiate sufficient resources and budgets and draw up an approved list of suppliers/consultants.

At implementation stage it is important to develop clear procedural guidelines for design and cross-functional teams with appropriate documentation and reporting systems.

The review stage monitors and evaluates performance against targets and communicates the findings to improve the strategic and tactical planning, thus completing the cycle.

Borja de Mozota (2003) showed that there are direct links between business objectives and the design requirements. A new or start-up company links to design by its immediate need for a logo and (in almost every case) a web presence. Many may be regarded as poorly designed since an appreciation of the power and quality of design is not so common. If the company gains such an appreciation and declares that it wishes to be an acknowledged design leader, then it becomes necessary to gain an understanding of how design is perceived across different cultures and international boundaries. When a company wishes to launch a new product/ service or establish a flagship or retail store, it needs design creative concepts and the expertise for a design development process. Launching a new brand adds the design activities from graphic design through to the design of the brand experience, including brand naming, brand values and delivering the brand promise. Most companies seek to increase their market share and designers can contribute design research to identify new opportunities and improvements to products and/or services. Also design may enhance performance through such areas as packaging and web site design. However when the market share is going down companies need designers for innovation and improvements and to review and redesign the consumer experience. Diversification into new markets also needs designers to develop new product/service extensions aligned with the brand. Finally the researcher offers the example of improving R&D policy whereby designers are needed for their creative thinking and constant feedback of new concepts. This can stimulate R&D into more relevant developments of technology.

These direct links are limited in scope since the real power of design lies in its ability to harness multi-disciplinary collaborations and generate new opportunities. They nevertheless establish clearly that business needs designers' input across a wide spectrum of business activities.

Example: Specsavers

Specsavers, the biggest optician in the UK, uses design management strategy to become a market leader. Although, design is not fully infused into the organization, it does make good use of tangible design (logo, store interiors, web site, retail displays) and intangible design (storytelling reflecting customers' lifestyles and how they address complicated eyesight problems). The design of the brand reflects their core offerings of "value for money quality eye care" and focuses on fashion and lifestyle more than functionality. All touch points of the customer experience reflect the core values. Shop interiors communicate simplicity, openness, hygiene and good quality service. The company invests in developing a good service design level making the whole process straightforward and relaxed. They have a small internal design department lead by a very experienced design manager and employ leading design consultancies in their quest to maintain a well-designed user experience and high level of customer satisfaction. The design manager communicates regularly with top management to interpret and integrate design and strategic business objectives.

1.4.4 Bottom Level: Design as Deliverables

The bottom level is vitally important because it is the stage at which the real designed experience is executed for delivery. Without this stage all other aspects of the strategy and process are a waste of time. This is the stage that the entire strategic approach is working towards: the delivery of a satisfying, pleasurable and memorable experience to every user. It addresses the need to satisfy both needs and desires. The key elements of its management can be seen in Table 1.7.

The real talents of creative "hands-on" designers are employed to design products/services/brands which interpret the organizational values and give

Table 1.7 Issues for attention at operational level

Stage	Activities
Planning	Ensure resources to help identify design trends and links to changing lifestyles (including ethnographic research).
	Interpret strategy and plan into practical design needs e.g. colours, shapes, style.
	Management and administration of the design function.
Organization	Employ designers with good skills and environmental awareness.
	Day-to-day budgetary control.
	Promote personal development; in particular multi-disciplinary teamwork.
Implementation	Carry out the design process from ideation/concept stage through to product/service launch.
	Carefully record all design project stages.
Review	Evaluate design performance against previously agreed targets and market feedback.

users satisfaction. Ideally the designers should go further to delight users, making happy memorable experiences at all touch points. The designers work to a "brief" and the quality of the brief is greatly influential on the outcome. If creative designers have been involved in the entire evolution of the organizational design philosophy and development of strategy, they may be better able to create added-value products, services and brand experiences. However designers must work within budget constraints and agreed time frames.

At the planning stage it is important to keep the designers aware of the changing world around them lest they become so absorbed in their studio-based work, involving drawing, model making and experimentation, that they lose sight of the end user. The management and administration processes must be supportive as distinct from rigid and strict as designers have a natural resistance to control especially if it threatens their creative freedom. The interpretation of the brief into colours, shapes, style etc. is the very special skill of the designer. In this practical arena it is vital that designers and the managers of design have respect and confidence in each other.

The organization requires designers with special creative skills but also a worldly awareness. This can be further developed through training which promotes successful collaboration. Management may expect careful attention to the budget in common with all organizational functions. Implementation at this practical level is first the design process, through all its stages but with frequent loops involving careful recording of all stages. Finally, the review stage measures how well design has performed against targets and market feedback. This intelligence is then used to further improve performance in a learning organization.

Example: Giant Bicycles

Giant Bicycles is a Taiwanese company which has grown to become a world leader, principally through operational level design management, in the design and manufacture of performance and quality bicycles. At the tactical level they addressed the design challenge as "creating exciting cycling solutions" and developing the "best cycling experience." Thus they see themselves as developing cycling culture not just making bicycles. This gave them a platform for developing technological innovations especially in frame design and use of composite materials. They achieved much success through, for example, reducing overall size, decreasing weight whilst increasing rigidity thereby allowing faster acceleration. Their attention to detail is acknowledged through Taiwan National Quality Awards.

1.4.5 Interrelationships of the Three Levels

All levels of design management can be seen as fundamentally interdependent. Strategic design management needs operational design management to turn the vision into tangible outcomes. At the same time, operational design management needs a clear direction from strategic and tactical design management. In order to be successful, a company needs all three levels of design management and each level must be well integrated. The work of Cooper and Press (1995) shows the emergent relationships.

Design Management	Design as a planner of:	Design as a creator of:	Design as an integrator of:	Design as a leader of:	Design as a catalyst for:
Strategic Level	Vision & Strategic Direction	Design Policy & Culture	Synergic Goals (Triple Bottom Line)	Brand Development (Brand Leadership)	Changes in Organization Culture
Tactical Level	Competitive Advantages	Design Strategy & Design Language	Value Delivery Network	Business Development	Changes in Business Models
Operational Level	Memorable Experiences	Design Activities & Design Projects	Multidisciplinary Innovation	Product Development (Product Champion)	Changes in Business Offerings

Figure 1.4 Inter-relationships of the three levels of design management

All three levels of design management can be used for planning, innovating, integrating, leading and fusing together the essentials of design-led change as can be seen in Figure 1.4. As a planner, strategy is about vision and future direction, tactics address competitiveness and operations are concerned with delivering the best experience. Creators formulate policies for innovation, strategies for design communication and operational design activities. Integrators seek synergy, establish networks and build multi-disciplinary teams and tools.

Design leaders can establish the best brands and develop the business through winning products/services. Designers as catalysts influence and change cultures, challenge and formulate new business (and social) models, and create new offerings. The three levels of design management, developed from the work of Borja de Mozota (2003), can be summarized as follows:

- The operational design management level is the practical small-d activity which creates design value through its distinctiveness and differentiates products/services from competitors, thus playing a major role in generating economic value.
- Tactical design management is concerned with planning the functions for the delivery of design value. The design planning impacts on all surrounding activities.
- At strategic level design management must establish the vision and has the capacity to transform and set the business/organization direction.

Design strategists must inevitably challenge established thinking and therefore have the capacity to generate new visions and directions across organizations, industries and communities.

Chapter 1 has explained the changing meaning of "design" and its evolution to becoming a key contributor to business strategy. Creative studio based design remains important but design strategy has the potential to deliver significant advantages to the successful management of organizations. Managing strategic design holds much promise for improving performance but it is challenging both as a concept and in terms of seeking new best practice design management tools and methods (see Figure 1.4)

1.5   GLOSSARY

Concurrent engineering is a management approach commonly used in the new product development (NPD) process. It encourages key business functions, namely research and development (R&D), design, engineering, marketing and manufacturing, to work in an integrated manner throughout the whole process in order to avoid downstream problems and improve time to market (BSI, 2008).

A cross-functional team is a group of people from different disciplines, e.g. finance, design, engineering, marketing, manufacturing and sales, working in a collaborative manner toward a mutual goal, normally to develop a new product/service. Members may come from disciplines inside or outside an organization (e.g. suppliers and consultants).

Crowdfunding is an emerging practice of funding projects, ventures or social/humanitarian causes by raising small amounts of money from a large number of individuals, typically via online platforms (Oxford Dictionaries, 2013).

Dematerialization is a sustainable trend encouraging the reduction of material usage in variety of economic activities, e.g. produce manufacturing. Using less material could lead to the reduction of energy used to extract, distribute and process raw materials.

Innovation management is a process for managing innovation in an organization.

Knowledge management is process to establish goals, identify, obtain, develop, share, utilize, retain and assess knowledge within an organization.

Network management is strategies and procedures for planning, developing and maintaining networks/relationships inside and outside an organization.

The **new product development (NPD)** is a process of developing a new offering (e.g. a product, a service, an experience and a system) for a marketplace.

Open design is an emerging approach/movement encouraging design information, e.g. technical drawings, to be publicly shared and used, typically via the Internet. Many experts see open design as a next step of open source. While an open source program makes source code available for people to use and modify freely, the open design approach makes the whole design information available for the public to share and use.

Peer-to-peer (P2P) lending is a practice enabling individuals to lend and borrow money without going through traditional financial institutions, e.g. a bank.

The **return on investment (ROI)** a performance measure used to appraise the efficiency of an investment. It can be calculated by dividing net profit by net cost.

Soft systems thinking is a systemic approach designed to tackle complex ill-defined problems. While "hard systems" thinking tends to break a problem into smaller components and then tackle each part, "soft systems" thinking does not try to deconstruct a problem – instead acknowledges its complexity – and tackles it in a holistic manner.

1.6 REFERENCES AND ADDITIONAL READING

Best, K. (2006) *Design Management: Managing Design Strategy, Process and Implementation.* London: AVA.

Best, K. (2010) *The Fundamentals of Design Management.* Lausanne: AVA.

Borja de Mozota, B. (2003) *Design Management: Using Design to Build Brand Value and Corporate Innovation.* New York: Allworth Press.

Borja de Mozota, B. (2006) The Four Powers of Design: A Value Model in Design Management, *Design Management Review*, 17 (2), 44 – 53.

Brown, T. (2008) Design Thinking. *Harvard Business Review*, 86 (6), 84–92.

Brown, T. (2009) *Change by Design: How Design Thinking Transforms Organizations and Inspires Innovation.* New York: HarperCollins.

BSI (British Standards Institute) (2008) *BS 7000-10:2008: Design Management Systems – Part 10: Vocabulary of Terms Used in Design Management.* London: British Standards Institute.

Clark, K. and Smith, R. (2008) Unleashing the Power of Design Thinking. *Design Management Review*, 19 (3), 8–15.

Cooper, R. and Press, M. (1995) *The Design Agenda*. Chichester: Wiley.

Cooper, R., Junginger, S., Lockwood, T. (2011) *The Handbook of Design Management*. Basingstoke: Berg.

Creasey, S. (2006) Only One Company can be the Cheapest, Everyone Else must use Design. *Design Council Magazine*, Winter, Issue 1, 36–39.

Design Council (2007) *Eleven Lessons: Managing Design in Eleven Global Companies: Desk Research Report*. London: Design Council.

Dumas, A. and Mintzberg, H. (1989) Managing Design/Designing Management. Design Management Journal, 1 (1), 37–43.

Design Management Institute (2010) *What Is Design Management?* [WWW] Design Management Institute. Available from: http://www.dmi.org/dmi/html/aboutdmi/design_management.htm [Accessed 14 February 2011].

Gorb, P. and Dumas, A. (1987) Silent Design. *Design Studies*, 8 (3), 150–156.

HM Treasury (2005) *Cox Review of Creativity in Business: Building on the UK's Strengths*. London: HM Treasury.

Lester, R., Piore, M. and Malek, K. (1998) Interpretive Management: What General Managers Can Learn From Design. *Harvard Business Review*, March–April, 86–96.

Lockwood, T. (2009) *Design Thinking: Integrating Innovation, Customer Experience, and Brand Value*. New York: Allworth Press.

Mintzberg, H. (1994) The Fall and Rise of Strategic Planning. *Harvard Business Review*, 72 (1), 107–114.

Norman, D. A. (2004) *Emotional Design: Why We Love (or Hate) Everyday Things*. New York: Basic Books.

Pink, D. H. (2006) *A Whole New Mind: Why Right-Brainers Will Rule the Future*. London: Marshall Cavendish.

Porter, M. E. (2004) The Five Competitive Forces that Shape Strategy. *Harvard Business Review*, January, 79–93.

Rich, H. (2004) Proving the Practical Power of Design. *Design Management Review*. 15 (4), 29–34.

Sanchez, R. (2006) Integrating Design into Strategic Management Processes. *Design Management Review*, 17 (4), 10–17.

Walsh, V., Roy, R., Bruce, M. and Potter, S. (1992) *Winning by Design: Technology, Product Design and International Competitiveness*. Oxford: Blackwell Business.

1.7 ONLINE RESOURCES

1. Design Business Association (DBA): www.dba.org.uk
2. Design Council: www.designcouncil.org.uk
3. Design Management Institute: www.dmi.org
4. TED: www.ted.com

Chapter 2
PLANNING STRATEGIC DESIGN

Having established the origins and nature of design strategy rooted in the development of design management and the importance of applying it at all levels, this chapter introduces approaches, frameworks and toolkits for understanding and using it. Conventional strategic planning tools offer some value but tend to be analytical, reflecting the schools of management thinking which were dominant over the last century. Therefore tools more sensitive to the contribution of design should be employed. A new simple cyclical model utilizing 4Ds is presented as a basis for determining present performance, defining visions, designing strategies and deliverables and deciding the quality of design performance. Several well-respected models and toolkits for measuring and monitoring performance are suggested to support the 4Ds framework.

Strategy is essentially a "game plan" to achieve carefully defined goals, but design strategy has the capacity to deliver added value at all levels and to generate powerful brand experiences integrating products and services at a deep emotional level. Numerous analogies have been offered to managers in recent years in an effort to improve strategy. Football and rugby are used, as in Chapter 1, plus many others like orchestras, mountaineers, mariners and even poets. They all add to the richness of the debate but none in themselves can handle the complexity of the variables required to achieve a successful contemporary, creative, robust organization.

With the introduction of design strategy, vision can be employed to provide a clear direction for the future and goes beyond the conventional economics-driven thinking. Design strategies provide the platform for creative enterprise and identification of opportunities. The design-led creative organizational model has been shown to deliver success. It leads to a willingness to be more open, challenging business norms and delivering value to users, frequently exceeding their expectations.

Design strategy needs to be based on mutual respect and close cooperation between Big-D and small-d designers who need to communicate well at all stages.

Objectives for this chapter:

- To introduce classic approaches to strategic planning;
- To show how new approaches to strategic planning are more flexible and adaptive;

- To explain the co-creative approach and compare it to the traditional approach;
- To discuss the relationship between design strategy and corporate strategy;
- To explain and evaluate established and emergent strategic planning tools;
- To set out the 4D design strategy framework;
- To discuss the rationale and introduce tools for using the framework;
- To present two further design management toolkits.

2.1 STRATEGIC DESIGN APPROACHES

2.1.1 Classic Approaches for Strategic Planning

In general, strategic design is based around four questions: Where are we? Where are we going? How do we get there? How do we know when we have got there? So in order to establish a clear sense of direction for the successful management of design it is essential to establish a clear goal based on well-defined steps which will deliver a measurable advantage through design.

Companies and other organizations usually begin with their *mission* which is a statement of the reason for their existence. Next they define their *values*, what they believe in and how they intend to behave in relation to these principles. An organization needs *visions* to determine where they want to be. This forms the foundation for a *strategy* for formulating the right competitive game plan and to implement, monitor, evaluate and review how the performance is going. Advantage is considered to be an essence of the strategy. Advantage or area of excellence is described as a skill, competence or capability that a company cultivates to a level of proficiency greater than anything else it does and particularly better than any competitor does.

Design contributes to addressing such key questions as: What does success look like? Where should we compete? How should we compete? Using design better than others is now accepted to be a key competence.

Most classical or analytical approaches for strategic planning were influenced by Michael Porter, a strategic management guru. According to Porter (1985), the fundamental question for strategic planning is how to create "sustainable competitive advantages" for an organization. The author suggested that there are two basic types of competitive advantage – one concentrates on cost and another on differentiation. Table 2.1 below shows how design may be used to reduce costs and/or seek uniqueness. Although Porter's two types of competitive advantage pre-date the emergence of design as a key competitive resource, he lays a valuable foundation for a clear understanding of how design may add value and, in particular, avoid the danger of competing on price alone, because constantly driving down prices leads to higher business failures.

Porter's approach to strategic planning is based on analytical thinking and tends to treat design as an upstream service function. However his famous "five forces" shown below set out the strategic challenges for corporate strategies to which design now contributes strongly.

Table 2.1 The contemporary advantages of design

Reduced costs	Uniqueness	Choice
Using design can keep down all costs e.g. manufacturing (most recently outsourced to China) Only one can be the lowest cost but design is used to minimize the costs wherever possible	Using design to be unique by creating own space for product/ service in often crowded markets Design researchers can gain a deep understanding of physical and psychological features most valued in quest for "brand excellence"	Generating future visions using design thinking as support for management decision making More design-led creative thinking about new opportunities throughout the organization
Targeting a niche market with a view to keeping costs down and carefully assessing the margins of profit	Using design for incremental innovation to maintain identifiable uniqueness	Modelling alternative future scenarios to assess levels of risk and potential return.

1. *Threat of new entrants*: New entrants are considered to be a threat, since they could bring in new capabilities that you may not have. Moreover, they could take advantage of the market that you spent a lot of investments to open up, as they could steal your market share, which directly affects your profits. This threat can be prevented/mitigated/avoided by making it difficult for new entrants, e.g. by developing strong networks with all key players, e.g. suppliers, within the industry.
2. *Bargaining power of suppliers*: Many suppliers have strong bargaining power toward a company, especially those who have unique expertise and special machinery, since it would be difficult for a company to switch from current suppliers to new ones. The bargaining power of suppliers could affect cost strategies as well as the quality of finished products and/ or parts.
3. *Bargaining power of buyers*: Customers have strong impacts on the strategic options that a company has. In the business-to-business (B2B) market where customers buy a large volume of product, the bargaining power is incredibly strong. They could negotiate for better services and so forth. Intermediate customers (e.g. retailers) also possess similar bargaining power, as they may decide to stop ordering your products and sell competing products instead.
4. *Threat of substitute products or services*: In all kinds of business, there are always substitute products or services. For examples in the fast-food market, substitute products are supermarket take-away food and ready-made meals. Substitutes are often overlooked, since they are indirect competitors. However, it is important to address this threat, as they could prevent your products/brands from growing and/or expanding into new markets. The threat is considerably higher when products/services offer similar values, e.g. Netflix and YouTube.
5. *Rivalry among the existing competitors*: These are your known, direct competitors. Kotler and Armstrong (2008) suggested that in order to compete

effectively, it is important to understand what drives your competitors and what they are currently doing and can do in the future. By studying them and anticipating what would be their next move, you can improve your business and shape your strategies in a way that limits their strategic options.

The application of the five forces can be seen in the case of Coca-Cola where:

1. The threat of *new entrants* is not strong. Coca-Cola and Pepsi still dominate the industry. Thus far, there has been no new innovation that could seriously shake up the industry.
2. Bargaining power of (intermediate) *buyers* (e.g. supermarkets and restaurants) is high, since they purchase in large volume. Hence, they can negotiate for discounted prices.
3. *Suppliers* (e.g. bottling equipment manufacturers) do not hold strong bargaining power, as they deliver basic products and there is no differentiation in their current offers. Thus, it is easy to switch to new suppliers. In this case, the switching costs are quite low.
4. Threat of *substitute* products, e.g. bottled water and sport drinks, is high. These substitutes have become increasingly popular due to the healthy-eating trend.
5. *Industry competitors* – the competition within the industry is high. Pepsi, the main rival, competes on every aspect ranging from products to corporate social responsibility campaigns, e.g. Coca-Cola's *Live Positively* vs Pepsi's *Refresh Project*.

The established approaches to strategic planning are largely analytical. Dating back to such classical management writers as Brech in his *Principles and Practice of Management* in 1954, managers have been encouraged to make their activities systematic and logical. The schools of management thinking which promoted the collection of detailed information as the basis for setting rigid programmes and control activities still pervade the management style of many modern organizations. Contemporary organizations cannot afford to be so rigid in the face of rapidly changing, unpredictable times. Mintzberg (1994) was one of the first to notice the dangers of over rigidity and openly criticized the analytical approach. He believed that "Planners should make their greatest contribution *around* the strategy-making process rather than *inside* it." Suggesting much wider vision was required. He summarized the pitfalls or fallacies of the analytical approach as follows:

- *Prediction*: Analyzing data alone for predicting markets, would not lead to breakthrough ideas and new innovations.
- *Detachment*: Because everything is planned based on research and analyses, decision makers will not take the blame and/or responsibility if anything goes wrong. This makes the "planners" less committed.
- *Formalization*: Formal procedures cannot "internalize," "comprehend" and "synthesize" knowledge to form compelling strategies. Planning cannot generate strategies when planners look for good ideas from others rather than initiate original ideas.

2.1.2 Emerging Approaches for Strategic Planning

The transition of strategic planning from the relatively formal and rigid methods of the past century to ones that meet the challenges of becoming more responsive has led to a range of new theories and practices. Conventional strategic planning was frequently considered scientific but Lafley *et al.* (2012) pointed out that it cannot be described as scientific when it lacks the creation of hypotheses and the careful generation of tests to prove or disprove them. All new ideas have the status of hypotheses until they are tested but the suggestion here is that there was a lack of creative thinking to generate ideas and an inadequate understanding of how to test them properly.

However, trying to anticipate everything in the rapidly changing unpredictable market is difficult, perhaps impossible to fully achieve. Thus organizations may choose to use the incremental strategy advocated by Tidd, Bessant and Pavitt (2005). It is referred to as a "trial and error" approach which encourages an organization to make actions towards business objectives and constantly evaluate the effects of these actions. Both objectives and actions may be adjusted if necessary to reflect the changes in the marketplace, customer demands and new technologies. They offered the two analogies that follow:

- The military applies the analytical approach to generate their strategies, where everything has to be meticulously planned, since people's lives are at stake.
- The incrementalist strategy can be compared to the approach medical doctors use to diagnose problems and cure illnesses. A doctor takes deliberate steps/changes toward curing the patient and continuously monitors the progress (or impacts of the actions) in order to adjust treatments accordingly.

Formulating the best strategic approach will be much influenced by the state of the industry and the market.

Whilst conventional approaches may still be relevant to quite static markets, more responsive and flexible methods may be required, such as those proposed by Reeves, Love and Tillmanns (2012).

Adaptive Approach

For an organization operating in the fast-moving, reactive environment (e.g. the high-street fashion industry), adaptability is the key to competitive advantage. It is not only strategies that have to be constantly adapted, but also corporate goals and objectives must be continuously refined to reflect the changes in the marketplace. In this case, a long-term view is impractical, since strategic plans are likely to be created on an on-going basis. A strategic plan should be regarded as "rough hypotheses" which is developed based on the best available data. These hypotheses need to be constantly tested out and refined.

How Design can Support the Adaptive Approach: Zara

Zara is a high-street fashion company famous for its effective supply chain and product forecasting. One of the key success factors is good use of design management. Zara has a dedicated team of designers and product managers who oversee the entire product development process starting from the design and development right through to the production. Good relationships between the design and the retail teams lead to the effectiveness of performance in terms of product forecasting. This makes sure that Zara produces what is in demand. It takes only two weeks for the company to get a new concept into a store.

Shaping Approach

For an organization operating in an industry where nothing can be taken as given (e.g. rules are often challenged and practices are frequently changed) and they are very likely to be affected by disruptive innovation (e.g. consider how iPhone shifted the path of the mobile industry and how YouTube transformed the entertainment industry), rather than trying to anticipate changes, it is better to shape the industry and become a pioneer in the field before someone else does. Similar to the adaptive approach, shaping strategies should be developed in short or continual planning cycles. However, the focus goes beyond the boundary of the company. The organization adopting this approach should aim to shape the whole ecosystem. Although Apple did not produce the first digital music players, iPod and iTunes redefined the rules, shaped new practices and established new norms for the music industry.

How Design can Support the Shaping Approach: Rovio's Angry Birds

Angry Birds has changed the gaming industry and has become one of the most successful mainstream games in the 2010s. After the success of the first iPhone, the developers foresaw that the smartphone could become a new mass medium for casual gaming. By combining strategic thinking with high-quality design that appealed to a wide range of audiences, the game was successfully launched and continues to expand. Effective use of design was evidenced in all elements, e.g. character design, interaction design (intuitive gestures) and graphic design.

Visionary Approach

Some visionary strategists or leaders can spot future trends long before someone else, and are capable of coming up with radical goals and strategic plans for realizing them (e.g. consider Amazon back in 1994 and Virgin Galactic more recently). Kim and Mauborgne (2004) coined the term *Blue Ocean Strategy* to describe this approach. Rather than wasting time and money competing in highly competitive market (dubbed the Red Ocean by Kim and Mauborgne), it is more lucrative to open up a new market (Blue Ocean proposed by Kim and Mauborgne) and become its leader. In this case, colour red is used as a metaphor for a hostile environment, while colour blue is referred to a peaceful environment – no competition and full rewards can be reaped. In order to do so, equal emphasis must be placed on (customers' perceived) *value* and (technological) *innovation*. Advanced technologies alone cannot attract customers. However, a new value proposition on its own can be vulnerable – since it may be easy to copy.

How Design can Support the Visionary Approach: Nestlé's Nespresso

One example of value innovation is Nespresso. The technology that allows consumers to brew the perfect cup of espresso in the comfort of their homes was invented and patented in the 1970s. However, without real demand from the market, the business did not take off until the late 1990s. To convince coffee lovers that espresso produced by the machine is as good as the one prepared by a well-trained barista, strategic design was used. The company used Nespresso experience (a beautifully-designed boutique café, where people can try Nespresso machines and different flavours) as a way to generate demand and it has become one of Nestlé fastest growing brands (more than 30% per annum between 2005 and 2010).

Of course there are still many opportunities to develop successful strategies in the highly competitive "red ocean" and it may be idealistic to expect to stay in tranquil waters for long.

Another way to handle the fearsome new environment may be to adopt a co-creative strategy by engaging and harnessing the creativity of all stakeholders. Ramaswamy and Gouillart (2010) identified several advantages of this approach and how design strategy may be used to develop them as follows:

- Design has been recognized for its potential to add value but a co-creative strategy has the capacity to identify changes and consumer needs quickly and make constant incremental and new product/service improvements.
- The aims of organizations and their design strategies should always complement each other but once fixed may be constraining: co-creation shows more confidence and maturity in allowing strategy to evolve and improve over time.
- The core business strategy of economic growth can develop into a more responsible approach to creating and delivering synergy among stakeholders, increasing commitment and loyalty and thus generating wider understanding and more opportunities.
- In place of the focus on using design to find cost savings, design thinking can be used to explore and create new interactions and experiences among the key stakeholders.

The process for co-creative strategy with stakeholders can be grouped into four main steps. Firstly, all key stakeholders involved in the value chain must be identified. Secondly, their current interactions should be mapped out to develop an in-depth understanding of their involvements and contributions. Next, planning of activities, e.g. organizing workshops, where they could share experiences, exchange ideas and imagine ways to improve current situations, which can lead to new strategic directions. Finally, implementing the agreed ideas and maintaining the conversations with all key stakeholders to continually improve ideas.

Ramaswamy and Gouillart (2010) claimed that many companies already successfully adopt this approach, namely Lego, Dell, Procter & Gamble and Unilever.

2.1.3   Design Approaches for Strategic Planning

"Good design is good business" said Thomas Watson, CEO of IBM in the 1950s. In more recent years the benefits have been made explicit by using design strategically. The potential of design strategy to make a significant contribution to business aims was recognized by Bessant (2002) and direct links may be summarized as shown in Table 2.2 below.

Hands (2009) regards designers as "unsung heroes of strategy development; they probe, test and stretch what is possible in the understanding of product development." Cooper and Press (1995) explained the strong relationships.

They established strong links between corporate strategy, the complementary objectives of design strategy and what design management ultimately delivers.

Corporate strategy is first and foremost for setting the goals, which are interpreted, visualized, clarified and communicated by the design strategy, and delivered through design management of a high quality visual and text-based communication of the corporate identity programme. At corporate strategy level management seek to drive the application of the aims, design strategy develops these applications into competitive goods and services and design management executes a design policy with a clear interpretation of the objectives.

Organizational goals require consistency since an unpredictable approach may serve to foster disharmony and misunderstanding. Design strategy can reflect and develop this consistency through the application of the design policy and clear standards and monitoring. Good leadership of design management is required for this. Whilst consistency inspires confidence, the rapidly changing market environment means that corporate strategy cannot be rigid and must be flexible enough to respond to changing conditions. Thus design strategy must mirror this flexibility and responsiveness and include environmental scanning and futures foresight. Design management delivers an outward-looking approach and develops a culture of innovation within the company.

Table 2.2   Relationship between companies' aims and design strategy

Company goals	Design strategy delivers
To enhance the company reputation and image by providing the best value to customers	• Adds value through product enhancements, styling, aesthetic quality and consistent reliability • Product/service differentiation • Designing for identity and total brand experience
To build an innovative and creative company culture in an environment of continuous improvement	• Design process for ideation, communication, synthesis and integration of functions • Product/service improvements and promotions
To identify and meet market needs rapidly and cost effectively	• Design thinking to reduce complexity, source new technology/materials and optimize logistics • Design to simplify manufacture, reduce production time and improve responsiveness.

In comparing the approaches of managers and designers to strategy development, it may first be noted that both should be based on a good understanding of corporate goals (e.g. missions and visions) and core capabilities as well as the competitive environment (user expectations and emerging trends). However the designers' approach may differ in that they use the design process to come up with new strategies. Designers always work with constraints (e.g. material properties, feasible technologies and viable manufacturing processes) although some are more aware of the constraints than others. So many design strategists examine these parameters (e.g. competitors' strategies) and come up with ideas which they then prototype, test and refine accordingly. Thus just like a product or service the strategy becomes a prototype.

Design disciplines also bring the extra dimension of visual skills to help communicate something which does not yet exist, for example a new product or even a new business model. Then they find create ways to test it, for example role playing.

An example is IDEO's strategy development process which is an iterative cycle of three key stages: *discovery*, *decision* and *delivery* (Weiss, 2008). *Discovery* is about contextualizing all key parameters, e.g. core brand values, business goals and key stakeholders' requirements. *Decision* is about choosing which angle the corporate seeks out to be different – to stand out from the crowd. This part focuses on synthesizing, designing and developing actionable ideas. Finally, *delivery* is about turning ideas into sustainable value propositions – using visualization tools/techniques, e.g. graphic iconography, which are easy to communicate to all key stakeholders or decision makers.

Since the different levels of design management require different types of strategic design planning, Best (2006) proposed three stages of design management, which have direct links to how strategic use of design is planned:

- *Strategic level*: The design leader sets the *vision* for how design could be used in an organization and gains buy-in from key stakeholders.
- *Tactical level*: The design manager ensures the design *processes*, procedures and internal functions are adding value to the organization.
- *Operational level*: Designers help unlock the potential of the proposal, and craft and *deliver* the solution.

Outsourcing Design

In order to use strategic design effectively, an organization does not have to establish an in-house design team. Many successful design-led organizations, such as Alessi and B&O, make a good use of external design resources, e.g. artists, designers and design consultancies.

Using external design resources is not necessarily cheaper. However, working with external designers could help a company re-examine its values, target markets and requirements. The rediscovery of what the company stands for, who it should be targeting and what opportunities it should be concentrating upon often helps the firm identify real needs and come up with new innovations. The "fresh" look (at problems) and "unbiased" thinking are considered very beneficial – even some in-house design teams decide to act like a design consultancy. For example, Philips Design team works like a design consultant. It treats the company as one of its clients and works for other companies as well (providing that these companies are not competitors). This practice helps its creative staff continue to develop new knowledge and stay sharp – working on the same products everyday could have negative effects on designers due to the lack of new challenges and opportunities to explore new areas.

However, working with external parties could lead to a leak of confidential information and intellectual property. Hence, "trust" is a serious issue that a company needs to take into consideration. Outsourcing design can be done through various practices. The simplest one is hiring a designer or a design consultancy to complete a design work according to a brief or a set of requirements set out by the company. Most experts agree that establishing a long-term relationship between the company and the designer/design consultancy is considered the most beneficial, since it promotes trust building, good understanding of each other's businesses and ways of working, as well as shortening the process (e.g. no need to re-establish the ground rules for each new project). This could be done in a form of strategic alliance or inter-organizational cooperation. By establishing mutual objectives, resources (e.g. financial and human resources) and intellectual properties can be shared. Many leading design/innovation consultancies, e.g. Seymour Powell, are interested in setting up a strategic alliance agreement with companies to pursue a shared vision (e.g. a new innovation) that they both believe in.

2.2   STRATEGIC DEVELOPMENT TOOLS

2.2.1   Established Tools

Many strategic design plans are developed using well-established business management tools such as SWOT analysis, PEST analysis, perceptual mapping, personas and scenarios, Ansoff's Matrix and the Boston Matrix. Each offers potential value and each has limitations. For design strategists they may all be seen as establishing the starting point before the tools for innovation and creative thinking take the strategy forward.

SWOT Analysis

SWOT is short for Strengths, Weaknesses, Opportunities and Threats. This tool excels at analyzing an organization prior to strategic planning. To ensure a thorough analysis, it important to cover all key aspects – ranging from management style and company functions right through to business performance such as market share. The tool helps designers to evaluate the current position in the broadest sense by showing the areas where design thinking is most needed, but does little to support the future directions and vision for design and innovation. Baxter (1995) identified how to use SWOT to analyze design effectiveness and identify the challenges for the design strategy to address. Table 2.3 shows how this can be done.

Table 2.3   Corporate strategy, design strategy and design management

Internal & current factors		External & future factors	
Strengths	Weaknesses	Opportunities	Threats
• Loyal customer base • Strong distribution chain • Brand well known • Experienced marketing staff	• Reducing profit margins • Maximum borrowing limit • Low technology manufacture • Long cycle for product development	• Good prospects for market expansion • Extend existing products/services • Product uniqueness in target sectors • Contracts for exclusive supply	• Failure to deliver new products/services which meet consumer needs • Reduced product quality • Resource constraints • Losing motivation and commitment of staff

PEST/PESTLE Analysis

PEST analysis is a framework for analyzing macrotrends potentially influencing an organization in the near future. It covers four key areas:

- *Political factors*: Changes in political climates – such as governmental policies
- *Economic factors*: Changes in the economic climate – such as growth or recession
- *Social factors*: Demographic and social trends – such as change in the population age structure, trends towards a multiracial and multicultural society
- *Technological factors*: Technological trends – such as new materials, processes, information systems, production techniques

Two more factors are often added, namely legal and environmental factors.

- *Legal factors*: Changes in laws and legislations – e.g. new health and safety laws
- *Environmental factors*: Changes in environmental practices and expectations

Again its value to designers is limited to identifying principally external forces and evaluating their influence on future design and innovation.

Ansoff's Matrix

Ansoff's Matrix is sometimes called the Product-Market Growth Matrix. It helps with planning product development and growth strategies. The tool suggests four generic options:

1. *Market penetration* (existing market, existing product): This strategy focuses on growing market shares in an organization's current market. For example, ASDA supermarkets use a low-price strategy to penetrate and maintain its share and the current market.
2. *Product development* (existing market, new product): This strategy is about growing through introductions of new products/services to existing

target audiences. For instance, high-street fashion companies introduce a new collection every season to existing customers. Focusing on existing targets has a lot of benefits, since a company has already developed a good understanding of their needs and wants. Moreover, it helps a company maintain and strengthen relationships with their customers. Even if the market share is not significantly improved, the money each customer spends could be increased.

3. *Market development* (new market, existing product): This strategy concentrates on expanding markets through introductions of existing products/ services to new target audiences (e.g. new geographic segments or new demographic segments). Lego bricks are construction toys designed for children. Recently, the company realized that Lego bricks could be used to assist people to generate, communicate, visualize and collaborate in creative workshops. For example, a development team wanting to create a new flagship store could use this toy to help them design and prototype their ideas together (see www.seriousplay.com). In this way, Lego gives new purposes to existing products and is able to introduce them to new target markets (e.g. creative professionals and developers) successfully.

4. *Diversification* (new market, new product): This strategy is probably the riskiest, since it explores how to grow businesses through introductions of new products/services to new markets. The Virgin Group is a good example of a company employing diversification strategy to grow businesses. Their products range from beverages to airlines. As a general rule few companies diversify widely, perhaps with one observed exception to be found in companies based in South Korea.

Designers may first see this tool as empowering but later find it a source of frustration when strategic managers show reluctance to take risks.

Boston Matrix

Boston Matrix is an analytical tool for appraising an organization's entire product/service portfolio. By categorizing current products into four different groups based on their market shares and growth rates, the company can make informed decisions regarding these products, e.g. proportion of resource allocation. Naturally an organization would tend to favour the best performers but ideas for regenerating under-performers may be considered and subsequently developed and a design strategy adopted to support the new business strategy.

1. *Question mark* – or sometimes called *problem child* (low market share, fast growth rate): Products belonging to this category grow rapidly and have yet to gain large enough market shares to generate sufficient profits to sustain themselves. They normally require a lot of resources to continue growing and could one day become *star* products.

2. *Star* (high market share, fast growth rate): Products belonging to this category have strong potential to become *cash cows* which help sustain and grow the company.

3. *Cash cow* (high market share, slow growth rate): Products belonged to this category typically reach maturity stage. The market shares are unlikely to

grow anymore, since they already reach most target audiences. However, these products continue to generate significant incomes, which helps support the company and new product development.

4. *Dog* (low market share, slow growth rate): Products belonging to this category typically have reached maturity stage, but market share is unlikely to grow anymore. They are unable to generate good returns like those in the *cash cow* category. In most cases, products in this category should be sold off and/or discontinued due to loss making.

Personas & Scenarios

Persona is a useful tool for the user-profiling process. Conducting thorough user research, attributes or characteristics that most target audiences have in common can be identified. Personas can help summarize and integrate these characteristics (e.g. demographic data, psychographic data, lifestyles and behaviours) in a meaningful way by creating "fictional" persons to represent the main target group. Using fictional characters as references, an organization can make plans, evaluate, select and implement strategic decisions effectively.

Scenarios are imaginative stories describing how fictional characters (personas) think about certain tasks and behave in certain situations. By creating these stories, an organization can visualize how users may interact with their brands, products and/or services. Scenarios can be presented in a variety of media, e.g. narrative stories, cartoons, storyboards, films, videos and/or short plays. One story can feature more than one persona.

Designers find these tools valuable but would argue that greater insights into human emotions and behaviour can be achieved using design research tools.

Perceptual Mapping

A perceptual map is a diagrammatic tool which excels at assisting an organization visualize positions of their existing products, product lines and brands in relation with those of competitors. This helps the organization make informed decisions regarding strategic options available to them, answering the question "Should/could they exploit the identified gap in the market?"

For designers this holds much promise because it assists them to argue their case for support (Figure 2.1).

The tool is used by luxury car manufacturers to establish their own space and keep as far away from competitors as possible in their quest for differentiation.

2.2.2 Emerging Tools

POINT

The name is short for Problems, Obstacles, Insight, Needs, and Themes. It is one example of an advanced tool to gain deeper insights as a basis for strategic planning. The technique was introduced by IDEO (2011) as part of

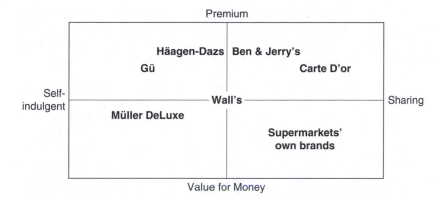

Figure 2.1 A perceptual map demonstrating positions of the cold dessert brands in the UK

the Human Centered Design Toolkit to help developers and strategic planners translate problems and opportunities into insights and themes. IDEO strongly encourage developers and strategic planners to actively collaborate with real users and key stakeholders in order to develop empathy for their situations, needs and wants.

By exchanging knowledge and ideas with these people, a truly innovative solution that benefits all parties can be realized. In this case, insight is defined both as the "unexpected" discovery that requires closer attention and examination and the identification of common factors/patterns that reoccurred in most users' stories. For example, elderly customers do not shop online – not because they cannot understand the Internet, but because they prefer to socialize with other people at actual stores. Insights into their behaviour and feelings could help developers and strategic planners to look at problems and opportunities in a new light. In this case, finding themes is about identifying similarities, differences and relationships of the insights extracted. For instance, some problems may be related to each other and/ or some ideas support each other. By clustering similar insights, needs and ideas together, key issues or themes can be extracted to guide strategic planning and developments further.

2.3 4DS OF STRATEGIC DESIGN MANAGEMENT

In order to bring together the established paradigms of management with the emergent paradigms of design strategy, it is first necessary to regard design as a resource. Management has long regarded money, physical property, human resources, technology know-how, markets, and (more recently) information as essential resources. Design and design thinking however, are frequently regarded as intangible and thus difficult to manage in the same rigorous manner. Thus although many strategic design tools/frameworks are available (a further list is provided later), they are often regarded as somewhat theoretical and academic.

Also many of these existing tools seek to promote design as "different" and suggest it must be managed in a manner markedly different from other resources. Managing the organizational design resource is challenging but it can be managed with the same degree of commitment as all other resources.

Organizations increasingly accept that creativity is a powerful resource for survival and growth. Consequently they turn to designers to generate new opportunities and directions. But having accepted design as a fundamental asset of the organization the question arises, "Can design be managed within the planning and control processes of the organization?"

Designers inherently resist control, particularly if it is seen as over rigid or detrimental to their creative freedom, but they respond well to management planning and control processes which respect their role and recognize their contribution. So the application of the planning and control principles to managing design may require much tact and sensitivity. In order to integrate management and design and bring design to the status of a recognized organizational resource, a framework is offered which emulates the management practice of establishing the current position of the organization, seeking and indicating new directions, planning the route to reach the goals and regularly reviewing progress. It is derived from the evolving pedagogy of design strategy education supported by leading practitioners and reflective of contemporary research.

The 4Ds of design management framework is developed to promote practical development and is based on the four fundamental questions: Where are we? Where are we going? How do we get there? How do we know when we have got there? This means tools are needed for each stage beginning with a robust assessment of an organization's current understanding and use of design, a thoroughly mastered sense of the direction the organization is going or wishes to go, a design strategy based on well-integrated management and design thinking, and methods of rigorously evaluating, maintaining and enhancing the quality of the outcomes.

Good cross-functional communication and feedback to designers is an embedded feature of the framework which comprises four stages:

- **Determining**: Objectively assessing perception and competence in the usage of design.
- **Defining**: Establishing visions, strategic directions and opportunities for design.
- **Designing**: Using design thinking to develop strategies and solutions.
- **Deciding**: Objectively evaluating the quality of the implementations.

The four steps of the 4Ds framework address the key elements of design at strategic, tactical and operational level as shown in the Table 2.4 below. The interrelationships of four key elements of the 4Ds framework are illustrated in Figure 2.2. These elements follow the cycle of managing all organizational resources, assessing the strengths and weaknesses at the starting point, establishing plans and strategies to move forward, executing them and evaluating performance as a platform for continuous improvement.

Table 2.4   Key elements of the 4Ds of design management

Strategic level	Tactical level	Operational level
Determining		
Attitude	**Organization**	**Implementation**
• Design commitment	• Design resources	• Products
• Design culture & policy	• Design processes	• Services
• Environment & facilities	• Team structure	• Experiences
Defining		
Visions	**Objectives**	**Deliverables**
• Design goals	• Design approach	• Design projects
• Design philosophy	• Design language	• Design activities
Designing		
Strategy	**Tactics**	**Design attributes**
• Brands & promises	• Unique selling point	• Differentiation
• Competitive advantages	• Product portfolio	• Touch points
Deciding		
Corporate performance	**Business performance**	**Product performance**
• Creative organizational development	• Return on investment	• Effectiveness
	• Market share	• Efficiency
• Vision and confidence	• Market growth	• Customer satisfaction

2.3.1   Determining Where We Are: Design Audit

The first D is about assessing the current situation. Two forms of audit based on assigning scores were developed by Kotler and Rath (1984) to assess sensitivity to design and design management effectiveness by assigning scores to a series of key questions. They provide a useful starting point to measure the degree to which design plays a role, if any, within the organization. The tool may be "tailored" to fit the organization but some examples of the questions may be:

Design Sensitivity Audit

- What is the relative importance assigned to design as part of the marketing strategy?
  - Design is largely ignored as part of marketing strategy – score 0
  - Design plays a minor subservient role in marketing tactics – score 1
  - Design is a major strategic integrated component of the marketing strategy – score 2
- How well is design thinking used to develop new products and/or services?
  - Design thinking cannot be identified in design development processes-score 0
  - There is some evidence of design thinking/research in product development – score 1
  - Good design thinking/research is evident in all design development – score 2

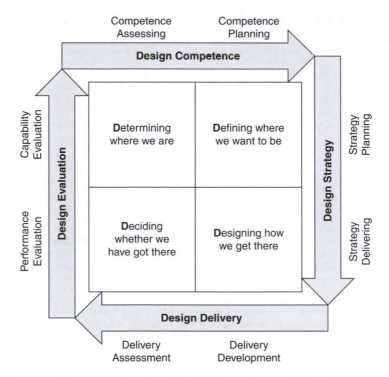

Figure 2.2 Interrelationships of four key elements of the 4Ds framework

The questions can be further extended to cover such aspects as environmental design awareness and practice, inclusiveness in design thinking, influence on corporate identity and brand, organizational culture and supporting resources for design and the ability to use creative designers effectively.

Design Management Effectiveness Audit

- How do the design staff approach their work?
  - The design staff focus is on artistic/ aesthetic concepts but they are unaware of the market and consumer needs – score 0
  - The design staff design what marketing requests in the brief – score 1
  - The design staff begin with awareness of the market and consumer needs before applying their creative thinking – score 2

- Does the management encourage and foster creative experimentation?
  - Creative experiment is regarded as a waste of time – score 0
  - Designers are given tight briefs and specifications but allowed small area of freedom- score 1
  - Designers have support for creative freedom with well-defined parameters – score 2

Further questions may relate to support for research and analysis, resources for design planning, allocation and monitoring of the budget, cross-functional relations, evaluation of outcomes and continuous learning.

In recent years many design audit approaches have emerged, some focussing on design and others on design management systems. A comparison may be made to the financial audit of a business which was once concerned with checking minutiae but evolved to become a sophisticated check of the effectiveness and security of systems.

In a similar way design management audit frameworks are now less prescriptive, more holistic and more flexible to encompass strategic design. To assess the value of a design audit tool, it is useful to follow Hands (2011), who outlines the general benefits of the audit process as follows:

- provision of knowledge of current practice;
- improvements in standards of process;
- highlighting of non-compliances;
- identification of potentially damaging practice;
- rewards which are intrinsically linked to accurate knowledge;
- securing of future cohesion;
- promotion of higher standards;
- facilitation of further planning;
- stimulation of learning.

A good example of design audit framework is Lockwood's (2007) ten categories for design measurement. His approach is a rather open framework and may thus require experience to drill down to the evidence of design performance. However its conceptual nature allows for skilful adaption to each organization. These ten categories are:

1. Purchase influence/emotion.
2. Enable strategy/enter new markets.
3. Build brand image and corporate reputation.
4. Improve time to market and development process.
5. Design return on investment (ROI)/cost savings.
6. Enable product and service innovation.
7. Increase customer satisfaction/develop communities of customers.
8. Design patents and trademarks/create intellectual property.
9. Improve usability.
10. Improve sustainability.

Whichever design audit tool or combination is adopted or formulated, it needs to cover all aspects of design from the top to the bottom of the organization. Table 2.5 below shows what needs to be determined at each level and the key considerations and questions.

The purpose will dictate the suitable time to carry out the design audit. While an annual audit might be conducted as part of continuous improvements, a one-off audit might be carried out as part of the preparation prior to strategic planning for particular projects.

Table 2.5 The 1st D – determining where we are

	Determining	Key considerations
Strategic level (attitude)	Design commitment	*Is design considered when planning corporate visions and objectives?*
	Design culture & policy	*Is there a culture of using design thinking and identifiable policy?*
	Environment & facilities	*Does the environment stimulate design? Is it conducive to creative thinking and sharing ideas?*
Tactical level (organization)	Design resources	*What is the relative investment in design? Are the resources adequate?(e.g. appropriate software)*
	Design processes	*What processes are used? How responsive are they? Are they appropriate and progressive?*
	Team structure	*How is the design team constituted? Is it multidisciplinary?*
Operational level (implementation)	Products	*Are products fit for purpose? Aesthetically pleasing? Pleasurable?*
	Services	*Is the service a consistent, high quality experience?*
	Experiences	*What is the real user experience and opportunities for enhancement?*

Experts agree that the design audit could be done by either an internal or an external team. While an external team could ensure the objectivity of the results, an internal team is likely to have better understanding of an organization. However, it is recommended that a combination of external and internal members is probably the most suitable compromise. Design Council (2001) discussed the advantages and disadvantages of involving different participants in the audit process as shown in Table 2.6.

2.3.2 Defining Where We Want To Be: Visions and Strategic Directions

Defining (the second D) is about setting goals and objectives, clearly establishing where the organization wants to be in the marketplace and in the customers' minds, and what design can do to achieve that. The highly respected Peter Drucker (1999) established that "mission defines strategy and strategy defines (organisational) structure, and strategy allows an organisation to be purposefully opportunistic." So clarity of purpose and shared visions across the organization are revealed as the critical prerequisites for developing a successful strategy. However business strategies may not be easy to identify, as shown by Collis and Ruskard (2008) who found that many executives could not summarize their corporate strategy.

To define the ideal or optimum use of design and design management, an organization needs the "designful mind," explained by Neumeier (2008)

Table 2.6   Advantages and disadvantages of different design audit approaches

Approach	Pros	Cons
Assessment by an internal individual		
One person takes responsibility for answering design audit questions.	One individual can quickly come up to speed with the issues highlighted within the design audit questions.	It can be difficult for one person to have a balanced insight into all the issues addressed within design audit questions.
Assessment by questionnaire		
One person co-ordinates the mailing out, collection and collation of design audit questions across an organization.	Quick and effective approach that encourages maximum participation.	Can be difficult to explain the background behind each area of questioning.
Assessment by working group		
A working group is established to answer design audit questions.	Provides the best opportunity for buy-in to the process and a healthy exchange of views.	Can be resource intensive due to the time required to attend working group meetings.
Assessment by external consultant		
An external consultant familiar with design audit questions undertakes a review on behalf of the business.	Has the potential to provide an objective external view on company activities – with ideally an insight into how other businesses are undertaking the activity.	External consultant needs to be selected carefully to ensure their understanding of the issues within design audit process. Careful management of the interface between the consultant and the business is essential.

Source: Reproduced from Design Council's *Design Atlas: A Tool for Auditing Design Capability* (http://www.designinbusiness.org.uk). Used with permission.

as the ability to generate the widest range of solutions to business challenges and problems. He argues that "design drives innovation, innovation powers brand, brand builds loyalty and loyalty sustains profits."

Goals need to be realistic and (preferably) measurable but should not be constrained by copying rivals. Effective use of design strategy will lead to the identification of alternative strategies to achieve the defined goals and support the use of creative artistic talents to differentiate the offer. Vision for designers differs from vision for business. Whilst business executives would all wish to claim some degree of vision, they tend to translate their visions into economic and financial performance indicators. Designers, especially those of artistic persuasion regard vision as a visual picture in their imagination of our futures. This is one of the principal challenges of reconciling design and business directions. Table 2.7 below shows key considerations for defining the strategic direction.

Table 2.7 Defining "where we want to be"

	Defining	Key considerations
Strategic level (visions)	Design goals	Set realistic goal(s) in terms of design capabilities. *What types of design expertise do we need to address identified opportunities and challenges?*
	Design philosophy	Establish clear design principles that will drive and guide all design decisions in an organization. *Which design philosophy will set us apart from competitors, motivate current staff and attract talented workforces?*
Tactical level (objectives)	Design approach	Organizational considerations. *Should we use an in-house design team? Should we use external consultancies? Or should we combine both?*
	Design language	Develop clear communication both internally and externally. *How should design convey the key message to our customers, partners, public audience and employees?*
Operational level (deliverables)	Design projects	Adopt good project management – monitoring and control. *Do we choose the right design project for our company/ brand? Do we manage the design project right?*
	Design activities	Promote well-focused creativity *How design activities are promoted and appraised?*

Example: Lenovo

Lenovo is a large Chinese corporation in the computer business. Having established their dominance of the Chinese market largely through innovation and product development, they acquired IBM's Personal Computing Division in an effort to become a major global brand.

Their vision is evident from their mission statement "to design innovative and exciting products and services to meet our customer's needs." They have placed design at the strategic management level. Their strategy is to combine Chinese expressive design with the Western emphasis on durability, reliability and ease of use. Their greatest strategic challenge may be to overcome the poor perception of "MADE in CHINA" which still holds back many Chinese organizations. The in-house design function is led by a visionary designer who is personally credited with many of the innovative developments of the Lenovo products.

2.3.3   Designing How We Get There – Design Activities and Cultures

The third D is concerned with planning the route forward. After rigorously assessing the current situation and realistically defining the strategic directions, now a plan is required to reach the goal(s). This stage is a combination of Big-D and small-d design in that it combines the systems design such as product planning and brand communication with the actual practical designing, such as product design, packaging design and interior design.

The close relationship of the two types of design is pivotal to the performance of the organization and mutual respect and good communication between the practitioners must be engendered.

BSI (2008) defined design strategy as:

> the chosen path formulated to achieve business and design objectives, supported by an indication of how resources will be committed.

However, to use design effectively organizations need to go beyond an indication and formulate a step by step plan for design activities at all levels.

Keinonen (2008) found that design strategy is needed at the nucleus of an organization as well as the operational level. At the strategic level, "the nucleus," it can generate visions and turn them into tangible opportunities, develop competences in using new technology, problem solving and information dissemination, and nurture attitudes, expectations and behaviours. At the operational level design can be used for managing and controlling collaborations internally and externally, delivering meaningful experiences to users, and establishing common ground for networking and alliances. To gain significant benefits from the design strategy it should also be extended to promote good leadership and multidisciplinary team working. Table 2.8 summarizes the two approaches to strategic planning.

Table 2.8 Summary of design strategies for the central and outer levels of the organization

At the centre of the organization	At the outer operational level
Design strategies offer design visions and competences in response to consumers' changing expectations.	Design strategies offer meaningful experiences and responsiveness to help identify business opportunities and deliver new products and services

In reality, design strategic planning is usually a hybrid of the linear and trial and error approaches. Indeed the two extremes may be considered dangerous because the first may lead to rigidity and lack of creativity whilst the second may lead to anarchy. Building a creative culture is essential. A culture that supports and nurtures design generates more creative ideas which can improve organizational performance. Such a culture must encourage and reward new ideas, make staff feel secure about expressing themselves freely and challenging conventions, promote a rich diversity of thinking and information sharing, be positive about risk taking, and even promote playfulness. A summary of the key design activities can be seen in Table 2.9.

Example: Google

Google use design to deliver their mission "to organize the world's information and make it universally accessible and useful." Their flat organizational structure enables the Google brand to be dynamic and adaptive to new environments, people, technology and emergent challenges. The culture of entrepreneurial, accessible and supportive team players embeds design thinking throughout the organization. Google's employees perceive the

Table 2.9 The 3rd D – designing how we get there

	Designing	Key considerations
Strategic level (strategy)	• Brand and promises	Design compelling values that capture people's imagination, inspire staff and attract new partners/investors.
	• Competitive advantages	Use design to create competitive advantages.
Tactical level (tactics)	• Unique selling points	Designing the communication of unique selling points at all stages.
	• Product portfolio	Develop a "family" of products/services.
Operational level (design attributes)	• Differentiation • Touch points	Stand out from the crowd. Make the experience special and memorable.

organization as innovative, fun, engaging, dynamic, intelligent, creative, original and smooth.

The architecture, outdoor landscaping, workspaces and even the parking lot reflect the Google brand. The exterior and interior of their office complex is designed around multidisciplinary collaboration and nomadic work styles. It is an open and imaginative work neighbourhood that inspires multidisciplinary thinking and cross-pollination of ideas. Google's brand has a diverse product portfolio and their founders and CEO are authentic brand champions. Andy Bernt, GLC managing director, described the team as "an eco-system of collaborators from designers to writers to agencies to production companies to every kind a creative resource." (This case study is derived from research by Bentley, 2009)

2.3.4 Deciding Whether We Have Got There: Evaluating Performance

The deciding "D" is about assessing the quality of the implementation and checking whether the outcomes meet the targets. To decide whether the organization has got there, it needs unambiguous performance targets. Because design strategy usually includes many intangible qualitative benefits it is often difficult to establish any rigorous measurement criteria. However the difficulty should not be used as an excuse, even the most intangible of benefits can be identified and highlighted and recently professionals are becoming more adept at "proving" the links between good design and organizational success.

At strategic level such questions as "Is the organization becoming more creative?" and "How well is design used to generate vision and self-belief?" Tactical level may be concerned with measuring profit generated, percentage of market share and growth rates. Operational level will include assessment of efficiency (e.g. output, budget compliance) and effectiveness, addressing questions like "Are we doing the right things?" and "Are we meeting/ exceeding customer expectations?" The organization's policy and practice in setting targets will much influence the motivation of designers and collaborating executives to achieve them.

In a design-led multidisciplinary team project it is vital that the artistic/ engineering designers are fully engaged in the setting of targets. If they are not respected and fully involved, it will lead to potential disenchantment and confusion. Recent design management audit frameworks, such as criteria for the Design Management Europe award: DME (2010) and Design Business Association's Design Effective award (2011) can be used as a basis for a thorough evaluation.

Criteria for the Design Management Europe (DME) Award

- *Leadership in design innovation*: Defining and implementing a vision for the whole organization; integrating design across a range of activities.
- *Driving change through design*: Identifying significant changes within an organization where design has played a major role.
- *Excellence in design coordination*: Demonstrating capabilities, processes, skills and resources in support of the application of design.
- *Strategic performance*: Demonstrating performance based on objectives, deliverables and overall effect on the organization.

Criteria for the Design Effectiveness Award – Design Management Category

1. Ability to plan strategically/analyze critically the overall objectives of the organization and design's subsequent role.
2. Capability to manage/integrate a wide variety of design disciplines.
3. Interface improvement between business managers and designers, leading to effective implementation of design initiatives.
4. Reduction of complex and costly operational practicalities.
5. Improvement in the organization's perceived reputation through the effective management of the visible elements of a corporation.
6. To manage design in building a sustainable global competitive advantage by integrating national cultures and design resources.
7. Successful implementation of a design programme.
8. Increased market share/brand value as a result of design management.
9. Increased share price.
10. Reduced brand communication and organizational costs.

Design has been proven to add value even in a recession (AMION Consulting, 2009). For example, good architectural design could increase the economic value of property, enhance the attractiveness of the area, and enrich quality of life of people who live in/nearby that property. While the value of houses fell generally across the UK in the late 2000s some of the best properties, well designed and in desirable locations such as parts of London, increased their value.

Indeed it is argued that design can shore up an organization's survival and even help to outperform rivals. The added value should cover economic, social and environmental values and must establish a recognizable continuity and futures focus. Deciding whether we have got there or whether there is some way to go requires close investigation of issues at all levels as well as a holistic assessment of how well they are integrated. A summary of the key deciding factors can be seen in Table 2.10.

Table 2.10 The 4th D – deciding whether we have got there

	Deciding	Key considerations
Strategic level (corporate performance)	Creative organizational development	Recruit the best creative people and develop a creative culture.
	Vision and confidence	A high level of vision and self-belief throughout the organization.
Tactical level (business performance)	Return on investment	Measurable financial outcomes recognising the design contributions.
	Market share	Use design as well as tactical know-how as a competitive weapon.
	Market growth	Sustain and grow through innovation and development of new products/ services.
Operational level (product performance)	Efficiency and effectiveness	Design helps an organization decrease cost of product/service development, increase the speed to market, reduce failures and improve efficiency.
	Customer satisfaction	Design helps an organization enhance customer satisfaction and loyalty.

2.4 CONCLUSION

Chapter 2 has introduced several approaches to strategic planning and showed how they are changing to meet new challenges for more flexibility and adaptation. Classic and emergent tools show how to build a strategy and bring together corporate strategy and design strategy.

In order to make the establishment of design strategy practical, as distinct from purely a set of theoretical ideas, a 4D strategic design framework is presented and tools for using the framework are suggested and explained. Subsequent chapters will explain in detail the application of the 4D model. This framework promotes design management as a catalyst for change, challenging the established models of strategic management. It shows the way forward to develop new integrated models that synthesize and harmonize the relationship between design strategy and corporate strategy.

Joziasse (2008) revealed three major roles for design management in the management of corporate strategy. First as catalyst and analyst the design manager should encourage management to think ahead and challenge management by constantly posing questions about key assumptions. Second as "sythesyst" and evaluator the design manager should transform the company's perceptions of its future into designs which harmonize with the corporate strategy, be a powerful advocate for new designs in close relationships with users. Third as implementer the design manager should deliver designs which interpret and celebrate the corporate strategy using natural talents and multidisciplinary teamwork.

2.5   STRATEGIC DESIGN TOOLKITS

2.5.1   Design Manager Toolbox (Taskbox)

Borja de Mozota (2003) summarized the roles and responsibilities of design managers as a toolbox. Since it is somewhat theoretical it may perhaps more accurately be described as a *taskbox* since it sets out the jobs to be done. A taskbox can also be developed to assess the potential contributions and relationships between design and other key business functions. Figure 2.3 should be viewed as an agenda for tools to be developed and tested. It highlights the need for continued research and learning from practice to address the successful application of design strategy.

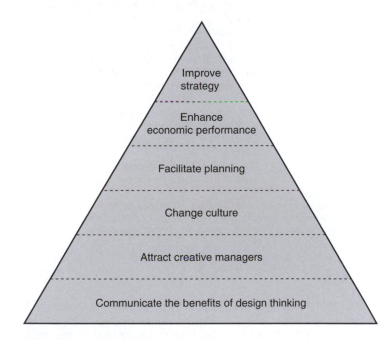

Figure 2.3   The design strategists required tools

2.5.2   Design Atlas

Design Atlas is a generic design audit framework introduced by the Design Council, UK that can be used to help any type of organization assess its design capability. The questions are grouped into five groups: (1) planning for design, (2) processes for design, (3) resources for design, (4) people for design, and (5) culture for design – see Table 2.11. A company can give a score from one to four for each question to identify current skills, as well as strengths and weaknesses. The full tool and guidance on how develop each area of design capability further can be downloaded from www.designin-business.org.

Table 2.11 below summarizes and extends the areas addressed by the tool:

Table 2.11   Design Atlas – summary of issues for evaluation

Design strategy domain	Issues for assessment
Planning	Awareness of purpose/value of strategy and plan
	Planning communication throughout the organization
	Integration of design into business strategy
	The design thinking underpinning the plan
	Focus of the design thinking and foresight
Processes	Awareness and understanding of the [underlying] processes
	Understanding of where and how design fits the business processes
	The level of the management of design
	Quality of the tools and methodologies used for design
Resources	Awareness of purpose/value of budgetary allocation and control
	Allocation of adequate budgets to design
People	Skills for effective design activity
	Development of cross-functional and multidisciplinary working
Culture	Support of senior management for design
	Attitudes to design throughout organization

Note: Level 1 = no evidence of design capability; Level 4 = clear evidence of strategic design
Source: Reproduced from Design Council's *Design Atlas: A Tool for Auditing Design Capability* (http://www.designinbusiness.org.uk/part_2/results_sheet.html). Used with permission.

2.6   GLOSSARY

Co-creation is defined as "any act of collective creativity, i.e. creativity that is shared by two or more people. Co-creation is a very broad term with applications ranging from the physical to the metaphysical and from the material to the spiritual, as can be seen by the output of search engines" (Sanders and Stappers, 2008).

Corporate social responsibility (CSR) is a concept suggesting that all organizations must be responsible and accountable for their conducts. Nowadays, most leading companies produce CSR reports alongside their annual reports to demonstrate their social and environmental targets and achievements, as well as financial ones.

Design audit is a systematic evaluation of design activities within an organization to establish the extent to which the targets/objectives have been met and identify areas for further improvements (BSI, 2008).

A Design brief is a document describing purposes, context (e.g. users), key deliverables and criteria of particular design work (BSI, 2008). A design brief is often used to set clear targets for a design project.

A Champion is a person dedicated and responsible for the promotion of and strategic thinking behind an initiative or a project. For example, a product champion is responsible for a new product development project, an innovation champion is responsible for innovation initiatives within an organization, and a design champion is responsible for the promotion of and strategic thinking behind design activities/directions.

A Design manager is a person responsible for managing design activities, ensuring that design outcomes support corporate strategies and objectives and making sure that required resources (e.g. finance and human resources) are in place to realize design goals.

Design policy is defined as general rules guiding design practices, directions and decision within an organization (BSI, 2008).

Human-centred design is a distinctive approach to design that focuses on needs/purposes, abilities/limitations and desires/aspirations of real people. Using the word "human" rather "user" signifies that design outcomes must fulfil beyond mere requirements of intended users, but add value to human life.

Prototype is an "approximation of the product along one or more dimensions of interest" (Ulrich and Eppinger, 2003). Thus, prototyping is a process of creating a prototype. While most people often associate the prototyping process with the new product development process, services and experiences can also be prototyped by simulating and enacting how users may interact with staff providing services.

Technology transfer is a process for passing on technological knowledge to others.

Trend spotting is an act of identifying future opportunities and reoccurring patterns in terms of style (e.g. fashion), user behaviours and potential markets.

2.7   REFERENCES AND ADDITIONAL READING

AMION Consulting. (2009) *Economic Value of Good Design in Recession: Final Report*. Liverpool: AMION Consulting.

Baxer, M. (1995) *Product Design: Practical Methods for the Systematic Development of New Product*. London: Chapman & Hall.

Bently, L. (2009) *Bonding through Branding*. Master Dissertation, Brunel University.

Bessant, J. (2002) Why Design? In M. Bruce and J. Bessant (eds) *Design in Business: Strategic Innovation through Design*. Harlow: Pearson Education, 3–17.

Best, K. (2006) *Design Management: Managing Design Strategy, Process and Implementation*. London: AVA Publishing.

Best, K. (2010) *The Fundamentals of Design Management*. Lausanne: AVA.

Borja de Mozota, B. (2003) *Design Management: Using Design to Build Brand Value and Corporate Innovation*. New York: Allworth.

Bruce, M. and Bassant J. (2002) *Design in Business*. Harlow: Pearson Education.

Bruce, M. and Cooper, R. (1997 *Marketing and Design Management*. London: International Thomson Business Press.

BSI (British Standards Institute). (2008) *BS 7000-10:2008: Design Management Systems – Part 10: Vocabulary of Terms Used in Design Management*. London: British Standards Institute.

Collis, D. J. and Ruskard, M. G. (2008) Can You Say What Your Strategy Is? *Harvard Business Review*, April 2008, 82–90.

Cooper, R., Junginger, S. and Lockwood, T. (2011) *The Handbook of Design Management*. Basingstoke: Berg.

Cooper, R. and Press, M. (1995) *The Design Agenda: A Guide to Successful Design Management*. Chichester: John Wiley & Sons.

Design Business Association. (2011) *DBA Design Effectiveness Awards – Design Management: Tips for Evaluating Effectiveness* [WWW] Design Business Association. Available from: http://www.dba.org.uk/awards/tips_for_success.asp [Accessed 14 February 2011].

Design Council. (2001) *Design Atlas: A Tool for Auditing Design Capability*. [WWW] Design in Business. Available from: http://www.designinbusiness.org.uk/get_a_hardcopy.html [Accessed 14 February 2011].

Design Management Europe. (2011) *DME 2010: Guideline for Entrance*. [WWW] Design Management Europe. Available from: http://www.designmanagementeurope.com/site/index.php?page=63 [Accessed 14 February 2011].

Drucker, P. (1999) *Management Challenges for the 21st Century*. Oxford: Butterworth – Heinemann.

Hands, D. (2009) *Vision and Values in Design Management*. Lausanne: AVA Academia.

Hands, D. (2011) Design Transformations: Measuring the Value of Design. In R. Cooper, S. Junginger and T. Lockwood (eds) *The Handbook of Design Management*. Basingstoke: Berg Publishers, 366–378.

IDEO (2011) Human Centered Design Toolkit. [WWW] IDEO. Available from: http://www.ideo.com/work/human-centered-design-toolkit/ [Accessed: 24/06/14]

Joziasse, F. (2008) Corporate Strategy: Brining Design Management into the Fold. In T. Lockwood and T. Walton (eds) *Building Design Strategy: Using Design to Achieve Key Business Objectives*. New York: Allworth Press, 23–32.

Keinonen, T. (2008) Design in Business: Views from the Nucleus and the Periphery. *Design Management Review*, 19 (3), 30–36.

Kim, W. C. and Mauborgne, R. (2004) Blue Ocean Strategy. *Harvard Business Review*, October, 76–85.

Kotler, P. and Armstrong, G. (2008) *Principles of Marketing*. Upper Saddle River: Pearson Prentice Hall.

Kotler, P. and Rath, G. A. (1984) Design: A Powerful but Neglect Tool. *The Journal of Business Strategy*, Autumn, 16–21.

Lafley, A. G., Martin, R. L., Rivkin, J. W. and Siggelkow, N. (2012) Bringing Science to the Art of Strategy. *Harvard Business Review*, September, 56–66.

Lockwood, T. (2007) Design Value: A Framework for Measurement. *Design Management Review*, 18 (4), 90–97.

Lockwood, T. and Walton, T. (2008) *Building Design Strategy: Using Design to Achieve Key Business Objectives*. New York: Allworth Press, 79–86.

Mintzberg, H. (1994) The Fall and Rise of Strategic Planning. *Harvard Business Review*, 72 (1), 107–114.

Neumeier, M. (2008) The Designful Company. *Design Management Review*, 19 (2), 10–15.

Porter, M.E. (1985) *Competitive Advantage: Creating and Sustaining Superior Performance*. London: Free Press.

Ramaswamy, V. and Gouillart, F. (2010) Building the Co-creating Enterprise. *Harvard Business Review*, October, 100–109.

Reeves, M., Love, C. and Tillmanns, P. (2012) Your Strategy Needs A Strategy. *Harvard Business Review*, September, 76–83.

Sanders, E. and Stappers, P. J. (2008) Co-creation and the New Landscapes of Design. *Co-Design*, 4 (1), 5–18.

Tidd, J. Bessant, J. and Pavitt, K. (2005) *Managing Innovation: Integrating Technological, Market and Organisational Change* (3rd edn). Chichester: Wiley.

Ulrich, K.L. and Eppinger, S.D. (2003) *Product Design and Development* (3rd edn). London: McGraw Hill.

Weiss, L. (2008) Developing Tangible Strategies. In T. Lockwood and T. Walton (eds) *Building Design Strategy: Using Design to Achieve Key Business Objectives*. New York: Allworth Press, 79–86.

2.8   ONLINE RESOURCES

1. Design Business Association (DBA): www.dba.org.uk
2. Design Council: www.designcouncil.org.uk
3. Design Management Institute: www.dmi.org
4. TED: www.ted.com

Part II

MANAGING STRATEGIC DESIGN AT CORE BUSINESS LEVEL

This part of the book addresses managing strategic design to improve organizational performance in commercial business organizations and other organizations which use business management practices. Design goes to the very heart of the business and the best users of design know it is vital for management to maintain competitiveness. The application of the 4Ds model supports the growth of creativity and confidence throughout the organization. It provides the framework by which design can be integrated as a core function.

One of the most powerful driving forces for the recognition of the importance of design strategy is in brand building which organizations accept as essential to success. Yet many do not use design effectively to develop and deliver great brand experiences. Established business models miss the opportunity to use designers' advanced creative thinking powers to establish new brands, revitalize existing brands and become market leaders. Chapter 3 introduces the application of design management strategy into branding and explains the benefits.

Innovation has also been recognized as the key to organizational survival and success. Yet the role of design in innovation is an ongoing challenge and the degree to which design is used varies considerably across organizations and sectors. Brands which do not innovate will be hard, or even impossible to sustain. So design should drive the delivery of the brand experience and brand should drive innovation. Chapter 4 shows how design can support the development of successful cultures for innovation and the development of new and enhanced products and services which deliver added value.

Maximum leverage of the design resource will only be achieved when design is integrated with all business functions and design thinking infused throughout the organization. Design can generate new thinking for strategic directions as part of top management endeavours. It can stimulate new ideas and develop new *modus operandi* in marketing, research and development (R&D), human resource management, finance and all other functions. Design research, which uses mainly qualitative soft research methods, can offer valuable insights and enrich the dialogue in the growing multi-disciplinary environment. Chapter 5 shows how to establish design in the organization and use design for successful collaboration and the resultant performance benefits.

Throughout the section there are examples given for further investigation, case studies and exemplars of good practice, analogies and questions to provoke further thinking and debate.

Chapter 3
DESIGN–LED BRANDING

Branding has become a global imperative for success across all organizational forms. Beginning with brand identity and recognition, organizations seek to build brand value and engender loyalty. Establishing the brand values and managing the development and process is usually seen as an extension of the marketing function responsibility. But increasingly designers are involved in the earlier stages of building new brands and refreshing existing brands.

Design-led branding reverses the process by which branding is often developed by business managers and marketers. Traditional models and processes of branding treat design as a "service function" and the designer is usually not involved in strategic and operational stages, but rather given a brief (often lacking in vision and clarity) and instructed to design, principally the organization identity and brand promotion. Emergent models and good contemporary practice reveal the benefits of using design and creative thinking from the very first stage of brand building, brand renewal or rebranding and all aspects of brand management. There is growing recognition of the power of design to lead brands as organizations strive to offer better, differentiated and often unique experiences to stand out from the overcrowded market place.

Big-D design thinking is integrated with branding to formulate how design can be used to add value and to bring the brand to life. The emphasis is on developing a strategy to use design to add tangible and intangible values and create memorable experiences which promote brand loyalty. Design-led brand strategy provides the platform for practical small-d design ideas to be developed concurrent with the strategy, using creative thinking and experimentation to generate new or enhanced products and services which deliver the winning brand experience.

The 4Ds model is important because it provides common ground for managers and designers. Managers can use the model to encourage design thinking and promote creative ideas for making their organization stand out from the crowd. Designers can feel a greater sense of ownership of the brands they design and deliver.

This chapter explains how design can act as a catalyst to advance the growing relationship between design and branding strategy and its influence on brand management. The difference between the established models of branding and emergent models which incorporate design is explored and the emergence of relatively new design-led branding models. The 4Ds model of design strategy is applied to branding to select and/or build the necessary design-led branding pragmatic tools. The first step is to establish where the brand currently is or, in the case of a new brand, where the organization wants it to be. Brand audit models incorporating design are the most valuable tools for this stage. The second step is to define what the brand stands for and identify its unique aspects. For this it is important to address the meaning of brand value and brand promise. This provides the intelligence and insights for the third stage, to design and build the brand strategy at strategic, tactical and operational levels. Finally the deciding stage evaluates the performance of the brand. Two case studies are offered to exemplify good practice and a thought provoking exercise is provided to test understanding and develop new thinking.

Objectives for this chapter:

- To contrast established business-led branding and design-led branding.
- To introduce new models and benefits of design-led branding.
- To explain the application of the 4Ds design strategy model to branding.
- To apply the brand audit to establish the current position of the brand.
- To define the brand value and the brand promise.
- To show how to design and develop design-led branding strategies.
- To offer tools for management to evaluate the brand performance and design role.
- To exemplify the good practice by case study examples.

3.1   DESIGN AS A CATALYST FOR BRAND DEVELOPMENT

The relationship between design and branding has long been misunderstood and educators and practitioners have locked themselves into a narrow perception. Almost all major texts and education programmes promulgate the idea that the designer's only major role in branding is the design of logos and promotional materials. Thus the field of design for branding is highly populated by graphic and visual communication designers creating new identities through logos and taglines and promotional campaigns. Many of them are very good at this. However this perpetuates the idea that designers generally have no major role in branding. Hence the branding strategy is often devised without the involvement of designers.

A brand is not just a logo, corporate identity or tagline. Experts describe a brand as a "promise." People should know what a particular brand stands for and what they can expect from it. For many loyal consumers, Coca-Cola's promise is "happiness in a bottle" whereas a BMW car promises to be the "ultimate driving machine." A strong brand starts with a compelling value proposition answering the key questions: What does it intend to offer? What are the purposes? In which ways does it seek to be different?

But it is even more important to establish the meaning of brand to the (potential) customer and Numeier (2003) defines it as "a person's gut feeling about a product, service or organisation." These feelings are hard to identify but they surely come from the real experience of interacting with the products, services and environment.

3.1.1 Design Strategy for Branding

Design plays an important role in all key aspects of brand. If the customer is going to get a strong clear message about the brand promise and the value they may expect, then all relevant contributions of design are needed. The brand can express what it stands for through various channels, namely physical elements such as products, interior spaces, furniture, uniforms; visual elements such as the logo and web site; and verbal elements such as the tone of voice in the commercials.

Management need to ensure the brand can be delivered as promised and, preferably with added value which goes a little beyond the promise. Failure to deliver makes it an empty promise and consumers will quickly punish the brand owner by switching their preferences. The challenge should not be underestimated. Any weak aspect of the design of the brand can undermine the promise. Thus the value proposition should be based on an organization's capabilities and expertise, especially their area of excellence. Moreover, the promise should reflect the vision of that organization. In other words it should be realistic.

If the management devise an unrealistic business strategy it makes the task of designers difficult, or even impossible, to design the required brand experience.

A design-led brand strategy is about delivering that promise in the most memorable manner so that people always think of this particular brand first when they need to acquire certain products and/or services again. The brand must occupy certain space in people's minds and have meaning to them.

Big-D strategic design thinking can help a company come up with a unique and compelling promise. Most importantly that promise can be delivered consistently and confidently and all features of the experience designed to deliver a holistic compelling experience. A strategy for the design of a branded physical environment can encourage employees to behave in a desirable way. People are good at picking up clues from their surroundings and deciding how best to behave. These employees reflect the brand. Indeed it could be said they *are* the brand, especially in service-based organizations. The customers will also have marked differences in their behaviour in contrasting environments, for example the way that people behave in a fine-dining restaurant is quite different from those in a fast-food restaurant.

A further example is the airline Easyjet which is a "no-frills" airline with a friendly personality. Good use of simplistic designs and bright colour schemes (seen in the airplane interior, web site and uniform for example) give staff a clear idea about the brand personality and desirable behaviours. Good use of interaction design also ensures that products/services behave in the way that reflects the value of the brand. The design strategy works well to give customers get what they expect, i.e. cheap and cheerful.

By contrast highly expensive luxury product and service brands need to reach a deeper emotional level of the customer experience. The design strategy will incorporate many intangible aspects such as self-identity, personal aspirations and social acceptance, even a spiritual dimension for some. Here Big-D design must work to create the story at the heart of all emotional and fantasy brand experiences. For example there are many attractive watches to buy but a Rolex gives membership of an exclusive "club" and speaks volumes about its wearer.

Small-d design translates the values into all tangible touch points – or points of contact at which people interact with the brand, e.g. visual identity, products, services, stores and advertisements. It is this design that essentially delivers the experience. The designers' challenge is to communicate and deliver the brand in an engaging and coherent manner. Therefore the creative practical designers need a good understanding of the brand values and the promise resulting from the business strategy and the Big-D design thinking. The earlier they are involved in the strategic thinking the better.

To design a total brand experience, designers must be deeply interested in the human condition. This goes beyond a fundamental understanding of consumer needs. A brand is not simply a logo or a product but rather a total experience, all aspects of which must be designed. The identity remains important, because if the brand is not identified, then no further engagement with it is like to follow. However, the product and service is important too, because the brand will not be successful if the product is not delivering its fundamental purposes. Gobé (2001) recognized that it is about giving the product/service long-term value "it is about sensorial experience, design that can make you feel the product, taste the product, buy the product." Thus brands have become a combination of rational and emotional experiences and designers must play a major part in both the planning and execution.

To summarize, design strategy for branding is about designing both tangible and intangible aspects of the experience and creating a consistent, added-value and memorable outcome.

3.1.2   Bringing Brands to Life

It is design which brings brands to life because it offers the opportunity for what Neumeier (2003) calls "logic and magic." This requires an integration of business strategy with creativity. Designers may enter the complex world of designing intangible benefits by following Gobé's (2001) findings on the transition to emotional branding and translating them to reveal the design challenges as follows:

- Customers become stakeholders as emotional brands engage them and designers adopt more human-centred approaches.
- Designers no longer design products and services but experiences with compelling stories.

- Brands go beyond trying to demonstrate honesty and reliability and develop trust like a true friend and designers develop open communications.
- From basic good quality and functionality brands seek to offer more variety and choice and designers creative skills help them to stand out.
- Formerly more concerned with reputation and status, brands change to addressing aspirations and fantasies and the designers must make the dream come true.
- Beyond recognition and identity (starting with logo) brands must show character and personality and designers interpret this "attitude" in all offerings.
- Boring brands are usually seen as out of date, and brands must reflect what is here and now, recently termed "cool", however contemporary life can be stressful and designers may offer simplicity to ameliorate pressures.
- Much effort in branding is directed at promotions and special offers but emotional branding promotes meaningful dialogue among the stakeholders and develops interfaces which allow designers to continually improve the brand experience.
- Fit for purpose and usable products/services need brands which engender feeling and engagement and designers introduce features to build associations through memory and lifestyle.
- The service design element within brands is critical to achieving brand reputation and designers must promote good practice and nurture networks.

Roberts (2005) argued that brands should go even further, to create *Lovemarks*, a mark that people both love and respect. If people love the brand but do not respect it, they might buy knockoff (copy) products rather than authentic ones – prevalent in the expensive luxury fashion industry for example. People want to associate themselves with the brands, but do not respect the quality of craftsmanship enough to buy genuine products. Respect alone may not convince people to buy the brand and/or stay loyal with the brand. Thus, this challenges designers to develop real love of the brand, reaching the sensual, spiritual and even iconic levels of the brand. Designers need to develop a strategy to build the love story: a powerful resonant story in the true tradition of great storytellers. More demanding than good copy writing which conveys information through narrative; the story must be the heart of the designed brand experience.

A truly great brand experience requires a combination of Big-D and small-d design to create, co-ordinate and deliver total sensorial experiences across all channels to optimize emotional impacts. The challenge is to build strong relationships, to make the brand truly loved, to move ahead of the generic and make it personal, to infuse it with sensuality and passion, and to wrap it in mystery and ultimately achieve iconic status.

Bringing brands to this higher plane of emotional connection requires designers with great passion, creativity and vision and a management team with an advanced appreciation of design and aesthetics. It also has implications for business and marketing strategy since the very high prices of some luxury brands invite copying and make the job of the design strategist and designer increasingly difficult.

Example: Superdry

While many high-street fashion brands struggle to survive, Superdry has become one of fastest growing brands due to the effective use of strategic design. Design is evident in all elements of its business. The brand identity is fun and distinctive. The products are innovative and high quality. The retail experiences are unique and memorable – the stores give a down-to-earth vibe rather than pretending to be "cool" like other fashion brands. While most high-street fashion brands tend to copy designs of famous fashion designers or catwalk trends and make them more affordable, Superdry invents its own styles, which helps it stand out in a highly saturated market and gives it a clear position in customers' minds.

3.2 BRANDING MODEL EVOLUTION

3.2.1 Established Branding Models

Most established models or frameworks focus on brand image, brand identity, brand value or equity and the composition of the organizations' brand portfolio. Some models barely mention design, and often the role is limited to creating visual identities – in particular logos – and ensuring a principally visual consistency of brand attributes through colours, shapes and patterns. Whilst recognizing that the tangible aspects are the backbone of any brand, many well-established brand models do not explicitly describe design contributions or include design as a core component.

The brand development process should begin with positioning. This is concerned with establishing the brand's standpoint, i.e. the position it will occupy in customers' minds.

Kapferer (2004) framed four questions to help establish the brand position: Why? For whom? When? Against Whom? By answering these questions, the purposes of the brand, target audiences, the occasions (or scenarios) that the brand will be needed and major competitors can be identified. He went on to show how to develop the brand identity by establishing his prism of six dimensions as extended in Table 3.1 below. *Externalization* defines the brand's external expression and *Internalization* focuses on the inner values that drive the brand.

One best ways to think of a brand is to see it as a person. We all have the physical identity (e.g. appearance) and personality. Our look and behaviours are guided by our beliefs and values, which continually evolve as we get older and gain more knowledge and experience – in the brand context, this could be compared to capabilities and expertise. Our personality influences the way we develop relationships with people around us. We also choose to project a certain image, which we believe suits us best, e.g. helpful,

Table 3.1   Examples to explain Kapferer's (2004) Brand Identity Prism

Externalization	Internalization
1. **Physique:** The tangible elements of the brand, e.g. products and services, the appearance of the brand (e.g. logo) and its functionality. Think about Chanel No. 5's iconic bottle and Tiffany & Co.'s blue box.	2. **Personality:** The brand's character. How does it behave? How does it communicate? Think about the tone of voice and brand ambassadors. Nike is about self-confidence. Ralph Lauren is elegant and cultured.
3. **Relationship:** A brand can develop relationships with consumers and partners in a similar way to people. Relationships are built through all experiences that people have with the brand. Mac OS treats you like a friend, while Windows serves you like a client.	4. **Culture:** Closely linked with the organization's values, visions and missions. What is the core belief or ideology that drives the brand?, Innocent is about being good to yourself and your planet. BMW exudes German cultures of engineering excellence.
5. **Reflection:** Deals with what a brand represents in customers' minds. Most high-street fashion brands portray themselves as a brand for stylish girls in their 20s even though their actual customers may be aged 30 and above.	6. **Self-image:** Is about what target groups think of themselves when they buy into the brand. People who want to identify with groups, cultures and subcultures. Most music brands strongly emphasize the sense of belonging to reflect self-image.

knowledgeable, stylish or easy-going. Think of IBM as a person – he is a middle-aged successful American man, working in a managerial position – definitely not a designer!

3.2.2   Branding Models Embracing Experience

In response to this changing world, Lindstrom (2005) summarized the evolution of branding as follows:

- 1950s: *Unique Selling Proposition:* No two products are alike
- 1960s: *Emotional Selling Proposition:* Products were perceived as different primarily because of an emotional attachment, e.g. Coca-Cola and Pepsi
- 1980s: *Organizational Selling Proposition*: The organization or corporation behind the brand in fact become the brand, e.g. Sony and Nike
- 1990s: *Brand Selling Proposition*: The brand was stronger than the physical dimensions of the product, e.g. Disney and Harley-Davidson
- Late 1990s: *Me Selling Proposition*: Consumers taking ownership of their brands
- 2000s: *Holistic Selling Proposition:* Brands anchor themselves in tradition but also adopt characteristics of religious sensory experience as a holistic way of spreading the news

Emerging models recognized the evolution in consumer demand and the emergence, in the 1990s, of the need to focus on brand experience

Table 3.2   Three decades of brand and design convergence

	Changing consumer demands	Successful brand strategies	Design used to address
1980s	Consumers sought new products & services	Building strong brand image	Design products and services with personality
1990s	Consumers sought new experiences	Developing the brand experience	Designing experiential customer encounters at all brand touch points
2000s	Consumers seek new and deeper meaningful experiences (emotional and spiritual)	Seeking brand truth, integrity, trust and engagement	Brand experiences with intangible inner meaning

(Norton, 2003). The age of abundance led to consumers seeking more meaningful experiences; experiences which need to be designed based on the core values and beliefs or brand truth – What does the brand actually stand for beyond making profits? Consider the brand LUSH, the handmade cosmetic brand, the whole experience is designed based on its core value – appreciating fresh organic ingredients and people's skills. Because of the rapid development of social networks, empty brands, those without any sense of purpose beyond making money, find it harder to exaggerate or lie. It is no longer acceptable to be seen to be interested only in making money. Table 3.2 shows the trend of consumer-driven brand and design imperatives over three decades.

The implications for designers are significant. Listening to consumers is now vital. They are the new brand owners. The shift of power to the consumer has been rapid and overwhelming. Many brands are still trying to adjust to this new era and address the challenge of designing new experiences. The design of communications requires a deep evaluation of the influence of social networks, lifestyle changes and the influence of global events.

Emerging brand models can no longer afford to be prescriptive but need to engender holistic and creative thinking to cope with change and complexity. Iwano (2006) observed that most emerging brand models can be categorized into rational, social, emotional and spiritual dimensions, see Figure 3.1. He went on to compare certain models and shows clearly how the designer must address the social, emotional and sometimes spiritual dimensions of designing brand experiences whilst ensuring that the product/service reflects and communicates both the tangible and intangible attributes, see Table 3.3.

Maio (1999) believes that spiritual values will be the key differentiator in the future and suggested brands become *soul brands* that inspire people. His brand positioning continuum shows industries at different levels from generic to inspirational. But designers are striving to push many products, services, industries, cities, social institutions, etc. up this scale, to create a "quasi-religious" fervour about the brand. Brands have become modern-day religion.

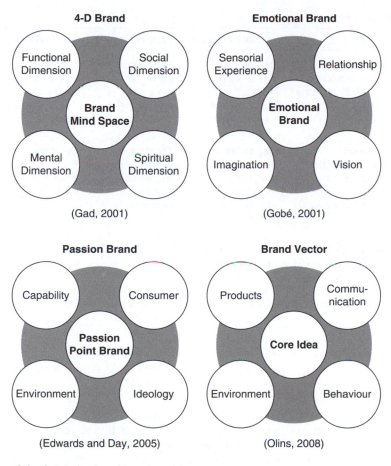

Figure 3.1 Categorization of brand models

Table 3.3 Comparison of emerging brand models

	4D branding	Emotional branding	Passion branding	Brand vectors
Rational	**The functional dimension** concerns the perception of benefit of the product or service associated with the brand.	**Sensorial experience** is used to create a memorable emotional brand contact that leads to brand preference and brand loyalty.	**The capability corner** concerns a company's abilities, and tangible and intangible assets, e.g. trade network.	**Products:** What the organization makes and sells.

Continued

Table 3.3   Continued

	4D branding	Emotional branding	Passion branding	Brand vectors
Social	**The social dimension** concerns the ability to create identification with a group.	**Relationship** is about being profoundly in touch with and showing respect for consumers.	**The environment corner** covers the entire competitive environment.	**Communication:** How it tells people about itself and what it's doing.
Emotional	**The mental dimension** concerns the ability to support the individual mentally.	**Imagination:** is about design executions, which continually surprise and delight customers	**The consumer corner** concerns people who buy, reject or otherwise influence the brand.	**Environment:** The physical environment of the brand, how it lays out its stall.
Spiritual	**The spiritual dimension** concerns the perception of global or local responsibility.	**Vision** is a brand's long-term goal; how it defines success; how it evolves and constantly reinvents itself.	**Ideology –** concerns the ethos of the company, all values associated and the foundation belief.	**Behaviour:** How its people behave to each other and to the world outside.

3.3   DESIGN-LED BRANDING MODELS

"Design-led" may be defined as putting design thinking at the heart of value generation and sustainable competitive advantage (Beverland and Farrelly, 2007). Although many branding writers acknowledge the need to integrate design or design thinking into brand strategy, they have limitations in showing how a brand can become design driven. The first essential requirement is a design-aware culture in which design is embedded in all functions. In such an environment the use of design is endemic. For every problem the question is posed, "How can we design a better way?" In terms of branding this makes design the main driver of the brand value and the means by which the brand is delivered in the real world.

Roscam Abbing (2010) posed the question "How do you create a brand that is visionary and inspiring, and then bring it back to earth with real tangible products?" This gets close to the core of the debate and acknowledges the critical role of design in translating brand ideas into meaningful experiences. He suggests design could drive and serve brand strategy by applying (Big-D) design at the strategic level (upstream territory) to help a company shape visions, brand values and brand strategy, then by applying (small-d) design at the operational level (downstream territory) to help a company implement brand strategy in a compelling manner and deliver memorable brand experience through coherent touch points. Rockwell (2008) proposed a formula for brand satisfaction and brand meaning which incorporates brand touch points over time. His formula equates brand satisfaction to the brand experience and the brand expectation over brand touch points over time. Brand meaning is formulated as brand satisfaction achieved over time. The complexity of branding does not readily lend itself to formulaic approaches but it underpins the importance of design as all touch points are real experiences and therefore the results of design, and the need for maintaining the quality of the design experience is evident. Aaker (2002) proposed a comprehensive framework wherein he suggested that the brand development process begins with contextualizing the environment in which the brand sits, through customer, competitor and self-analyses, see Table 3.4.

Table 3.4 Design strategy implications for Aaker's strategic brand analysis

Core elements	Descriptions
Design trends	Trend analysis is considered to be a good place to start, as it helps developers understand changes in the marketplace and demands, e.g. health and environmental concerns.
Users' motivations	This analysis helps developers understand functional, emotional and social drivers behind users' decisions. It is important to identify actual and perceived benefits, as well as their priorities from their customers' point of view. Think about major reasons that motivate people to choose a car: fuel efficiency, appearance and social status.
Segments/ inclusiveness	Examine how the market is currently segmented (e.g. demographic or psychographic segmentation) and how each segment may respond to the value proposition. Segmentation is no longer simply about age groups. Indeed the development of inclusive design makes major challenges to segmentation.
Unmet needs	In order to differentiate the brand/offers and exceed customers' expectations, it is fundamental to find out their unmet needs, e.g. fast fashion for the silver market.
Brand image/position	To find out the gap in the marketplace, it is useful to understand how target audiences perceive competing brands and what are their positions in customer's minds. Bentley cars are adept at finding their own position/space.
Strengths/vulnerabilities	To compete with competitors effectively, it is also important to find out their strengths and weaknesses. Many businesses protect such information determinedly.
Existing brand image	To develop the brand further, it is necessary to understand how the brand is currently perceived. How is it different from others? If a brand is a person, who would he/she be like? For example, a successful American man.
Brand heritage	To plan for the future, it is essential to understand the past. How the brand was originated? Where does it come from? Why it was created in the first place. Successful brands like Chanel and Levi's make good use of their heritage.

Continued

Table 3.4 Continued

Core elements	Descriptions
Strengths/ weaknesses	To create a sustainable brand, it is crucial to offer core values that are based on organizational strengths. For example, MUJI utilizes their strengths in simplistic design.
The heart and soul of the brand	To create an authentic brand, it is vital to identify the soul or core belief behind the brand. For example, the Body Shop is about campaigning for the better society.
Links to other brands	A brand cannot be created in isolation, it is critical to define its roles in relation to other brands/organizations. Just like a person, a brand needs to understand how it connects, supports and works with other key players.

3.3.1 Design and Brand Identity

After developing a good understanding of the brand and its environment through thorough contextual analyses, the next stage is planning the core and extended identity. While Aaker (2002) defined the core identity as "the timeless essence of the brand," the extended identity is described as "details that help portray what the brand stands for." For example, Alessi core identity is about redefining everyday products and delighting customers through design. Its extended values are colourful, playful designs and collaborations with top designers. In order to plan the identity, an organization should examine the brand from four different perspectives – brand as product, as organization, as person and as symbol.

The central core elements of brand as product comprise product scope, product attributes, quality and value, uses, users and country of origin. The scope of the product is directly linked to the brand identity and it is thus necessary to define the scope of the offering. For example, Gü offers premium desserts for self-indulgence while Carte D'Or provides luxury desserts for sharing. The product attributes make the product stand out and McDonalds is an example of a brand which achieves and delivers consistent worldwide differentiation. Quality and value as perceived by consumers are key differentiators. There are major differences for example, in the perception of the quality and value of leading furniture brands IKEA and Cassina.

Some brands are defined by their uses thus becoming the essence of the task, examples are Google and Hoover where people more often state, "I will google it" when they seek information online or "I will hoover" when they mean vacuum clean. Many brands have strong associations with groups of users, such as Johnson and Johnson linked strongly to mothers and babies. This can be a great strength but may also be a hindrance if the brand wants to expand into a new market, for example male skin care. Gillette has the opposite problem as it is so strongly linked to male grooming it is very hard to reach the female consumer. Country of origin can also influence the perception of the brand. Prada, Armani and Gucci are proudly Italian as Italy is seen as a leading fashion trendsetter. Building international Chinese brands by comparison has the challenge of overcoming the perception that China is predominantly about manufacture and relatively new to innovation.

The second of Aaker's categories is brand as organization. This perspective looks at the brand attributes of the organization as distinct from the product/service, including such matters as capability for innovation, organization management and style. Examples are the Gore Group and 3M which have unique organizational cultures and structures which promote collaboration and innovation development. Brands choose local or global brand identities, although some, e.g. HSBC, try to achieve both. Unilever chose to develop brands to meet local needs whilst P&G develop global products to meet the needs of a wide range of consumers across continents.

Category three is brand as person and encompasses giving the brand a personality like a human being, such characteristics as friendly, sincere, reliable, fun and smart may be sought. The objective is to reflect the personality of the target group so first they may say "I can identify with this brand" and ultimately they may accept that "this brand is me". The personality of the brand also indicates how it will approach, interact, communicate and serve its customers. Powerful brands often use famous celebrities to represent the face of the brand, e.g. David Beckham and H&M. This is of course highly expensive and some brand owners have encountered problems when celebrities lose their popularity or become controversial. For example, Nike had to remove the strapline in its 2013 advertisement saying "I am the bullet in the chamber" featuring Oscar Pistorius after the athlete was accused of murdering his girlfriend.

The final category is brand as symbol, although this is often the first when non- designers consider the role of design in branding. This category relates to visual imagery and metaphor, what the consumer sees and what it stands for. A strong symbol can improve brand recognition and brand recall aiming to achieve recognition and recall without any prompting. Good use of metaphor enhances symbolic meaning such as Nike's "swoosh" and FedEx's "arrow" which signify speed. According to Aaker, the identity influences functional, emotional and self-expressive benefits of the brand or its value proposition. In the final stage of brand development, the brand identity and position will be implemented and monitored to ensure the quality of the outcome.

3.4   4Ds OF DESIGN-LED BRANDING

The former conceptual models can help to establish the issues, elements and (to some extent) relationships of the design-led brand strategy, but in order to generate momentum towards usable strategies and tools, it is necessary to apply the 4Ds of design management to the branding context. Four strategic design stages are applied to branding as follows:

1. **Determining** – Objectively assessing the current position of a brand and the roles of design (brand audit).
2. **Defining** – Establishing what a brand stands for and why it will be unique, and identifying opportunities for design (brand value proposition).

3. **Designing** – Using design thinking and creativity to deliver promises and resonant experiences (brand strategy and brand experience).
4. **Deciding** – Objectively evaluating whether a brand delivers its promises (brand evaluation).

Table 3.5 and Figure 3.2 show the key elements of the 4Ds of design-led branding at strategic, tactical and operational level.

Example: Shanghai Tang

Huppatz (2009) described Shanghai Tang as "branding Chineseness" and "luxurious kitsch." In an interview with Mortimer (2007), the chairman of Shanghai Tang stated that "it would be very myopic to think that China – with 5,000 years of history – will remain the factory of the world forever." He claimed that Shanghai Tang was "the ambassador of modern China." The mission statement on the official web site said:

> Shanghai Tang sets out to create the first global Chinese lifestyle brand by revitalising Chinese design – interweaving Chinese culture with dynamism of the twenty-first century.
>
> (www.shanghaitang.com)

Table 3.5 Key elements of the 4Ds of design-led branding

Strategic level	Tactical level	Operational level
Determining		
Brand DNA audit • Meaning • Reputation • Advocacy	Brand strategy audit • Communication • Performance • Differentiation	Brand execution audit • Design • Behaviour • Experience
Defining		
Design-led brand value/ promise • Core values • Belief • Aspirations	Design-led brand strategy • Creativity • Behaviour • Cultures	Brand experience design • Emotional dimension • Rational dimension • Resonance
Designing		
Design-led brand DNA • Brand position • Brand story	Design-led brand tactics • Brand equity • Brand expression	Multi-sensory design • Interaction/experience • Aesthetics/functionality
Deciding		
Perception of image • Uniqueness • Relevance • Robustness	Perception of performance • Rational/emotional • Social/ethical • Economic	Perception of delivery • Memorable • Desirable • Enriching

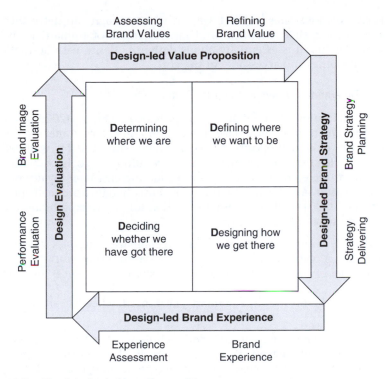

Figure 3.2   4Ds of design-led branding model

Mortimer (2007) observed that Shanghai Tang was inspired by Japanese brands, such as Kenzo, which successfully changed the negative image of the "MADE in JAPAN" label.

The brand has been focusing on bringing back the glamorous pre-war Shanghai (1930s) and traditional Shanghainese tailoring skills. As a result, its tailoring service offered "unique hand-cut, hand-sewn, made-to-measure fashion in luxurious materials." The nostalgic and playful designs using a variety of Chinese cultural references (e.g. kitsch Maoist propaganda posters) were the key factors behind the success of the brand. Store designs reflect its mission statement, as they are a combination of Shanghai Art Decor furniture and a vibrant colour scheme (e.g. purple, bright yellow, pink, orange, fuchsia and lime-green).

According to Huppatz (2009), Shanghai Tang could be seen as:

a Chinese version of Ralph Lauren's polo brand that recycled the nostalgic styles from American 'history' in the 1970s and 1980s. Lauren based his collections on Hollywood-filtered American fantasies including mythical figures such as the pioneers, the cowboys, the Indians, and the British aristocracy.

This case demonstrates well the way in which design can delve into the emotional, nostalgic, mythical and fantasy levels of human needs and desires. The brand is essentially about designing desire with aesthetically beautiful clothes and accessories at the core.

3.4.1 Determining Where a Brand Is: Brand Audit

A useful definition of brand audit was provided by Smith (2009) as "regular measurement of brand image, reputation and the customer experience against the desired proposition." This implies the need for well-defined goals and effective measurement tools. The ultimate goals of brands are to create strong emotional bonding engendering customer loyalty beyond rational reason. An effective brand audit must therefore probe deeply into what Gobé (2001) called the emotional bonding between a brand and its targets. He suggested four steps:

- *Cultural relevance*: A brand is relevant to audiences' lifestyles (*I need it*).
- *Meaning*: A brand has a place in audiences' minds (*I want it*).
- *Emotional connection*: A brand occupies a space in audiences' heart (*I will take it*).
- *Loyalty*: A brand has a permanent place in audiences' heart (*I will take more*).

Experts offer a range of audit tools and techniques. The late esteemed Olins (2008) for example suggests there are five distinctive domains to the audit: communications, behaviour, brand architecture, competitors and design. A complete audit would go on to integrate and evaluate these findings from all areas. This section introduces a selection of appropriate audit tools for strategic, tactical and operational levels to establish the performance of the brand.

Brand Audit at the Strategic Level

Brand audit at the strategic level is about assessing the very core ideas of a brand. Some experts refer to this as the brand DNA, brand value or core idea. Just as a human's DNA is unique, so it is argued that each brand is unique. This may be examined under three headings:

1. *Meaning*: Determining whether what the brand stands for is still considered inspiring, visionary (creative) and relevant to stakeholders;
2. *Reputation*: Assessing if people perceive a brand as respectful and trustworthy;
3. *Advocacy*: Checking whether customers love, are loyal to and advocate the brand.

Brand Trampoline Framework

This framework (Edwards and Day, 2005) uses an analogy of the trampoline to generate passion and leap higher than competitors. Four key components are identified: ideology, capability, environment and consumer. For each component the audit may seek potential weaknesses, and a weakness in any single area may cause serious problems for the success of the brand strategy. Design, especially through design research which excels at building user empathy and contextualizing the changing environments, could prevent a brand from becoming irrelevant. Moreover, good use of Big-D design helps a brand define a sense of purpose and builds innovation capacity.

The categories are explained as:

1. *Hollow brands* which have little or no character or clarity about what they stand for.
2. *Question mark brands* which are over hyped but fall short of consumer expectations.
3. *Irrelevant brands*, out of step with contemporary needs.
4. *Blind brands*, unaware of the changing world.

Design strategy issues to address the weaknesses can be seen in Table 3.6.

Brand Trust Pyramid

This framework (Ryder, 2003) uses an analogy of human relationships to describe how a brand builds trust with people. The author recommends keeping full records of customer satisfaction and superior user experience to build trust. Design plays an important role in trust building. The first step is about creating an appearance that engenders trust, beginning with the logo and web site. Next, all experiences must reinforce the message that this brand is reliable and trustworthy – e.g. providing a transparent trans-action process. Effective use of experience design can help create strong relationships in a long term. In order to achieve a convincing brand, the brand owner has to work hard to establish a relationship, especially if it is the first experience. Examples of businesses at this level may be estate

Table 3.6 Using the brand trampoline to evaluate the brand

Category	Design strategy issues
No personality or charisma	Brands need strong core values to survive in the marketplace which must be communicated clearly by design to consumers who seek honesty, meaning and authenticity.
Disappoint consumers	Brands must deliver their promises; if there is a mismatch between belief and capability customers will be disappointed, so design is required to ensure satisfaction and added value.
Not in the here and now	Brands must stay relevant to changing world or their market will shrink; designers must be aware of the changing environment.
Inflexible to environmental changes	Brands must gather good intelligence about people's changing lifestyles and aspirations as a platform for designers to meet (and sometimes exceed) their expectations.

agents, car sales and timeshare salespersons, all of whom may inherently be mistrusted. To reach the second level of measured belief, the brand needs time to become established. However the overall perception must be that the brand will never let you down, thus it becomes a good friend and occasional failure is tolerated and quickly fixed. The highest level of the pyramid is total belief and requires the design and management of a brand to the level that it never lets you down. It is as reliable as your closest family. Achievement of the highest level is the ultimate challenge for designers as everything must be consistent and reliable down to the last detail.

Lovemarks

Lovemarks (Roberts, 2005) are at the top level of the brand pyramid and need both love and respect. Brands that are loved but not respected will not last. To engender respect brands must be honest and responsible. The design-led brand strategy must demand that they perform well at every touch point, continually improve and never fail the customer, examples are Apple, Google and Ferrari.

Below the level of Lovemark, Roberts places the category "brands", which are marked by high respect but not loved, examples are brands such as HSBC, TESCO and Marks & Spencer. Further down the scale comes "Fads" which stimulate high love but low respect, such as certain celebrities and sports heroes. Finally, bottom of the pyramid comes "Commodities" which have low scores in both respect and love and are often the fast-moving consumer goods with which consumers make no significant emotional engagement.

Brand Audit at the Tactical/Business Level

At the tactical (or business) level brand audit is about assessing the effectiveness of the brand strategy. It is a question of determining whether the brand strategy is sufficient to execute the brand core values and promises. Hence, the audit must address:

1. *Communication*: Checking the frequency and consistency of brand presence and how it influences customers' perceptions and persuades them to get involved – *does the brand message reach and appeal to all potential customers?*
2. *Performance*: Assessing the reliability and accountability of the brand – *does the brand deliver its promises and always satisfy or exceed expectation?*
3. *Differentiation*: Determining whether a brand stands out from the crowd – *does it have unique brand strategy and offerings (products, services or experiences)?*

BrandDynamics™ Pyramid

This brand framework (Edwards and Day, 2006) helps to measure brand advocacy. For example, if brand A starts with 25 people and brand B with 75 people, but they both end up with ten people, then brand A performs better in terms of bonding. Since the cost of attracting new customers is generally higher than maintaining existing ones, it is in a brand's best interest to build strong relationships with customers. As peer-to-peer comments become increasingly important in the current market, it is vital to turn customers into loyal brand ambassadors.

The aim is to achieve bonding, rational and emotional attachments to the brand to the exclusion of most other brands. Customers with this high degree of bonding are likely to be advocates of the brand and are thus immensely valuable is spreading the brand reputation. On the route to reaching the "bonding" level, brands establish presence, relevance, performance and advantage. Presence is related to familiarity based on past trial, saliency or knowledge of the brand promise; thus awareness builds presence. Relevance means it meets the customers' needs, in terms of price and/or other criteria set. Performance involves getting the product on to the customer's shortlist. Finally, before the ultimate level of bonding, the brand seeks an emotional, rational or saliency-based advantage.

Emphasis on the importance of differentiation is provided by Gad (2001) in the form of the differentiation and dramatization matrix. He asserted that:

> if you're not different in business your whole existence is in danger. If you're not different you will be replaceable, and you will be under constant pressure to lower your price. Sometimes the only difference you need is not in the product you deliver, but in *the way* it is delivered.

The brand auditor can use Gad's categories to assess whether the brand is differentiated through innovation or dramatization or both.

Gad calls the most successful the *killer brand* wherein both differentiation and dramatization are high. Differentiation makes the brand distinctively different from all competitor brand offerings and high level dramatization means the brand is delivered in a significantly different way from all competitor offerings. The designer needs to be aware of the unique selling points (USPs) of the product/service and how it is effectively promoted and delivered to the target market. ASOS is an example of such a brand.

The second type of brand he identified he termed *invention brand* which displays high differentiation and gains leadership through innovation sometimes with intellectual property (IP) protection. But this type of brand may have nothing distinctive in delivery. The designer may identify the USPs but needs to improve how they are communicated and subsequently delivered. Hewlett Packard provides an interesting case study of such a brand.

The third type Gad calls *campaign brand* where the opposite of the invention brand can be observed. The product/service has low differentiation and there is nothing distinctive about it. However the dramatization is high and it is delivered in an engaging and creative manner. Designers may be aware that the product/service is not inherently attractive and may focus of making the model(s) on offer engaging and exciting. This should not of course preclude them from seeking to improve the core offer. An example of this brand type may be HSBC, indeed many banks may find dramatization essential to delivering their services.

The final brand type is where no brand manager wishes to be and is termed *no brand*. This type has low differentiation and low dramatization. It is urgently in need of creative thinking and design to take it above the threat of extinction. Some brands slide into this category and look to designers to find a way out. Sunny Delight brand has this challenge in the early 2010s.

Brand Audit at the Operational Level

Brand audit at the operations levels evaluates the effectiveness of the delivery of the brand attributes at the interface with all stakeholders. It is audited through examining design effectiveness, behaviour of all associated with the brand and the assessment of the real brand experience. This may be examined under three headings:

1. *Design:* Assessing the appropriateness and quality of design implementations (e.g. visual identity) – *do (tangible) designs reflect brand values and strategy?*
2. *Behaviour:* Checking whether the brand behaves the way that it promises – *Are all representatives (e.g. employees and spokespersons) living the brand?*
3. *Experience:* Examining the consistency and the quality of brand experience across all touch points – *does the brand have a 100% record in terms of customer satisfaction? Has the brand ever let customers down?* Lindstrom (2005) argued that the more senses (e.g. sight, small, touch, sound and taste) the brand employs to engage with customers, the more memorable it becomes. Hence, he proposed a check on how many senses the brand currently uses to engage their audience and how effective they are.

According to Olins (2008), the execution of the brand core idea should be assessed by:

1. *Communication audit* examines what the organization says, how it says it, to whom it says it – and how hard it listens back.
2. *Behavioural audit* examines fundamental attitudes towards people both inside and outside the organization.
3. *Visual audit* examines the way in which different parts of the organization present themselves in terms of their physical evidence.
4. *Brand architecture audit* examines main brands, subsidiaries, co-brands, joint ventures and all competitors – the audit helps to show how brands are organized, what the hierarchies are, how close are the relationships between brands.
5. *Presentation audit* examines the presentations of brands whether they are clear, logical relevant and comprehensive.

3.4.2 Defining What a Brand Stands For & Why It Is Unique: Brand Values

Definitions of Brand Value/Brand Promise

Brand value is connected to the brand promise. The value can be measured in economic terms or human values or both. Economic value is the sum deemed to be the amount representing the asset value to an organization. Interbrand (2007) put it simply as "the dollar value of the brand."

By contrast Gad (2001) defined "values" as the rules of life, and indicated the need to assess a deeper personality and elements which make a brand as trustworthy as a friend.

Brand promise is the core purpose of a brand (Allen, 2000). It addresses the question "What does the brand stand for?" He suggested that "the brand promise sit in the centre of the brand, driving all of a company's communications and business actions." ...thus it becomes "the basis for the way in which the brand is expressed, from corporate identity to environment to communications" and provides "a means for measuring the success of the organization's brand action." Many leading global companies follow his maxim on arriving at a central idea that provides a focus for the organization's strategy, values and personality. This way they keep their brand promise and stay ahead of their competitors in meeting and exceeding customer expectations.

Value Creation at the Strategic Level

Creating design-led brands at the strategic level is concerned with generating belief. This can only be achieved through a deep engagement with human emotional needs and increasingly spiritual needs. First basic rule is to promise only what can be delivered. This is a powerful central pillar of the brand value (Ryder, 2003).

Another very fundamental explanation comes from Anholt and Van Gelder (2003). They explained that:

> value is created when people reckon that a brand offers them something worth their while and they are persuaded to provide something in return, e.g. their time, money, attention, allegiance, brainpower and so on. Value is thus an intangible substance made up of qualities like trust, reassurance, excitement, snobbery, efficiency, and so forth. Thus, they concluded that "branding is a way of thinking about how an organization aligns its goals and abilities with the demands of its stakeholders.

Reaching the deeper spiritual level is becoming more and more significant. Whilst it is clear that some brands address the spiritual level, e.g. health spas, it is a new dimension of brand thinking in many fields, e.g. cosmetics, food. It involves understanding how humans connect to the past, tapping into happy memories, even going back to childhood memories and dreams. It also seeks to develop self-awareness, through the design of sensorial experiences which engender self-reflection and help to develop self-image. Dugree (2001) says "soul brands connect users to their pasts, to themselves, to each other, to a 'big picture' life plan or force, and to general societal concerns, such as the environment and positive labour." The real challenge for designers is to create strong bonding of the stakeholders to the brand. Examples of how designers may use Dugrees' deep or high soul brand types can be seen in Table 3.7.

More and more, researchers are seeing brand as a part of society. They are exploring not only rational and financial values, but also social and cultural values of brands. To gain understanding and insights into these values, the

Table 3.7 Designing for deep or high soul consumption experience

Type of experience	Examples	Role of design
Re-living the "good times" from the past and generating happy memories	VW Beetle	• Create emotional bonding based on the fondest memory. • Nostalgia has become a strong force in design-led branding (even former Communist-era brands has successfully re-launched).
All about you – as a human being, self-reflection, self-image, personal aspirations and desires	Harley-Davidson Disney iMac	• Provide sensorial experiences that require full attention and promote slow consumption so that users can reach a self-reflective state. • The brands are often called "iconic" or "classic" or they have embedded themselves deep into the human psyche.
Bigger than you – the mega experience which captivates	Olympics	• Amplify soulful experiences, e.g. wonders of nature and religions. • Mega sports events have become a modern phenomenon for lifting human spirits.
Close relationships	Skype	• Enhance social connections, such as offering communal products. • Social networks burgeoning to generate a feeling of belonging.
Caring for the world	Body Shop	• Produce products/services that follow triple-bottom-line principles. • Organizations are now expected to "give back" positive contributions to sustainability.

psychological theory of a Hierarchy of Needs developed by Maslow (1943) remains a useful platform to develop brand values.

- *Physiological needs:* the most basic requirements for survival, such as breathing, food, water and sleep. If these requirements are not met, a human cannot function properly. These requirements are basic but the most important.
- *Safety needs:* once physiological needs are met, people seek their safety needs, security of body, employment, resources, morality, family, health and property.
- *Love/Belonging needs:* after physiological and safety needs are fulfilled, people seek to satisfy their emotional needs in terms of love and a sense of belonging. The requirements in this category include friendship, family and sexual intimacy.

- *Esteem needs:* upon fulfilling all needs in the first three categories, people want to feel respected. These emotional requirements include self-esteem, confidence, achievement, respect of others and respect by others.
- *Self-actualization needs:* the highest level of needs is about "being the best person you can be." Hence, this level of needs focuses on morality, creativity, spontaneity, problem solving, lack of prejudice and acceptance of facts.

Based on this theory, Meads and Sharma (2008) developed a brand model entitled "three dimensions of aspirational brand values and consumer choice" set out below with examples:

- *Need-driven* brand value (tangible – rational consumer choice) relates to tangible material and biological consumer needs stressing impersonal factors – think about commodity products and services, e.g. water, electricity, gas and food. People make decisions based on tangible and rational values (e.g. high-quality ingredients)
- *Inner-directed* brand value (intangible – emotional consumer choice) relates to a consumer's need for self-actualization and stresses emotional personal factors – think about ethical products and services, e.g. Fairtrade goods. People make decisions based on moral values (e.g. brands certified by NGOs)
- *Outer-directed* brand value (intangible – cultural consumer choice) refers to consumers' relational needs stressing social and cultural relations – think about products/ services that signify consumers' social groups and cultural preferences, e.g. fashion brands like Prada. People's decisions are affected by social values, e.g. status.

Example: Starbucks

Starbucks is an example of how design thinking can change the value proposition of the brand. Originally, Starbucks was created for "coffee connoisseurs." Offering too many choices made the menu complex and, hence, only appealed to certain groups of customers. In order to expand its business, Starbucks re-examined its value proposition and rebranded itself as "the third place" or a social space where people congregate other than home and workplace (home is the first place and workplace is the second place). To redefine its brand and values, sophisticated, yet friendly design is used in all elements, e.g. interiors, exteriors, services, product offerings and other experiences. The use of strategic design has helped the brand become synonymous with good experiences and successfully expand its business to many countries across the globe. Starbucks continues to re-invent the "third place" concept by regularly introducing new ideas to make services more personable and engaging.

Value Creation at the Tactical/Business Level

Value at the tactical level is about competitive advantage. According to Aaker's conceptual model discussed in Section 3.3.1, several issues have to

Table 3.8 Design for brand alignment

Key questions	Actions
What do we represent presently?	Critically evaluate real strengths and weaknesses of the designed brand – focus on a company's strategy, values and personality.
What is our complete offer including every detail of what is expected of us?	Extract key points from the discovery stage to define/redefine a brand promise that is credible, inspiring and meaningful for all stakeholders.
How can we best promote our brand promise through design?	Design coherent touch-points that send a clear message about the brand promise.
How can design help to deliver and sustain our brand promise over time?	Get people in an organization to "live" the brand – fully involved in the process. Design for an innovative and creative environment.

be taken into consideration when building a brand. Firstly, external environments must be contextualized through appropriate tools, such as customer and competitor analyses and self-audit. Next, a holistic brand identity system, which covers all key aspects, namely product, personality, heritage and value proposition, must be generated. Finally, a thorough implementation plan including brand positioning, brand execution and realistic monitoring processes can be drawn.

The *brand alignment* tool (Allen, 2000) can help to build a strong brand. This technique consists of four stages: brand discovery, brand promise, brand expression and brand action to which key questions and actions related to the design strategy may be added. To execute the design of a strong brand the strategist needs to address four key questions as shown in Table 3.8.

Example: Cath Kidston

Cath Kidston is an example of how strategic design could create competitive advantages and USPs for the brand. This lifestyle brand is famous for its distinctive designs: nostalgic floral prints and polka dot patterns. While its modern vintage designs do not appeal to everyone, they effectively evoke happy childhood memories for many consumers across the world. The clever use of design has helped the company differentiate the brand and its products. The design language has proven to be very versatile, as it has been applied to a wide range of products, e.g. clothing, bags, accessories and home furnishing.

Value Creation at the Operational Level

Operational level value creation is at the interface between and with users. It expresses and delivers the practical real life designed experience and carries all of the attributes of the differentiation and/or uniqueness of the brand, referred to as the "brand signature."

Example: Singapore Airlines

An example of highly successful operational level design-led branding can be found in Singapore Airlines. In the fiercely competitive airline market, they manage to stand out from the crowd due to their unique brand values. Singapore Airlines focus on designing memorable experiences and creating emotional connections. They deliver their promise to "rediscover the romance of flying once again" through clever use of experience designs. They were ranked number one in the world top sensory brands – ahead of other top brands such as Apple, Disney and Mercedes Benz (Lindstrom, 2005).

3.4.3 Designing How to Deliver Promises: Brand Strategy & Brand Experience

The effective delivery of promises involves connecting the brand strategy to the real life brand experience. Brand strategy is a contentious term. Whilst most agree that it is ultimately about delivering the promise, they emphasize different methods to achieve it.

Brand Strategy Development at the Strategic Level

Collins and Ruskstad (2008) argue that strategic development should start from the mission and the vision of the company and should include three basic elements: objectives (end), scope (domain) and advantages (means). Emphasis on "being different" should be the main feature of the strategy which should be regarded as competitive strategy, according to Borja de Mozota (2003). However, Ellwood (2009) suggested that it was about brand positioning which involves key steps as follows:

- *Define the market and customer target*: Gain in-depth understanding of potential users' behaviours and attitudes through proper research and user profiling.
- *Audit and identify opportunities*: Apply qualitative and quantitative research to assess the firm and its market environments in order to find out new opportunities.
- *Model positioning territories*: Define the boundary that a brand can take an ownership of by applying the **Opportunity Model**, which consists of four key aspects:
  - *Differentiation*: clearly distinguish itself from other competitors in the market.
  - *Credibility*: align the new position with a firm's capability, culture and personality.
  - *Stretch*: ensure the brand will continue to be relevant to future markets/needs
  - *Relevance*: be functionally and emotionally relevant to customers
- *Refine final positioning:* The position or the boundary must be validated with potential users and then refined based on user test results.
- *Bring positioning to life:* Turn the positioning into tangible products/services, people behaviours, communication and environment through

the **Quadrant Model** containing four key aspects as shown below to ensure the design consistency across all touch points.
- *Products & Services* – What products and services do we offer?
- *Communication* – What is our core message/strap line?
- *Environment* – How do we present ourselves?
- *Behaviour* – How should we and our people behave?
- *Measure results:* The outcomes of brand positioning programme can be checked through the **Brand Positioning Matrix** developed by Ellwood (2009). Managers may use design strategy to measure and enhance the brand position by addressing questions such as:
  - *Are employees projecting and promoting the brand image in their appearance, deportment and behaviour?*
  - *Are employees proud of the brand and advocates for the brand among their family and friends?*
  - *How do employees show their pride in their employer and brand(s)?*
  - *Are employees loyal and long serving?*
  - *Does the image perception of the brand among customers match with the design aims?*
  - *How strongly do customers recommend the brand to others?*
  - *Are customers given incentives to recommend the brand?*
  - *How likely are customers to buy the brand again or buy more products/ services of the brand?*
  - *Which of our competitors is trying to encroach upon or occupy our brand space?*
  - *How loyal are our customers to our brand?*
  - *How well does design generate eager expectation of forthcoming offers?*
  - *What is the brand impact on business growth measured by financial and management accounts and future forecasts?*
  - *Is the brand delivered efficiently- which generally means at the lowest possible cost?*
  - *How profitable is the brand as measured by financial accounts and models?*
  - *What is the brand valuation in relation to its current and projected earnings?*

Example: Nike

Nike is an example of a brand that truly understands its mission. Nike's mission statement is "to bring inspiration and innovation to every athlete in the world." In this case, the word "athlete" refers to everyone, since its co-founder strongly believed that "if you have a body, you are an athlete." Hence, the brand has always focussed on empowering people – remember its famous slogan, *Just Do It*, innovative products that make real impacts to sport practitioners' performance (e.g. Nike Air and Nike Shox ranges) and incredible flagship store experiences (Nike Town), which set a standard for many flagship stores in various sectors.

Design is always at the heart of Nike's brand. Design is effectively employed in brand identity, product and service design and experience design (both offline and online touchpoints). Nike is well known for its bold design statements (e.g. strong colours and graphics) – this unique design language has helped communicate the brand's mission and vision, as well as reinforce core values, e.g. innovation, empowerment, confidence and performance.

Brand Strategy Development at the Tactical/ Business Level

Ellwood (2009) suggested developing next the brand portfolio strategy and competitive growth strategy. While the former focused on how to leverage brand equity across all brands (master brands, sub brands and endorsed brands), the latter concentrates on developing good understanding of competing brands so that the brand could plan how to respond accordingly. Press and Cooper (2003) made it clear that "small-d" are integral parts of brand experience and that "the role of design and designers is central to the success" converting the ideas into products/services, packaging, retail stores, brand messages across all communication channels, workplace environments and so forth.

Therefore whilst at the strategic level design is used to create inspiring stories for the core message and establish a clear brand position, the tactical/business level design is employed to develop brand assets (e.g. brand identity, products/services and communication channels) and compelling brand expressions, which direct the overall *brand experiences*. The brand experience can simply be explained as what customers feel or think of a brand based on their encounters with the brand over a period of time through various sensorial touchpoints, e.g. TV commercials, retails, products and customer help lines. Several experts broadly divide brand experiences into three stages: pre-purchase experience, purchase experience and post-purchase experience. Purchase, can refer to such things as buying a product, having a haircut, visiting a city or watching a film. In order to design coherent and compelling brand experiences, an aspirational brand story and a clear brand position are required. Hence, the effective use of design at the strategic level is crucial to the success of brand experiences.

Since the way people form their opinions about the brand is influenced by their social and cultural backgrounds (e.g. where and how they were brought up), in order to design positive and memorable brand experiences, the company needs to develop a good understanding of its target audiences. The ways customers interact with the brand is equally important. Therefore, the company must identify and develop their preferred channels of engaging with the brand (e.g. suitable medium to raise awareness, influence decisions and stay in touch).

Example: Virgin Atlantic

Virgin Atlantic is an example of how brand experiences can be used as competitive advantages. After identifying that travelling to and from airports and checking in as the main stages that most travellers dislike, the company redesigned its check-in procedures. Passengers of Upper Class are now offered a range of transport options that will take them to and from airports at both ends of their journeys. By collecting passenger information as part of the transport booking, this helps speed up the check-in process.

Moreover, the company used design to create distinctive experiences in all major touchpoints, e.g. Clubhouse, airplane interiors and seats, amenity products and soft furnishing (e.g. pillows and blankets).

Brand Strategy Development at the Operational Level

This is the stage of delivery. The creative talents of designers are a critical factor at this stage and brand managers need to have a highly developed sense of what constitutes good design.

Lindstrom's BRAND Sense (2005) says it is about synergy across all sensory touch points, dramatization of the brand personality and defining the unique statement/design expression – think about the harmonious experience you may expect to receive in luxury hotels (see Six Senses Resorts and Spas, for example). It carries the opportunity to "release the latent potential within the brand's image, its audience, and its company." According to Lindstrom (2005), the delivery is about:

1. *Brand staging*: ensuring a design synergy across sensory touch points;
2. *Brand dramatization*: designing brand personality – *who the brand is;*
3. *Brand signature*: defining the unique statement/design expression.

To summarize, design-led brand strategy development requires designers to identify real benefits, values and promise through Big-D design then develop tactics for delivering real benefits through small-d design, in a balanced and integrated manner. The chief of design for BMW Group emphasized that: "where there is meaning, there is design" (Breen, 2002).

Example: Tate Modern

The coherent design of multi-sensory experiences has helped the Tate gallery become one of the top tourist attractions in London. The effective use of design, e.g. brand identity, exhibition designs and products, has helped attract a number of collaborators and supporters.

3.4.4 Deciding Whether a Brand Delivers Its Promises

Brand evaluation is the assessment of brand performance now and its inherent strength for the future. From a business perspective, the brand should have a high financial value.

Indeed many brands are bought and sold on the basis of the perceived monetary value.

The consultancy Interbrand (2007) focus on three main issues: financial analysis, role of brand and brand strength. *Financial analysis* is used to estimate current and futures revenues attributable to the brand. The *role of brand analysis* measures how the brand influences consumer demand at the point of purchase. *Brand strength analysis* establishes a benchmark of a brand's ability to secure on-going customer demand through loyalty, repurchase and retention.

Whilst ultimately a business is concerned with the economic performance of a brand, measuring the brand performance in delivering its promise involves the identification and critical assessment of many intangible factors. The evaluation must be rigorous. This means preparing well-designed evaluation instruments which seek deep insights and this in turn means asking the right questions. Building long-term value is the key challenge and Gad (2001) proposed ten most important rules to assess the future potential of the brand. The "rules" are updated and further design thinking introduced as follows:

- The brand becomes the story/fantasy created by designers in a person's mind
- Design communicates what the brand signifies (its stance, attitude, ideology, ethics)
- People learn to love it like their closest friends and family
- It has value, indeed may be worth more than the owning company's market valuation
- It is used by management to design the experience and to drive the company
- It needs to be clear and transparent about its role among all stakeholders
- It encourages creativity, and opens up co-creation opportunities
- It builds alliances with other brands rather than aggressively maintaining exclusivity
- It is better to be protected by leadership in design than by trademark laws
- It consistently delivers value and frequently adds value

Brand Evaluation at the Strategic Level

The brand performance at the strategic level seeks to answer the question, "How well does the brand deliver its promise?" Ryder (2003) emphasized that delivering or even exceeding the brand promise is crucial to success. He showed the connections and consequences of three levels of brand performance. Brands which excel make a promise and beat the promise, thereby gaining customer advocacy and acquisition of new customers. Brands which deliver make a promise and keep the promise. They too can be successful in retaining customers and acquiring some new ones. But brands which make a promise and break the promise fail and this leads to customer loss and disaffection which quickly spreads negative influences.

Brand authenticity to maintain brand strength is advocated by Lindstrom (2005), by keeping it real, making sure it is relevant to people and the marketplace, and creating rituals for the product and establishing an engaging story. A good example is Kit Kat, the famous chocolate biscuit snack – the recital: "have a break, have a Kit Kat."

Brand Evaluation at the Tactical/Business Level

At the tactical/business level the evaluation is about measuring against the established plan. Appropriate assessment tools and techniques need to be developed to facilitate comprehensive measurement of the multifaceted aspects of the brand.

Gobé (2001) proposed a brand personality assessment tool called Brand Presence Management (BPM). Whilst the tool can be used for any brand, Tables 3.9 and 3.10 show how the tool may be used for a hotel brand by

Table 3.9 BPM – emotional IMPACT

Emotional CONTACT	Sensory	Brand impact → Brand contact						
		1	2	3	4	5	6	7
	Hotel lounge						×	
	Hotel interior					×		
	Menu/food				×			
	Entertainment					×		
	Facilities (e.g. gym)						×	
	Furniture & bedding							×
	Special events				×			
	Human touch	1	2	3	4	5	6	7
	Reception						×	
	Room services					×		
	Uniform					×		
	Amenities				×			
	Concierge					×		

Table 3.10 BPM – practical IMPACT

Practical IMPACT	Information	Brand impact → Brand contact						
		1	2	3	4	5	6	7
	Web site		×					
	Signage			×				
	Corporate graphic		×					
	Advertising				×			
	Bill/receipt							
	Stationery			×				
	Information/leaflets			×				

assigning scores. This tool can "allow an expanded exploration of the many facets of a brand's personality in all its expressions in the marketplace, from 'impact' to emotional 'contact.'" While practical aspects, e.g. corporate identity and signage, could leave a good impression in customers' minds, these aspects are unlikely to create a strong relationships. There is a need to make people "feel" the brand or create emotional contact. Giving the scores in the example, impact is creating presence, e.g. getting people to recognize the hotel from afar, whilst contact is building relationships with people through elements that people will come in contact with (e.g. furniture and facilities) over a long period. Thus, high scores equate to close contact.

Edward and Day (2005) suggested a series of brand assessment tools to link measurements to actions (e.g. improvement plans). They group the measurement under four categories:

1. Brand perception – focuses on measuring brand recognition (prompted awareness) and brand recall (spontaneous/unprompted awareness). It

also covers the areas of brand image from customer point of view and current level of customer satisfaction.
2. *Brand performance* – concentrates on practical elements, which, in most cases, directly impacts profitability of the brand, such as brand loyalty, frequency of purchase, ability to attract new customers and ability to retain existing customers.
3. *Brand inside* – measures the internal elements of the brand, e.g. knowledge and commitment of people working for the brand. Hence, it includes key aspects, such as employees' and partners' brand knowledge and the effectiveness of internal branding.
4. *Brand currency* – assesses social capital and goodwill of the brand, embracing social values like corporate reputation, brand trust and brand community.

In order to connect the measurement with actionable plans, the integration of the future planning elements may be assessed using a Balance Scorecard template. The template comprises a straightforward structure inviting the assessor to evaluate performance in four categories set out above. The scorecard user assigns their own measurement criteria under each category and then records scores in answer to the questions:

- What did we hope for?
- What did we get?
- What will we change?

The first two questions highlight the gap between the aims and the actual performance and the third question affords the invitation to decide on future actions.

Brand Evaluation at the Operational Level

Operational level evaluation involves a constant monitoring of the experience at the customer interface. This is particularly challenging because of the vulnerability of the brand to any failures or inconsistencies in the customer experience. For example, every small failure or deficiency at this level can undermine the strategic vision and careful planning in just one moment.

Schmitt (1999) identified five types of customer experience that a brand should deliver to provide a holistic experience and gradually influence customers' thoughts and behaviours.

He also proposed a framework to plan and assess the experience:

1. *Sense*: Using sensual and tangible aspects of a product or experience to appeal to the five senses of sight, sound, scent, taste and touch – see Hotel Chocolat for example.
2. *Feel*: Promoting positive feelings toward a product or service – think about the Harry Potter franchise: books, merchandises, films and a theme park.
3. *Think*: Encouraging customers to engage in elaborative and creative thinking that may result in a re-evaluation of the company and products – see LEGO Games Creationary board game, for example. It allows people to build their own board games and create the rules by themselves using LEGO bricks.

4. *Act*: Changing long-term behaviour and habits in favour of the particular product or service – see the success of the Android smartphone as an example.
5. *Relate*: Expanding beyond the individual's private sensations, feelings, cognitions and actions by relating the individual self to the broader social and cultural context reflected in a brand – e.g. riding a Harley Davidson means being a member of a brotherhood.

Assessing the effectiveness of design in relation to each of Schmitt's five factors requires a close investigation into how well design is used to communicate (the entire experience), the designed identity and personality, the relevance and innovative nature of the core product(s) and/or service(s), the synergy from co-branding, the design of physical and virtual environments, the impact of web site design and finally, but perhaps most importantly, the design of the delivery through people.

3.5   CASE STUDY 1 – DESIGN-LED BRANDING: DESIGN BRIDGE

Design Bridge is a leading London consultancy that "bridges" the gap between design and branding. Indeed they develop enduring and memorable brand experiences using design thinking. Their approach is highly creative and founded on the belief that every good brand is based on the power of great ideas. Every brand strategy they develop seeks to uncover the big idea behind the brand personality as a basis for inspiring creativity. They use strategic analysis to get a deep understanding of the true meaning of the brand (reflecting the operational level model above). Audits are used to evaluate strength and assess effectiveness, and ease of navigation which equates to the clarity and comfort of the customer journey. The brand signature tool and workshops are used to address complexity and develop vision.

An integration of Big-D and small-d thinking is evident throughout their work. Designers are involved in every stage of the process, thereby bringing their best creative ideas to the on-going development of the brand idea. Design Bridge describes this as "bring the creative brief to life." This combination of creativity and strategic insight has helped them to grow successfully, currently employing 200 people and working in over 40 countries and 30 languages.

An example of their client work is Beefeater Gin: creating, naming and positioning Beefeater's new premium gin brand for (client) Pernod Ricard. The consultancy had already successfully rebranded the Beefeater core gin product and were now required to develop a strategy to "turn heads" in an overcrowded market for alcoholic spirits and cocktails.

The solution is expressed in their own words as:

> for the brand's personality and positioning, we looked to London's and Beefeater's *heritage* and *provenance*. With the formula 20% history to 80% modern, we distilled the brand's essence into "*Daring*

London Glamour" and named it after its 24-hour botanical processing and London's edgy 24-hour culture. Like London, our bottle and label designs are rich in detail, full of hidden treasures and unexpected turns. There are nods and winks to emblems of London old and new, from keys and ravens to Saville Row and gleaming gin palaces. Our brand guidelines carry the luxurious underground London mood and imagery into every nook and cranny of Beefeater 24's bar territory.

The differentiation was identified as: "the only London gin still made in London." They sought the real Londoner and a brand that is steeped in tradition and heritage, yet also contemporary. What they call "authentic yet vibrant." So the brand needed to capture the past, present and future, and get the right balance, in this case 20% history, 80% modern. The semiotic of the bottle was achieved through the shape of the London stock brick.

Some questions for discussion:

- How can design research reveal the "big idea"?
- Compare this brand with Jack Daniels – both brands exude mood and mystery but one is based on real heritage and the other on myth.
- Can all brands exploit heritage without appearing staid?

3.6 SUMMARY OF KEY POINTS

Brand experience means going way beyond the design of the product and the logo. It involves the application of Big-D and small-d design thinking throughout the process to deliver a truly added-value experience. Brand models provide a useful platform but relatively few incorporate design and even fewer are design led. However there is a trend to integrate design into the branding strategic and planning stages which goes beyond the use of design at only operational level. Design is at the heart of many highly successful brands.

The 4Ds tool can be applied as a strategic tool for branding and should be viewed as a cyclical process. First determine the current situation with emphasis on the role of design in the performance of the brand. Next define clearly what the brand stands for and why it is unique by establishing what is the brand promise and how added value is to be delivered. Then design the system and all delivery points to a consistent level of sensory experiences which characterize the brand. Finally decide objectively and rigorously whether it is working, and what may be designed to repair, evolve and enhance the experience.

3.7 FURTHER CONSIDERATION

3.7.1 Exercise the Mind...

Using the principles introduced in the book so far, readers are invited to consider the following issues in relation to their own experiences and environment.

1. Select any famous iconic design in the world, for example a product or a building, and consider how big-D systems design played its part in creating this famous icon.
2. Identify any major design project which was reported to have got out of control. A recent example was the Scottish Parliament. How could design strategy prevent such problems?
3. Consider your favourite design – it could be a product, a building, an interior, or any design experience. Why do you like it? What makes it special? Be a design critic!
4. Think about what the purpose of a brand really is. If a product/service is well designed, why is the brand needed? What is the relationship between brands and designs?
5. What are your favourite brands? Can you explain why you prefer them? What is the brand saying to you? Does the product/service say this too?
6. Which of your favourite brands are considered "design led"? Can you identify design contributions in their deliverables?
7. Identify brands that do not make good use of design and consider how to make them more design led. Think further about how to convince these firms to invest in design.
8. Remember your last brand experience and record the customer journey in detail. Was it good, bad or indifferent? Did the brand deliver its promise? Did the feeling last? What could a designer do to improve the experience? (if your memory is not that reliable go on a deliberate journey to evaluate a chosen brand!)
9. Why does the entire brand experience need to be designed? What special aspects could only be delivered through design creativity? Consider the consequences of poorly designed experiences.
10. If and when branding loses its credibility or integrity, should designers disassociate with it?

To develop design-led thinking, it is suggested that the practice of "positive discontent" is employed. That is not to say that a negative attitude is promoted but that, rather like cultural caretakers, we adopt an attitude of vigilance towards identifying those frailties that are endemic to human society in order to identify opportunities for designing improvements. This may lead to many creative ideas and the appropriate formulation of strategies to address or develop them.

3.8 GLOSSARY

Brand architecture is a structure of brands within an organization. Some companies may use one brand for all products (e.g. Heinz). Some may introduce sub-brands for different product lines (e.g. Nintendo Wii and Nintendo DS; Sony Walkman and Sony PlayStation). Some companies may create brands for individual products. For example, Linx, Persil, Comfort, Dove, Wall's and Flora are brands owned by Unilever.

Brand identity covers all unique features that help people identify brands, e.g. a logo, colours, patterns (see Louis Vuitton and Burberry for examples), product shapes (e.g. Coca-Cola's bottle and Volkswagen's beetle), names, fonts, sounds (e.g. Intel's jingle) and straplines (Nike's Just Do It). Strong identity is timeless and derived from the core value of the brand/organization. Good identity sends a clear message about the brand.

Brand image – While brand identity focuses on sending a message (what a brand is all about) to potential and existing customers, brand image is what people interpret based on the message and an overall experience that they received.

Brand portfolio is the total collection of brands in an organization. The term is rather similar to "Brand Architecture". While brand architecture focuses on the structure or how brands are organized, brand portfolio concentrates on making sure that all market segments that a company is interested in are covered and complement each other.

Brand touchpoint includes every point of contact that people have with a brand. According to Wheeler (2006), the touchpoints include various aspects: such as visual elements (e.g. signage, packaging and business cards), verbal communications (e.g. emails and voicemails), product/service components (e.g. employees, vehicles and environments), and public relations (e.g. trade shows and exhibits).

Co-branding is an arrangement of two or more brands to associate their identities with a new product (range), e.g. Sony Ericsson phones, Nike + iPod, Philips Nivea grooming products and Adidas Goodyear shoes. The idea is to combine the strengths (e.g. reputation and expertise) of two or more brands and overcome certain limitations.

3.9 REFERENCES AND ADDITIONAL READING

Aaker, D. (2002), *Building Strong Brands*. London: Simon & Schuster.

Aaker, D. (2004), *Brand Portfolio Strategy*. New York: The Free Press.

Allen, D. (2000) Living the Brand. *Design Management Journal*, 11 (1), 35–40.

Anholt, S. and Van geler, S. (2003) Branding for good? In N. Ind (ed.) *Beyond Branding: How the New Values of Transparency and Integrity are Changing the World of Brand*. London: Kogan Page.

Beverland, M. B. and Farrelly, F. J. (2007) What Does it Mean to be Design-led? *Design Management Review*, 18 (4), 10–17.

Borja de Mozota, B. (2003), *Design Management: Using Design to Build Brand Value and Corporate Innovation*. New York: Allworth.

Breen, B. (2002) BMW: Driven by Design. *Fast Company* [WWW] http://www.fastcompany.com/magazine/62/bmw.html [Accessed 28 March 2011].

Clifton, R. and Simmons, J. (eds) (2003), *Brands and Branding*. London: The Economist.

Collins, D. J. and Ruskstad, M. G. (2008) Can You Say What Your Strategy Is? *Harvard Business Review*, April, pp. 82–90.

Dugree, J. F. (2001) Soul Branding: How to Do It. *Design Management Journal*, 12 (1), 40–45.

Edwards, H. and Day, D. (2005), *Creating Passion Brands: Getting to the Heart of Branding*. London: Kogan Page.

Ellwood, I. (2009) Brand Strategy. In R. Clifton (ed.) *Brand and Branding* (2nd edn). New York: Bloomberg Press, 73–95.

Gad, T. (2001), *4Ds Branding: Cracking the Corporate Code of the Network Economy*. London: Financial Times Prentice Hall.

Gilmore, F. (1999) *Brand Warriors: Corporate Leaders Share Their Winning Strategies*. London: Harper Collins Business.

Gobé, M. (2001), *Emotional Branding: The New Paradigm for Connecting Brands for People*. New York: Allworth Press.

Harvard Business Review (1999), *Harvard Business Review of Brand Management*. Boston: Harvard Business School Press.

Huppatz, D. J. (2009) Designer Nostalgia in Hong Kong. *Design Issues*, 25 (2), 14–28.

Ind, N. (ed.) (2003), *Beyond Branding: How the New Values of Transparency and Integrity are Changing the World of Brands*. London: Kogan Page.

Interbrand (2007) *All Brands are not Created Equal: Best Global Brands 2007*. London: Interbrand.

Iwano, T. (2006) *Brand Spirituality: The New Generation of Brand Thinking*. Masters Dissertation, Design and Branding Strategy, Brunel University.

Kapferer, J. N. (2004), *The New Strategic Brand Management: Creating and Sustaining Brand Equity Long term*. London: Kogan Page.

Klein, N. (2000), *No Logo*. London: Flamingo.

Lindstrom, M. (2005) *BRAND sense: Sensory Secrets Behind the Stuff We Buy: Build Powerful Brands Through Touch, Taste, Smell, Sight, and Sound*. New York: Free Press.

Maio, E. (1999), The Next Wave: Soul Branding. *Design Management Journal*, 10 (1), 10–16.

Meads, C. A. A. and Sharma, P. (2008) The Social-Cultural Role of Brand in Business Value Creation. *Design Management Review*, 19 (2), 29–37.

Morgan A. (2009) *Eating the Big Fish: How Challenger Brands Can Compete against Brand Leaders* (2nd edn). Hoboken: John Wiley & Sons.

Mortimer, R. (2007) Shanghai Tang Brings Chichi Shops from China. *Brand Strategy*, June 2007, 48–49.

Norton, D. (2003) Toward Meaningful Brand Experiences. *Design Management Review*, 14 (1), 19–25.

Nuemeier, M. (2003), *The Brand Gap: How to Bridge the Distance between Business Strategy and Design*. Berkeley: New Riders.

Olins, W. (2004) *Wally Olins on Brand*. London: Thames & Hudson.

Olins, W. (2008), *Wally Olins: The Brand Handbook*. London: Thames and Hudson

Press, M. and Cooper, R. (2003) *The Design Experience: The Role of Design and Designers in the Twenty-first Century*. Basingstoke: Ashgate.

Roberts, K. (2005), *Lovemarks: The Future Beyond Brands*. New York: Power House.

Rockwell, C. (2008) The Mathematics of Brand Satisfaction. *Design Management Review*, 19 (2), 75–81.

Roscam Abbing, E. (2010), *Brand-Driven Innovation: Strategies for Development and Design*. Lausanne: AVA Academia.

Ryder, I. (2003) Anthropology and the Brand. In N. Ind (2003) *Beyond Branding: How the new values of transparency and integrity are changing the world of brand*. London: Kogan Page, 139–160.

Schmitt, B. H. (1999) *Experiential Marketing*. New York: Free Press. Wheeler, A. (2006) *Designing Brand Identity: A Complete Guide to Creating, Building, and Maintaining Strong Brands*. Hoboken: Wiley.

Smith, S. (2009) Brand Experience. In R. Clifton (ed.) *Brand and Branding* (2nd edn). New York: Bloomberg Press.

3.10   ONLINE RESOURCES

1. Emotional branding: http://www.emotionalbranding.com/
2. Interbrand: www.interbrand.com/
3. Place branding: http://www.simonanholt.com
4. Design Management Institute: www.dmi.org
5. *TED:* www.ted.com

Chapter 4
DESIGN–DRIVEN INNOVATION

This chapter establishes the meaning of innovation and explores the relationship of design management and innovation. It is firmly established that innovation is critical to organizational success and this means developing design management-led models to promote idea generation in a vibrant and creative climate. Innovation can be driven by an integration of design management research and design creative thinking. The creative thinking extends to the design of the entire climate and methods adopted to achieve an innovative organizational culture.

Conventional innovation models are reviewed and their relationship to the design process is established. Two emergent models of innovation are introduced to show how innovation can be brand driven and used to establish added value. Design-driven innovation models show opposing schools of thought whereby one approach favours user-needs-driven innovation and the other designer-driven innovation. Guidance on how to select and/or reconcile the approaches is given. Case study examples of the application of principles are presented.

Design strategy can be formulated to utilize design thinking to assess the capability of the organization to innovate, to support management to establish clear directions for future innovation and identify design opportunities, to improve the environment for creativity, and to evaluate the effectiveness of the innovation strategy. Design concepts for new and incremental innovation can thus be developed concurrent with the organizational goals, leading to viable value-added solutions.

Examples of design-driven innovation models are introduced and the application of the 4Ds design management model explained.

Objectives for this chapter:

- To define and discuss the meaning of innovation in organizations;
- To establish the relationship and impact of design on innovation;
- To explain conventional innovation models and their influence of the design process;
- To introduce two contemporary models which show brand-driven innovation and how to add value;

- To discuss the user needs and designer led approaches to design-driven innovation;
- To show how to apply the 4Ds design strategy model to build innovation strategies;
- To show how to develop a successful culture for innovation;
- To provoke questions about convergence of mindsets for further consideration.

4.1   INNOVATION THROUGH DESIGN STRATEGY & CREATIVE THINKING

Innovation is the "successful exploitation of ideas" (British Standards Institute, 2008). But in order to exploit the ideas there must be some process, some method by which the ideas can be turned into reality, otherwise they remain concepts only. The challenge for management and designers therefore is to shape the ideas into practical added-value propositions for users, customers and related stakeholders. Many experts perceive design as an integral part of innovation. Sir George Cox told the UK government that "design links creativity and innovation" (The Cox Report, HM Treasury, 2005). Experts like Smith (2006) and Von Stamm (2008) argued that innovation is not just invention but requires the essential activities of design, marketing, distribution and product support for exploitation and possible commercialization. Innovation can be expressed as the equation:

$$\text{innovation} = \text{creativity} + \text{commercialization}$$

4.1.1   Different Types of Innovation

Whilst many people relate the term innovation with high-tech products, it covers a wide spectrum. Tidd, Bessant and Pavitt (2005) grouped innovation into:

1. *Product innovation*: Change in things which an organization offers, e.g. new models of electric vehicle and new generations of smartphone.
2. *Process innovation*: Change in the ways in which products/services are created and delivered, e.g. Toyota's just-in-time practices or Dell's made-to-order process.
3. *Position innovation*: Change in the context in which the products/services are introduced. For instance Swatch changed the market position of Swiss analogue watches.
4. *Paradigm innovation*: Changes in the underlying concepts. For example, no-frills airlines changed the perception of air travel from luxury to easy and affordable.

Keeley, Pikkel, Quinn and Walters (2013) proposed a more comprehensive structure for categorizing innovation. They suggested that innovation can be broadly divided into three types – each type can be broken down further as shown below.

(A) *Configuration*: This type of innovation focuses on an underlying concept of an enterprise and how it operates. It can be divided further into four groups:

1. **Profit model**: This innovation model focuses on finding new ways of generating incomes, for example creating revenues through multiple channels or reinventing how to run a business. One example is Netflix. Rather than adopting a traditional pay-per-rent approach and making customers pay "late fees" if they do not return videos on time, the company introduce a flat-rate subscription – you can borrow DVDs or watch as on-demand streaming videos as many or as few as you like. You can keep a DVD as long as you like, but you will not get another one until you return the DVD that you borrow. This profit model demonstrates good use of creative thinking and a true understanding of users and has helped the company outperform well-established brands, such as Blockbuster.

2. **Network:** This type of innovation focuses on finding new ways of capitalizing on external relationships and taking advantage of other people's or organizations' assets, for example tapping into strategic partners' facilities, know-how, expertise and skills. One example is LEGO. The company collaborate with various groups, such as film producers and loyal fans. Good use of networking results in many successful ranges, like the Star Wars and Harry Potter ranges. Realizing that adult fans do not want to buy children products, LEGO introduced products designed specifically for adults, for example the Architecture range. This clever use of networks shows remarkable holistic thinking and creativity.

3. **Structure:** This type focuses on finding new ways of organizing and making the most of a company's existing assets (both tangible and intangible), such as machines, human resources and intellectual property. For example, a company may rent out their office space during the night for other organization(s) working night shift. This can maximize the utilization of office space and generate profit. One example is John Lewis. The company treats their employees as partners or co-owners of their business by ensuring that their jobs are fulfilling and rewarding. By making employees happy, the company achieves a high level of service quality and customer satisfaction. This organizational structure shows how good use of systematic and creative thinking can motivate people in the way that financial incentives and promotion alone cannot achieve.

4. **Process:** This type focuses on finding new ways of creating and delivering values – think about Toyota's just-in-time process, McDonald's global standardization process and Dell's personalization process. Another example is IKEA. The company offers flat-pack furniture worldwide with very minor variations, an example is larger-size furniture for the US market and smaller-size furniture for Japan. This practice ensures cost-effectiveness throughout the value chain, especially in production and distribution.

(B) *Offering*: The type of innovation focuses on an enterprise's offerings (e.g., products, and services) and can be divided further into two groups:

5. **Product performance:** This focuses on innovation in designing and developing new features, new products or new solutions – think about the superior performance of Dyson's vacuum cleaners, Alessi's iconic design and Apple's intuitive interface. One example is MUJI. The name can be directly translated as "no brand quality good." Subsequently, the product performance in terms of practical functions and aesthetic values are the key to their success. Interesting choices of material and minimalistic design have helped differentiate the brand and create a clear position in customers' minds, as well as reduce the cost of manufacturing and dissembling at the end of product life.

6. **Product system:** This type focuses on finding new ways of combining a company's offerings together to create holistic solutions – think about IBM's IT solution packages. One further example is Microsoft Office package. Although each product (e.g. MS Word, MS PowerPoint and MS Excel) can work on its own, because they are designed to support each other, users are willing to buy the whole package. Evidently, good use of systematic and creative thinking can help a company create more revenues.

(C) *Experience*: The type of innovation strand focuses on customer-facing elements of an enterprise and can be divided further into four groups:

7. **Service:** This type focuses on finding new ways of enhancing customers' experience through services, e.g. offering unique guarantees, warranties or other forms of assurance and establishing good systems or communities to support customers. One example is Metro Bank, which is one of the fastest growing retail banks in the UK. While most banks in the UK only open on weekdays and operate during office hours, Metro Bank opens seven days a week and after office hours. This practice is favourable for many working professionals with busy lifestyles. Other policies, e.g. pet friendly, are also well received by the British public. This example shows that good use of service design can help differentiate the brand and accelerate user acceptance and growth rate.

8. **Channel:** This type focuses on finding new ways of connecting the offerings with users, e.g. using multiple channels in complementary ways and creating memorable interactions with customers (think about Apple Store and NIKE Town). One example is BBC. Starting as a radio broadcasting organization, before moving into television, the BBC now employs various channels to provide services and engage with audiences – ranging from traditional broadcast media (e.g. TV and radio channels), to social media (e.g. Twitter and Facebook), on-demand streaming services (e.g. BBC iPlayer) and publicity events.

9. **Brand:** This area of innovation focuses on creating distinctive promises, memorable identity and desirable values – a company that makes good use of this type of innovation tends to have a unique value proposition that allows it to diversify itself across sectors – think about the

Virgin Group – the philosophy of its brand (e.g. challenging the norms and going the extra mile for customers) has helped the company to build a large portfolio covering various industries, e.g. finance, media, health & fitness and travelling. Effective use of holistic thinking, brand identity and service design is evident throughout.

10. **Customer engagement:** This type focuses on finding new ways of creating meaningful connections with users. One example is YO! Sushi. Its playful design (e.g. bright colours and Japanese-style graphics) has helped this franchise restaurant successfully introduce the concept of conveyer-belt sushi bar to UK consumers and those in the other countries. While most restaurants focus on delivering high quality services when people come to their places, YO! Sushi goes an extra mile in terms of customer engagement. It uses various social media to connect with customers, e.g. Twitter. Its official web site encourages people to upload interesting photographs capturing their fantastic time at YO! Sushi restaurant. It also offers cooking classes where customers can learn how to prepare sushi. Good use of customer engagement has helped the company become one of the leading franchise sushi restaurants in the UK.

Keeley, Pikkel, Quinn and Walters (2013) argued that the structure that they applied to categorize different types of innovation can also be used by a company to assess their current strategies and plans for the future. This idea is discussed further in Section 4.4.1.

4.1.2   Different Degrees of Newness

Innovation implies a certain degree of novelty or newness. However, it does not mean that all innovations have to be completely new to the world. Small improvements are the most common form of innovation and such small changes can add high value. Designers often show a tendency to want to be celebrities by making high impact artistically compelling products, buildings and experiences. But there is only room in our world for a few such stars who create controversy and challenge thinking. The majority of designers must cooperate with management to develop changes to maintain competitiveness and seek advantage.

Two dimensions of novelty are suggested by Tidd, Bessant and Pavitt (2005):

- *The level of implementation:* Was the new idea implemented at a component level? For example, introducing a more durable coating on a car's panel. Or was the new idea implemented at systems level? For example, introducing a new way to fuel a car.
- *The degree of newness:* How novel was the idea? Is it new to an organization, to the industry/sector, to the market, to a country or to the whole world?

They help to explain the difference between innovation at the basic level of improving or introducing new components and the higher risk systems level which addresses more radical ideas. At the basic components level the organization may seek to improve components by, for example, using higher quality materials and/or finishing techniques. They may also offer new components for existing products, like the Dyson ball for the wheelbarrow. Finally they may use the fruits of their R&D to improve performance, e.g. flexible LCD screens. At the higher, more radical level they can develop new versions of existing products e.g. cars, planes and fridges. They may also introduce new generations of existing products which render the previous generation obsolete, e.g. CDs and cassettes became MP3 and downloads.

Finally, at the most radical end of the spectrum, new concepts that did not exist before are introduced, like steam power, ICT revolutions and biotechnology outcomes.

The altogether most prevalent form of innovation is incremental, defined by the British Standards Institute (2008) as "change that involves one or more relatively minor innovations that are predictable extrapolations from the present state." These relatively minor changes and improvements in products and/or services may be seamlessly integrated into existing technologies and infrastructures. This kind of innovation is referred to as a minor improvement or extension to an existing product and may result in only minor changes in consumer behaviours. Examples of incremental innovation are computer operating system upgrades (e.g. MS Windows), software packages (Adobe graphic design package) and new models of hybrid cars. Small improvements have been made every year. Many of the longest lasting brands have shown patience and caution by innovating slowly, e.g. Kelloggs and Coca-Cola.

Radical innovation is defined as "innovation resulting in significant (sometimes step) changes that could not have been extrapolated from present state" (BSI, 2008). Hence, this kind of innovation often contains "disruptive" technologies or technologies that significantly change the entire ecosystem of the product and industry – consider the impact that the first generation of iPhone had on the mobile communication industry. Radical innovations are likely to lead to changes in infrastructures, e.g. the introduction of the electric car. This type of vehicle requires new infrastructures so that the car's battery can be charged at petrol stations. Charging stations must be made available in car parks of both public and residential spaces, e.g. supermarkets, offices, flats/apartments and universities. Radical innovations tend to change consumers' behaviours significantly – think, for example, about eBooks, which changed the way people look for, carry, purchase and read a book.

In general, for radical innovation Big-D design will be needed to address strategic technological, cultural and behavioural changes and for incremental innovation small-d design will be used to constantly improve the product/service at the customer interface. Borja de Mozota (2003) identified how the role of design has been expanded to incorporate the entire spectrum of innovation and impacts on all aspects of organizational performance. Table 4.1 shows the growing influence of design on innovation.

Formerly designers were constrained to improving or refining products/ services – often simply through styling. Now organizations are using design to engender innovative cultures, add value and generate higher profits.

Table 4.1 The influence of design on innovation

Innovation	Design contribution	Long-term benefits
• Products/services to market	• Ideation, alternative scenarios, faster response to changing environment, reduced time to market	• Product/services leadership • Offering consumers new and improved experiences • Increased confidence in cross-functional development
• Developing internal culture	• Cross-functional team working, sharing ownership of ideas and responsibility	
• Developing external collaboration	• Improved communication (especially visual communication)	• Strong internal and external relations and cohesiveness based on trust and shared experiences
• Building knowledge resources	• Building good networks with all key stakeholders • Stimulating learning and dissemination of ideas and knowledge	• Valuable knowledge base in a learning organizational culture

Brown (2008) refers to this as "the former role is tactical and results in limited value creation; the latter is strategic and leads to dramatic new form of value." This exemplifies the convergence of management and design through the evolution of strategic design management wherein there is agreement that it is about creating value through innovative products and services and widespread acknowledgement that competitiveness can be enhanced through good design.

A study of Norwegian companies conducted by Solum, Smith and Karlson (1998) cited in Von Stamm (2004) demonstrated that "companies using design consciously have (a) higher levels of innovation activity, (b) generate more revenue from innovation, and (c) are overall more profitable than companies that do not use design." By returning to the original meaning of the word "design" (*de + signare*), Verganti (2008) concluded that design was about making sense (of things) or making things more meaningful. Thus, the role of design is about *(re)defining the meaning* of products/services/experiences and effectively innovating our futures.

4.2 CONVENTIONAL & EMERGING INNOVATION MODELS

4.2.1 Conventional Innovation Models

Since the middle of the last century innovation models have evolved from linear, somewhat rigid processes, to open and more responsive models. In the early 1990s, the most well-known model was Cooper's (1993) Stage-Gate process which went to the heart of the design process and consists of six stages: (1) preliminary investigation, (2) detailed investigation, (3) development, (4) testing and validation, (5) full production and (6) market launch. Between the stages are gates, which function as quality control and go/kill check points. The idea is that if the results of any stage are not "up to scratch," it is better to keep the gate closed and stop or redo the work again rather than let poor quality outcomes pass to the next stage. In this way, problems can be identified and addressed before the product/service reaches the market.

Cooper's idea influenced research and developments in this field, and many innovation models in the middle of 1990s still divided key design development and innovation activities into five to seven stages. Although they used different names for each stage, the ideas are similar to those shown below:

- Stage 1: *Ideation* – focuses on exploring and identifying new opportunities, unmet needs or unsolved problems as well as developing new ideas.
- Stage 2: *Feasibility study* – evaluates and refines ideas through a wide range of research (e.g. market research, trend forecasting and user research) to ensure that problems and/or opportunities are properly examined from all angles. This stage often results in a business development plan or a specification of a new product/service.
- Stage 3: *Concept development* – concentrates on turning innovative ideas into tangible concepts. The key is to create as many plausible options as possible so that an organization will not miss any good opportunities.
- Stage 4: *Implementation* – tends to focus on screening all concepts, identifying the ones with strong potential and developing these ideas further in detail.
- Stage 5: *Validation & verification* – concentrates on evaluating outcomes with all key stakeholders, e.g. potential users, suppliers, retailers and salespersons.
- Stage 6: *Realization* – producing and delivering the new solution to the target audiences. Since an innovation does not have to be a product, it could be a novel manufacturing process. Thus, it could mean applying the new process in a factory.
- Stage 7: *Commercialization* – focuses on activities, such as advertising, marketing, distribution and retailing. Sometimes practitioners combined the last two stages together.

Since the middle of the 1990s, models were simplified and often presented in the "funnel" shape, such as conceptual models developed by Wheelwright and Clarkin (1992) and Baxter (1995).The wider end of the funnel represents the ideation stage and the process narrows the focus towards the final selection and launch. Some models contained only three stages – searching, screening and implementing ideas. A similar model was proposed by the BSI (2008) to emphasize the need to search for new ideas and screen potential solutions. Trott (2008) summarized the six generations of innovation models as shown in Table 4.2 to which are added the influences on the growth of design-led innovation.

The relationship of innovation processes and design thinking can be seen by comparing the innovation stages identified by Tidd, Bessant and Pavitt (2005) with the "spaces" of design thinking derived from Brown (2008).The relationship and similarities can be seen in Table 4.3. Although the word

Table 4.2 The chronological development of models of innovation

Year	Type of model	Influence on design-led innovation
1950/1960s	Technology push	Simple linear sequential process with the emphasis on R&D; the market received the outcomes but with limited artistic input.
1970s	Market pull	Beginnings of a reversal whereby market/consumers were asked what they needed and R&D set about providing it – but continued emphasis on technical performance to the detriment of fashion.
1980s	Coupling model	The influence of R&D and marketing became more balanced and integrated. Designers' influence grew in helping to develop new products to reconcile their needs.
1980/1990s	Interactive model	Emergence of teamwork with varying levels of multidisciplinary skills. Closer external relationships with suppliers and customers. More integration of R&D with design and manufacture.
1990s	System integrating and network model	Fully integrated parallel development; use of expert systems and simulation modelling in R&D; strong linkages with leading customers (customer focused at the forefront of strategy); strategic integration with primary suppliers including co-development of new products and linked CAD systems; horizontal linkages; joint ventures; collaborative research groupings; collaborative marketing arrangement, etc.; emphasis on flexibility and speed of development (time-based strategy) increased focus on quality and other non-price factors.
2000s	Open innovation	This model, developed by Chesbrough (2003), focuses on making the best use of knowledge from internal and external sources. It encourages organizations to exchange knowledge/ideas as a means to sharing risks and rewards.

Table 4.3 Comparison of innovation's stages and design thinking's spaces

Three stages of innovation	Three spaces of design thinking
1. **Search** – detecting signals in the environment about potential for changes – new technologies, changing requirements of markets.	1. **Inspiration** is the problem or opportunity that motivates the search for solutions.
2. **Selection** – making sure that the choices fit with the overall business strategy of the firm.	2. **Ideation** is the process of generating, developing, and testing ideas.
3. **Implementing** – turning potential ideas into reality.	3. **Implementation** is the path that leads from the project stage into people's lives.

stage is used to describe key tasks in the innovation process, these activities could be regarded as *spaces* since they may be overlapped and do not have to be carried out sequentially.

It can be seen that the importance of the design contribution to innovation has been increasingly recognized as a key factor in developing multidisciplinary collaborations, knowledge sharing and decision making by generating, visualizing and implementing ideas, allowing objective selection and testing. Big-D and small-d design can be recognized as fundamental contributions to innovation for ideation, feasibility, concept development, implementation, validation and verification, realization and commercialization.

Design and R&D identify and explore new opportunities and/or ideas. Design research plays a major role in the business development or specification by testing and evaluating ideas. In concept development design takes a leading role. For implementation design takes the major responsibility for rigorous testing of all details, to make sure the product/service works as intended. Validation and verification will often involve designed prototypes to be tested both inside and outside the organization. If the product/service is to be successfully realized, design supports other functions such as engineering and manufacture and contributes to communication and staff training. Finally commercialization activities such as advertising, marketing and selling benefit from good design and creative thinking to design and deliver a compelling experience, e.g. promotional campaigns and unique retail environments.

4.2.2   Emerging Innovation Models

The first example is the brand-driven innovation model presented by Roscam Abbing (2010) who argued that "innovation and branding need each other, derive value from each other and strengthen each other in an on-going synergy. They are caught in an eternal loop of mutual symbiosis. Design is the mechanism that keeps the symbiosis going." He proposed the new model titled *brand-driven innovation*, which includes four main stages:

- *Building a human-centred brand*: The method starts with the brand promise. In order to use a brand as a foundation for innovation, it cannot be an empty promise – the brand must be developed based on people.
- *Building an innovation strategy*: This stage is about using design thinking to create a strategy that fulfils the promise and takes the aspirations of the organization and all key stakeholders into consideration.
- *Building a design strategy*: This step concentrates on strategic use of design in order to bring the innovation strategy to life in a meaningful way – it is about how to use design and what to do with it.
- *Orchestrating touchpoints*: This stage is about managing design of all touchpoints to deliver a holistic, meaningful, compelling experience.

Further he identified nine roles of design in the context of brand-driven innovation, thereby establishing the importance of design throughout:

1. To enhance creativity and innovation.

2. To enhance empathy and user-centredness.
3. To bridge silos and connect departments with different agendas.
4. To envisage possible futures for the organization.
5. To resolve conflicting interests and demands into one fitting solution.
6. To make plans and ideas tangible and concrete.
7. To make innovations usable and relevant for end users.
8. To create coherent experiences that satisfy all the senses.
9. To create aesthetics that communicate the right story to the right people.

The second example of brand-driven innovation is Kim and Mauborgnes' (1997) Value Innovation model. They explained that many high-growth companies concentrated on making their competitors irrelevant. The authors claimed that "value innovation is about offering unprecedented value, not technology or competencies. It is not the same as being first to market. When a company's value curve is fundamentally different from that of the rest of the industry – and the difference is valued by most customers". They offered CNN as a good example as it was the first all-news television channel in the US. CNN's value innovation was not challenged for almost ten years.

The authors suggested that a company should ask themselves the key questions: Which of the factors that our industry takes for granted should be eliminated? Which factors should be reduced well below the industry's standard? Which factors should be raised well above the industry's standard? Which factors should be created that the industry has never offered?

This concept was later developed into the *Blue Ocean Strategy* – which explores the simultaneous pursuit of differentiation and low cost. In this way, a company can open up a new market and offer new value without being challenged for a long period of time.

By comparing conventional innovation logic with value innovation logic they identified differences along five basic dimensions of strategy.

First they pointed to industry assumptions which, under conventional logic, regard conditions as fixed. Value innovation logic suggests the conditions can be shaped. Second the strategic focus is conventionally aimed at securing competitive advantages as in a race to be the winner. Application of value innovation logic suggests abandoning competitiveness in favour of the quest to add value to the company as a means to dominate the market. Third, conventional logic dictates that the company should expand through segmentation and customization of its offers, whereas value added logic suggests looking for a broader spectrum of commonalities among customers and a willingness to let some existing customers go. The fourth factor addresses assets and capabilities. It shows conventional logic as leverage of existing assets and capabilities. However value added logic invites the question "What would we do if we were starting anew?" and thus shaking off the constraints of existing assets. Finally the products and service offerings conventionally operate within an industry's traditional boundaries. A value innovator starts with a close understanding of customers' changing needs, then throws off the constraints of traditional industry offerings. The self-imposed constraints of conventional logic can be seen in industries in many countries but there are companies in South Korea which seem to find it natural to diversify well beyond the accepted norms.

This value added approach could certainly be viewed as higher risk but the rewards may be much higher too. Whilst many organizations would like to occupy the calm blue ocean where they can stay out of the aggressive competitive red ocean and profit unchallenged, there are many opportunities for good returns on investment in the highly competitive red ocean.

4.3   DESIGN-DRIVEN INNOVATION MODELS

There are two schools of thought about whether design-driven innovation should respond to user needs or create user needs. Best (2010), in common with many other authors, argues that innovation is driven by the needs of users and customers and should thus be user centred. Verganti (2008) describes the role of design as "aiming to radically change the emotional and symbolic content of products (i.e. their meaning and languages) through a deep understanding of broader changes in society, culture and technology." His study was based on successful Italian firms, such as Alessi, and suggests that design-driven innovation is not user centred. Design-driven innovation has some similarity to a technology push approach but instead of developing radical technologies, it is about using design to create new meanings.

Table 4.4   Three types of innovation with examples

	Functionality (technology)	Meaning (language)	Descriptions & examples
Market-pull innovation	Small changes only in response to findings of market research		These are incremental or user-centred innovations resulting from market and user research, e.g. new generation of washing machines.
Technology-push innovation	Radical change as new technology makes breakthroughs	May introduce new meanings	These are radical and disruptive innovations resulting from new technological developments, e.g. high-performance sports equipment.
Design-driven innovation	May be related to new technologies	Major changes in the way people think and feel about the innovation	Radical innovations that may not have most advanced technologies, but introduce new expressions that change the way people think about certain products or services, e.g. iPod – not the first MP3 player, but it set the "language" of the product category.

It also implies that design should go beyond responding to user needs, even expectations, and users may not have the vision to articulate their future needs. Table 4.4 gives examples of the changing functionality and meanings of market pull, technology push and design-led innovation.

However the two approaches are not mutually exclusive and user-centred design remains a major influence in design-driven innovation as reflected in IDEO's approach outlined below.

4.3.1 IDEO's Methodology

1. *Understand* the market, the client, the technology and the perceived constraints on the problems.
2. *Observe* real people in real-life situations to find out what makes them tick; what confuses them; what they like; what they hate; where they have latent needs not addressed by current products and services.
3. *Visualize* new-to-the-world concepts and the customers who will use them.
4. *Evaluate and refine* the prototype through a series of quick iterations.
5. *Implement* the new concept for commercialization. This phase is often the longest and most technologically challenging in the development process.

At the centre of IDEO's innovation approach (Kelly and Littman, 2001) lies design thinking which Brown (2008) defined as "a discipline that uses the designer's sensibility and methods to match people's needs with what is technologically feasible and what a viable business strategy can convert into customer value and market opportunity" and described by Weiss (2002) as "the innovation engine" comprising desirability (human factors), viability (business factors) and feasibility (technological factors), involving close cooperation with the client. This approach to innovation was developed further into IDEO's Human-centred Design Toolkit. It was suggested that the process should start with desirability followed by feasibility and viability. Thus, the key questions are: *Desirability*: What do people desire? *Feasibility*: What is technologically and organizationally feasible? *Viability*: What can be financially viable?

IDEO's Human-centred design (HCD) process has three stages: *Hear (H)* – collect stories and inspiration from people through field research. *Create (C)* – work together with people to translate stories into frameworks, opportunities, solutions and prototypes. *Deliver (D)* – realize the solutions through rapid revenue and cost modelling, capability assessment and implementation planning.

It can be seen that the process begins with observations where the design team collects stories and inspirations from people. Next, the design team identifies key themes and opportunities from the real stories. Then the process explores how ideas could be transformed into tangible solutions. Suitable prototypes are made to develop and evaluate solutions with real users. Finally, the implementation (or commercialization) plan is developed.

Recent studies explored not only relationships between design and innovation, but also between design management and innovation management. Acklin (2010) argued that good use of design research and *design leadership* or proactive design management can make significant contributions to innovation management and deliverables. The word "leadership" is used to emphasize that, in order to make major contributions, design management must be applied at the strategic level to set the agenda for an organization to use design for core competitive advantages.

At the first stage of idea generation, design leadership and design research can be used to identify signals from the internal and external environment and turn them into innovation hypotheses as a basis for developing the design-led innovation strategy. At the second stage of idea selection, again design leadership and design research are required. Leaders take the responsibility for selecting the ideas with the highest potential for success with the support of observational and experiential research. During the third stage of concept development, the practical design skills come into play supported by continued design research for the purpose of concept development, design, evaluation and testing. The design may be progressed through prototyping and customer feedback must be sought to test the likely reaction to the market.

Finally the fourth stage addresses implementation and here design management and design research can be used for the implementation planning, product/service launch and subsequent promotion and brand communication. The main contribution of design is to create a value proposition for the product/service and a value-added customer experience.

4.4   4Ds OF DESIGN-DRIVEN INNOVATION

The 4Ds design management model shows the 4Ds of design-driven innovation as follows and provides the framework for management and designers to review and enhance their use of design strategy for innovation.

1. Determining – Objectively assessing the level of readiness for innovations (innovation audit).
2. Defining – Establishing strategic directions for innovation and identifying opportunities for design (innovation directions and policy).
3. Designing – Using design thinking to create environments that support innovations and generate new concepts (innovation culture and teams).
4. Deciding – Rigorously assessing performance of the innovations against corporate targets (innovation evaluation).

The strong relationships and interdependence of the three levels of design-driven innovation are illustrated in Figure 4.1.

Crawford (1997) proposed a similar model with vision leading innovation strategy as the basis for the tactical product line strategy and the operational product development. The core strategic vision is derived from the questions: Where are we going? How do we get there? Why will we be successful? The mid-level strategy (innovation and product line strategy) focuses

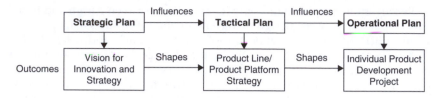

Figure 4.1 Dimensions of innovation and innovation strategies

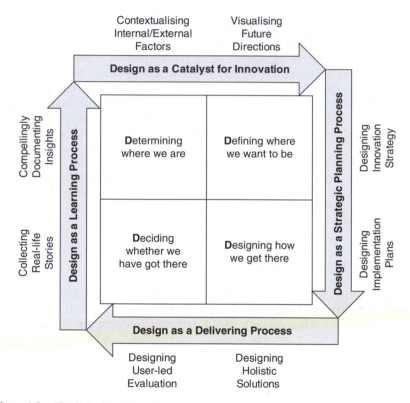

Figure 4.2 4Ds of design-driven innovation model

on addressing practical innovation development plans, e.g. defining target markets and technologies, planning product portfolio architecture, creating product line plans and managing the innovation development process.

The 4Ds model of design-driven innovation is presented as Figure 4.2 and the key elements to be addressed in using the 4Ds model are shown in Table 4.5. This is followed by two case studies of organizations that successfully embraced the principles and practical guidance and tools for using the model to enhance innovation.

Table 4.5 Key elements of the 4Ds of design-driven innovation

Strategic level	Tactical level	Operational level
Determining		
Readiness to innovate • Current visions • Organization culture • Established policies	Present platform • Existing tactics • Planning environments • Resources available	Execution effectiveness • Projects and activities • Processes and methods used • Infrastructure and facilities
Defining		
Vision for innovation • Aspirations • Opportunities • Goals	Scope and range • Product portfolio architecture • Product line planning	Innovation projects • Product/service developments • Allocation of tasks • Supporting activities
Designing		
Climate for innovation • Creative culture • Supporting policies	Creative resources • Creative capacity • Teams • Physical environments	Innovative products/services • Process and methods • Communication channels • Prototypes, trials
Deciding		
Assessing innovation strategies • Assessment against goals/targets • Evaluation of future robustness	Assessing planning effectiveness • Individual/ group performance • Adequacy of resources • Conduciveness of environment	Assessing quality of product/service • Overall design quality and consistency • Individual product/service design quality • Perceived level of innovation

Example: LEGO

LEGO is the world's sixth largest toy maker with well-established design heritage. An increase of competitors from East Asia and a rapid growth of computer-based toys in recent years forced LEGO management to rethink its innovation model. A case study investigation conducted by Design Council (2011) pointed out that a lack of business considerations in the past resulted in massive losses and many commercially unsuccessful products. As a result, LEGO developed the new innovation process called Design for Business (D4B) which ensures the alignment between corporate objectives and design strategy. The process comprises an innovation model, a foundation overview and a road map, which allow the teams to align key objectives, tasks and deliverables during the development stage.

This new approach has helped LEGO move from a primarily product-focused innovation approach to a broader view of innovation in the organization. A more holistic approach has opened up new possibilities and led to many successful innovations, such as the MINDSTORMS (http://mindstorms.lego.com) and Serious Play ranges (www.seriousplay.com).

Example: Bang & Olufsen (B&O)

B&O is an innovative producer of high-end audio-video systems. Its ability to create a synergy of aesthetic and technology is driven by its vision: "courage to constantly question the ordinary in search of surprising, long-lasting experiences." Design is recognized as one of its eight key competencies and the company claims that design is "at the core of everything we do." Since 1974, B&O's unique design philosophy was codified in the seven *Corporate Identity Components* (CIC) that guided all design and communication policies (Ravasi and Lojacono, 2005). It was observed that in the mid-1980s, the designs seemed to have lost touch with customers' needs and the communications concentrated on luxury symbols instead of the unique quality and product experiences. The decline in sales caused the company to refocus its innovation development efforts and seek the true "essence" of its brand. This helped a company to re-discover its core competencies (picture, sound, user interaction, system integration, moving mechanics, design, materials and finish, and quality). B&O chooses to work with freelance designers to maintain "a broad creative horizon."

4.4.1 Determining the Level of Readiness for Innovation: Innovation Audit

Innovation is risky, as Baxter (1995) pointed out "for every 10 ideas for new products, 3 will be developed, 1.3 will be launched, only 1 will make any profit." So the innovation audit needs to be thorough and rigorous. Baxter (1995) also found that:

- Strong market orientation = five times more likely to achieve new product success;
- Early planning and specification = three times more likely to achieve new product success;
- Company factors (e.g. cultures) = 2.5 times more likely to achieve new product success.

Benefits to the market are important as the BSI (2008) stress that "innovation might not be right for every organisation, or for every product of innovative organisations. Furthermore, customer and markets do not always welcome innovation unless the benefits are obvious." Regarding all innovation as inherently "good" could be dangerous. Thus the audit should incorporate a wide range of questions on issues outlined in Table 4.6.

Innovation Audit at the Strategic Level

An innovation audit at the strategic level is about assessing the "mindset" for innovation. This should be examined under two headings:

- *Strategic approach* – evaluating missions, visions and aspirations of an organization and deciding which strategic approaches suit the organization best.
- *Culture and policy* – assessing if current organizational cultures encourage people to come up with innovative ideas. Are there supporting mechanisms in place to help employees develop ideas further? Is there any

Table 4.6   Innovation audit at different levels

Level	Key areas for auditing	Key questions
Strategic	1. Vision and mission	• *Are our visions still relevant to all stakeholders and the market environment?*
	2. Corporate culture	• *Do we have innovation cultures? If so, do we effectively nurture these cultures? Do we have the right climate to promote innovation development and innovation cultures?*
	3. Corporate policy	• *What are our policies regarding innovation? Do they support our visions and cultures?*
Tactical	1. Innovation strategy	• *Does our innovation strategy help us stand out, fulfil our visions and answer user latent needs?*
	2. Capabilities	• *Do we have mechanisms/processes in place to support our strategic directions?*
	3. Resources for innovation	• *Do we have all required resources (e.g. people, know-how and financial support) in place?*
Operational	1. Activities & projects	• *Do our innovation activities and new product development projects match our strategy?*
	2. Infrastructures & facilities	• *Do we have adequate infrastructures and facilities to support current projects?*
	3. Processes & methods	• *Do we employ appropriate innovation development processes and methods?*

incentive for innovative idea development? Some organizational cultures can discourage innovation, such as when a benevolent autocratic CEO inadvertently creates fear among subordinates to express themselves freely.

Although external factors (e.g. social trends) play significant roles in shaping innovation directions, visions for innovation should be based on the aspirations of a company rather than simply responding to market demands. Baxter (1995) suggested that an innovation approach should be directly linked to an organization's mission and vision. For example, if a company aspires to be a leader of their industry, they should aim to the "best" at something, e.g. cheapest, safest, the most energy efficient, friendliest or the most reliable. Their innovation strategies should be built upon their goals. Not every organization wants to be a leader. It is very difficult to maintain the leading position. It may be safer and, sometimes, more profitable to be a fast followers. Hence, it is important to assess an organization's "mindset" toward innovation, e.g. its attitudes toward risks and radical changes, in the context of its current organizational culture.

To help with this assessment the *Innovation Self-assessment Questionnaire* (BSI, 2008) is useful. As the first of a series of self-assessment questionnaires to help an organization assess their current innovation practices, it is designed to assist an organization in investigating its current perception

Table 4.7 Examples of the issues assessed using BSI's self-assessment questionnaire

Where is your organization on these issues? Mark an "x" in the relevant box on the scale.

	1	2	3	4	5	
Innovation is too disruptive and not easy to plan within our management structure	☐	☐	☐	☐	☐	Innovation is essential and we make a 100% effort to promote it to sustain and improve our organization
Our focus is on survival and what needs to be done now	☐	☐	☐	☐	☐	We subject every facet to long term planning.
We do not promote change as we believe it is bad for us and our stakeholders	☐	☐	☐	☐	☐	We embrace and engage with all required changes to maintain our competitive strength.
We emphasize making our existing products better	☐	☐	☐	☐	☐	We re-invest our income to develop new products/services
We seek to avoid failure	☐	☐	☐	☐	☐	We accept failure as necessary to learning

of innovation, the responsiveness to changes, the attitude toward failure and the priorities (e.g. a leading position or profits). An example of how the questionnaire works is shown in Table 4.7 but the detailed instrument is available on subscription.

Another approach to connecting innovation directions with a company's vision proposed by Abbing (2010), is making sure that innovation strategy is developed based on a brand promise. However, some brand promises are more visionary than others. Hence, not all companies will be able to use their brands as a catalyst for innovation.

Abbing proposed that suitable innovation approaches should be determined by (1) the brand usability and (2) the innovation potential. Brand usability is referred to as "the extent to which the brand is suitable as a driver for innovation and the extent to which there is room for innovation to be led by the brand" and innovation potential is defined as "the extent to which an organisation has room in its competitive field for proactive creation of new meaningful value." He identified possible innovation approaches as follows:

- *Opportunity-driven innovation*: If both brand usability and innovation potential are low, a company will not have the luxury to use its brand as a driver for innovation. It will need to grasp any opportunity for innovation it gets.
- *Innovation-driven branding*: If brand usability is low but innovation potential is high, a firm should look for opportunities for innovation based on other drivers (e.g. technology) and use innovation as a foundation to build the brand on.

- *Co-branding*: If brand usability is high but innovation potential is low, a firm may not develop innovation on its own. It should seek partners/alliances with appropriate innovation capabilities to unlock the full potential of its brand.
- *Brand-driven innovation*: If both brand usability and innovation potential are high, a company has an option to use its brand promise as a driver for innovation.

It is important to ensure that all members of staff share the same mindset and attitude toward innovation. Hence, a company must create organizational cultures and climate that reinforces the desirable mindset and enables innovation to happen at all levels. In *Managing Creativity and Innovation* (Harvard Business Essentials, 2003) it is pointed out that there are six organizational characteristics that influence the creativity and innovation cultures: (1) acceptance of risk taking; (2) welcoming new ideas and ways of doing things; (3) ensuring a free flow of information; (4) giving employees access to knowledge sources; (5) support of good ideas by executives; and (6) rewarding innovators. A simple scorecard can be used to assess strengths and weaknesses and further features added as appropriate – see example shown in Table 4.8.

Keeley, Pikkel, Quinn and Walters (2013) pointed out that while most companies (average innovators) tend to use only one or two types of innovation, leading companies (top innovators) are likely to employ more than three types of innovation (see their ten types of innovation concept in Section 4.1.1). According to their research, integrating more types of innovation into a company's practices could lead to superior financial return and business success. Hence, a company should assess how many types of innovation they currently use and identify how to improve as well as how to build upon their current strengths.

Table 4.8 Checklist of organizational characteristics that support creativity and innovation

Features of the organization	Enter score – 1 to 5 where 1=weak 5=strong
CEO and top management encourage risk taking and reward innovation.	
Information is open and available to all (across functional boundaries).	
Employees have support and access to all internal and external knowledge sources (open transparency).	
All employees encouraged to contribute ideas by senior management.	
An open and fair reward system gives recognition to those employees who add value.	

Innovation Audit at the Tactical and Operational Levels

An innovation audit at the tactical and operational levels is about assessing whether an organization has the required ability to achieve its aspirations, e.g. resources (including physical, human and financial), infrastructures or facilities and mechanisms and processes to nurture innovative ideas and support the implementation. This may be examined by first considering capabilities. There are several strategic options available to a company, which were identified by Baxter (1995) and Freeman (1982) cited in Walsh *et al.* (1992). The types of strategy identified are largely complementary and are summarized below to further explain their implications for design strategy. Thus, it is vital to find what options are available based on current capabilities.

Baxter's four strategic options may be addressed by design strategy as follows:

1. *Pioneering*: A pioneering organization is one which seeks to lead the way forward, and this usually means it invests much in scientific development and user/lifestyle research and development. The rewards may be long term. (Examples: Nike, Bio-fuel development.)
2. *Responsive*: The organization that allows others to take the new product/ service risks and test the market response but are geared up to bring better innovations onto the market rapidly.(Examples: Cannon, low-cost airlines.)
3. *Traditional*: This type of organization sees the market as quite static – they do not expect to innovate except very conservatively and are thus unprepared and vulnerable to change. (Examples: Wedgewood, traditional furniture companies.)
4. *Dependent*: An organization that leaves all the innovation to others – principally parent companies and/or customers. In-house innovation is limited to process innovation making them most vulnerable to sudden environmental changes. (Examples: parts suppliers, manufacturers with no own brand.)

Relationships between innovation strategies and a company's priorities investigated by Baxter (1995) revealed, perhaps not surprisingly, that pioneering companies lead the way in innovative design, R&D and marketing and often gain patents, whilst giving strong attention to production engineering and time to market. Responsive companies are on time to market with innovative designs and rapid production but neglect R&D. Traditional and dependent companies show concern only for production engineering.

Freeman (1982) offered six strategic options and their issues for design strategy may be summarized as:

1. *Offensive*: The organization wants to be the technical and market leader, staying ahead of its competitors by offering new products/services/experiences. (Examples: Tesla Motor, Microsoft.)
2. *Defensive*: The close follower company which tracks the leader and follows up rapidly to be seen to be up to speed. (Examples: Vax.)

3. *Imitative*: The race participant company but a long way back, looking for opportunities to gain advantage, for example by using local knowledge or lower labour costs. (Examples: Fake and cheaper product producers – like mobile communications companies.)
4. *Dependent*: Subsidiary of main company with no pressure to innovate because others provide the required technical and design support. (Examples: Fashion sweat shops, parts suppliers.)
5. *Traditional*: Companies that produce products which change very little technically and are often craft based. Design may change in response to technology more than fashion. (Examples: Montblanc pens and wallets, Wedgewood.)
6. *Opportunist*: The organization that sees new opportunities in changing markets instinctively and by observation and research, providing something no-one else thought of – radical new to the world innovations. (Examples: Amazon, the Virgin Group.)

Further investigation by Freeman (1982) cited in Walsh *et al.* (1992) show the relationships between the types of strategy they found and the company capabilities in their in-house scientific and technical functions. Using a scorecard whereby 1 = underdeveloped relationship and 5= fully developed and utilized relationship, they measured the six strategies against the provision of fundamental research, applied research, experimental research, design engineering, production engineering and quality control, technical service, patents, scientific and technical information, education and training and long range forecasting and product planning.

They found offensive strategy users to be strong across all categories. Defensive strategy companies showed strengths in experimental research, design engineering and scientific and technical information but were notably weak in fundamental research. Imitative strategists were strong in production engineering and scientific and technical information but weak in applied research, technical service and patents and very weak in fundamental research. Users of dependent strategy were strong only in production engineering and only moderate (score 3) in design engineering, scientific and technical information and education and training. The traditional approach showed strength only in production engineering with every other category weak. Opportunist strategy adopters were shown to be strong in long-range forecasting and scientific and technical information whilst very weak in all other aspects.

The most significant finding for the management of design is the would-be leaders generate great pressure to be highly capable across a wide range of related functions and contemporary practices indicate the importance of integrating them strongly. However, follower strategies may also be risky as choosing which leaders and which trends to follow is also complex.

These tables can formulated to match the organization's need for self-evaluation and used to assess and understand an organization's strengths and weaknesses and support the management decision-making process in preparing for the future. Good use of design audit tools as well as other strategic analysis tools, such as SWOT, can help a company to uncover its

Table 4.9 Examples of self-assessment questionnaire

Where is your organization on these issues? Mark an "x" in the relevant box on the scale.

	1	2	3	4	5	
New product/service briefs follow standard practice from former projects	☐	☐	☐	☐	☐	Project briefs are formulated with great care and insight.
Project teams tend to be fixed and staff are under pressure.	☐	☐	☐	☐	☐	Project teams eschew appropriate skills and experience.
Senior management do not communicate closely with project teams.	☐	☐	☐	☐	☐	Top manager leads each project.
Tools and techniques vary according to individual choice.	☐	☐	☐	☐	☐	Advanced tools are used to support creative thinking.
Our technologies are comfortably familiar with no intellectual property to protect.	☐	☐	☐	☐	☐	Our products/services have significant protected unique intellectual property.

strengths, realistically acknowledge its weaknesses and identify areas of excellence. For example, it would be dangerous to choose the offensive or pioneering strategy if a company does not have well-established R&D strengths to enable this strategic choice.

The BSI (2008) also produced a self-assessment questionnaire to help an organization assess their capabilities (e.g. processes and team structure) and resources (e.g. staff and intellectual property) at the tactical and operational levels. An example of an innovation self-assessment questionnaire is reproduced in Table 4.9 and the full questionnaire is available on subscription.

Naturally, as with all self-assessment, its use in practice will depend on the degree to which the organization is ready to be objective in assigning the scores. If the management of the organization have concerns about the objectivity, it may be best to engage an experienced independent consultant.

4.4.2 Defining Directions for Innovations: Innovation Directions and Policy

Step 1: Having Clear, Long-term Goals

Management must set clear goals and directions as the basis for building a strategy and implementation plan. The strategy should be "creative and visionary, yet critically functional. The overall aim of strategy is to identify and secure a long-term competitive advantage for the enterprise" (Cooper and Press, 1995). The extent of innovation will vary between organizations but most will recognize many compelling reasons to innovate, see Table 4.10.

An organization may wish to constantly improve, maintain and enhance competitiveness, attract and retain good staff and sustain their existence. Innovative organizations thrive on ideas to open up opportunities. They

Table 4.10   Why organizations must innovate

Driving forces	Design strategy action points
To maintain and improve present situation.	• Design to minimize costs and maximize profitability. • Secure and enhance market position and respond to threats. • Develop a loyal, stable, confident and creative workforce.
To identify new directions.	• Help organization to establish its perspective, i.e. its place in the world. • Identify opportunities to develop new products/services/experiences for competitive advantage. • Outclass the competition.
To be legally compliant and socially and environmentally responsible.	• Be fully compliant with law but go further by being aware of impending changes. • Actively seek opportunities to demonstrate "good citizenship" through addressing social and environmental needs.
To enhance organizational image, reputation and trust.	• Develop trusted image and identity. • Gain the best staff by being the most desirable organization to work for. • Attract leading collaborators e.g. for co-branding.

are responsible bodies, legally compliant but also showing they care about social and environmental concerns. This way they gain a strong reputation and attract funding and good partners.

Defining future directions is complex and challenging. At extremes an organization can be a follower or a leader. The follower waits for competitors to take the first (sometimes risky) steps and, having satisfied themselves the direction is potentially lucrative, joins the competition with an adaptation of the offering. The leader takes more risks but, when they can protect the intellectual property and/or achieve market dominance, they can reap greater rewards. Followers wait for the leaders and try to exploit their weaknesses. Leaders are often the acknowledged technical experts and rely on retaining their superior R&D capacity.

Step 2: Planning How to Realize the Goals

The next step in developing and managing the design strategy for innovation is planning how to realize the goals. A useful tool for planning innovation strategy was developed by Jacoby and Rodriguez (2007). It is based on Ansoff's Product/Market Matrix and helps to identify growth factors and key activities. The authors explained that good use of management can help a firm grow by making more profits, increasing and expanding market shares. However, this is considered to be an incremental innovation, since this practice is unlikely to lead to any significant improvement in products/services/experiences. Growing by *adapting* or *extending* is a natural evolution process. In general, most companies either rely on their existing customer bases when developing new products or introduce products/

Table 4.11 Relationships between innovation outcomes and strategic choices

Ways to grow	Users	Offerings	Design strategy addresses	Examples
Management strategy	Existing users	Existing offerings Products/ services	• Raising perceived value • Raising consumption • Winning greater share of market	Tesco's Finest range Eva Airways Elite class
Extension strategy	Existing users	New offerings	• Extending brands • Share of wallets • Leveraging users	Microsoft's Windows 8
Adaption strategy	New users	Existing offerings	• Expanding footprints • Winning shares	Skype's business accounts
Creation strategy	New users	New offerings	• Creating markets • Disrupting markets	Nintendo Wii

services in new markets. They further argued that growing through *creating* leads to revolutionary outcomes. Nintendo Wii is a good example of how a company can think "outside the box" and develop games for non-mainstream gamers. It successfully attracts female and older audiences who are normally not interested in digital games. Table 4.11 shows the relationships of growth strategies to design strategies with examples of resulting sub brands.

Most experts suggest that innovation strategy contains four to seven key elements. Despite some small differences, there is general agreement that innovation strategy must be placed in context (e.g. market conditions) and have a clear focus and well-defined criteria and milestones so that the outcomes can be objectively assessed – the main components of three leading researchers are compared in Table 4.12.

A valuable and pragmatic agenda for the stages of developing design-led innovation strategy was set by Roscam Abbing (2010). Most activities included in his Stage 2 are likely to be carried out as part of the innovation audit and are encompassed under four main headings as follows:

- *Create the future vision*: In order to create the future it is necessary to get powerful thinking and inputs from all stakeholders. They must all understand and share ownership of the organizations vision of the future, its mission and goals. Their challenge is to translate this into desires based on the value proposition and develop future scenarios which explain what future success may look like.

- *Scan for internal opportunities*: First match the internal resources to the desires to ensure they are realistic. Ensure the resources, especially creative people, have the capability to deliver the future vision. Check the level and quality of the internal resources and the trends, in answer to the question "Are they improving?" Revisit the scenarios and change them as required following this evaluation.

- *Scan for external opportunities*: By modelling how the external drivers influence the scenarios and how the environment may, in turn, be changing them, the organization may identify the most significant forces and further improve on the future scenarios.

- *Create and implement innovation strategy*: Having identified the key areas wherein the best opportunities may be found, innovation strategy criteria can be established based on the self-assessments and used to assess the potential of each area. This provides the foundation upon which to select and plan futures products/services/experiences and prepare a programme with project times, teams and resources.

Table 4.12 A comparison of key components of innovation strategy

Boike and Staley (1996)	Crawford (1997)	Grant (1991, cited in Von Stamm [2008])
1. Statement of consumer needs.	1. **Background:** Key ideas from the analysis.	1. The unambiguous long-term goals.
2. Market conditions and response.	2. **Focus:** At least one clear technology dimension and one clear market dimension. They match and have good potential.	2. The insightful understanding of the external environments.
3. Product attributes and specifications.		
4. Development schedule and milestones.	3. **Goals/objectives:** What the project will accomplish, e.g. profit, growth and market status.	3. The intimate self-knowledge of organization's capabilities.
5. Resource requirement and purchasing.		
6. Product financials.	4. **Guidelines:** Any "rules of the roads," requirements imposed by the situation or by upper management.	4. The committed and well-coordinated implementation.
7. Key (internal and external) interfaces.		

The same process is applied at all levels. However, the scope and the results are different. At the highest level the strategic managers must aim to create an innovation strategy to guide the long-term developments and innovation management. Hence, all factors, including brand values, emerging trends and core competencies, have to be taken into consideration.

The strategic management at the tactical level focuses developing product line strategy, platform strategy and product portfolio architecture.

As strategic directions of the entire organization have already been defined, the scope of contextualization is narrower, for example responding to the strategies of direct competitors and the demands of chosen target audiences. The strategic management at the operational level concentrates on designing the strategy for individual projects and/or services, team structures, innovation development processes as well as roles and responsibilities of all key stakeholders. As directions for individual projects have already been defined at the higher levels, the contextual study becomes even more specific, for example the requirements of particular segments and performance of existing products/services in the same category.

4.4.3   Designing Environments to Support Innovation: Culture & Teams

Maintaining momentum and direction for innovation requires well-designed environments, which are conducive to the design of successful products and services. This means innovative culture and innovative teams. The objective is to develop an "innovation climate" which supports innovation. Innovative companies develop their own practices. For example, Google has the 70/20/10 model for managing innovation. This model suggests that employees should divide their time in the following ratio:

- 70% of time should be dedicated to core business tasks;
- 20% of time should be dedicated to projects related to the core business;
- 10% of time should be dedicated to projects unrelated to the core business (side projects).

Working on projects outside of the core business tasks allows employees to work on different projects and gain new experiences, which helps them to stay creative. Moreover, it encourages employees to continually develop new skills and knowledge. Nowadays, many big organizations, e.g. Nike and 3M, recognize that their successful products (e.g. Post-it notes) started off as side projects – projects that companies do not assign their employees to work on. However, these people choose to dedicate their own time (and sometimes their own resources) to work on them because they truly believe that these ideas have strong potential. This level of commitment needs to be recognized, rewarded and encouraged. Allowing people to work on side projects also shows a high level of trust that a company has in its employees.

Another interesting example is the innovation culture at W. L. Gore & Associates (www.gore.com).The story began when Bill Gore left DuPont and co-founded the company in 1958. The real motivation behind his major decision was that he would like to create a new kind of company that unleashes people's creativity, and fosters personal initiative. His company, which now has more than 10,000 employees, termed "associates", generates $3.2 billion annual sales and owns more than 2,000 patents worldwide, and is a team-based, flat organization – no chain of command, no hierarchy. People have freedom to work with and communicate with anyone – there is no predetermined channel of communication. People can choose projects that they want to work on. Teams are organized around opportunities which certain groups of people are interested in. Team leaders emerge naturally – not by being assigned by the top management. Some may wonder: If these people are not closely monitored and managed, why should they work? The company believes that if people are passionate about their work, they are highly motivated to do good jobs. Moreover, associates are fairly rewarded for their achievements and commitment. Gore's culture has successfully promoted innovation at individual, group and organizational level and encouraged positive behaviours.

Step 1: Understanding Factors Influencing Innovation Culture

The first step towards making the organizational climate more creative is to understand creativity in the organizational context. Patterson, *et al.* (2009)

investigated how to enhance innovative working and identified employees' characteristics and behaviours that contribute toward innovative working as (in order of priority): openness to ideas, problem solving, motivation/personal initiative, strategic thinking, leadership and management skills, self-belief/ confidence, willingness to take risks, emotional intelligence and tolerance of ambiguity. These are characteristics are frequently found in designers and thus it may be surmised that designer characteristics should be developed and nurtured throughout the organization to promote innovative working.

Goffee and Jones (1998) cited in Von Stamm (2008) argued that the solidarity and sociability in an organizational context can significantly influence the innovation process and outcomes. It can be seen that while personal initiative, interests and individual abilities play an important role in the innovation process, a combined effort of committed, cohesive and highly motivated teams results in superior outcomes and better implementation. Table 4.13 shows the implications of the degree of cohesion on the design strategy for innovation. The highly cohesive team emerges as potentially the most favourable for design and innovation but the profit-driven team can be very effective in a more mechanistic manner, even though they have less fun.

Three key factors to promote creativity and innovation culture were identified by Teresa (1996) and cited in Harvard Business Essentials (2003). The first is *expertise*, i.e. the technical, procedural and intellectual knowledge of employees. In second place was *motivation*, employees' extrinsic motivation (driven by outcomes or external factors) and/or intrinsic motivation (driven by an inner passion or personal interests). The third factor identified was *creative thinking* skills, or how flexibly and imaginatively employees approach problems.

Table 4.13   Group cohesiveness and design strategy for innovation

Degree of cohesion	Features	Design strategy
Highly cohesive, mutually supportive teams	High commitment and participation. Good social relationships	Excel at longer term complex problem solving. Spawn innovation and visionary design leadership.
Well connected but no strong goal-directed bonds.	Lower team commitment but good social relationships.	Tendency to be more radical and diverse but may be lax about design management procedures.
Profit-driven, concerned mainly with being first to market.	High team commitment to achieving set goals but weak social connections.	Rigidly pursuing well-focussed goals with good planning and defined roles. Faster implementation.
Individuals with very limited connections and/or interactions.	Lacking team commitment, focus and co-ordination. Often a mismatch of people.	More individuals who do their own thing. No team spirit or teamwork development.

Apart from understanding how innovation happens in an organization and which factors promote innovation culture, it is important to recognize current barriers. Patterson *et al.* (2009) identified a number of major barriers that need to be overcome. The most significant barriers were revealed as excessive financial constraints and lack of time.

This may indicate risk aversion at times of economic pressure and a natural tendency to caution among financial controllers. Constant pressure to be first to market and to maintain competitiveness leads to lower priority of time allocated to generating new ideas. Lack of resources was also found to be a significant barrier, which indicates the allocation of resources is controlled to minimize costs. Risk aversion and fear of failure, a rigidity in organizational structure and unclear leadership and strategy for innovation were also seen to be holding organizations back from innovation success. Less significant but influencing barriers were insufficient incentives, insufficient training and insufficient talent, all indicative of an unwillingness to invest in creating an innovative environment. The final factor found to be inhibiting innovation were found to be lack of autonomy in job roles, insufficient opportunity to share ideas and lack of support by management. The first two of these final three factors suggest a restrictive environment but the last one is particularly interesting because seemingly the respondents did not blame management for lack of support, so "blame culture" was cited by only 14% of those surveyed.

Step 2: Assessing Current Situation and Identifying Areas for Improvement

The second step for management to build a design-led innovation culture is to assess the current climate in an organization in order to identify areas for improvement. Johnson (1999) cited in Goffin and Mitchel (2005) identified the main factors for assessing the corporate culture as: (a) *organizational structures* which demonstrate what is important to an organization, e.g. a hierarchical structure shows that authority and control is crucial for a company; (b) *power structures* showing where the power and authority lie, such as chains of command and channels of communication which demonstrate who is in charge; (c) *symbols* which visualize the beliefs, like office environments and dress code which can reinforce the message about core values and beliefs; (d) *routine and rituals* by which unwritten rules guiding employees' behaviours can be identified, for example behaviours of people in managerial roles can influence behaviours of their staff; (e) *control system* showing what is valued and focussed on, such as formal processes, measurement systems, promotion criteria, recognition and rewards; and (f) *paradigm* which is how an organization "thinks" and "acts," its code of conduct.

Table 4.14 is based on the work of Patterson *et al.* (2009) which identified measures of employees' characteristics and behaviours in terms of their readiness to innovate. The checklist has been modified to incorporate the characteristics of designers to lead innovation. It is a generic example of how such a checklist may be formulated but managers of design should be ready to adapt the checklist to match the requirements of their organizations. Central issues will be motivation and attitude to change, readiness to

Table 4.14   Tool for measuring designers' readiness to innovate

Category A: High design innovation characteristics	1	2	3	Category B: Low design innovation characteristics	1	2	3
Motivation and attitude: • Actively seeks and embraces change. • Confident about solving complex problems. • Discontented (even bored) with current "solutions" .				**Motivation and attitude:** • Needs encouragement and support to try new ideas/approaches. • Persistent but reflective. • Requires high degree of direction and detailed guidance.			
Challenge norms and champion changes: • Strong, assertive and independent. • Difficult to manage conventionally. • Determined and formidable in promoting own ideas.				**Challenge norms and champion changes:** • Favours harmonious relationships. • Reticent to argue and conformist. • Looks for social acceptance.			
Adaptability: • Challenges the boundaries. • Uses instincts at least equally to facts. • Wants to be seen as different.				**Adaptability:** • Assigns high value to facts and evidence. • Keeps within established boundaries. • Concentrates on refining approaches.			
Working practices: • Wide range of methods/styles for each new project. • Thrives on variety. • Does not need detailed specifications.				**Working practices:** • Prefer good planning and structure. • Follows the rules. • Methodical and efficient.			

challenge behavioural norms, creativity and adaptation and consistency of working practices.

The first aspect aims to measure to what extent a designer is open and willing to change. The second aspect tests the designer's readiness to champion changes and challenge conventional behaviour and ways of thinking and working. The third aspect is intended to evaluate whether an individual prefers to use proven methods or is willing to try new ways of thinking, working and solving problems. The last aspect could help a company see whether a designer prefers structured or unstructured tasks. Unstructured tasks allow individuals to express themselves more than well-defined tasks.

A high score in category A indicates the designers are well prepared to play a leading role in innovation, whereas a high score is category B indicates a lack of preparedness. Score 1 = weak relationship, 3 = strong relationship, and 2 = neutral. A scale of 5, 7 or 9 may be used if preferred. The tool can then be used to identify and further investigate any areas of weakness revealed. By gaining a better understanding of their designers and related employees, management is able to identify areas for improvement and develop practical plans such as group training and personal development schemes.

Step 3: Continually Improving and Creating Environments for Innovation

The next step is to address continually improving and promoting the innovation culture. Kanter (1983) cited in Von Stamm (2008) suggested five ways for managers to improve an organization's environment for innovation: (1) *encourage a culture of pride* – highlight achievements of people in the company; (2) *enlarge access to power tools for innovative problem solving* – provide vehicles to support proposals for experiments and innovation; (2) *improve lateral communication* – bring departments together. encourage cross-fertilization through exchange of people, create cross-functional links; (3) *reduce unnecessary layers of hierarchy* – eliminate barriers to resources access; (4) *increase, and provide earlier, information about company plans* – increase security by making future plans known in advance, empower and involve people at the lower levels at an earlier point.

Three management practices by Harvard Business Essentials (2003) summarize what matters the most in terms of enriching creativity and innovation cultures in an organization as:

1. *Getting the right match* – matching the right people with the right assignments;
2. *Giving freedom* – setting the goals and letting people plan their own processes;
3. *Providing sufficient time and resources* – setting unrealistic deadlines and allocating insufficient resources prevent people from trying new/creative ideas.

The degree of freedom for allowing designers to plan their own approaches is particularly challenging for management. The favoured characteristics for design-led innovators lean towards autonomy and freedom. This was further confirmed by Patterson *et al.* (2009) and supported Kanter's suggestions for improvement, as most participants in the research perceived support from the top management, incentives and opportunities to collaborate and exchange of ideas as the most important factors.

The most important catalysts for design-led innovation are good leadership, openness and support for the design and innovation functions, building teams of creative thinkers with the right characteristics and giving them freedom to do the job. To do this successfully means developing and agreeing on a strategy, communicating it well and constantly reinforcing the messages. This in turn strengthens the networks and increases confidence in further investing in design-led innovation. Evaluation of outcomes can also be improved as confidence grows in the metrics adopted. Provided these catalysts are constantly improved, the organizational structure mutates to reflect the practices and thus the traditional concentration on structuring and restructuring becomes less relevant.

Forming the right teams and acknowledging contributions each member can make are essential for success. The most influential work on team formation is that of Belbin, whose "dream team" identifies nine different team role descriptions, see Table 4.15. The ideal composition of creative teams is both controversial and challenging. Members of the team each have their own personality which may often cross the boundaries of the "types" identified by leading researchers. Thus psychometric tests of personality based

Table 4.15   Team-role descriptions

Team role	Contribution	Allowable weakness
Plant	Creative, imaginative, unorthodox. Solves difficult problems	Ignores incidentals. Too pre-occupied to communicate effectively.
Resource investigator	Extrovert, enthusiastic, communicative. Explores opportunities, develops contacts.	Over-optimistic. Loses interest once initial enthusiasm has passed.
Co-ordinator	Mature, confident, a good chairperson. Clarifies goals, promotes decision making, delegates well.	Can be seen as manipulative. Offloads personal work.
Shaper	Challenging, dynamic, thrives on pressure. The drive and courage to overcome obstacles.	Prone to provocation. Offends people's feelings.
Monitor evaluator	Sober, strategic and discerning. Sees all options. Judges accurately.	Lacks drive and ability to inspire others.
Team worker	Cooperative, mild, perceptive and diplomatic. Listens, builds averts friction.	Indecisive in crunch situations.
Implementer	Disciplined, reliable, conservative and efficient. Turns ideas into practical actions.	Somewhat inflexible. Slow to respond to new possibilities.
Completer/finisher	Painstaking, conscientious, anxious. Searches out errors and omissions. Delivers on time.	Inclined to worry unduly. Reluctant to delegate.
Specialist	Single-minded, self-starting, dedicated. Provides knowledge and skills in rare supply	Contributes on only a narrow front. Dwells on technicalities

Source: www.belbin.com

Table 4.16 Ten Faces of Innovation

Personas	Roles
Learning personas	
1. Anthropologist	Brings new learning and insights into the organization by observing human behaviour and developing a deep understanding of how people interact physically and emotionally with products, services and spaces.
2. Experimenter	Prototypes new ideas continuously, learning by a process of enlightened trial and error.
3. Cross-pollinator	Explores other industries and cultures, then translates those findings and revelations to fit the unique needs of your enterprise.
Organizing personas	
4. Hurdler	Knows the path to innovation is strewn with obstacles and develops a knack for overcoming or outsmarting those roadblocks.
5. Collaborator	Helps bring eclectic groups together, and often leads from the middle of the pack to create new combinations and multidisciplinary solutions.
6. Director	Not only gathers together a talented cast and crew but also helps to spark their creative talents.
Building personas	
7. Experience architect	Designs compelling experiences that go beyond mere functionality to connect at a deeper level with customers' latent or expressed needs.
8. Set designer	Creates a stage on which innovation team members can do their best work, transforming physical environments into powerful tools to influence behaviours and attitude.
9. Caregiver	Builds on the metaphor of a health care professional to deliver customer care in a manner that goes beyond mere service.
10. Storyteller	Builds both internal morale and external awareness through compelling narratives that communicate a fundamental human value or reinforce a specific cultural trait.

Source: Kelly and Littman (2006).

on research of character and roles should be regarded as a guide to team building and part of the foundation for a deeper insightful quest to achieve the optimum balance. Some talented designers still cling proudly to their "rebel" status and may find it difficult to cooperate in teams.

A more recent work on personas and roles was developed by Kelley and Littman (2006) as the Ten Faces of Innovation, see Table 4.16.

The climate for innovation has to be created and reinforced at all levels. While the strategic level focuses on promoting creative cultures through suitable policies, the tactical level deals with more practical aspects, such as developing employees' knowledge and skills, building creative teams and using tangible designs such as office environments, to reinforce key messages from above. The operational level concentrates on creating an innovation culture at project/departmental level, e.g. introducing employees to creative tools and techniques.

4.4.4   Deciding Whether Innovations Meet Corporate Objectives

Innovation evaluation is an assessment of whether the organization met its established targets, the extent to which the organizational climate promotes, nurtures and rewards innovation and the quality of the resultant designed/manufactured outputs. Roper *et al.* (2009) proposed that innovation capability should be broadly evaluated by examining the way the organization accesses knowledge, builds innovation and commercializes it. Accessing knowledge refers to the way the organization sources or creates knowledge through R&D and design which either complements or substitutes for external knowledge sources.

Accessing knowledge can be an indicator of the sectors' level of engagement with open innovation. Building innovation is done through knowledge transformation into new products, processes or organizational forms. It will usually involve multi-skill teams working with external partners to capture deeper level "hidden" innovations such as improvements in organizational and marketing activities. The commercialization is concerned with translating the innovations into added productivity or sales. It may encompass different forms of customer involvement, internal spending on reputation and branding and intellectual property protection. Overall the study highlighted the relationship between openness and innovation success within sectors and added to the growing support for open innovation.

Evaluation should be conducted rigorously and as objectively as possible based on searching questions formulated to address the nature and effectiveness of the strategy. The evaluation should be conducted as an ongoing process, as distinct from a periodic exercise. The findings from the evaluation can direct vigorous debate and feed into the audit as a cyclical process, thus promoting constant learning within the organization. Useful self-assessment checklists have been introduced in previous sections and further guidance can be found in BSI's *Design Management Systems – Part 1: Guide to Managing Innovation.*

4.5   CASE STUDY 2 – DESIGN-LED INNOVATION: PHILIPS

Philips is one of the largest design-led organizations in the world. It has seven studios in Europe, Asia and North America, 400 design professionals from 35+ nationalities, and uses multidisciplinary design teams. Philips Design is guided by two core design principles, "high design" and sustainability. High design is their holistic approach, based on thorough research and generating insights from social sciences and anthropology to support the designers. It is a powerful combination of good traditional design skills (small-d design) and contemporary design-related skills, such as systems thinking (Big-D design) and anthropology. The sustainability principle focuses on environmental impacts and ethical issues.

For more than half a century design and research has been an integral part of Philips' innovation process. Design research projects, such as their

Vision of the Future, allow the design teams to develop knowledge and competence at three levels:

- *Level 1, Research for design:* Obtaining knowledge to improve the quality of design;
- *Level 2, Research into design:* Exploring new methodologies and design languages;
- *Level 3, Research through design*: Investigating new business options and high potential values and building strategic partnerships with the Philips product divisions.

According to Gardien (2006) Philips' innovation model was underpinned by two theories: the "Alchemy of Growth" (Baghai et al., 2000) and the "Hype Cycle" developed by Gartner, a technology market research firm in 1995. Based on the Alchemy of Growth's principles, the innovation territory can be divided into defending and extending the company's core business, developing new business and creating viable options. While most organizations will start with defending their current core business and then expand into new product categories and new markets, Philips Design team begins by investigating unexplored territories, identifying viable options and coming up with visionary concepts. Subsequently, suitable applications for particular concepts will be identified, followed by a roadmap on how to expand new opportunities further.

Another example of their approach is Nebula. This project was created to probe into unexplored territory for enriching the experience of going to bed and waking up through an interactive projection system. Simple body movements and gestures are used to interact with the system and control the ambience of a bedroom, such as colours and brightness of light. Although the original concept might sound very futuristic, it allowed Philips Design team to explore relationships between people's emotional well-being and their surrounding environments. This investigation resulted in innovative applications in the areas of medical ambient experience. This human-centred design approach helps humanize hospital experiences of many patients, especially children.

Some questions for discussion:

- What is the risk in focussing on new opportunities rather than defending core products/services?
- Why does Phillips use multinational, multidisciplinary teams to gain foresight into the future?
- How are humans in different environments and cultures affected by colour and levels of light?

4.6   SUMMARY OF KEY POINTS

Design-driven innovation harnesses the power of design creative thinking to influence the entire culture and practices of the organization. The application of Big-D design addresses the tangible and intangible aspects of the innovation strategy and small-d design delivers more concepts and added-value products and/or services. Innovation models have evolved to integrate design and, in some cases, to lead the innovation strategy. There is a growing recognition of the need for open, flexible models of innovation to share knowledge and stimulate creative ideas and solutions. The design creative thinking runs concurrent with the strategy and planning and the 4Ds design management model enables to assessment of readiness, the definition of future directions, enhancement of the creative environment for innovation and the review of performance.

4.7   FURTHER CONSIDERATIONS

Utilizing design strategy to drive innovation requires the fusing of managerial and design "mindsets." Walker (1990) cited in Bruce and Cooper (1997) argued that they would never agree. His argument which he titled "two tribes at war" showed managers and designers as having diametrically opposed thinking styles, aspirations, education and visions. These differences can still be recognized in design and management education and in the practice of many organizations. However the need for organizations to be innovative is now a prerequisite for survival and innovation requires the best creative thinkers within a supportive and well-directed framework. Leading organizations and brands such as Samsung, Apple, Philips and Starbucks use design throughout the innovation process, utilizing multidisciplinary teams to evaluate and develop ideas and maintain their strong strategic focus.

4.7.1   Exercise the Mind...

1. Select any product and/or service which you consider to be an impressive innovation and deconstruct the process by which the organization created and developed the concept to an impressive offering.
2. Identify long-established products and prepare a timeline of incremental design changes which have contributed to keeping the product popular.
3. Compare the performance of organizations which are innovation leaders and followers.
4. Consider how to encourage designers to generate viable added-value concepts.
5. Express your own emotions related to a work environment you have experienced.
6. To what extent does the environment encourage your creativity?

4.8   GLOSSARY

Design research: "The overall aim of design research is to develop an accessible, robust body of knowledge that enhances our understanding of design processes, applications, methods and contexts. Often, this knowledge helps to define best practice and workable methods in dealing with design and design related problems. It therefore has considerable potential for improving our use and management of design" (Cooper and Press, 2007).

Disruptive technology is described as "technology that significantly alters the status quo of a product" (BSI, 2008b). Good examples are MP3s and downloading music files, cloud computing, eBooks and streaming movies and TV programmes.

Open innovation is "the use of purposive inflows and outflows of knowledge to accelerate innovation. With knowledge now widely distributed, companies cannot rely entirely on their own research, but should acquire inventions or intellectual property from other companies when it advances the business model" (Haas School of Business, University of California, Berkeley, 2013).

Organizational culture is often referred to as what Charles Handy calls "the way we do things around here." In this case, organizational culture includes visions, values, beliefs, common practices (or norms), systems, symbols and habits. The culture guides behaviours of all members of an organization. Hence, it may support or impede innovation development and management within the organization.

Product architecture is a layout or a structure of a specific product.

Product portfolio is an organization's entire collection of products/services.

Product portfolio architecture is a layout or a structure of a whole product line. Thus, it is often described as a plan/system/strategy of shared components within that line.

Platform strategy is described as the system strategy for laying out components and systems on multiple products to best satisfy current and future market needs (Otto and Wood, 2001). It sets clear strategic directions on how products/services under the same platform share components, modules, or sub-systems to meet market variety. One of most common platforms in the computing industry is the Windows-Intel platform.

4.9   REFERENCES AND ADDITIONAL READING

Acklin, C. (2010) Design-Driven Innovation Process Model. *Design Management Journal*, 5 (1), 50–60.

Baghai, M., Coley, S. and White, D. (2000) *The Alchemy of Growth*. New York: HarperCollins Publishers.

Baxter, M. (1995), *Product Design: Practical Methods for the Systematic Development of new Product*. London: Chapman and Hall.

Best, K. (2010), *The Fundamentals of Design Management*. Lausanne: AVA Academic.

Boike, D. G. and Staley, J. L. (1996) Developing a Strategy and Plan for a New Product. In M.D. Rosenau, A. Griffin, G. A. Castellion and N. F. Anschuetz (eds) *The PDMA Handbook of New Product Development*. New York: Wiley, pp. 139–151.

Borja de Mozota, B. (2003) *Design Management: Using Design to Build Brand Value and Corporate Innovation*. New York: Allworth.

Brown, T. (2008) Design Thinking. *Harvard Business Review*, 86 (6), 84–92.

Brown, T. (2009), *Change by Design: How Design Thinking Creates New Alternatives for Business and Society: How Design Thinking Can Transform Organizations and Inspire Innovation*. New York: HarperCollins Publisher.

Bruce M. and Cooper, R. (1997) Marketing and Design: A Working Relationship. In M. Bruce and R. Cooper (eds). *Marketing and Design Management*. London: International Thompson Business Press, 35–57.

BSI (British Standards Institute). (2008), *BS 7000-10:2008: Design Management Systems – Part 10: Vocabulary of Terms Used in Design Management*. London: British Standards Institute.

Chesbrough, H. (2003) *Open Innovation: The New Imperative for Creating and Profiting from Technology*. Boston: Harvard Business School Press.

Cooper, R.G. (1993), *Winning at New Products: Accelerating the Process From Idea to Launch* (2nd edn). Addison-Wesley: Reading.

Cooper, R. and Press, M. (1995), *The Design Agenda*. Chichester: Wiley.

Cooper, R. and Press, M. (2007) *Academic Design Research*. London: Design Council.

Crawford, C.M. (1997), *New Product Management* (5th edn). London: Irwin.

Design Council. (2011) Eleven Lessons: Managing Design in Eleven Global Brands: Design at LEGO. [WWW] Available from: http://www.designcouncil.org.uk/Documents/Documents/ Publications/Eleven%20Lessons/PDF%20Design%20at%20LEGO.pdf [Accessed 5 April 2011].

Gardien, P. (2006), *Breathing Life into Delicate Ideas: Developing a Network of Options to Increase the Chance of Innovation Success*. [WWW] Available from: http://www.design.philips.com/philips/shared/assets/design_assets/downloads/news/Breathing_life_into_delicate_ideas.pdf [Accessed 6 April 2011].

Gartner (2005) Gartner's Hype Cycle Special Report for 2005 [WWW] Gartner Available from: https://www.gartner.com/doc/484424/gartners-hype-cycle-special-report [Accessed 26 June 2014]

Goffin, K. and Mitchel R. (2005) *Innovation Management: Strategy and Implementation Using the Pentathlon Framework*. New York: Palgrave Macmillan.

Harvard Business Essentials. (2003) *Managing Creativity and Innovation*. Boston: Harvard Business School Press.

HM Treasury. (2005) *Cox Review of Creativity in Business: Building on the UK's Strengths*. London: HM Treasury.

IDEO. (2009) Human-centred Design Toolkit (2nd edn.) [WWW] Available from: http://www.ideo.com/work/human-centered-design-toolkit/ [Accessed 2 April 2011].

Jacoby, R. and Rodriguez, D. (2007) Innovation, Growth, and Getting to Where You Want to Go. *Design Management Review*, 18 (1), 10–15.

Keeley, L., Pikkel, R., Quinn, B. and Walters, H. (2013), *Ten Types of Innovation: The Discipline of Building Breakthroughs*. Hoboken: John Wiley & Sons.

Kelley, T. and Littman, J. (2001), *The Art of Innovation: Lessons in Creativity from IDEO, America's Leading Design Firm*. London: Profile Books.

Kelley, T. and Littman, J. (2006), *The Ten Faces of Innovation: Strategies for Heightening Creativity*. London: Profile Books.

Kim, W. C. and Mauborgne, R. (1997) Value Innovation: The Strategic Logic of High Growth. *Harvard Business Review*, January–February 1997, 103–111.

Kumar, V. (2013), *101 Design Methods: A Structured Approach for Driving Innovation in Your Organisation*. Hoboken: John Wiley & Sons.

Lockwood, T. (2009), *Design Thinking: Integrating Innovation, Customer Experience, and Brand Value*. New York: Allworth Press.

Lockwood, T. and Walton, T. (2008), *Building Design Strategy: Using Design to Achieve Key Business Objectives*. New York: Allworth Press, 79–86.

Otto, K. and Wood, K. (2001) *Product Design: Techniques in Reverse Engineering and New Product Development*. New Jersey: Prentice Hall.

Patterson, F., Kerrin, M., Gatto-Roissard, G. and Coan, P. (2009) *Everyday Innovation: How to Enhance Innovative Working in Employees and Organisations*. London: NESTA.

Ravasi, D. and Lojacono, G. (2005) Managing Design and Designers for Strategic Renewal. *Long Range Planning Journal*, 38, 51–77.

Roper, S., Hales, C., Bryson, J. R. and Love, J. (2009) *Measuring Sectoral Innovation Capability in Nine Areas of the UK Economy*. London: NESTA.

Roscam Abbing, E. (2010), *Brand-driven Innovation: Strategies for Development and Design*. Lausanne: AVA Academic.

Smith, D. (2006), *Exploring Innovation*. London: McGraw Hill Education.

Tidd, J., Bessant, J. and Pavitt, K. (2005), *Managing Innovation*. Chichester: Wiley.

Trott, P. (2008), *Innovation Management and New Product Development* (4th edn). Harlow: Prentice Hall.

Verganti, R. (2008) Design, Meaning, and Radical Innovation: A Metamodel and a Research Agenda. *Journal of Product Innovation Management*, 25, 436–456.

Verganti, R. (2009), *Design Driven Innovation: Changing the Rules of Competition by Radically Innovating What Things Mean*. Boston: Harvard Business School Publishing.

Von Stamm, B. (2004) Innovation – What's Design Got to Do with It? *Design Management Review*, 15 (1), 10–19.

Von Stamm, B. (2008), *Managing Innovation, Design and Creativity*. Chichester: John Wiley & Sons.

Walsh, V., Roy, R., Bruce, M. and Potter, S. (1992) *Winning by Design: Technology, Product Design and International Competitiveness*. Oxford: Blackwell Business.

Weiss, L. (2002) Developing Tangible Strategies. *Design Management Review*, 13 (1), 33–38.

4.10 ONLINE RESOURCES

1. Design Business Association (DBA): www.dba.org.uk
2. Design Council – CABE: www.designcouncil.org.uk
3. Design Management Institute:www.dmi.org
4. NESTA: http://www.nesta.org.uk
5. Technology Strategy Board: http://www.innovateuk.org

Chapter 5
ESTABLISHING DESIGN IN THE ORGANIZATION

Design has a profound influence on the management and performance of all kinds of organizations and yet its place in the organizational structure and relationships with other functions varies widely. Its principal acknowledged power is in generating new thinking, potential solution strategies and directions, yet it still retains some "mythical" status among management as noted at the outset of the book in the introduction to Part I. Using design strategically can help other functions to achieve their goals and synergies. Close examination of business functions in many organizations often reveals a degree of design thinking embedded in the activities but often it is not recognized as design and the design function is given no credit for it.

By contrast some of the most successful companies try to infuse design thinking throughout their entire operation. They work in increasingly cross-disciplinary ways, blurring and sometimes eliminating barriers between functional areas. Some of the functions get new names as the organization continuously learns and improves.

However, integrating and managing design strategy is challenging and relatively new (when compared to the theories of management established more than a century ago). One of the greatest challenges is bringing together the thinking styles and subsequent practices of managers and designers. Management models are still seen as analytical and rigid which designers regard as an anathema. This sections focuses on the potential for contribution of design to top management and four main functions and the application of the 4Ds design management model to achieve effective partnerships and integration is explained.

Objectives for this chapter:

- To demonstrate how design strategy and design thinking influences and supports all functions across the organization.
- To show how design thinking can help to find new strategic directions for management.
- To identify the performance benefits of becoming a design capable organization.
- To evaluate the different thinking and problem-solving styles of managers and designers and discuss how they may converge.

- To establish the need for cross-disciplinary knowledge and skills development.
- To show how to leverage design at top management level.
- To make a case for integrating design with HR management, R&D, marketing, finance and other functions.
- To explain the benefits and insights from design research.
- To explain how the 4Ds model can be used to enhance collaboration and performance.
- To discuss how effectiveness of design strategy may be measured.

5.1 RELATIONSHIPS BETWEEN DESIGN AND BUSINESS

Design has been customarily linked to marketing and R&D. Indeed many of challenges of marketing, R&D and design functions overlap and complement each other. The place of design in the organizational structure continues to be problematic. Some organizations have not yet recognized the potential of design as a resource and continue to treat it as a lowly function

Table 5.1 Responses to Design Council survey question: Over the last three years, to which of the following would you say that design, innovation and creativity have contributed a great extent/fair extent within your firm?

	Percentage of all respondents (column percentages)						
	All firms	Primary, construction, communication	Manufactures	Financial & business services	Trade & leisure services	Stayed the same size	Grown moderately/rapidly
Improved quality of services/products	17	10	50	13	16	11	24
Improved image of organization	13	11	26	12	12	9	18
Competitiveness	11	10	33	9	8	7	16
Improved customer communications	10	11	22	8	9	8	14
New products/services	9	8	31	9	5	4	14
Increased turnover	8	8	29	5	6	3	13
Productivity	8	8	27	6	5	5	12
Development of new markets	8	8	26	7	5	4	13
Increased profit	8	8	24	4	7	3	13
Increased market share	7	9	24	5	4	2	12
Increased employment	4	1	19	4	2	2	7
Improved internal communications	4	3	17	4	3	1	7
Reduced costs	3	1	15	3	1	1	5

Source: Design Council National Survey of Firms (cited in Tether, 2005).

usually under the control of the marketing function. Leading companies and other organizations have come to accept that design should be given a more central role and its creative capacity used as a major driver throughout the entire enterprise. Such organizations have infused design thinking to good effect. There is no single "ideal" place for the design function and its place is reflective of the degree to which the organization has come to respect the power of design and manage it effectively.

The UK Design Council regularly publishes studies showing growing recognition of the influence of design in improving quality of products and services, reducing costs, increasing competitiveness and market share, see Table 5.1. Their 2012 project revealed that "for every £1 businesses invest in design, they can expect over £20 increased revenues, over £4 increase in net operating profit and over £5 in increased exports" (Design Council, 2012).

Moreover, another study demonstrated that companies that invest in design can avoid competing on price alone. "In the UK, 45% firms that do not use design compete mainly on price while only 21% of firms where design is significant do so" (Design Council, 2007). The survey in Table 5.1 shows 13 categories of benefits of investing in design and compelling evidence of the added value good design can provide. Competing mainly on price can be high risk as the business becomes caught in the downward spiral of increasing competitiveness. The highest level of benefits was found to relate to manufacturing thereby showing that design has the potential to drive innovation in reviving the manufacturing sector.

The survey findings matched those of the Danish Design Centre (2003) which also showed that design could contribute to business performance in key areas, namely gross revenue, exports and employment. The results revealed that organizations investing in design (internally and/or externally) outperformed those that did not in all areas (Danish Design Centre, 2003). They found that Danish companies which use design:

- Generate greater revenue;
- Have higher exports as percentage of sales;
- Develop more employment opportunities.

Several experts suggest that the special ability of design to generate many solution strategies is particularly important in an increasingly complex world where there are more "wicked problems" deemed as impossible to solve because of incomplete and/or contradictory information. Neumeier (2008) argues that design excels at addressing such problems and can contribute many benefits across the organization. He explains that design disciplines look at problems from different angles and generate solutions. The more the potential solutions the more likely is the chance of successfully overcoming problems. Table 5.2 presents examples of these complex problems and how design strategy may address them.

Roger Martin, the dean of Rotman School of Management, University of Toronto, (2004) developed this idea even further, as he suggested that: "Business people don't need to understand designers better: they need to be designers. They need to think and work like designers, have attitudes like designers, and learn to evaluate each other as designers do."

Table 5.2 Design strategy response to complex questions

Complex question	Design strategy challenge
How to keep up with the seemingly increasing speed of change?	Design should monitor the changing environment aligned with longer-term vision.
How to evaluate which concepts will be most profitable?	Design strategists must develop rigorous tests and charge designers with addressing commercial considerations.
How to engender successful cross-functional collaboration?	Design to infuse "design thinking" throughout the organization.
How to attract the most creative and talented people?	Design the most attractive working environment.
How to find new unexploited market opportunities?	Design should seek new opportunities for products/ services and especially experiences.
How to satisfy short-term needs whilst setting longer-term aims?	Design must closely monitor consumer needs and contribute to scenarios and future visions.
How to demonstrate social responsibility whilst generating profit?	Design to identify and communicate how the organization can best deliver its social and environmental obligations.
How to ensure the organization strategy focuses on customer experience?	Design should maintain customer-centric focus and use design research methods to gain deep insights into their experience in order to constantly add value.

The centre of his argument lies in the belief that design is crucial to value creation in the 21st century. According to Martin, a learning process of individuals and organizations can be divided into three steps: mysteries, heuristics and algorithms. When we first observe any phenomena (e.g. lightning and unconventional consumer behaviours), we register them as "mysteries;" we notice them, but do not understand why they happen in certain ways.

Through careful thoughtful studies, we begin to make sense of these phenomena although this way of understanding or learning (*heuristics*) is not necessarily correct. It simply helps increase the possibilities of coming up with successful outcomes. Further research/analyses could result in a formula (*algorithm*) to explain these phenomena. The author noted that value creation in the 20th century follows these steps – first noticing emerging demands/changes in user behaviours (as mysteries), carrying out research to understand these demands/changes heuristically, then developing a formula (or a recipe for success or algorithm) and applying it in every market – a study of McDonalds and Wal-Mart shows they adopted this pattern.

The author argued that value creation in the 21st century cannot afford to follow these steps because in the increasing complex world it is impossible to develop a formula that can be applied to all markets. Rather than trying to generate a rigid formula or algorithm, it is more useful to become a master of heuristics. In general, designers are good at heuristics or experienced-based learning processes, as they often learn by doing e.g. designing, prototyping and testing. While most organizations use inductive research to develop a theory in a bottom-up manner and deductive reasoning based on research to test a theory in a top-down manner, designers also add *abductive reasoning*, which is the best explanation/guess based on available information, into the mix. This more open way of thinking allows a greater degree of flexibility and accommodates complexity.

As a result, Martin recommended businesses should develop design skills and become more like design shops (or design studios).His argument presents design as having a great deal more to offer to an organization than just supporting marketing and R&D functions. It demonstrates the need for a new business mindset and sets the scene for explorations of the wider role and contribution of design across key business functions, such as management, marketing, finance, human resources and R&D. Table 5.3 develops the manner in which businesses may be encouraged to transform to "design shops."

The transition of thinking to embrace the full benefits of design is captured succinctly by Cooper and Junginger (2011) showing how successful organizations have moved through two former paradigms to achieve design capability. Organizations which use design fully are more flexible, more confident about dealing with complexity and develop and improve creativity at the individual and organizational levels to support all business functions in fulfilling missions, visions and corporate objectives.

The researchers show how organizations that have achieved full design capability went through the design practice paradigm and the design management paradigm. Of course some organizations remain in these paradigms.

Table 5.3   Business transformation to "design shops"

From traditional focus	To design shop focus
Efficiency of completing established tasks, (what management author Peter Drucker calls "doing things right").	Effectiveness through questioning existing practices (what management author Peter Drucker calls "doing the right things").
Measured by size of budget and relating it to the size of department.	Questioning the purpose and sometimes the very existence of departments by addressing the "wicked problems."
Fixed clear roles and expectations – often tortuous route to solutions.	Emphasis on cooperation, sharing ideas, flexibility, responsiveness and responsibility.
Somewhat mechanistic "left brain" thinking	Abductive – best guestimate – thinking using "right brain."
Constrained by resources – particularly money.	Nothing is impossible and constraints seen as a challenge.

The earliest of the three paradigms was *design practice* and sought to add value through aesthetics, product innovation and differentiation. It addressed complex (wicked) problems by focussing on products, brands and services. It sought to foster design competence and creativity among top management, board members, design leaders, design consultants, design teams and cross-disciplinary teams. It saw its objectives as designing products and services that are beautiful and functional, create a brand and make profit for the organization. The second and higher paradigm used *design management* and emphasized interpreting the need, writing the brief, selecting the designer and managing the design and delivery process as the means to add value. It expanded to encompass all aspects of design in the organization and thus contributed to addressing wider business strategy issues. It continued to foster design awareness and competence among top and senior management but brought in more design consultants to help. Finally it laid strong foundations for managing design to achieve strategic goals. The highest level termed *design capability* uses humanistic, comprehensive, integrative and more visual approaches to add value. Organizations in this paradigm show advanced awareness of changes in environment, society, economy, politics and other organizations: they feel the "pulse" of change. They have infused design into every area of the organization and positioned themselves as sustainable organizations in the context of societal and global wellbeing.

Example of Good Relationship between Design & Business: Giffgaff

The concept of Giffgaff, a UK mobile telecommunication network provider powered by people, is an interesting example of how design thinking can revolutionize a business model. The name, Giffgaff, is an old Scottish word meaning "mutual giving." This concept was inspired by the success of collaborative developments, such as *Wikipedia*. Giffgaff encourage customers to play an active role in its operation by rewarding those who get involved. By getting users to help answer other users' enquiries and recruit new members, the company have made a significant saving on call centres, marketing campaigns and advertising. This saving is used to pay back to the user community, e.g. giving active users up to 100% top-up money. This creative business model has won the company many awards including the Most Innovative Community at the Social CRM Customer Excellence Awards in 2010. For more information visit: http://giffgaff.com

5.2 RELATIONSHIPS BETWEEN DESIGN AND STRATEGIC MANAGEMENT

Strategic management may be defined as "the process by which an organisation establishes its objectives, formulates actions (strategies) designed to meet these objectives in the desired time-scale, implements the actions, and addresses progress and results" (Thompson, 2001). Gluck, Kaufman and Walleck (1980) show strategic management as a merger of strategic planning and management. It is about developing strategies that drive a company and create competitive advantages. Design is also about creating value and yet conventional models rarely give credit to the contribution of design. For example, one of the most influential models, Porter's *Value Chain* model, covers business functions such as human resources, sales and marketing, but does not recognize the direct influence of design.

Strategic management is traditionally built around three key elements (Thompson, 2001):

1. *Strategic awareness*: The authors prefer to use the word *awareness* instead of *analysis*, since new directions or opportunities may result from a leader's vision instead of market research and analysis. It is about being aware of a company's visions, capabilities, performances and changes in the marketplace. Design can be at the heart of the process by integrating all key factors to create a leadership vision.
2. *Strategic ideas and choice*: This element is about "establishing just what courses of strategic actions are available to an organization and how these might be evaluated." Normally, they are divided into three levels: corporate, competitive and functional, in other words, strategic, tactic/business and operational. A company could use the power of design thinking to explore many potential strategic directions.
3. *Strategic implementation*: The last element is about converting ideas into reality and preparing infrastructures, systems and facilities to support the strategic actions. This is a key step which can utilize Big-D and small-d design throughout.

Table 5.4, which reflects the work of Gluck, Kaufman and Walleck (1980), shows four phases in the evolution of strategic planning. It may be seen that design has a growing role in particular in the highest strategic phase as it is about creating futures. All phases share a common aim to add value to the bottom line but the very meaning of bottom line is also a changing concept and in contemporary business incorporates social, ethical and environmental values.

Table 5.4 The evolution of strategic planning

Hierarchy of levels	Strategy
Strategic level	The organization becomes an adaptable, flexible, confident and creative open system.
Systems level	More holistic thinking is employed to identify opportunities and alternative directions.
Planning level	Environmental scanning and analysis used to inform the planning process.
Financial base level	Tight control maintained by fixed budgets with little or no flexibility.

Thompson (2001) acknowledged that strategic management is a dynamic process which is constantly influenced by internal factors, e.g. leadership and culture, and external factors, e.g. changing consumer demands, and therefore continuously evolves. His idea is rather similar to Mintzberg's *5Ps for strategy* (Plan, Pattern, Ploy, Position and Perspective), which recognizes the need to address cultural aspects.

The understanding of the nature of strategy is at the heart of the strategic management process. Hence, he summarizes *ten key elements* of strategy as follows:

1. *Perspective of strategy* embraces all stakeholders' viewpoints.
2. *Corporate strategy* directs a company towards its goals, e.g. corporate portfolio.
3. *Strategic positioning and competitive advantage* concerns how an organization will sustain and grow in the competitive market environment.
4. *Strategy creation* is about change. It is observed that strategy is largely influenced by leadership styles and corporate cultures.
5. *Strategy implementation and structure* is about turning ideas into reality.
6. *Crisis avoiding* can be achieved by addressing the first five issues properly. A company with significant weaknesses is likely to be more "crisis prone".
7. *Resources and opportunities* are key concerns of in terms of opportunity identification. A company may choose the *opportunity-driven* approach, which concentrates on identifying external opportunities, or the *resource-based* approach which focuses on utilizing current capabilities, competent and resources.
8. *Strategic competency* can be accomplished by addressing the above issues. A firm should develop strategic competency which goes beyond technological expertise.
9. *E-V-R congruence* – "successful organisations create and sustain congruency between the external environment (the source of fresh opportunities and threats), resources (competencies, capabilities and strengths) and their values."
10. *Strategic paradox* is about finding the best way to deal with uncertainty.

Since 1987, Gorb and Dumas observed that "a great deal of design activity goes on in organisations which is not called design. It is carried out by individuals who are not called designers." What they call *silent design* is in fact Big-D design which supports strategic management and all kinds of functions within an organization. Some design leaders e.g. Coca-Cola's head of design, report that they rarely if ever use the word "design" as it causes confusion among strategic managers, preferring to talk of "innovation" and "new directions", but underlying these practices is powerful design thinking linked to business awareness. The extent to which design plays a role in the formulation of management strategy will depend on the approach of the organization (Francis, 2002). This approach is determined by their awareness, attitude and confidence in applying design management thinking. He identified four fundamental approaches and Table 5.5 explains how design can play its role.

Table 5.5   The design role in strategy formulation

	Strategy set by management	Design strategy role	Design activities
Positioning	Strategists determine *in advance*, where they want to be in defined markets and all sub-plans are set to the goals.	• Identification of the needs of the target market • Build design competences to address the chosen market(s) • Develop products/services/new experiences for the target market • Maintain competitiveness through design-led innovation and technology • Promote the design superiority/differentiation of products/services	The designer acts as a craftsperson. The designer's role is to design compelling products and/or services to attract targets.
Momentum	Strategists determine *in advance*, their primary organizational strengths and which competencies they wish to invest in, acquire and develop.	• Define required creative competences and enhance them • Maintain competitiveness through design competences and technology • Leverage the design and creative competences to offer the best products/services	Design is seen as a dynamic resource for the firm. The designers play the key role in innovation development.
Agile	Strategists decide *in real time*, which competencies they wish to develop or acquire temporarily and what opportunities they wish to exploit.	• Identify and pursue new opportunities as design/development projects • Buy in required creative competencies only for the duration of the projects • Develop an organizational culture that is opportunistic and flexible and responsible in terms of delivery of on time, high quality outcomes	The designer is part of the strategy team, perhaps its leader – initiating and realizing opportunities.
Me-too	Strategists seek to exploit potential rich opportunities that *others* have pioneered (follower strategy).	• Use design to model and assess the potential and the risks • Design used to improve the new products/services identified • Design used to lower development and manufacturing costs to afford competitive pricing	The designer is not an originator but an improver. Design helps enrich values and reduce cost.

Example of Good Relationship between Design & Strategic Management: d.school

The Institute of Design at Stanford (or d.school) is one of the good examples of organizations promoting the use of design thinking in strategic management. The institute believes that an ability to apply design thinking strategically is essential for all "innovators." Hence, it was designed to support all kinds of disciplines (ranging from preschool teachers to senior managers) develop design thinking skills through real-world problems/projects. For more information visit: http://dschool.stanford.edu/

5.3   ROLES OF DESIGN IN AN ORGANIZATION

The role and influence of design in organizations ranges over a very wide spectrum, from organizations that are proud to be seen a design-led to organizations that claim that design has no role to play in the organization. The UK Design Council National Survey of Firms – see Table 5.6 – shows only the manufacturing sector as fully integrating design in the operation in two out of five companies. The largest category at 37% showed design as having no role. So whilst the trend to adopting design is upward, the rate remains slow. A closer examination may well reveal much silent design activity among those who dismiss design as irrelevant and the survey participants may have narrowly defined design, but it seems that about one third of companies do not acknowledge the contribution of design.

A more recent study carried out by the Institute for Manufacturing (IfM), University of Cambridge, revealed that design investment is still relatively small. According to a survey of 358 companies in the UK, the total spending on design was £92 million, which represented 2.1% of their turnover (Livesey and Moultrie, 2009). The study also showed that design spending can be categorized into four groups as shown below. Based on the survey results, most participating companies (66%) invested in promotional design.

- *Technical:* Design is used to solve technical issues, for example in mechanical engineering or software design.
- *User:* Design which considers the user experience, user interaction and aesthetics of product and services.
- *Promotional design:* Design of advertising and promotional activities for specific products and services.
- *Identity design:* Design focused on company identity, including branding.

Since the late 1990s, many strategic experts recognize the strategic value of design and showed how to harness design strategy. Close examination of companies usually reveals that it is integrated into a company and crosses functions. Borja de Mozota (2003) summarized some basic domains as the CEO, corporate communication, R&D and production and marketing.

She linked the CEO to corporate identity using graphic design, innovation using product design and workspaces/factory using environment design. The corporate communication function is similarly concerned with corporate identity and uses environmental design for promotion events and trade shows. R&D and production use graphic design for technical documentation, packaging design for logistics and packaging, product design to develop innovation and environmental design for the factory. Marketing use all four types of design: graphic for brand and web site, package for product promotion, product to develop the range of offers and environmental for trade shows and stores. Through this research she demonstrated that design is indeed integrated into a company whether or not it is the

Table 5.6   Design Council National Survey of Firms undertaken by PACEC

Which of the following most closely represents the role design plays in your firm?

	All firms	Primary, construction, communication	Manufactures	Financial & business services	Trade & leisure services	Stayed the same size	Grown moderately/ rapidly
It is integral to the firm's operation	12	8	41	15	6	6	17
It has a significant role to play	16	8	35	18	15	16	16
It has a limited role to play	35	18	15	39	42	24	47
It has no role to play at all	37	66	9	28	37	54	19

Percentage of all respondents (column percentages)

Source: Tether (2005); PACEC is short for public & corporate economic consultants.

result of proactive strategy. Nevertheless it may be expected that a well-formulated design strategy would identify many more relationships and opportunities for integration and synergy.

An increase of appreciation and utilization of design in a company might be because design thinking can help bridge business and creative thinking. Roscam Abbing (2010) shows that business thinkers are predominantly left-brain rational thinking types, reluctant to take risks until a detailed analysis of a problem has been carried out and discussed. They seek certainty and are more risk averse. By contrast the creative thinkers use their right brain more and use emotional, intuitive approaches and are more comfortable about risk and complexity. Business thinkers are inclined to think in a rational, structured way and creative thinkers are, by contrast, emotional and intuitive. Design thinking encompasses both mindsets and acts as a bridge between both sides of the brain – having the capacity to switch from one style of thinking to the other.

Whilst business thinkers customarily focus on analysis, creative thinkers prefer intuition and are much influenced by emotions. Big-D design thinkers can iterate between the two extremes. Business thinkers prefer well-defined problems but creative thinkers see the definitions as boundaries and favour freedom to think uninhibited by definitions. Design thinking uses the best of both to address undefined problems, avoiding rigidity but establishing a framework by consensus. Problems may be seen more quickly by business thinkers, who are often impatient to solve them. Creative thinkers are inherently optimistic and say, "What problem?" Design thinking views the problem as the start of the process of solving it. The apparent impatience in business thinking is evident in the thinking process which goes from analysis to decision making. Creative thinkers perceive a need or opportunity, create the concept, and then decide if it has potential. Design thinking may go through more stages of analysis, ideation, prototyping, evaluating and only then deciding, though this may not always mean the process is slow. Finally it can be seen that business thinkers tend to solve problems by reducing them to component parts whereas creative thinkers are more holistic, seeing the problem as a whole and considering the influences of the environment. Big-D design thinkers are often natural systems thinkers who can use mental models of the soft elements or problems and zoom in and out to assemble and reassemble aspects of the problem in different ways.

Similar observations were made by Martin (2006), who showed how design thinking helps bridge analytical thinking and intuitive thinking. The author argued that design thinking also helps a company achieve an optimum balance between reliability and validity. To obtain reliable results, a process has to reduce the number of variables and use quantitative bias-free measurement. On the other hand, to reach valid outcomes, all relevant variables must be taken into consideration and rich qualitative information is required.

Martin suggested that design thinking has an inherent bias toward validity, since designers seek in-depth understanding of the users and context. Moreover, designers are more interested in valid outcomes rather than replicating the process. They have learned to value rigorous studies and analyses required to justify and support their ideas. He pointed out that most entrepreneurs started off as intuitive and design thinkers as they used their gut feeling and creativity to come up with a new-to-the-world business idea. They did not ask: How can we be sure that this idea would work? However, as the company begins to grow, it leans more and more towards analytical thinking and systematic processes focussed on reliability, addressing the question: How can we prove that this idea will work? Thus start-up business people usually start by using design thinking and it is important to persuade them to return to this style of thinking. Business thinking and design thinking can be reconciled. Table 5.7 sets out some of the ways in which Big-D design thinking can merge the two thinking styles.

As design becomes more integrated in an organization, strategic design managers need the necessary skills, e.g. financial management, to collaborate with other functions. It is just as difficult for the creative designer to learn left-brain-based thinking as it is for the rational business thinker to learn right-brain creative thinking.

Many charismatic leaders have shown natural ability to combine both styles of thinking and have significantly influenced organizational theory and practice in recent years. Many leaders are seen as designers and/or creative humans, such as Steve Jobs of Apple Inc., Sir Richard Branson of Virgin and Sir Terence Conran of Habitat. Handy (1999) identified many such individuals whom he dubbed *The New Alchemists*, visionary people who make something out of nothing. As designers and creative thinkers themselves their organizations and strategy are immersed in integrated Big-D and small-d thinking. They represent the new creative leadership which many organizations try to emulate.

Table 5.7 Reconciling business and creative thinking

Left brain thinking	Whole brain thinking	Right brain thinking
• Emphasize business/ analytical thinking and detailed analysis of information	• Big-D design thinking • Integration of both styles of thinking	• Emphasis on intuition, emotion and envisioning
• Seeking concrete proof from reasoning and facts	• Integration of analytical outcomes and intuitive judgment	• Trusting intuition and judgment – distrusting analysis
• Using established knowledge based on past performance indicators	• Integration of past experience with futures foresights	• Seeking new knowledge/visions and forecasting the future
• Identifying potential problems and risks	• Reconciling and evaluating opportunities and risks	• Presenting new scenarios and alternative choices
• Decisions based on reliable facts	• New processes and models to integrate research and creative thinking	• Decisions based on perceptions and feelings

Not all organizations have such natural creative leaders, so first they must fully engage with the idea that design needs to be welcomed and cross-examined for its ability to renew and refresh thinking at all levels., thus infusing the organization with new ideas and confidence.

Bruder (2011) found that strategic design management can contribute at all levels as follows:

- At corporate level it can infuse creative leadership through brand design and the design of the products, services and communications which contribute to the brand experience.
- At tactical business level it can support the design of the business, build new tools, methods and processes to improve design thinking and make the design function operate in a business aware fashion.
- At operational level it can champion design thinking and the development of new processes using multidisciplinary design teams.

It can be seen that, at the strategic level, design can be used as a catalyst to create aspirational visions, distinctive brands and memorable brand experiences. A bold vision, like that of TOMS Shoes: "with ever pair you purchase, TOMS will give a pair of new shoes to a child in need," could benefit from creative inputs from the design function to communicate and deliver a unique, memorable brand experience. At the business/tactical levels, design thinking can support improvement of other business functions in delivering their work. While *design of business* explores how to use design to drive business activities, e.g. designing a business model of a new product range, *business of design* concerns how to integrate design into business practices. Lastly, at the operational level, design practices, especially design thinking and design processes, can build multidisciplinary working and help other departments implement their strategic and business plans in a creative manner.

5.4 DESIGN AS STRATEGIC PARTNER

5.4.1 Top Management

Relationship of Design and Top Management

Whilst a few contemporary organizations place design at the top table, with a design director who is a full board member, most place design within the organization as an integrated function. Borja de Mozota (2003) categorized design's place in a firm into four groups.

First she identified design as an R&D/production department, common in technology-driven companies and used to generate creative ideas that meet technical constraints imposed by the engineering or R&D departments. Second she found design as a marketing department, often adopted in commercially driven firms and saw design used as a tactical tool concerned with trends, market conditions and brand management. Third she categorized design as a corporate communications department for firms concerned primarily with their corporate identity where design is used as a communication tool. Finally she identified design as an independent department where the independent design department has the greatest opportunity to use its competencies, where design is recognized as a "key strategic resource" and long-term goals for design are established and included in corporate objectives.

In the fourth category design is placed at the same level as other corporate resources and may be represented by a design director on the board of directors.

Design Contributions to Strategic Management

Many experts urge organizations to adopt the last approach, design as an independent department, and consider design as a key strategic resource. It has been noted that design can increase profits and market share and give competitive advantages. It can be used to identify new strategic opportunities and directions, breathe new life into tired or failing products and services, launch new products and/or services, deliver memorable brand experiences and deliver cost savings. Design should not be viewed as an expensive luxury but as a powerful weapon for organizational performance. In helping to accomplish vital goals design can also deliver many valuable skills into the organization as Bruce and Harun (2001; cited in Bruce and Bessant, 2002) identified. Table 5.8 shows a summary of the principal contributions which design can offer to the organizational skills.

An organization has to adopt a continuous learning approach which, according to Shani and Docherty (2003) is essential for them to sustain and grow in the increasingly complex and uncertain market environment. This

Table 5.8 Design contributions to organizational skills

Practical skills	Knowledge skills	Operational skills	Potential added value
• Craft-based design and making skills • Creative problem solving techniques • Visual presentation of alternative visions and candidate solutions	• Advanced design and development process • Technical know-how, materials science and market intelligence	• Design research, visualizing, scenario building • Innovation, adaptation and invention • Intuition, synthesis • Presenting alternatives • Reconciling diverse needs of stakeholders	• Future foresights • Bringing clarity to complexity • Raising confidence in risk taking • Catalyst for developing relationships

enables the organization to remain adaptive and responsive to emerging business conditions. They argue that the "design process" can be used as a tool to restructure a company to become a learning organization. This is because design thinking excels at contextualizing the issues, identifying real problems, providing creative and practical solutions and implementing outcomes. Their recommendations range from redesigning individual works to organizational processes and corporate structures.

Example of Design Contributions to Strategic Management: Pixar

Pixar, an American computer animation film studio with 27 Oscars under its belt, is an example of how design and creative thinking can help build a strong innovative culture and bring the financial success. The key characteristics of design thinking, e.g. empathic, people-centred, positive, collaborative and holistic, are evident in the way the company was structured and operated. For example, it encourages all staff (not only the senior executives) to give comments on new ideas for its animation films at the very early stage of the development right through to the end. The company truly values its people and, hence, the goal is to tell a story or create an animation film that the employees feel is the best thing that they could possibly make. Staff's passion and commitment are key factors behind its success.

Design Contributions to Internal Branding

In the highly competitive market, in order to build a strong brand as well as high-quality products and services, an organization needs to make sure that all employees "live the brand" and deliver memorable customer experiences. Brands have come to be regarded as the soul of the company and internal branding as essential to building brand equity. Thus, internal branding has increasingly become as important as, and possibly more important than, external branding. While most organizations are familiar with the concept of external branding which begins with communicating their brand to customers and potential collaborators, the idea of internal branding, which involves selling your brand to your employees, has not been so commonly adopted.

A study commissioned by the Canadian Marketing Association defined the term internal branding as:

> the set of strategic processes that align and empower employees to deliver the appropriate customer experience in a consistent fashion. These processes include, but are not limited to, internal communications, training support, leadership practices, reward & recognition programs, recruitment practices and sustainability factors. (MacLaverty, McQuillan and Oddie, 2007)

Big-D and small-d designs have potential to support the top management in planning and implementing internal branding activities, see Table 5.9.

As with external branding, every brand touchpoint counts. Big-D and small-d designs play a key role in reinforcing the brand message through all physical clues, e.g. office interiors and uniforms, and intangible clues – telling stories in a compelling manner. Design can encourage desired

Table 5.9 Internal branding techniques and tools

Current techniques/tools	Best practice	Challenges	Design inputs
1. Internal communications			
Employee newsletters; Push messages from president; Walk-the-talk (communication through behaviour); Videos with messaging demonstrating brand; Employee story telling; Involvement in customer promise through a range of communication tactics; Senior management site visits.	Senior management "on-brand" behaviour; Relevant personal communication; Vehicles that enable sustained consistency of message.	The trade-off between reaching efficiency and personalization; Constant communication is necessary for consistent execution.	Big-D and small-d designs could help reinforce the brand message and deliver brand values in a memorable and motivating manner.
2. Training support			
New hire orientation including explanation of brand attributes and roles; Brand workshops; Customer sensitization; e-learning; Brand values imbedded in training; Brand tool kits; Customer videos recording "what works".	Brand workshops (train-the-trainer); Clarify effect of each division on customer experience; Customer enthusiasm programs.	Refresh brand training programs; Consistency; E-learning impersonal; Continued employee connection and motivation to live the brand. Establishing good feedback loops.	Big-D and small-d designs could help make the training programme engaging and interesting. Also embed creative thinking skills.

Continued

Table 5.9 Continued

Current techniques/tools	Best practice	Challenges	Design inputs
3. Leadership practices Management development programs; Senior team personal site visits; Employee rating of leaders through regular performance reviews.	Leadership practicing "on-brand" behaviours; Explicit senior management endorsement of brand behaviours.	Consistent application of brand requirements with annual planning process. Reliance on good leadership exemplars.	Design thinking can help make the practices, e.g. site visits, more meaningful and disseminate outcomes.
4. Reward & recognition Special events commemorating success milestones; Peer recognition programs; Performance reviews encompassing brand behaviours; 360 degree feedback including peer, boss and customer feedback; In some cases, directly linked to compensation.	Peer recognition programs; Reinforcement of storytelling of on-brand behaviour; Special events celebrating living the brand values.	Connection of desired behaviours to brand values; Getting personal values aligned with clear company values.	Design thinking could help make the reward schemes and programmes more interesting, relevant and personal.
5. Recruitment practices Longer-term strategy to continually build the skill within an organization to deliver the brand promise.	Internal partnership with HR and marketing; Research recruitment practices within the industry; Measure success of recruitments, number of responses, retention, why or why not retained.	Cross-functional nature of task within HR and within the enterprise.	Big-D and small-d designs could help attract talented workforce and make HR and marketing more attractive for people externally and internally. Making the company "the" place to work.
6. Sustainable factors Internal communications; Internal focus groups with front-line staff to identify what they could do better and deepen engagement; Continuous customer contact groups – fresh input to service experience.	Consistent, customer and employee relevant messaging.	How to keep it real and relevant.	Design thinking could help support ongoing in-depth research to identify key issues to be developed further.
7. Other Measure project outcomes; Planning broader employee input.	Identify brand impact on projects	Consistent application.	Design thinking into criteria used.

Source: Adapted from MacLaverty, McQuillan and Oddie (2007).

cultures. According to Mauzy and Harriman (2003), the climate for creativity and innovation in an enterprise can be designed. Since a person tends to behave in the way that meets corporate expectations, by clearly signalling that an organization values curiosity and is not risk averse and providing relevant support, such as internal forums, people are likely to explore new ways to doing things.

Example of Design Contributions to Internal Branding: Whole Foods Market

Whole Foods Market is a socially responsible and environmentally friendly supermarket chain. It is committed to provide high-quality natural and organic products for the customers as well as support its employees and suppliers. Good use of design goes beyond tangible aspects, e.g. brand identity, web sites, publicity material and retail spaces. The key characteristics of design thinking, e.g. people empowerment and collaborative development, are evident in the way the company communicates its values and organizes its teams. The fundamental units of the organizational structure are self-directed teams. Good design of team structure and internal communication system encourages people to have regular dialogues to share ideas and solve problems. As a result, the company was listed in the Fortune 100 best companies to work for every year since the ranking started in 1998.

5.4.2 Marketing

Relationship of Design and Marketing

Kotler and Armstrong (2008) defined marketing as "managing profitable customer relationship." The two main goals of the marketing function are attracting new customers and keeping and growing current customers. Therefore marketing needs design contributions to achieve their goals, since good designs, e.g. product design, service design, corporate identity design, advertising design and retail design, can draw more customers and retain existing customers. The work of Bruce (2002) shows design must contribute to all triggers in the market. When marketing launch a new product or service, design contributes the new concepts and development. An increase in market share requires design to create promotional aids such as point of sale displays and web sites. To recover a lost market share, marketing needs design to rekindle the offering through incremental design innovations. Finally diversification into a new product and/or services market will need design concepts and development for product/service extension and new promotion and packaging designs to meet the needs of the new sector.

Design can play a major role in the core elements of marketing strategy: segmentation, targeting, differentiation and positioning. For example, good use of design helps marketers satisfy different needs and wants of various segments while keeping the cost down. Effective use of the product platform (discussed in the previous chapter) can offer a greater variety, while allowing core components to be shared across the product line. Well-designed quality offerings can help marketers to retain current customers and attract new buyers, as well as position a brand in a desirable spot, and help marketers build and maintain brand reputation.

Bruce (2011) summarized the added value of design to marketing activities in four key areas: financial, brand strength, increased innovation and faster change. She showed design delivering prestige and thus able to charge higher prices, whilst achieving savings in both production and marketing costs. Through design-led distinctiveness, the brand reputation will rise and greater loyalty among customers results. More innovation generates more ideas and potential intellectual property and helps the firm to be first to market. Internally, the flexibility supported by design thinking can mean the company is faster to change to meet changing external conditions. The company learns more quickly to engage with such issues as social changes, e.g. aging population, and take responsibility for the environment.

However, rivalries are evident between marketing and design which often compete for the budget and authority (Svengren, Holm and Johansson, 2005). For example, both functions claim the ownership of branding and new product developments and related budgets. Marketing have long viewed themselves as the controllers of design activity and find it difficult to accept the growing influence of design. In 1990 Walker presented this as "two tribes at war." Bruce and Cooper (1997) further developed Walker's (1990) ideas that there are serious polarities in thinking and characteristics of marketers and designers. However, whilst the researchers pointed to the main differences in thinking styles and characteristics there are now major drivers of convergence which encourage using the whole brain (see also Table 5.7).

The divergence of aims was identified as managers addressing the long term whist designers address the short term. Managers were seen as more interested in profits and returns but designers focussed on their perceived view of the aesthetic and functional quality of the product and/or service. Managers prioritized how to survive whilst designers were always looking to reform and introduce new experiences. Growth was at the forefront of the managers' minds, but designers sought prestige, acclaim for their output. Finally they were noted to diverge through commitment, managers to building a strong organization and designers to building their own image and gaining recognition. The drivers for the convergence of aims include:

- Next generation of products and service, intense competition, pressure on life cycles.
- The need to develop profitable products and services using design to add the value.
- A managed evolution, more flexibility and incremental innovation.
- Growth seen as achievable through design-led innovation.
- Embracing of creativity as core business need.
- More design thinking infused in leadership.

Managers were formerly seen to be concerned with managing people as their most immediate resource, whereas designers (especially within the studio) were mostly focussed on "things," e.g. drawings, models, prototypes. Developing systems for organizing resources dominated managers thinking, but designers were more concerned about improving the environment, sometimes rather narrowly construed as their personal environment and the world of their own – principally young – age group. Drivers for the convergence of this form of thinking will include:

- The recognition that products and services must satisfy people; trending to a much more user-centred approach.
- Growing confidence in using holistic/systems thinking as a tool for creativity.

Education of managers and designers continues to be quite different. Managers generally study more quantitative-based subjects like accountancy and engineering. They learn to express themselves verbally and in writing. By contrast designers pursue art and crafts and develop visual communication skills. They are more concerned with shape than numbers.

Convergence of education has been slow but the driving forces are becoming stronger:

- Organizations are seeking to employ people who have skills which can add value and this includes their ability to work across disciplines.
- The development of successful brands requires the integration of the narrative with the environment.
- The emergent digital revolution enforces artists and engineers to collaborate and new types of professionals to emerge.
- Addressing complexity can best be achieved through combined quantitative and qualitative methods.

As noted in earlier sections, managers had spent a century using serial, linear, analytical and immediate problem identification thinking. Designers had always tended to the holistic, lateral-thinking approach preferring synthesis to analysis and intent on achieving a solution.

Drivers for the convergence of their thinking styles include:

- The need for growing holistic style thinking to support strategic planning.
- Recognition by organizations that it is acceptable for all staff to be creative.
- Combining the analysis and synthesis styles in multidisciplinary teams.
- Seeking optimum creative solutions for well-defined problems (in turn developing better design briefs),

The behaviour and culture of managers was hitherto seen as pessimistic, adaptive, cautious, and inclined to conformity. Designers on the whole were seen as optimistic, full of new ideas, inclined to experimentation and enjoying diversity. Convergence may be principally driven by:

- Recognition that design-led innovation delivers rewards at the core of the organization's strategy.
- More models of measuring the influence of creativity and managing risk are emerging.
- Pessimism may be seen as over cautious and optimism as risky as they converge to become "realism" about the context.

Marketing and design functions in progressive organizations are trying to close the communication gap, as designers develop a greater awareness of business and marketing needs and marketers gain a better understanding of the value added by design thinking. However it is interesting to note that marketing is still reluctant to address the issues deeply in research as there is a low percentage of marketing research papers which include the relationship with design. Cooper and Jones (1995, cited in Bruce and Cooper, 1997) suggested that the relationships can be enhanced through:

- Good understanding of each other's roles and responsibilities;
- Awareness of each other's needs;
- Good communication in terms of content and frequency;
- Commitment to the project, e.g. a new product development, and organization.

Design Contributions to Marketing Mix

A closer collaboration between design and marketing is considered to be very beneficial, since design plays a key role in every component of the "Marketing Mix" (Bruce, 2002):

1. *Product:* Design is directly involved in this factor, as it influences quality, function, usability and appearance of products/services. Design also helps differentiate the offerings and reinforce brand messages through users' interactions and experiences.
2. *Price:* Design can help reduce cost, e.g. reduce materials, production processes, energy consumption and wastes, while concurrently increasing values of the product/service. Some experts argue that price has nothing to do with cost, for example, the price of a Rolex watch is higher than the price of a Tata Nano car! Price is about perceived value and design could help increase it through the look and feel, as well as the functionality of the product/service. But design ideas are not restricted to products/services, they are about every aspect of performance and design thinking frequently generates cheaper methods for making, packaging, distributing, displaying and selling.
3. *Place:* Design can support the distribution and logistics in many different ways. Good packaging design can reduce transport costs, e.g. stackable packaging, and prolong a product's shelf life, e.g. reducing transport damage. Good design can attract consumers even without costly display units or point-of-purchase (POP) advertising in stores.
4. *Promotion:* Design excels at capturing people's attention and communicating brand messages. The visual quality of design is vital to the success of all kind of advertising, e.g. brochures, printed advertisements, photography, viral videos and publicity events. Good use of design can help convey messages through new media, e.g. social networking sites and sponsorship.

Design can also contribute to the extended elements of the Marketing Mix (i.e., people, process and physical evidence), which was developed in

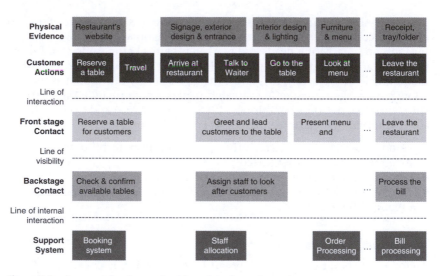

Figure 5.1 An example of a service blueprint of a restaurant

response to the service economy. Figure 5.1 shows an example of a service blueprint where every element of the experience needs to be designed coherently and consistently.

Emerging design disciplines, e.g. service design, address all issues related to staff, processes and all tangible service touchpoints. The term *service design* has been defined as "the design of the overall experience of a service as well as the design of the process and strategy to provide that services" (Moritz, 2005). Good use of service design in all points of contact or service touchpoints can deliver positive experiences while reducing negative ones (Saco and Goncalves, 2008). For example, in a restaurant, small-d design can be used to create a memorable front stage, the environments and interactions that customers will experience, such as the dining area, the waiting area and the bar, while Big-D design can help create a practical backstage, the processes and systems that customers will not see, but are important to the quality of the service, e.g. the order processing system. Good businesses never lost sight of the importance of service design for delivering a good experience but it seems now that many need the help of designers to recover and/or enhance their service offerings. Designing the service experience is essential to the brand as discussed in Chapter 3.

Design Contributions to Marketing Research

One key role of the marketing function is to anticipate needs and changes in the marketplace, as well as customer feedback on the current products/services/experiences that the company provides. Design research can complement marketing research, since both designers and marketers seek an in-depth understanding of current and potential customers, that is, their needs, wants, aspirations, lifestyles, preferences, expectations, behaviours and the context of use. While marketers are good at collecting and analyzing verbal information, for example through interviews, questionnaire surveys and focus groups, design disciplines excel at gathering and making sense of visual information like user interaction observations, visual ethnography and product trend analyses. Good collaboration between marketing and design teams can lead to a more complete set of data and richer, more insightful research outcomes. Evidently, more and more designers and marketers share research methods and analysis tools, e.g. personas, scenarios, storytelling and perceptual maps. There is thus a stronger chance in the future for further collaboration and idea exchange.

Example of Design Contributions to Marketing: Comparethemarket.com

Compare the Meerkat is an interesting example of how humour and playful design can help create likable personality for a characterless company.

The online price comparison service is one of the fastest growing sectors in the UK since 2005. In this highly competitive market, many key players found it difficult to differentiate themselves due to similar service offers. In 2009, comparethemarket.com, a UK price comparison web site, launched its *Compare the Meerkat* marketing campaign featuring Aleksandr Orlov, a fictional CGI Russian aristocratic meerkat who founded comparethemeerkat.com. The TV commercials were centred on his frustration over the confusion between his web site and comparethemarket.com. The campaign is considered a commercial success. Humour and playful design have been used beyond TV adverts – for example, the web site (www.comparethemeerkat.com) and Orlov's Facebook page (https://www.facebook.com/Comparethemeerkat) were created and regularly updated. This successful marketing campaign has set the standard for its sector. The idea of creating a fictional character to represent a company has been copied by many competitors in the UK.

5.4.3   Research & Development

Relationship of Design and Research & Development

There is a strong connection between design and research and development (R&D), as observed by Swann and Birke (2005) They pointed out that both functions are rooted in creativity and use creative thinking to generate innovation and productivity for an organization, which in turn influences business performance. While R&D and design functions on their own can create innovation, arguably, a closer collaboration between the two disciplines could lead to better outcomes. R&D without design inputs can come up with technologically advanced applications. However, they might not be attractive and desirable from the consumers' point of view. Design without R&D inputs could bring about aesthetically pleasing and highly functional products. However, they might not be technologically superior or significantly different from those of competitors. The interdependence of value, innovation and technology is expressed by Kim and Maborgne (2005) as "value without (technological) innovation tends to focus on an incremental scale ... innovation without value tends to be technology driven."

A report published by the Department of Trade and Industry (DTI), UK (2005) suggested that the linkage between design and R&D is rather complex. For some organizations, design function is considered as part of R&D. This might be because there are certain overlaps between design and R&D. For example, skills and expertise of technical design disciplines, such as engineering design and system design, fall inside the competencies of R&D. The importance of a good relationship between design and research and development (R&D) can be seen by the practices of the world's most innovative companies, see Table 5.10. All of these identified companies create value through design and technological development and consistently deliver successful new products/services.

Example of Synergy between Design & Technological Development: Salesforce.com

Salesforce.com (http://www.salesforce.com) ranked number one in Table 5.10 is a good example of a company that integrates design and technology. It offers cloud computing applications to other businesses worldwide. The company specializes in the practice of customer and collaboration relationship management (CRM) applications. Their applications are well designed and practical, simple to use and can be customized as well as integrated with other software applications. The company has become one of the fastest growing companies because of effective use of design and technological developments. While many "world most innovative companies" rankings are based on past performance (people were asked to vote for organizations they think are most innovative), Forbes asked investors to vote for the ones they are willing to invest in based on past and future

Table 5.10   Forbes' world's most innovative companies

Rank	Company	Five-year average sales growth (%)	Five-year average net income growth (%)	Enterprise value ($billion)	Innovation premium*
1	Salesforce.com	39.5	78.7	20.7	75.1
2	Amazon.com	32.0	37.6	92.7	58.9
3	Intuitive Surgical	43.4	36.4	13.4	57.6
4	Tendcent Holding	69.0	75.4	46.5	52.3
5	Apple	35.1	60.7	303.4	48.2
6	Hindustan Unilever	10.0	4.0	15.5	47.7
7	Google	35.0	37.1	138.1	44.9
8	Natural Cosmetics	17.0	13.5	10.2	44.5
9	Bharat Heavy Electrical	27.2	25.0	19.5	43.6
10	Monsanto	13.4	44.7	41.3	42.6

Source: Forbes (2012).
* The innovation premium is a measure of how much investors have bid up the stock price of a company above the value of its existing business based on expectations of future innovative results (new products, services and markets). Members of the list must have $10 billion in market capitalization, spend at least 1% of their asset base on R&D and have seven years of public data.

performance. The fact that Salesforce.com came top shows that it has strong potential to grow and attract investors.

Design Contributions to R&D

Design and R&D generally collaborate in most new product developments. Cooper and Press (1995) emphasize how R&D information feeds the creative process and enables designers to develop innovative and leading edge concepts. They encourage R&D teams to gain design understanding, the use of design research to help R&D teams to generate new applications based on design ideas and insights from design practice to open up new avenues for scientific research and technology. Design, especially through design research, can contribute to R&D.

Press and Cooper (2003) explained that design research can be categorized into three types:

1. *Searching for understanding* of the context which designers are working on. It includes various types of research, namely market and competitor research, anthropology/ethnography research, lifestyle research, contextual and trend research, technology research, participatory research and practice-centred research. The new insight gained from it could help R&D teams better understand their target markets.
2. *Searching for ideas* to formulate new concepts. It concentrates on the idea generation and the creative process, e.g. practice-centred research. Visionary ideas can inspire R&D teams to find new applications, test and explore new territories.
3. *Searching for solutions* for identified problems/opportunities. Designers use various techniques to design, prototype and test their ideas, e.g. experience prototyping, user trials and experiments. The new insight from such design practices could lead to new ideas for scientific research and technological applications.

Design disciplines can bring a number of additional emerging research tools to help R&D gain better understanding of users and other factors influencing the outcomes, such as soft trends. Examples are as follows:

- *Design ethnography:* This method is considered to be open-ended, holistic and discovery-oriented. It utilizes "ethnographic skills" to tackle design problems. Consider a group of social scientists who spend a certain period of time with a small tribe in Africa trying to understand their cultures, beliefs and customs, and then summarize all key insights into stories, which allow people who did not have the first-hand experience to empathize with the people. That is what ethnographic research is about. In this case, ethnographic techniques are employed to understand people, e.g. their cultures and lifestyles, in order to serve them better. Design ethnography uses a combination of tools, like diaries and disposal cameras, in order to see people's world through their eyes.
- *Contextual enquiry:* This method was designed to gain knowledge of hidden user interactions and latent needs. The principle is going to observe users in real-life situations, like the place where they use the product.

Through a balanced combination of observing users and asking them to explain what is going on, researchers can help people articulate their experiences with products, services or systems. This combination helps overcome problems caused by misinterpretation. It is important to assume nothing. For example, a researcher may notice that a user always uses Control-C (Ctrl + C) to copy information onscreen. Rather than assuming that it is his/her preference, it is better to ask. It might turn out that the user does not know other ways to copy information, such as right click on a computer mouse or a copy button on a menu bar. Because participants are questioned while using a product, their responses are based on on-going experience rather than generalized answers based on overall experience that they have with the product. Moreover, this method allows researchers and participants to determine what participants' words and actions mean together. Participants do not set out to mislead researchers but there is often a wide difference between what they perceive they do and what they actually do in practice.

- *Cultural probes:* This method was designed to inspire and sensitize developers to people's needs, wants, dreams and aspirations. It uses a number of prompts, such as postcards and maps, in order to probe deeply into people's thoughts. While design ethnography relies on researchers' observation skills and interpretation, cultural probes encourage participants to tell researchers what certain things mean to them. In general, researchers create and give each participant a probe pack which may contain a disposable camera with requests for certain pictures (e.g. please take a picture of the best part of your house), a set of postcards asking open-ended questions (e.g. what place does chocolate have in your daily life?) and maps for demonstrating user emotional relationships with certain groups of people or areas (e.g. what it is your favourite spot in your workplace?).

- *Experience prototyping:* This method is a form of role-playing that enables developers, users and other key stakeholders, such as frontline staff, to gain first-hand appreciation of existing or future conditions. By allowing different stakeholders to "experience it themselves" rather than imagining or observing others, they can get a better idea about the context of use. It is important to act out how the experience will be delivered and received. Existing products or simple physical models may be used as props to support role-playing and make it as close to the real experience as possible. For example, to design a new experience for a supermarket, tables and chairs may be arranged in certain ways to represent shelves and checkout counters. It is useful to film the all the interactions during the role plays for further discussions afterwards.

- *Participatory design:* The method was first used as a means to empower workers at the workplace by letting them take part in the design of the technology they were going to use. Nowadays, participatory design focuses on bringing all key stakeholders (e.g. designers, users, marketers, engineers, researchers and business representatives) to work together towards a design solution. It helps increase the usability of the design outcomes, enhance/accelerate user acceptance and gain supports from business functions, since they are involved in the development process from the start.

It can be seen that design research tools are valuable for collecting qualitative information which can complement scientific data obtained by R&D. A close collaboration could lead to more radical innovation which meets consumers' requirements, lifestyles and preferences. For an example of a consultancy which excels in such research see www.seymourpowell.com

5.4.4 Human Resources

Relationship of Design and Human Resources

Human resources (HR) function can increase the awareness and effectiveness of design throughout the organization through recruitment, on-going policy and communications and training and development. Design supports the HR function in communicating corporate strategy, developing brand awareness (internal branding) and creating a climate to attract and nurture creative people. Design and HR can work together to achieve a well-structured but flexible and responsive environment that promotes an innovative culture. A new breed of *T-shaped* design manager can help bridge the gap between functions, with the horizontal of the "T" representing breadth of knowledge across disciplines and the vertical of the "T" representing in-depth design knowledge/skills (Hansen and Von Oetiger, 2001).

Glick (2006) urged organizations to explore how to convert the talent of their staff into business performance. The author identified key elements which influence organizational performance, namely motivation, ability and corporate culture and proposed a simple formula as shown below:

$$\text{Performance} = (\text{motivation}) \times (\text{ability}) \text{ as moderated by the environment (corporate culture)}$$

To increase motivation an organization must focus on intrinsic rewards, which Fraser (2011) described as an "important fuel" for creativity. It is about encouraging people to do what they love, what they are passionate about or what they have a genuine curiosity about. To get people interested or excited about their jobs, it is important to make the job rewarding in its own right, for example allowing staff to use their imagination and express themselves freely.

Glick (2006) recommends five dimensions of a motivating job as: skill variety – the use of different skills in one job; task identity – requires completion of whole (or identifiable piece of work); task significance – impact on the organization and/or larger society; autonomy – amount of freedom, independence and discretion; feedback – ability to tell how well one is doing from the job itself. Managers may recognize these as "hygiene factors" from the famous motivation theory of Frederick Herzberg.

HR strives to achieve a balance between the degree of freedom for creative individuals and teams and their need to function within a constrained

Table 5.11 Time/creativity matrix

		Time pressure	
		Low	**High**
Creative thinking	High	Designers exploring, wandering around	Designers share ownership and goals and feel valued
	Low	Designers dreaming but not constructively sharing	Designers unduly pressed and stressed and somewhat disorganized

organizational framework. Time and budget constraints are likely to be the biggest direct influence on design creativity. A study conducted by Amabile *et al.* (2002; cited in Harvard Business School, 2003) demonstrated the relationship of creative thinking and time pressure. Table 5.11 summarizes the effect on designers of time pressure on creative thinking. It can be seen that the best results come from high time pressure coupled with clear directions and goals and a sense of ownership of the project and outcomes.

In order to improve the abilities of staff, Glick (2006) suggested that managers need to provide feedback, so that staff members know how they are doing and where they need to improve, and opportunities for staff to learn new things and improve. But ultimately it is important to create corporate cultures where creativity and innovation can flourish. This is probably the area where both Big-D and small-d designs can contribute the most.

Design Contributions to Human Resources

The main contributions are in the areas of internal branding and training programmes. Design can be used to ensure that all touchpoints (e.g. staff handbook, intranet pages, forms, office furniture) convey brand messages effectively and make all training materials engaging and easy to follow. Design can also help HR develop and strengthen desirable organizational cultures and behaviours. Many experts have also suggested that emotional and/or soul branding should be employed to create strong relationships with employees.

Example of Design Contributions to Human Resources: VALVE Corporation

VALVE (www.valvesoftware.com), a company behind many successful games, such as *Half-Life®*, is an example of how design thinking can attract and nurture innovators as well as an innovative environment in an organization. The structure of the company is completely flat – no bosses, no managers, no hierarchy. According to the staff handbook, even the founder is not considered the boss! People who work at VALVE either invent their own projects or work on projects that they strongly believe in. The company is not risk averse – mistakes are perceived as part of the creative process. The company has worked a fair system to reward staff according to their contributions. Instead of employing common practices, such as appraisals, VALVE uses peer reviews and "stack ranking", which ensure that the payments reflect the value that individual members give to the company (the more value you give to the company, the more money you receive). This practice has been expanded beyond the internal structure, as the company has recently introduced Steam, a platform to support independent small developers to connect, collaborate, distribute and share their digital creations.

5.4.5   Finance

Relationship of Design and Finance

Designers, as a body, show an inherent dislike of finance. Yet most business decisions are based on financial judgment. Best (2010) described finance as "the lifeblood of any company or business." Thus, designers need to become acutely aware that their proposals must meet financial criteria, particularly return on investment and cash flow. Return on investment is the percentage profit to expenditure ratio over time, and most organizations calculate the effect of inflation to assess the real potential value of new proposals. Financial management focus on good cash flow, so designers will be encouraged to show the cash generated and in particular how quickly the new product/service will achieve positive cash income. A cash flow forecast will enable managers to know whether they have enough liquid assets to support new projects and to decide the best time frame. Finance directors consider how much to invest in design. They have a limited resource to manage and, whether the organization is financially strong or not, they see their prime responsibility as allocating the available money to generate sustainable growth. When an organization is cash rich, it may have more confidence in investing in design. When it is financially weak, it may show more caution but needs strong support from design to achieve a turnaround. Both money and design should provide the "lifeblood."

Design Contributions to Finance

Convincing the financial function of the benefits of investing in design is challenging because design value is hard to measure and in particular to isolate from other contributors to value. However many studies demonstrate that a commitment to design yields benefits. Cooper and Press (1995) identified six broad areas of contribution and Table 5.12 presents their implications for design management strategists.

In considering the benefits of convergence of design thinking into finance, it should be remembered that both have the same ultimate goal, to identify opportunities and generate growth. However the language of the two domains may be seen as "foreign" and this may slow the process of understanding. Real cooperation will only be achieved when designers are confident to engage with economic issues and finance managers show respect for the creative and artistic contribution of designers and their ability to directly impact the bottom line, e.g. profitability measured in economic, social and environmental terms.

Designers need to understand the mindset of accountants and financial managers when they are bidding for contracts and/or internal support for their proposals. Since designers have a natural leaning towards presenting

Table 5.12 Design contributions to finance

Area of financial management	Implications for design
Planning in terms of project/ product and marketing plans	Design can help to successfully plan and manage the portfolio of offerings, propose new cost-effective projects and give much creative input into marketing plans.
Forecasting sales and growth profits	Using trend analysis and soft research techniques, design can offer valuable information for forecasting future performance of products and services.
Resources planning and allocation	Finance want to identify the "winners" from the range of alternatives placed before them: design can generate more possible alternative directions and assist to identify which products and/or services may yield the best returns, and should therefore be allocated sufficient resources.
Project cost monitoring	The greatest concern of finance is that projects may exceed the budget allocated and the results may fall short of expectations: careful control of design and related projects can use appropriate evaluation techniques to monitor and review the progress and expected outcomes, thus avoiding the risks of expensive aborted projects.
Project authorization and expenditure	The financial function will authorize only projects they regard as viable and potentially beneficial: they need design to give them reliable estimates and a clear view of the expected performance, and they need it set out in figures not just artistic or even technology-based images and diagrams.
Project evaluation	Design can contribute by demonstrating the effectiveness of the design process to ideate, develop, test and launch new products and services and measure the added value which design brings to brand equity and brand experience.

Source: Cooper and Press (1995).

the aesthetic appeal of their proposals, it is easy to forget that the powerful decision makers include finance experts who have little or no interest in the artistic argument but a primary interest in the return on capital which may be generated from the project.

The financial manager will customarily calculate the return on capital using one of two methods. Capital is the total resource required to run the project expressed as a sum of money. The first method is payback, and simply seeks how long it will be before the money invested is paid back. Naturally the quicker the money is paid back, the more the finance manager likes it. So designers can gain an edge on competitors by demonstrating the outflows of moneys and the expected inflows, especially if the cash inflow can be generated quickly. The second and most common method uses a technique called internal rate of return and is based on discounted cash flow. The main difference from the first method is that the finance manager will apply a percentage "discount" to all the future cash income to reflect the future cost of capital. Of course this can only be an estimate and much depends on prevailing interest rates and the economy, but the objective is to get a realistic financial assessment of the project *now*, thus the calculation shows the net present value.

Designers might expect that the financial manager will always favour the project proposal which give the highest financial return as shown by the net present value, but there are also risks to be considered and the availability of financial resources to meet competing bids. So the financial manager may prepare financial projections based on many variables. In any event the financial decision makers are unlikely to support a design proposal which does not generate cash rapidly and yields less than 8% return on capital. Examples where design has made a significant impact on finance may be found in many fields, such as health care, open space community benefits, energy and green buildings. Management consultants McKinsey report a successful case of using a product designers approach to designing a benefits package for employees, thus combining design, HR and finance thinking (www.mckinseyquarterly.com) and the UK Design Council publish case studies of reversing business downturn and achieving savings (www.designcouncil.org.uk).

Example of Design Contributions to Finance: Swatch

Swatch is an example of how design could help reduce costs and gain market shares. Back in 1960s and 1970s, Swiss analogue watch producers suffered the loss of significant market shares to Japanese digital watch manufacturers, such as Seiko and Citizen. Design was strategically employed to re-popularize analogue watches. In the 1980s, most people still perceived Swiss watches as premium products – something that you would not buy very often; something that would be passed from one generation to another. As a result, it was hard to grow the market. Nicholas Hayek, the founder of the Swatch Group explained that the name "Swatch" refers to the plural of watch (s + watch). Hence, strategic design was used to encourage consumers to buy more than one watch and change people's perceptions of Swiss watches from luxury products to affordable fashion accessories. In order to achieve competitive prices, design was also used to reduce the number of components. Consequently, the concept of Swatch became a great financial success due to good use of strategic design.

5.4.6   Summary

Design should be a strategic partner of all functional areas and make significant contributions to (extended) departments as shown in the Table 5.13.

Example: Samsung

Samsung is an example of an excellent user of design. Using design as a catalyst for change, Samsung successfully transformed itself from an original equipment manufacturer (OEM) into a global leader. They utilize Big-D design to integrate business direction and product/service development. Their small-d designs demonstrate the fusing of technical innovation with changing lifestyles and emotional values, communicating the "story" behind the experience. *Business Week* (2004) reported that the organization loosened several

Table 5.13 Design contributions and roles of design as strategic partner

Functions	Key design contributions	Roles of design in partnership
Top management	• Visualize "bold" strategic ideas • Help explore emerging opportunities • Create sustainable competencies	• To create inspiring visions, strategies and policies.
Marketing	• Support marketing activities (Marketing Mix) • Help attract and retain customers • Differentiate brands and enrich experiences	• To develop tactics for long-lasting customer relationships.
Finance	• Increase share price and brand value • Reduce operational and manufacturing costs • Accelerate the return on investment	• To estimate realistic design management budgets.
R&D	• Provide user and market insight through appropriate design research • Convert technological knowledge into desirable products/services • Offer visionary and inspiring ideas	• To set research directions and plan implementation process in order to achieve value innovation.
HR	• Communicate corporate strategy and policy • Create the right climate for innovation • Support internal branding and motivate staff • Promote knowledge exchange	• To enhance effective internal communication and suitable climate for innovation.
Legal	• Exploit existing intellectual property • Advance current intellectual property • Generate new intellectual property	• To accelerate the process of obtaining legal protection.
Engineering	• Integrate functionality with aesthetics • Bridge the communication gap between business and engineering disciplines	• To achieve the synergistic effect of design and engineering.
Production	• Showcase manufacturing capabilities • Ensure that designs meet technical constraints • Reduce operational complexity and costs	• To optimize product quality and reduce potential failures.
Sales	• Provide unique selling points • Create attractive products that are easy to sell • Supply user insight through design research	• To develop business plans for new products/services.

traditional cultures to develop the right climate for creativity and appointed a high-ranking chief design officer to represent design at top management level.

5.5   4Ds OF STRATEGIC DESIGN PARTNERSHIPS

The 4Ds design management model can be used to develop internal and external strategic partnerships. Thus it can energize and infuse new ideas into the learning curve for cooperation across all major functions. Steinhilber (2008) says strategic alliances need the right framework, the right organization, people and environment and trust in relationships.

Design helps to build such an organization and establish such a framework which provides a platform for integrating design strategy across all activities. The four stages of the 4Ds model can be used as shown below and the key elements of successful design partnerships is shown in Table 5.14 followed by the conceptual model for cross functional cooperation.

1. Determining the current use of design – finding out how and what other functions perceive, use and expect from design; identifying opportunities for new contributions in all areas, products, services, systems, and experiences.

Table 5.14   Key elements of the 4Ds of design partnerships

Strategic level	Tactical level	Operational level
Determining		
Perception of design • Design as strategic resources • Design as strategic partner/alliance	Collaboration with design • Balance of multidisciplinary contributions • Synergy of design and business activities	Usage of design • Tangible designs • Intangible designs • Internal resources • External resources
Defining		
Goals • Mutual Benefits • Targets – *What does success look like?*	Behaviours • Working environment • Ground rules – *How should we collaborate?*	Responsibilities • Staff/team structure • Tasks – *How can we complement each other?*
Designing		
Policies • Long-term relationships • Trust building	Systems • Processes • Synergy • Team building	Services • Design activities • Design projects • Related support
Deciding		
Strategic roles of design • Influencer – *Does design bring positive changes/ new assets?*	Tactical roles of design • Partner –*Does design enhance performance and competencies?*	Practical roles of design • Team and individual –*Does design deliver high-quality services?*

2. Defining design activities to co-ordinate achievement of business objectives – establishing realistic goals: *How can design help other functions accomplish their objectives? What types of design do partners require?*
3. Designing services and systems to support other business units – servicing other business functions by designing products, services, identities, etc and building systems that enhance/support long-term relationships based on mutual respect and trust.
4. Deciding whether the design activities meet organizational goals and push the organization towards new visions. This checks the alignment of the business and design strategy but is ultimately about how to infuse design thinking throughout the people comprising an organization to help them to make their future. (Figure 5.2)

Oakley (2011) pointed out that design managers can bring different perspectives and different sets of skills to integrate with and challenge the established skills in other functional areas. Table 5.15 supports the argument discussed in the previous section that design should be treated as an independent unit, since using the traditional management style to manage design teams might not bring the best out of them, and further extends the contemporary practice of the design manager. Of course many management groups may regard themselves as progressive but the researcher

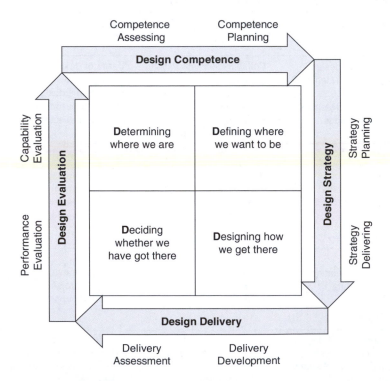

Figure 5.2 4Ds of cross functional cooperation model

Table 5.15   The design managers view of management

Traditional approach of managers	Design manager extended perspective
• Management practice based on education with limited opportunities taken for further professional development.	• Managerial approach based on continuous learning.
• Strong analytical and technical know-how and skills based on current state of technology.	• Skills under continuous development for addressing ambiguity, complexity and conflict.
• Behaviour conditioned by continuity and established practices of established organizational experiences.	• Outward-looking perspective to ensure flexibility and adaptability to rapid changes in environment.
• Makes and follows the rules which are hard to change.	• Works within (broader) boundaries but responds to environmental and other inputs.
• Inward looking towards internal issues and politics.	• Encompasses internal and external issues through holistic thinking and tact.
• Maintains stability of structures, relationships and trust.	• Accepts transient nature of relationships.
• Favours logic and rational approaches and tends to deride intuition.	• Argues powerfully with integrated objective and subjective evidence.
• Completing each task efficiently to required standard.	• Achieving goals with added value and striving to add more.
• Showing busy/active approach – running around and exuding stress.	• Mix of thinking/reflecting time and intense action.
• Individual responsibility to solve problems and make decisions.	• Interdisciplinary team approach to complex problem solving and building consensus.

Source: Based on Oakley (2011).

clearly found much evidence of "traditional," somewhat rigid mechanistic approaches and some reluctance towards cross-functional working. The differences highlight how a design manager may bring new approaches and will certainly need excellent communication skills and a well-developed sense of diplomacy and tact.

5.5.1   Determining the Current Use of Design

A good starting point to establish the organization's current integration of design and other functions as partners is Kotler and Rath's (1984) *design sensitivity audit* presented in Chapter 2. Another useful framework is the design ladder developed by Danish Design Centre, see Table 5.16. It is useful for a company to carry out a self-assessment to determine the current role of design.

The study showed that the higher the place of a company on the design ladder, the stronger the business performance. Companies using design as

Table 5.16 The design ladder

Step	Description
1	Design is an inconspicuous part of, for instance, product development and performed by members of staff, who are not design professionals. Design solutions are based on the perception of functionality and aesthetics shared by the people involved. The points of view of end-users play very little or no part at all.
2	Design as styling. Design is perceived as a final aesthetic finish of a product. In some cases, professional designers may perform the task, but generally other professions are involved.
3	Design as process. Design is not a finite part of a process but a work method adopted very early in product development. The design solution is adapted to the task and focused on the end-user and requires a multidisciplinary approach, e.g. involving process technicians, material technologists, marketing and organizational people.
4	Design as innovation. The designer collaborates with the owner/management in adopting an innovative approach to all – or substantial parts – of the business foundation. The design process combined with the company vision and future role in the value chain are important elements.

Source: Danish Design Centre (2003).

innovation were revealed as the top performers in measurements of gross revenue, exports and increasing employment. Design as process and design as styling were placed second and third respectively whilst companies which do not use professional designers were placed bottom in each category. Hence, it showed evidence that it is in a firm's best interest to become an effective user of design and make sure that design has a role to play in shaping future visions. The highest performing companies in the top two categories (innovation and process) represented about 50% of those surveyed and non-design users were just over one third (Danish Design Centre, 2003)

However, it can be observed that one of the most influential barriers to the effective integration of design is embedded in the respective education programmes of designers and business managers. They continue to be educated in markedly different ways. Many design schools throughout the world include only a cursory introduction to business and management, frequently through including a programme about marketing design services, delivered in whole or in part by a design consultant/practitioner. Design practice educators argue that there is insufficient time for business studies and giving too many non-studio assignments can diminish the student designer's ability to achieve their optimum creative potential. There is an on-going debate about how much designers need to be taught about business and management and who should teach it. Design schools may lack business know-how and business schools lack design know-how. Meantime, Abram (2007) reported that the skills designers lack the most were business skills (Table 5.17).

Table 5.17 Which skills do designers lack the most?

Business management	72%
Understanding client's business	60%
Verbal communication	44%
Team working	24%
Drawing skills	19%
Creativity	18%

Source: Design Council questionnaire (2006; cited in Abram, 2007).

By contrast, a study of 15 top business programmes by Lockwood (2002) revealed a major lack of design exposure for business graduates with only one elective design class on offer.

He found that none of the programmes offered design as a core class. Two-thirds of the courses introduced design as part of another class (almost certainly marketing) and only as power point fundamentals. A similar pattern was identified for design management, except that two elective classes from 15 were offered. There were no core classes in creativity or innovation but both were incorporated as part of other classes.

Clearly, there is still much to be done in the field of education to allow design and business management academics, practitioners, students and researchers to learn from each other and bring about meaningful collaboration. Many leading universities have set up design management programmes but they are still relatively few compared with conventional largely studio-based design courses. Business schools are trying to make a transition to more open creative approaches but the majority of programmes continue to treat design as a relatively low-status service function. Some of the programmes have failed for lack of committed leadership, cultural resistance and disputes about ownership, that is to say whether the programme rightly belongs in the design school or the business school.

5.5.2 Defining Design Activities to Coordinate Achievement of Business Objectives

A national survey commissioned by Design Council, UK, demonstrated that design has begun to integrate into other business functions across many industries – ranging from the manufactures right through to the finance and business services sector (see Table 5.18). Although design is still commonly employed to create tangible artefacts, e.g. packaging and advertisements, it has now been used to support strategic planning and research.

This survey shows about three-quarters of the participants are able to identify the contribution made by design in several areas of the firm's activities including areas which were not considered the territory of design until recent years. So there is evidence of a willingness to accept design thinking and the design activities can be planned accordingly. For the one-quarter who do not acknowledge the role of design there remains the challenge to identify and demonstrate the value which design may bring to them.

Table 5.18 Which of the following functions or activities do you consider make use of design?

	Percentage of all respondents (column percentages)						
	All firms	Primary, construction, communication	Manufactures	Financial & business services	Trade & leisure services	Stayed the same size	Grown moderately/rapidly
Advertising & corporate communication	60	52	40	78	58	52	66
Product development	53	39	84	81	41	46	56
Packaging	53	46	50	59	54	46	57
Research and development	40	18	42	72	33	30	43
Marketing	38	29	33	44	40	30	48
Production engineering/service delivery	26	24	29	50	16	20	30
Don't know	23	23	20	14	27	20	22
Marketing research	18	7	21	25	18	13	24
Sales and distribution	16	5	20	25	14	8	18
Corporate/strategic planning	14	4	14	34	8	9	18
Others	2	0	0	0	3	4	0
None	1	0	0	0	2	1	1

Source: Design Council National Survey of Firms undertaken by PACEC (cited in Tether, 2005).

The roles, responsibilities and activities of the design function should be carefully planned and defined in order to ensure that they help a firm achieve its business objectives.

Svengren Holm (2011) suggested that the integration of design as a strategic resource can be accomplished as follows:

1. *Functional integration*: This level of integration focuses on practical values of design. Hence, the author recommended that the design function should become an integral part of the innovation development process. Design teams should be involved in the new product development from the beginning right through to the end of the process. This level of integration is about design contributions at the operational level.
2. *Visual integration*: This level of integration concentrates on communication skills of design. As a result, it was proposed that the design function should play a leading role in managing visual coherence and coordinating all design elements in an organization. This suggests that design teams should work closely with marketing, brand management and human resources to convey brand message to employees, customers,

business partners and the general public effectively. In this case, visual elements cover everything people see – ranging from the look and feel of a product right through to the office signage. This level of integration highlights design contributions at the business/tactical level.

3. *Conceptual integration*: This level of integration focuses on design thinking. Thus, the author recommended that design thinking and design methods should be used to explore and develop relationships between an organization and its surroundings (e.g. the marketplace) and create meaningful offers at the strategic level – such as visions for innovation. This level of integration highlights design contributions at the strategic level.

For maximum leverage, partnerships between design and other functions need to go beyond the development of products and services and deliver value through differentiation and new experiences. Inevitably, in the future, all companies will have to compete on experiences – not just products or services. Joseph Pine II and Gilmore (1998) pointed out that:

> an experience occurs when a company intentionally uses services as the stage, and goods as props, to engage individual customers in a way that creates a memorable event. Commodities are fungible, goods tangible, services intangible, and experiences memorable.

They showed how the economic offer has metamorphosed from fungible, tangible commodities and goods to intangible and memorable services and experiences. The service and experience economy delivers and stages experiences, emphasizes the benefits and emotions by creating sensations and treats the customer as valued client and guest. An example may be considered in the form of butter whereby New Zealand continues to offer a trusted product based on agrarian and tangible features and Ireland manufacturers have sold butter through the storytelling of Celtic myth and mystery for many years. Whilst the former product remains popular for its quality and perceived healthy attributes, the latter became storytellers of "butter in culture" and have increased their sales and built up strong connections and brand loyalty.

The objective of collaborative working is to deliver a complete and consistently good quality experience. One weak link, e.g. poor customer service, can undermine the perception of all the positive elements and thus damage the design-led brand. According to Joseph Pine II and Gilmore (1998), there are five steps to a memorable experience:

1. *Theme the experience:* Creating a well-designed theme to help people envision what type of experience they are going to receive. Examples are Hard Rock Café and Ice Hotel.

2. *Harmonize impressions with positive cues:* Delivering the promised experience, harmonizing all touchpoints and making sure the experience unfolds in a logical manner. BMW cars are good at this.

3. *Eliminate negative cues:* Removing everything that is contradictory or could distract customers from the key theme. Consider the case of

Disneyland, everything is about fantasy. Each touchpoint contributes to the main theme – even the rubbish bin!

4. *Mix in memorabilia:* Good design of memorabilia can help remind people of a great time that they have. If your experience is unforgettable, people want to get something to preserve their happy memories. Many theme parks do this well.

5. *Engage all five senses:* The more senses the experience engages, the stronger the memory will be. Thus, it is important to design to please more than one sense. Starbucks showed the way.

It can be seen in order to deliver a memorable and distinctive experience, all functions must work together. One department is unable to plan, coordinate and deliver an experience on its own. Design activities must be identified and defined for every stage of the customer journey and to enhance the overall experience. Identifying the touchpoints at each stage of the customer journey can help to define the design requirements for maintaining and enhancing the experience to achieve business objectives. A similar degree of careful planning must be employed in designing the employee experience in support of the HR function and internal branding. Using service delivery in the hotel industry as an example (see Figure 5.3), it can be seen that the needs for a cross-departmental collaboration occur in nearly every touchpoint of the service.

Example: World Match Racing Tour

The World Match Racing Tour is a good example of how the world professional sailing series achieves its business objectives through design. All the experiences are designed to the highest level. Every touchpoint of the experience is designed as a stage for a spectacular and memorable experience. Maintaining the consistency and high quality of the experience requires the coordination of many design activities across all functions.

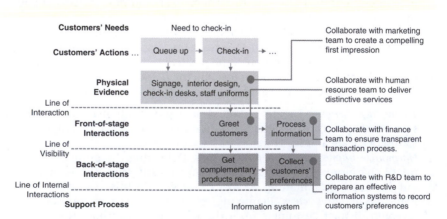

Figure 5.3 Opportunities for collaboration

5.5.3 Designing Services and Systems to Support Other Business Units

At *strategic level*, Big-D and small-d designs can contribute to elements which according to McKinsey's 7S model determine organizational success (Table 5.19).

The *tactical level* is where design helps other business functions perform their key tasks and enrich the results – some examples of which are shown in Table 5.20.

At *operational level*, small-d design seeks to make aesthetically pleasing products and environments to increase satisfaction and happiness. Norman (2004) argues that beautiful designs appear to be easy to use. Whilst they may not always be so easy to use as they appear, people are intrinsically motivated to overcome problems and explore new possibilities. There is strong emerging evidence that pleasurable products deliver longer lasting happiness and memorable experiences. Some experts argue that well-designed environments and equipment could enhance employees' creativity and

Table 5.19 The relationships between design and the 7S model

Seven elements	Description	Design contributions
Soft elements		
Shared values	Long-terms goals – e.g. vision and beliefs that shape an organization's behaviours	Initiate and communicate long-term goals and values
Style	Cultural style – e.g. leadership style	Visual thinking and creative enterprise
Staff	The employees and their capabilities	Enhance knowledge sharing and development among staff
Skills	Expertise, competencies, know-how, skills	
Hard elements		
Strategy	Plans – which competencies could help a company achieve long-term goals	Identify opportunities and build relevant competencies
System	Processes, procedures and routines that characterize an organization	Create transparent and user-friendly systems
Structure	The internal relationship – e.g. the hierarchy of authority and accountability	Design the climate that supports collaborations

Table 5.20 Services and systems designed to support other business units

Functions	Examples of key tasks	Without design inputs	With design inputs
Marketing	marketing campaigns	talk the talk	walk the walk
Finance	annual financial reports	financial facts and figures	easy-to-understand reports
R&D	technological development	new technologies	new applications
HR	internal branding	announcement	interactive dialogue

performance. When people feel happy, they tend to think more creatively and search for new effective ways of doing their work.

Chung and Kim (2011) offered another way of explaining how design could be integrated into an organization using strategic roles as follows:

- *Initiative roles*: Design can initiate new ideas and identify new opportunities for a company. Big-D design can also plan how these opportunities could be realized, e.g. by providing product strategies, design guidelines and/or new concepts. This role places design at the fulcrum of strategy formulation within the senior management group.

Table 5.21 Design performance measures

Design activity	Design goals	Measurements	Business functions impacted by design performance
Product/ service	Desirability	• Sales against targets/profit margins • Satisfaction surveys from customers	• Sales/finance/R&D
	Functionality Reliability	• Awards in the trade press • Warranty claims/liabilities/ recalled products	• PR/marketing • PR/marketing/legal
Process	Speed – meeting targets	• Concept to launch time relative to competitors	• Marketing/sales
	Efficiency of manufacture/ assembly	• Engineering hours per component • Level of skilled staff • Length of production runs • Cost of components and assembly • Time to reach optimum productivity	• Finance/engineering • HR • Finance/engineering • Purchasing • Finance/production
	Quality control	• Time to reach required quality levels • Percentage deviation from schedule • Actual vs forecast cost per product • Cost of late/unexpected changes in requirements	• R&D/engineering • Finance/marketing • Finance • Marketing/ engineering
Other outcomes	High earning capacity and extended life cycle of product/service	• Product cost as proportion of percent retail product: PRP (%) • Cash flow generated to end of reporting period and over product life • Recovery of development cost as proportion of gross profit (%) • Success in the market	• Finance/production • Finance • Finance/R&D • PR/marketing

- *Participative roles*: Design can direct, manage and coordinate strategic implementations of ideas initiated by other functions. In this case, design plays a supporting role, participating in strategic formulation, but does not lead the strategic planning. Design contributes to strategy formulation and implementation with senior and middle management.
- *Subordinating roles*: These are general roles of design, which mainly focus on implementing corporate strategies and solving problems and addressing issues identified by the management or other core business functions. Design is used only for implementation at the middle and lower management levels.

Example: Xerox

Xerox is a good example of how design can become a strategic partner of other business units. Xerox is an engineering-led company with strong heritage in R&D. Traditionally, the design department (Industrial Design and Human Factors) was not integrated in the whole new product development process. The design team was brought in after business opportunities and product specifications were already defined. Moreover, they were not involved in the implementation process. The recent shift from product producing to delivering customer experience made Xerox rethink about design contributions. The company now invests in design research as well as technological research. Further, design is now an integral part of the new product development (NPD) process. Having design inputs in the front end of the NPD process helps business development and marketing teams explore all possibilities, visualize new ideas and accelerate product realization. In addition, designers help bridge the gap between R&D and marketing strategies including design contributions at the end of the NPD process to ensure that the design quality will not be compromised.

5.5.4 Deciding Whether Design Activities Meet and Push Organizational Goals

Measuring the success of design activities involves evaluating all design processes, products and services. Oliver (2002) argued that, generally, the measurement either concentrates on the quality of outcomes (product focus) or quality of process (process focus). While criteria for the former tend to include aesthetic quality, novelty, functionality, price, intellectual property and product longevity, the criteria for the latter covers areas such as variety of idea, time to market, ease of manufacturing, ability to deliver on budget and schedule, and the involvement of key stakeholders. Frequently the measurement ends at this point but the author identified a number of further key design performance areas and measures which have a direct impact on other functions and these ideas are further developed in Table 5.21.

For the design performance measurement at the project level, Oliver (2002) grouped key criteria into four groups as follows:

1. Time to market – *How long does it take to bring a new idea to the market?*
2. Development effort – *How many staff hours are required to develop this product?*

3. Schedule and cost adherence – *Was the product completed on time and on budget?*
4. Late changes – *Were there many last-minute changes in the design?*

Design strategists need to be aware that these measures, and in particular financial measures, are considered a vital tool of business practice. Like every other function, design has to be monitored and controlled for its effectiveness.

Borja de Mozota (2011) posed a series of key questions that could help an organization decide whether design activities meet and push organizational goals as follows:

- *How should we appear, through design, to our customers in order to achieve our vision?* Design knowledge applied to corporate difference-building and strategic market positioning.
- *To satisfy our stakeholders how can design help in the business processes in which we excel?* Design provides improvements in company performance and processes, these innovations in processes being totally invisible to outsiders.
- *How will we sustain, through design, our ability to change and improve?* Design-explicit knowledge is applied to strategic change, perspective, personnel empowerment and talent search.
- *To succeed financially, how should design appear to our shareholders?* Design explicit and measurable value of company reputation, stock market performance and societal responsibility.

She also offered a more generic approach for measuring design performance in relation to business goals and objectives. It was observed that design can add value to the market position, the development process, the personnel and knowledge management, and the financial performance. As a result, she proposed a framework for measurement, which she called the Design Balance Scorecard. Her example of measuring the success of a business objective extended the criteria to include workers' interaction and flexibility. By moving people and equipment around the physical space, instead of furniture and cables, the example showed a 72% saving in workplace costs of moves, additions and changes. This reflects Big-D thinking about using design for optimum workplace design and flexibility to support frequently changing multidisciplinary teams. This in turn delivers benefits to the knowledge base, the development process and the market share.

Good use of design evaluation of tangible outcomes such as product development, can show the effectiveness of cross-functional collaboration and lead to continuous improvement in manufacturing, engineering, other supporting functions and management (*Kaisen* in Japanese). Results help to make the role of design more visible in stimulating new ideas for informed management decisions regarding new target markets, product portfolios, brand identity/values and technology directions. Evaluating intangible aspects such as communication and culture for collaboration can help to plan policies and training programmes to enrich the design ethos and innovation culture further.

5.6   CASE STUDY 3 – DESIGN-LED MARKETING STRATEGY: BENTLEY MOTORS LIMITED

Bentley Motors Limited is a long-established British luxury car operating in a niche market. Their attention to design is unmistakable. Bentley has a distinctive design language which underpins the marketing plans and delivers a resonant customer experience. At strategic level Bentley seeks to differentiate through linking the design attributes and the brand. Design helps them to maintain a clear position in the market and to keep them distinctive from their main competitors. Design is dedicated to the effective expression and delivery of the brand promise.

The marketing communications team manages the customer and brand experience, communicating across all channels and using design at every touchpoint. Products are aesthetically pleasing, coherent and have brand-related qualities "engineered-in." Bespoke design and craftsmanship make Bentley unique in the automotive field. They continue to value the Mulliner (coachbuilder) tradition of handcraft, employing the best craftspeople to customize their products. Bentley design highly distinctive products based on design research which deeply evaluates the customer mind-set, and uses design craft skills to customize and deliver a unique experience.

Marketing strategy of Bentley is rather subtle compared to other high-end automobile companies, such as Audi, Jaguar and Lexus. Bentley does not actively advertise its prestige brand or luxurious products. The marketing is considered design-led, since the company lets design "do the talking." Dr Marcus Abbott, the head of product marketing at Bentley Motors Limited describes Bentley's approach below:

> The Bentley product has an emotional appeal for a customer that is largely based upon the embodiment of the brand's values in the product. Therefore, we find a strong relationship between customer satisfaction and the design and engineering of the multi-sensory "touch-points" of the car, from the vehicle concept and overall style through to graphic interfaces on the infotainment system; from the engines torque characteristics to the softness of the leather. Organizationally, the link between the customer and the design and engineering functions is made through Product Marketing, where the two-way conversation between the customer and the car's specifications and performance is facilitated. Through the Product Marketing function and their defined processes, concepts, features and attributes are set that exemplify, reinforce and develop the brands values. In a complementary role, the Product Marketing function acts as a channel for the engaging and insightful communication of the detailed design "stories", the cars performance and capabilities that bring the

product to life for the customer and make the brand and its products, unique within the marketplace.

Some questions/issues for discussion:

- To what extent can the product (car) represent the brand?
- What is the role of design in maintaining and enhancing quality?
- Consider the need for design/craftspeople to customize the product

5.7   SUMMARY OF KEY POINTS

- Design impacts on all functions and can be used for generating many solution strategies.
- Management strategy can utilize design thinking to identify new directions.
- Real business benefits can be derived from achieving design capability.
- Organizations which embrace design and use it strategically usually out-perform others.
- Business and design thinking have different characteristics but can be reconciled.
- Design managers need cross-disciplinary knowledge and skills.
- Design should be represented at board of directors level for maximum leverage.
- HR management can benefit from cooperating with design for internal branding.
- Design can assist HR to develop a creative environment and culture.
- Marketing and design should work closely to achieve profitable customer relationships.
- Design research can identify and offer many valuable insights.
- R&D need design for value-added innovation.
- Finance and design converge around the common goals of profit and return on investment.
- The 4Ds design management model can be used for collaboration and better performance.
- Firms use design across a wide spectrum of activities.
- Design is best at delivering experiences.
- Effectiveness of the design input can be measured

5.8   FURTHER CONSIDERATIONS

Progressive companies and public sector organizations throughout the world are learning to harness design and to use the methods and thinking styles of designers to inject fresh ideas into their activities. But by far the greatest majority of organizations are locked into the paradigm of design as adding artistic elements like styling and producing promotional materials and websites. This is to vastly underestimate the power of design to break away from the school of management thinking which dominated the last century, based on analytical rigour and mechanistic systems. Management writers identified the need among managers for more holistic thinking over 50 years ago, yet many business organizations show reluctance to change from their established systematic thinking. Designers are natural systems thinkers but they are educated in a manner which encourages them to resist analytical approaches and, beyond conducting basic market research, they are often intolerant of the demands research places upon them, They want to draw, model and make. In other functional areas, professionals like lawyers and accountants surround themselves in an impenetrable language partly because of the complexity but to some extent because they want to be seen as specialists and protect themselves with the language barrier.

To become a valued design strategist the designer must overcome such barriers to communicate well across functions. That means learning about business and organizations.

A new language is emerging, especially around branding, which helps business and design to converge but it needs a renaissance in education to support it.

Organizations may usefully be compared to a football team, some treat design like the substitute player who comes on only when needed and sometimes when the team is struggling. By contrast some organizations have become so excited by what design can offer, the use it like a "show boating" football player to dazzle their audiences. It is generally agreed that the quality of BBC and CNN news is high but both find it necessary to package their core offerings with imagery which uses up much of the broadcasting time.

5.8.1 Exercise the Mind...

- In relation to an organization you have worked in (or studied – select a case study), what are the principal barriers to creative thinking?
- Draw a model of the relationships between design and the other main organizational functions.
- Add to the model a statement of the main purpose of each function.
- Consider the extent to which the functions are (a) complementary (b) conflicting.
- Between design and each function add a statement of how you would seek to promote more effective collaboration.
- Evaluate the effectiveness of internal branding in your chosen company and formulate design ideas to improve it.
- As design manager, what steps would you recommend to raise design awareness in the organization and enhance cross-functional collaboration?

5.9 GLOSSARY

Cash flow forecast: is related to managing the flow of cash in an organization to optimize the use of excess cash generated and avoid the risk of not having sufficient liquidity to remain operational

Continuous learning: in organizations is the process by which people and teams continue to expand and improve their capacity to achieve added value through creativity, new thinking and methodologies and learning how to learn.

Gross revenue: the money (income) generated by all the organization's activities before deducting any expenses.

Intrinsic rewards: an intangible award of recognition (like "well done" or "thank you") for something seen as a good job or contribution leading to a feeling of satisfaction, and motivation to continue to perform well.

Kaisen: Japanese word used to mean continuous improvement in manufacturing, engineering and business.

Qualitative information: information (or basic data) based on characteristics and qualities which are not easy to measure, and may be impossible to measure,

Return on investment: a performance measure used to evaluate the efficiency (usually expressed in money terms) or allocating capital (money available) or to compare a number of alternatives options for allocation of the available money.

Silos: is a term used to denote rigid barriers between functions which inhibit cooperation.

Systems thinking is understanding how systems (e.g. social systems) interact; it is used as a problem solving tool to explore the wider context.

Turnover: generally applied to mean the money generated from sales but can also refer to staff, i.e. employee turnover.

5.10   REFERENCES AND ADDITIONAL READING

Abram, R. (2007) Why UK Designers Need an Extreme Makeover. *Design Council Magazine*, Winter (3), 46–49.

Best, K. (2010) *The Fundamentals of Design Management*. Lausanne: AVA Academic.

Borja de Mozota, B. (2003) *Design Management: Using Design to Build Brand Value and Corporate Innovation*. New York: Allworth.

Borja de Mozota, B. (2011) Design Strategic Value Revisited: A Dynamic Theory for Design as Organisational Function. In R. Cooper, S. Junginger and T. Lockwood (eds.), *The Handbook of Design Management*. Oxford: Berg, 276–293.

Bruce, M. (2002) Marketing and Design. In M. Bruce and J. Bessant (eds), *Design in Business*. Harlow: Pearson Education, 76–111.

Bruce, M. (2011) Connecting Marketing and Design. In R. Cooper, S. Junginger and T. Lockwood (eds), *The Handbook of Design Management*. Oxford: Berg, 331–346.

Bruce, M. and Bessant, J. (2002) Managing Design as a Process. In M. Bruce and J. Bessant (eds), *Design in Business*. Harlow: Pearson Education, 36–58.

Bruce M. and Cooper, R. (1997) Marketing and Design: A Working Relationship. In M. Bruce and R. Cooper (eds), *Marketing and Design Management*. London: International Thompson Business Press, 35–57.

Bruder, R. (2011) Mutual Inspiration and Learning between Management and Design. In R. Cooper, S. Junginger and T. Lockwood (eds), *The Handbook of Design Management*. Oxford: Berg, 144–160.

Business Week (2004) *Samsung Design.* [WWW] Available from: http://www.busi nessweek.com/magazine/ content/04_48/b3910003.htm [Accessed 16 April 2011]

Chung, K. and Kim, Y. J. (2011) Changes in the Roles of Designers in Strategy. In R. Cooper, S. Junginger and T. Lockwood (eds.), *The Handbook of Design Management.* Oxford: Berg, 260–275.

Cooper, R. and Junginger, S. (2011) General Introduction: Design Management – A Reflection. In R. Cooper, S. Junginger and T. Lockwood (eds.), *The Handbook of Design Management.* Oxford: Berg, 1–32.

Cooper, R. and Press, M. (1995), *The Design Agenda.* Chichester: Wiley.

Danish Design Centre (2003), *The Economic Effects of Design – The Report for the National Agency for Enterprise and Housing.* Copenhagen: Danish Design Centre.

Design Council (2007), *The Value of Design: Factfinder Report* [WWW] Available from: http://www.designcouncil.org.uk/Documents/Documents/Publications/Re search/TheValueOfDesignFactfinder_Design_Council.pdf [Accessed6 April 2013].

Design Council (2012) *Designing Demand: Executive Summary* [WWW] Available from: http://www.designcouncil.org.uk/Documents/Documents/OurWork/Design ing%20Demand/Designing%20Demand_Executive_Sumary_Final.pdf [Accessed 6 April 2013].

Department of Trade and Industry (2005) *DTI Economics Paper No. 15: Creativity, Design and Business Performance.* London: Department of Trade and Industry.

Forbes (2012), *The World Most Innovative Companies* [WWW] Available from: http://www.forbes.com/special-features/innovative-companies.html [Accessed 10 April 2013].

Francis, D. (2002) Strategy and Design. In M. Bruce and J. Bessant (eds.), *Design in Business.* Harlow: Pearson Education.

Fraser, H. (2011), *Business Design: Becoming a Bilateral Thinker.* [WWW] Available from: http://www.ideo.com/images/uploads/news/pdfs/BusinessDesign.pdf [Ac cessed 13 April 2013].

Glick, L.J. (2006) Lessons for Managing Creative Staff. *Design Management Review,* 17 (3), 73–77.

Gluck, F. W. and Kaufman, S. P. and Walleck, A. S. (1980) Strategic Management for Competitive Advantage. *Harvard Business Review,* 58 (4), 154–161.

Gorb, P. and Dumas, A. (1987) Silent Design. In M. Bruce. and R. Cooper (eds.), *Marketing and Design Management.* London: International Thompson Business Press, 159–174.

Handy, C. (1999) *The New Alchemists.* London: Hutchinson

Hansen, M. T. and Von Oetiger, B. (2001) Introducing T-shaped Managers: Knowledge Management Next Generation. *Harvard Business Review,* March, 107–116.

Harvard Business School (2003), *Harvard Business Essentials: Managing Creativity and Innovation.* Boston: Harvard Business Press

Joseph Pine II, B. and Gilmore, J. H. (1998) Welcome to the Experience Economy. *Harvard Business Review,* July–August 1998, 97–105.

Kim, W. C. and Maborgne, R. (2005), *Blue Ocean Strategy: How to Create Uncontested Market Space and Make the Competition Irrelevant.* Boston: Harvard Business School Press.

Kotler, P. and Armstorng, G. (2008), *Principles of Marketing*, 12th edn Upper Saddle River: Pearson/Prentice Hall.

Livesey, F. and Moultrie, J. (2009), *Company Spending on Design: Exploratory Survey of UK Firms 2008*. Cambridge: Institute for Manufacturing, University of Cambridge.

Lockwood, T. (2002) Design in Business Education – A Square Peg in a Round World. *Design Management Review*, 13 (3), 19–24.

MacLaverty, N., McQuillan, P. and Oddie, H. (2007), *Internal Branding Best Practices Study – The report for Canadian Marketing Association* [WWW] Available from: http://www.odditie.com/pdf/InternalBranding.pdf [Accessed 13 April 2013].

Martin, R. (2004) The Design of Business. *Rotman Management Magazine*, Winter, 7–11.

Martin, R. (2006) Designing in Hostile Territory. *Rotman Management Magazine*, Spring/Summer, 4–9.

Martin, R. (2009), *The Design of Business: Why Design Thinking Is the Next Competitive Advantage*. Boston: Harvard Business Press.

Mauzy, J. and Harriman, R. (2003) *Creative, Inc.: Building an Inventive Organisation*. Boston: Harvard Business School Press.

Moritz, S. (2005), *Service Design – Practical Access to an Evolving Field*. Cologne: Köln International School of Design.

Neumeier, M. (2008) The Designful Company. *Design Management Review*, 19 (2), 10–15.

Norman, D. A. (2004) *Emotional Design: Why we Love (or Hate) Everyday Things*. New York: Basic Books.

Oakley, M. (2011) Organising Design Activities. In R. Cooper, S. Junginger and T. Lockwood (eds.), *The Handbook of Design Management*. Oxford: Berg, 74–86.

Oliver, N. (2002) Performance Measurement and Benchmarking. In M. Bruce and J. Bessant (eds.), *Design in Business*. Harlow: Pearson Education.

Peters, T. (2003), *Re-imagine!* London: Dorling Kindersley.

Press, M. and Cooper, R. (2003) *The Design Experience: The Role of Design and Designers in the Twenty-first Century*. Aldershot: Ashgate.

Roscam Abbing, E. (2010) *Brand-driven Innovation: Strategies for Development and Design*. Lausanne: AVA Academic.

Saco, R. M. and Goncalves, A. P. (2008) Service Design: An Appraisal, *Design Management Review*, 19(1), 10–19.

Shani, A. B. and Docherty, P. (2003), *Learning by Design: Building Sustainable Organisation*. Oxford: Blackwell Publishing.

Steinhilber, S. (2008), *Strategic Alliances: Three Ways to Make Them Work (Memo to the CEO)*. Boston: Harvard Business School Press.

Stickdorn, M. and Schneider, J. (2010), *This is Service Design Thinking*. Amsterdam: BIS.

Svengren Holm, L. (2011) Design Management as Integrative Strategy. In R. Cooper, S. Junginger and T. Lockwood (eds.), *The Handbook of Design Management*. Oxford: Berg, 294–315.

Svengren Holm, L. and Johansson, U. (2005) Marketing and Design: Rivals or Partners. *Design Management Review*, 16 (2), 36–41.

Swann, P. and Birke, D. (2005), *How Do Creativity and Design Enhance Business Performance? A Framework for Interpreting the Evidence – Think Piece for DTI Strategy Unit*. Nottingham: Nottingham University Business School.

Tether, B. (2005), *Think Piece on the Role of Design in Business Performance* [WWW] Available from: http://www.bis.gov.uk/files/file14796.pdf [Accessed 9 April 2011].

Thompson, J. L. (2001), *Strategic Management,* 4th edn London: Thompson Learning.

Walker, D. (1990) Two tribes at war?. In Oakley M. (ed.) *Design Management: A Handbook of Issues and Methods*. Oxford: Blackwell.

5.11 ONLINE RESOURCES

1. Design Council – CABE: www.designcouncil.org.uk
2. Design Management Institute:www.dmi.org
3. The Department of Trade and Industry: www.dti.gov.uk

Part III

MANAGING STRATEGIC DESIGN TO DRIVE CHANGE

Design has the power to drive change at corporate level and is impacting daily on contemporary management thinking and practice. Conventional business models may lack the agility needed for survival and growth in the 21st century. In an era of rapid change, design can help to address complexity, bring clarity and find new directions in addressing business, social and environmental problems. Because it is essentially creative and pragmatic, design thinking can be used to address the big problems of our age.

Much progress has been made in exposing the power of design to support management but only the most progressive corporations and organizations have learned how to use design to drive their businesses to new levels of achievement. This section will identify many of these leaders, discuss their approach to fusing design and management thinking and practice and show the challenges they face.

Society is evolving new values, demanding that all organizations behave responsibly and are seen to add value beyond returns for investors. New forms of business are emerging, driven by the demands for social and environmental contributions and accelerated by the digital age.

All modern organizations are now expected to add value, not just commercial and economic value but demonstrable social and environmental value. Our networked and interactive world means that organizations must learn to respond and adapt quickly to collective opinions among their stakeholders. They are now obliged to behave responsibly and do good deeds. Networks can make and break organizations, brands and even governments.

Public sector organizations are using design for planning and developing new approaches to such areas as transport, education and health. Charities use design to differentiate, communicate powerfully, motivate and inspire commitment. For design management strategists there are many complex challenges and no lack of fertile areas for the improvement of the human condition.

Design thinking and its influence on strategy, organizational cultures and forms may be regarded as the most powerful driving force for change in organizational behaviour and practice.

Chapter 6
DESIGN–DRIVEN ORGANIZATIONS

Design has the capacity to drive organizations and to find new opportunities and directions. Chapters 3 and 4 showed design taking a more prominent role in building better brand experiences and driving innovation. In Chapter 5 the means of integrating design into the organization was discussed. Whilst relatively few organizations have developed the confidence to use design strategically, a few very well-known ones are establishing leading positions and powerful brands through their advanced use of design. They may be correctly termed "design-driven organizations."

Traditional business management models fail to recognize design as a significant resource but contemporary progressive models show the power of design to drive innovation, create value and redefine the world around us. For more than one century, organizations have been primarily driven by a strong focus on management control and economic considerations. Later the importance of listening to customers and building markets became paramount. Then came the battle for technological supremacy. Amidst all of these models, designers have been quietly turning ideas into real experiences and trying to deliver life-changing enhancements, largely unnoticed.

Organizations must seek new ideas for survival and sustainability. Design can lead the response to new challenges like social responsibility, improving wellbeing and generating greater understanding and alternative choices about our environment and how we communicate. Business managers must identify the common goals and characteristics of core business and design elements. They need design to position the business as essentially "good," that is, responsible and caring about their place and role in making a better world.

A design-driven business model needs "design thinking" at the heart of management. The benefits to be derived from changing the mindset and developing the confidence to integrate design into mainstream business models are explained throughout the chapter, together with many examples of organizations which encompass design in this manner.

Objectives for this chapter:

- To demonstrate the potential of design to drive business.
- To show the relationship of core business elements to design.

- To explain the power of design to generate new ideas and drive value.
- To identify how design can help make a business "good."
- To evaluate how design can address global issues.
- To show how design can contribute to sustainable futures.
- To examine the role of design in online business.
- To explain how design can be used to deal with the ageing population.
- To show the potential of integrated design/business to improve performance.

6.1 DESIGN AS A DRIVER FOR ORGANIZATIONAL SUCCESS

The world famous management guru Tom Peters was one of the first to acknowledge design as having the potential to transform organizations. Over the past three decades design has made great progress as an agent of change. However, many organizations still treat design passively, using it as a function to serve identified needs. It is difficult to identify the point at which an organization can be deemed design driven, but the influence is shifting from passive to active. Leading business management pioneers continue to promote the power of design and there are many leading organizations proud to claim they are led by design thinking, such as IDEO and Philips, all of which treat design as a core competency.

It can be seen that all business activities are inextricably linked to design as the function which brings the business to the real world. Borja de Mozota (2003) identified a number of triggers which instigate demand for design, which are expanded as follows:

- *To start a new company or subsidiary:* product/service development, logo, visual identity, brand image (independent or under holding company).
- *To increase market share:* design-led product/service innovation, promotion materials, new packaging, and attractive retail environments.
- *To launch a new product or store:* New concepts and NPD process.
- *To develop a brand:* Brand naming, graphic design and design of all brand touchpoints: designing the brand experience.
- *To rebrand a company:* Consistent redesigning of corporate logo, all environments, livery, web sites and packaging.
- *To regain a market share:* Product/service enhancements, promotional aids.
- *To diversify into a new market:* New product/service design and/or brand extension promotion.
- *To make R&D policy more effective:* Ideation, new concepts based on user needs and trends.

Stanford University (2010) argue that "great innovators and leaders need to be great design thinkers". They established a "d.school" as a hub for multidisciplinary practitioners of design thinking to work together to solve big problems in a human-centred way. This is founded on their belief that all problems, however complex, are amenable to design thinking and this forms the basis for the solution strategy (see the example in Chapter 5, section 5.2).

At the strategic level design can influence the whole organization, transform the value chain and the industry vision (Hetzel, 1993 cited in Borja de Mozota, 2003). In other words, design can change the way a company "sees" its business, the nature and scope of the market environment and competitive strategy. One good example is Dyson, who used design to challenge established practices and became a leading company within their industry sector. Verganti's research (2008) supports this through studies of leading Italian organizations such as Alessi and Kartell, demonstrating that design can be used to create visions and build unbeatable and sustainable competitive advantages.

6.2   CONVENTIONAL & EMERGING BUSINESS MODELS

The purpose of a business model is to show the rationale for how the organization creates, delivers and captures value in economic, social, cultural and other contexts.

Conventional frameworks/models tend to identify the core elements of a business model but do not demonstrate their relationships. Emerging models show similar elements but are generally perceived as a closed loop, self-sustaining and self-reinforcing ecosystem. For example, Casadesus-Masanell and Ricart (2011) suggested that a company needs to create a "virtuous cycle" and make good strategic choices which lead to favourable consequences and enable further positive choices. Choices in terms of pricing strategies could affect the sales volume, market growth and rate of return on investment. Choices of innovation may influence in-house technological developments, manufacturing processes, technical services and distribution channels. They noted that when it comes to creating a business model, a company have to make strategic choices as follows:

- *Policy choices* – help guide a company's actions across the board, such as incentives and promotions, locations of factory and criteria for recruitment.
- *Asset choices* – directly related to tangible resources, such as facilities, information systems, factories and machines and retail shops. This type of strategic choice will shape how a company can acquire, develop and deploy tangible assets.
- *Governance choices* – guide a company's decision making regarding management issues, e.g. should we have in-house designers or outsource design work?

The main point to bear in mind is that every choice has consequences which can be broadly grouped into two categories: flexible or rigid. Casadesus-Masanell and Ricart explained that a flexible consequence is one that responds quickly when the underlying choice changes. For instance, deciding to lower prices could increase sales volume in a short period of time. By contrast, some strategic choices cause consequences that are difficult to change even though the underlying choices have changed. For example, Toyota had been successful in delivering affordable mass-produced cars for a number of years. It takes a while to change people's perceptions that Toyota can actually deliver cutting-edge technologies and produce truly luxury cars. Seemingly however, even rigid consequences can be changed, as Toyota has proven, but a large amount of effort is required. Since developing a business model is about choosing appropriate strategic choices, the authors proposed three questions for assessing its effectiveness: (1) Is it aligned with the company goals? (2) Is it self-reinforcing? (3) Is it robust? These questions will be developed later in the chapter.

6.2.1 Conventional Business Models

Many business models were developed by researchers and practitioners over the last century and for convenience of distinction are broadly divided into "conventional" models and "emerging" models. The discussion of conventional and emerging innovation models in Chapter 4 (Sections 4.2.1 and 4.2.2) may be said to reflect the same paradigm. The first branding models were also predominantly built on the foundation of conventional business models and thus failed to incorporate design (see Chapter 3, Section 3.2.1).

Conventional models were based on the earlier schools of management thinking, the classical school, scientific management, human relations school and systems approach. Most pre-date the emergence of design as a recognized resource and thus make no reference to design and/or design strategy. Many such models continue to exclude design. It may also be noted that whilst management writers and researchers frequently refer to "designing" the business model, they fail to acknowledge the role of design, in particular for creating wealth.

One such definition of a business model was provided by Joan Magretta (cited in Casadesus-Masanell and Ricart, 2011) as "a story that explains how an enterprise works." Elements of what constitutes a successful business model were identified by Johnson, Christensen and Kagermann (2008) as: creating a customer value proposition, designing a profit formula and identifying key process and resources. Their business model comprises four main components:

1. *Customer value proposition*: Establishing the market needs, target customer, jobs to be done (to meet their needs) and offerings – both what is to be sold and how.
2. *Profit formula*: Calculating the cash flow generated, and the costs and sales volume required to be profitable.
3. *Key processes*: Setting up the procedures, rules, metrics and norms which make the profitable delivery of the customer value proposition repeatable and scalable.
4. *Key resources*: The principal resources needed to deliver the customer value proposition profitably, including money, people, technology, equipment and knowledge.

In summing up his chronicle of The Management Century (i.e., 20th century) Crainer (2000) writes "managers find themselves in the uncomfortable and discomforting world of chaos and complexity theory ... uncertainty and ambiguity are the new realities." Thus, all new business models need to deal with complexity and generate many questions amid new forms of organization. These models may benefit from using design thinking to envision future scenarios and enhance agility.

6.2.2 Emerging Business Models

Osterwalder and Pigneur (2010) offered a valuable contemporary definition of a business model: "the rationale of how an organization creates, delivers, and captures value." The authors identified nine building blocks of a business model as shown below:

1. *Customer segment*: It is recommended that the planning start with the identification of target groups. An organization must be clear which groups it wants to serve. Choosing the right target groups is a challenging task. The groups must be big enough to justify the business. They must stay attractive for a number of years. It will be even better if there are not many competitors targeting these particular groups. It is important to decide whether to go for a mass or niche market. Then, a company can start exploring the needs, wants, expectations and aspirations of these groups. Design, especially design research, can help management study and evaluate potential targets before making a final decision.
2. *Value propositions*: The next step is to come up with ideas on how to fulfil needs, wants and dreams of chosen targets. The value propositions are reasons why target groups chose our company and not competitors. Hence, these values must be unique, meaningful and not easy to copy. A number of values were identified, e.g. newness, more superior performance, customization, brand/status and quality of design. Indeed design can be used to make a difference in all these values by improving functionality, reducing production costs, as well as making the appearance more appealing.
3. *Channels*: There is no point in coming up with good ideas unless a company has means to communicate with and reach target audiences. Therefore, this building block is about planning suitable channels to raise awareness about a brand and offerings, persuade target groups to give a product/service a try and deliver the values that a company has promised. Identifying an appropriate mix of channels can be challenging especially in the era where people obtain information from various sources and often jump from one channel to another. Good use of design, especially experience design, can ensure that all channels and/or touchpoints convey coherent messages and deliver superior experience.
4. *Customer relationships*: This is about planning what types of relationships a company would like to establish with target customers. Some relationships are more intimate than others. While some companies aim to create communities and get people involved in designing products/services in order to serve them even better, some organizations are about enabling people to take charge and providing automated services. Taking a Eurostar train, for example, is different from boarding an underground tube – corporate objectives are different and, of course, customer

relationships are different. Flying Singapore Airlines is not same as flying EasyJet! But they all need design, especially interaction design, to establish desirable relationships.

5. *Revenue streams*: A business cannot sustain and/or grow without revenue streams. Thus, after planning what values it wants to offer and how it would like to deliver them, it is important to plan how to obtain income streams to support your business. Even not-for-profit organizations (NPOs) need to think about revenue streams. They cannot just think about people whom they would like to help and how to help them. They have to plan how to sustain their organizations so that they can continue to deliver valuable services to disadvantaged people in our society. Creative/design thinking is required to explore all options available to an organization. See the Natural History Museum as an example – its main purpose is about education, but having a beautiful building in Central London means it can make money through venue hiring.

6. *Key resources*: After planning what the organization would like to happen, the next step is thinking how to make it happen. Thus, a company needs to identify key resources to make the business model work. In this case, key resources cover all kinds of assets – ranging from physical assets, such as factories, machines, offices and retail shops, to intellectual ones, e.g. knowledge, customer databases and brand values. Design can help a company unlock the potential of its assets, for example by developing applications based on existing patents.

7. *Key activities*: Similar to the previous building block, but this one goes on to cover all activities required to make the business model work and deliver value propositions. In this case, key activities include all kinds of actions – ranging from those directly related to value creation and delivery, such as design, engineering, marketing and production, to supporting activities, e.g. finance and customer services. Design, especially design thinking can support many of these activities and make them more effective.

8. *Key partnerships*: No man is an island and thus a business cannot be isolated, especially in this era. Strategic partnerships are crucial to deliver values in an exceptional, yet effective way. Good partnerships could help reduce risks, minimize costs, enhance efficiency, e.g. through economies of scale, and make offerings more complete. Partnerships can range from a supplier–buyer relationship to co-branding. Good use of design thinking can help promote a synergy effect (whereby $1 + 1 = 3$ or more). Most successful strategic alliances emphasize the need for trust, transparency, mutual benefits and clear ground rules for collaboration.

9. *Cost structure*: The last building block is about planning all elements related to costs. In this case, all kinds of costs must be taken into consideration, e.g. fixed costs – costs that stay the same despite the change in volume of products produced, e.g. staff salaries and office rent, and variable costs – costs that vary according to the volume of goods produced, e.g. energy consumption and raw materials. Design, especially small-d design can help increase values while reducing costs – see IKEA for an example. In order to deliver its promise, stylish furniture at an affordable

Table 6.1   Relationships between design and the effectiveness of a business model

Criteria for assessing business model	Design contributions to addressing these questions
Is it aligned with the company goals?	Design can envision new possibilities, new horizons and deliver new value-added experiences
Is it self-reinforcing?	Design can build sustainable virtuous cycles
Is it robust?	Design can lead the race for success through competitiveness and self-learning

Note: questions posed by Johnson, Christensen and Kagermann (2008).

price, IKEA carefully plans its cost structure. Activities that lead to serious cost implications (e.g. assembling and distribution) have largely been eliminated, many through clever designs. For example, designing flat-pack furniture helps save space during transportation and allows customers to carry it home and assemble it by themselves. In fact, IKEA starts each product development process by deciding on the price that customers are willing to pay and works backwards to achieve the desirable outcomes at the right costs.

Whilst design rarely gets a mention in conventional business models, both Big-D and small-d design can contribute much to the value proposition, the creation of key creative resources, building good customer relationships and the processes to support them. Borja de Mozota (2003) identified ways to embrace design into business models as follows:

- *The innate model*: where design is treated as a core competency due to the founder's design appreciation and/or visions, such as Habitat, Braun and Hermann Miller.
- *The experience model*: where design is acquired or learned through experience – examples include Philips, Sony and Samsung.

The influence of design on business models reflects the level of confidence of an organization to integrate design into the management decision-making process. Design thinking always generates new ideas and possible directions and thus constantly challenges the status quo. Thus, the degree of design management influence may be directly linked to the emotional maturity of the organization or its willingness to learn and self-reflect. Design thinking can help management to answer the key questions posed by Johnson, Christensen and Kagermann (2008), see Table 6.1.

6.3   IMPLICATIONS OF NEW OPPORTUNITIES AND CHALLENGES

Leaving behind the era of industrial and knowledge economies presents opportunities and challenges for design to contribute to the new conceptual economy lead by ideas. Organizations need to use design to stand out in an age of abundance, where cheap products from cheap labour locations flood

202

Table 6.2   Key questions and essential senses

Key questions
- *What can I offer that can create a demand when seemingly people have everything they need?*
- *If I identify a new opportunity can my competitors offer it at lower cost? In recent years it has become customary to expect Chinese manufacturers to copy and manufacture cheaper alternatives.*
- *Can technology make the product or deliver the service faster?*

Utilizing design senses
- *Design*: Moving beyond function to engage human senses and emotions
- *Story*: The offer is the story behind the products and services
- *Symphony*: Holistic thinking to add richness, harmony and inspiration
- *Empathy*: Maintaining simplicity but going further to engage intuition
- *Play*: Bringing out fun and playfulness in business, products and services
- *Meaning*: Making explicit the underlying meanings behind products and/or services

Source: Adapted from Pink (2006).

Table 6.3   Implications of emerging expectations

	New expectations	Implications for businesses
Social	Social responsibility	Delivering products/services that are good for brand(s) and society.
	Ethical consumption	Offering ethical products without passing additional costs to users.
	Transparency	Making sure that your business conducts transparent and enhancing two-way dialogues between the organization and customers.
	Democratization	Designing products/services "with" people instead of "for" people.
	Sustainability	Ensuring sustainability in both environmental and commercial senses.
	Inclusive design	Designing for all ages and abilities, and including non-mainstream users.
Technological	Open source	Promoting "collective" developments and ideas.
	Open innovation	Making good uses of internal and external ideas and research.
	Open design	Helping people design and produce products by themselves.
	Social networking	Taking advantages of emerging social networking tools to build/maintain strong relationships with customers.
	Digital economy	Exploiting new possibilities provided by the digital and ICT technologies.
	E-business	Utilizing electronic business platforms to reach new markets, find new partners and enhance effectiveness.

the world's markets. Businesses are encouraged to assess their core values by asking certain fundamental questions as proposed by Pink (2006) and embracing six essential senses as updated in Table 6.2.

People are demanding more of organizations than the delivery of products and services. They expect organizations to behave responsibly and to be essentially "good." Thus, using only small-d design may deliver quality products and services but it is no longer enough. Big-D design must be used to engage with these new expectations and push the boundaries. Some of the expectations and implications can be seen in Table 6.3.

Design can provide solutions to most, if not all of the challenges in Table 6.3.

Integration of design into all organizational activities can help to embrace new possibilities, the imperative for survival. This will certainly lead to the need for significant restructuring and cultural change in businesses and other organizations. Challenges for design integration can be identified and considered by building a matrix with management functions listed in the vertical column and major design roles listed across the horizontal. In this way it is possible to see the relationship of each business activity to the design endeavours.

Borja de Mozota (2003) proposed such a matrix with CEO, management, corporate communications, R&D and production and marketing in the vertical column, and sustainable design, inclusive design, social responsibility and digital/interaction design in the horizontal. The matrix can be adapted to reflect the main business and design functions and can be used as a strategic tool by entering the relationship at the intersections. It can be a useful starting point to assess the level and effectiveness of the integration.

6.3.1 Emerging Global Issues

Designers tend to be altruistic and the opportunities for design to "make a difference" in addressing world economic and social problems is now a reality. Currently the global financial crisis indicates that demand from developed countries will remain weak whilst developing economies will offer the greatest opportunities (Ghemawat, 2010). He proposes five new strategic directions for business which will generate new design opportunities.

The first relates to strategy and competition where he advises adapting to local conditions, investing more selectively and watching out for emergence of competitors. Design can support this by identifying user requirements and often latent needs and tailoring product and service offers to meet them.

The second key strategy concerns markets and products and suggests seeking underserved segments, i.e. neglected opportunities, recognition of price pressures (where others can undercut the price) and the cultivation of requisite variety, which means meeting the complex needs of human beings with a rich variety of meaningful offers. Such a challenge is natural to designers who consider it their duty to add value, fulfil users' needs and frequently find solutions to reducing costs.

The third key area for the strategic attention of management is operations and innovations. Here the author advises rethinking the scope of offshoring, principally outsourcing manufacture, simplifying supply chains, importing process innovations from emerging economies and moving R&D closer to where the organization's researchers and growth markets are located. Design thinking can be used to simplify and make robust supply chains and attention to design for manufacture and disassembly can improve processes.

The next issue concerns organization and people and recommends the re-creation of country manager functions, relocation of key functions, the development of a globally representative talent pool, and the exploitation of communication technologies. It may be noted that the large Korean corporations Samsung and LG are currently taking such steps and introducing foreign nationals into their design teams. Design thinking can be used to attract the most talented people, bring clarity to the organizational structure and promote cross-cultural learning and collaboration.

The final key strategic area is identity and reputation and calls for the building of a strong corporate identity, emphasis on corporate citizenship and the restoration of the reputation of business in general. Design can demonstrably help build the business reputation through winning products/services and compelling messages. Raising the reputation of business in general is a more demanding issue and design can play its part in helping businesses to be ethical, responsible and caring, all qualities which are demanded of the modern business.

Left-brain and right-brain thinkers are needed to respond to turbulent times and Rigby, Gruver and Allen (2009) show they are the key requirements for success. Former USA President Bill Clinton (2009) urges business to rethink their value creation strategy by doing "good," investing in socially responsible and sustainable developments. An example of a successful response strategy is Virgin Atlantic Airlines. The company responded to the economic downturn caused by the 9/11 terrorist attack by investing more in design and innovation, effectively designing their way out of a crisis. Organizations must be acutely aware of emerging global issues and their implications for businesses and learn to apply strategic design management to address the challenges.

6.3.2 Ethics and Social Responsibility

Organizations were generally slow to identify the advantages of being seen to be socially responsible. First they needed to be coerced by the force of law and showed reluctance to invest more than the minimum effort or money to comply. Even now there are many examples around the world of organizations who do not think it wrong to pollute or take risks with human life and wellbeing. But whilst there is a long way to go, over the last decade most progressive organizations have come to regard corporate social responsibility (CSR) as an essential element of their strategy and many have learned how to use it for competitive advantage and reputation (and thus brand) enhancement.

CSR is a self-regulation mechanism whereby businesses identify their impacts on society and ensure that they comply with social standards, e.g. human rights and fair trade (Collings, 2010). CSR is increasingly regarded as a crucial aspect of economic competitiveness as it can encourage product uptake on aspects beyond functionality and price sensitivity. Olins (2001), a brand guru, stated that "the next big thing in brands is CSR ... it will be clever to say there is nothing different about our product or service, but we do behave well." Design has the potential to be a critical aspect of CSR, broadening activities from corporate sponsorship and certification to the incorporation of CSR principles throughout product development.

There is evidence to suggest that businesses are responding to CSR imperatives. The majority of the FTSE100 and two-thirds of the FTSE's Global 100 now produce CSR reports (Rare Corporate, 2011). Nevertheless, most of these reports present a narrow view of CSR. Senior management appears to often associate CSR practices solely with Fairtrade or additional social activities. Supporting charities and governmental initiatives alone are insufficient for the delivery of significant social impacts. To accelerate the effects, Bill Gates urges companies to align business interests (profits) with wider interests, such as global issues (Bill and Melinda Gates Foundation, 2008). His *Creative Capitalism* idea suggests that CSR practices could be integrated in every business activity. Research conducted a decade ago revealed that 83% of consumers intend to behave ethically but only 18% were doing so, principally because they chose the cheaper price (Doane, 2003). The consumers were reluctant to change their habits. Thus, designers must address many behavioural and economic issues if they are to support ethical business.

Nowadays, consumers have become more socially and environmentally conscious. A rapid increase in services providing information about environmental and social performance of products and companies, e.g. GoodGuide (www.goodguide.com), demonstrate growing demands for reliable data regarding social impacts of products/services. The popular perception that buying ethical products is a more effective way of tackling global poverty than giving to charity shows that there are commercial benefits in ensuring sufficient social values in product offerings (*The Times*, 2008). Nevertheless, consumers will not purchase products/services simply because they are branded as "ethical." People demand good functionality, attractive appearance, intuitive interaction and reasonable price, and now honesty.

In relation to developing design-led brands which embrace social responsibility, Hilton (2003) proposed a framework entitled *Seven Social Wins of Brand* to help a firm move towards ethical and social practices. This framework includes seven steps as shown below.

1. *Wealth creation*: At the very least, a company should create jobs and wealth for surrounding communities where it operates. The first step toward becoming a socially responsible organization is being a good employer – help employees develop themselves further and be the best they can be! Customers nowadays do care about the way a company treats its workers. As a result, numerous good governance ranking sites appears all over the Internet. Big-D and small-d design can be used to support local developments and develop skills of the workforce on an

on-going basis. For example, good use of small-d design can ensure that a product can be produced using local materials.

2. *Consumer protection*: The second step is about protecting consumers by enforcing and raising standards in terms of products/services. A good example in this category is Volvo. The company's goal, "being the safest on the road," has driven the safety standard of the industry. The modern three-point safety belt was invented and patented by Volvo engineers. To ensure that all vehicles are safe, Volvo allows other companies to use their invention. The example shows how good use of small-d designs can help achieve this CSR goal.

3. *Product and service leadership:* To raise the standard even further, a company should aim to be a leader and deliver innovations with direct identifiable social impacts. A good contemporary example in this category is Patagonia Clothing. The firm is keen to promote fair labour practices and sustainable design. Fair labour policy is employed throughout the supplier chains and all products embrace sustainable design principles, e.g. reduce, repair, reuse and recycle. To showcase its good practices, the company has a *Footprint Chronicles* section on its web site where people can track the carbon footprint of its products. This example demonstrates that both Big-D and small-d designs are used to achieve their CSR targets set by the management.

4. *Corporate social responsibility*: The next step is about embracing the corporate social responsibility principles in the way a company runs its business. Some experts criticize this practice as being rather reactive, since a company simply responds to the public demands regarding social conduct. For instance, Nike was seriously criticized in the past due to its poor conduct, e.g. using child labour. The company has been working hard to overcome this image, e.g. launching a socially and environmentally conscious sub-brand, called Nike Considered, and showcasing its sustainable practices through its Nike Environmental Design Tool. But since damage has already been done, it is hard to change people's perceptions entirely.

5. *Corporate social leadership*: Many experts argue that rather than reacting to the demands, it is better to be proactive and act responsibly from the start. Companies, such as The Body Shop, LUSH and People Tree Clothing, are good examples in this category. These examples also exemplify how Big-D thinking and small-d designs are used well.

6. *Social change*: Apart from applying corporate social responsibility principles within an organization, a company can support other organizations, e.g. enabling charities, non-governmental organizations (NGOs) and multilateral institutions to accomplish their social goals. Good collaboration between global brands and not-for-profit organizations can lead to mutual benefits. However, Big-D design is needed to make the relation work and overcome sceptical views.

7. *Social cohesion*: The final step of this framework is the suggestion that a company should seek to become a social unifier, e.g. Dove's campaign for real beauty, which celebrates body diversity and Coca-Cola's campaign

I'd Like to Teach the World to Sing (in Perfect Harmony) in the 1970s, which aimed to promote social cohesion among different races and cultures. The power of the brand and Big-D design can help raise awareness of and tackle serious social issues, like poverty and economic inequality.

To evaluate how well the organization is performing and the role of design, a checklist can be developed which should include such questions as:

1. Behaves responsibly towards employees and external partners?
2. Delivers high standard products and/or services?
3. Offers innovations with direct positive social impacts?
4. Complies with CSR law?
5. Works towards raising CSR standards?
6. Uses CSR to enhance performance and brand?
7. Cooperates with others to achieve positive changes?
8. Campaigns actively for social change?

With its established power of creative thinking and envisioning, strategic design management can lead the way to finding new opportunities to become an acknowledged leader in social change and deliver a credible message about the "caring" character of the organization.

Example: Ecover

Ecover was established 30 years ago. The brand offers all kinds of cleaning products ranging from hand soaps to bathroom cleaners. The company aims to offer "a washing and cleaning product that is efficient and truly ecological." The commitment to sustainability is evident in everything. Products are made from plant-based ingredients. It uses as little material for packaging as possible. Moreover, all packaging can be reused and recycled. Even the printing process is environmentally friendly. It recently launched the Refill System which allows people to refill the bottles up to 50 times. Ecover is a good example of CSR because the company helps raise the standard in its field. The firm works with the European Union to establish a certification scheme in order to raise environmental standards worldwide. Strategic design is integrated in all parts of the business – strong brand identity and brand communication, sustainable packaging design, etc.

6.3.3 Sustainability

The area of sustainability is complicated by myriad definitions and different national, industry and academic approaches. Therefore designers need to establish clearly what design for sustainability means for their purpose. Often sustainability in design is expressed as design for the environment and Roy (2006) summarized the key concepts as:

- *Green design*: An approach that reduces environmental impact but limited by focussing on one or two environmental objectives, e.g. conserving materials and energy by manufacturing with recycled materials or increasing energy efficiency.

- *Eco-design*: An approach that reduces total environmental impact by considering a product's impact over its life cycle (cradle to grave).
- *Sustainable design*: A radical approach for reducing environmental impacts by using an alternative technical method to carry out the product's essential function. Often includes social and economic as well as environmental impacts. A good example is the disruptive innovation in the music industry. Allowing people to download music files instead of buying CDs can help reduce environmental impacts, e.g. reducing materials, waste and energy used during production and transportation. At the same time, it brings a lot of benefits for consumers, like increasing flexibility, personalization and convenience. Moreover, it helps independent artists raise their profiles and sell their music.

Following green design and eco-design concepts, there are many opportunities for designers to reduce environmental impacts throughout the entire product life cycle, see examples provided by the Sustainable Design Awards Online (www.sda-uk.org) in Table 6.4.

However, many experts have urged designers and companies to go beyond green design and eco-design, and adopt sustainable design practices, but in some cases simply trying to use more recycled or recyclable materials could do more harm than good. Possible consequences of design choices must be thoroughly examined. Holistic thinking is required to address the inherent complexity in terms of environmental impacts.

Table 6.4 Different approaches of design for environment

Step	Design choices
Concept	De-materialization, increase shared use, provide a service
Physical optimization	Integrate functions, optimize functions, increase reliability and durability, easy maintenance and repair, design for modularity, promote product–user relationships
Material selection	Cleaner materials, renewable materials, low energy content materials, recycled materials, recyclable materials, reduce material use
Optimize production	Choose alternate production processes, fewer production steps, lower/cleaner production energy consumption, less production waste, fewer/cleaner production consumables
Optimize distribution	Less/cleaner/reusable packaging, energy efficient transport mode, energy efficient logistics
Product use	Lower energy consumption, cleaner energy sources, reduce consumables, cleaner consumables, reduce consumable waste
End of life	Reuse of product, re-manufacturing, refurbishment of product, recycling of materials, safer incineration, design for disassembly

White, Belletire and St Pierre (2007) pointed out the possible negative consequences of design choices which are further extended as follows:

• Using recycled materials	→	Quality may be compromised and consumers may perceive the product as inferior but possibly more expensive.
• Lowering energy consumption	→	Higher development costs to achieve savings and loss of jobs for workers in traditional power supply companies.
• Product/service life cycle extension	→	Risk of competitors launching new superior products/services or enhancements of existing products/services first.
• Design for ease of disassembly	→	Higher development and production costs, new machinery and training programmes.
• Biodegradability	→	May reduce life and risk disaffected users if product degrades too soon.
• Local production to support local economy	→	Limited by availability of local skills and aptitudes, possible high cost of training.
• Renting/leasing rather than owning	→	Constraints on usage and possible extra transport and insurance costs.
• Reducing quantity of materials used	→	Lighter may equate to perceived inferiority, tendency to discard and shorter life.
• Excessive attention to green marketing	→	Over hyping of green credentials may be perceived as lacking robustness.

By adopting sustainable design principles, opportunities for designers to make contributions to environmental impacts can be more profound, since they could change the way values are delivered to consumers entirely – seven strategic options are shown in Table 6.5. The findings of White, Belletire, and St Pierre (2007) provide the foundation for this table adapted to address how design can help to achieve the objectives.

Many companies may think that embracing sustainable design principles means high costs and complex product development processes. Good use of sustainable design can improve business performance and margins. The World Business Council for Sustainable Development (WBCSD) proposed a management philosophy called *Eco-Efficiency*, which encourages business to search for environmental improvements that yield parallel economic benefits. For example, simple design can reduce the number of production processes, energy consumption and environmental impacts, while

Table 6.5 Sustainable design strategic options

Strategic options	How to achieve	Examples
Sustainable innovation	• By using nature and living organisms ethically to generate ideas and develop new products and services. • Focussing on inclusive user needs and their changing attitudes to responsibility for environment. • Design for future enhancements allowing for modifications and/or additional features as R&D provides know-how. • Design the product and the service contemporaneously.	Soundbug, a small device that can turn nearly any flat surface into a sound board using a clever design to deliver the same value as big Hi-Fi systems.
Low-impact on the environment materials	• Use minimal quantities of materials proven to have high safety and low environmental impact and sourced from renewable resources. • Design using waste by-products and recycled materials whilst maintaining quality and robustness.	Invotek's strawboard uses good product design to transform agricultural waste to produce an attractive and functional product.
Optimize manufacturing and production	• Design with full consideration of manufacturing, production and quality control. • Simplify components and processes. • Design for lowest possible energy consumption and reduced waste.	MUJI's flat-packed cardboard speakers use good product design to reduce product parts and simplify the manufacturing process.
Efficient distribution	• Design distribution system to reduce delivery costs by manufacturing and/or assembling products close to market. • Reduce product and packaging weight and design shape to use maximum carrying space. • Use transport systems which seek sustainability but operate reliably.	Foo Go's biodegradable packaging use plant-based materials for packaging.
Low-impact use	• Design using cleaner, renewable and efficient energy sources. • Minimize use of water.	The Eastgate Centre, Zimbabwe uses smart architectural design to reduce energy required to function the building.

Continued

Table 6.5 Continued

Strategic options	How to achieve	Examples
Extend product lifetime	• Design for timeless looks which transcend fashion. • Design and manufacture for durability plus ease of repair and enhanced additions: and final disassembly. • Design for extended life with new or different functions.	Philips and Alessi's kitchen appliance range explores how to achieve a timeless classic design to prolong product lifespan.
End of life	• Design safe disposal and/ or reuse/recycling methods including collection and disassembly.	Kodak's recycling programme uses systems design to increase the number of parts that can be reused in new cameras (77% to 90% by weight).

Source: Adapted from White, Belletire, and St Pierre (2007).

concurrently reducing production costs and speeding up the process. The philosophy consists of three broad objectives:

- *Reducing consumption of resources*: Minimizing the use of energy, materials, water and land, enhancing recyclability and product durability, and closing material loops.
- *Reducing impact on nature*: Minimizing air emissions, water discharges, waste disposal and the dispersion of toxic substances, and fostering the sustainable use of renewable resources.
- *Increasing product or service value*: Providing more benefits to customers through product functionality, flexibility and modularity, providing additional services and focusing on selling the functional needs that customers actually want. Thus the customer can get the same functional need with fewer materials and less resources.

WBCSD also suggested seven elements for Eco-Efficiency improvement. First reduce material intensity by using less material. Second reduce energy consumption. Next avoid toxic substances. Enhancing recyclability, maximizes the use of renewables (such as reusing agricultural waste), extending the product lifespan and switching to service delivery.

Producing a product requires a lot of materials and energy. Delivering a service only needs thoughtful human interactions. For example, in order to help a person gets from A to B a company does not need to sell him/her a car. In fact, it could offer a car hire service instead. In this way, the value proposition is even better, since the customer does not have to worry about maintenance, road tax, parking and so forth.

Solutions driven solely by technology are often found to exacerbate sustainability problems, but strategic design management can play a major role in all related issues by stimulating the debate about designing environmental benefits and applying creative thinking to lead the manner in which technology is used.

Example: Masdar City

Masdar City in the United Arab Emirates is designed to be the world most sustainable city. It is positioned as a new hub for sustainable development where current and future renewable energy and clean technologies are showcased, marketed, researched, developed, tested and implemented. The city sets a great example of sustainable urban development, as it aims to deliver the "highest quality living and working environment with the lowest possible ecological footprint." Its iconic buildings are both functional and aesthetically pleasing. For example, "solar umbrellas," which are inspired by flowers, open up during the day and close up at night in order to regulate the temperature. Other clever sustainable design features include adaptive building facades that can adjust and angle themselves to receive more or less sun, and wall surface materials that respond to changing temperatures and contain minimal embedded energy. For more information: www.masdarcity.ae

6.3.4 E-businesses and Digital Economy

In his book *Being Digital*, Negroponte (1995) predicted that the digital age would be about decentralizing, globalizing, harmonizing and empowering. It seems he was right. The digital age has created an entire new set of driving forces for industry, government and society. Business models, now often emulated by social organizations previously resistant to business practices, are responding to the challenges and opportunities presented. Experts point to five main revenue streams for e-business:(1) connection – providing connection to the internet, e.g. BT Broadband; (2) commercial – obtaining revenue from advertisers, e.g. Google; (3) commerce – providing services or selling products, e.g. Amazon; (4) content – gaining revenue from the content, e.g. online database; (5) community – obtaining revenues from membership fees, e.g. online dating sites.

Online business is free of geographical and time-zone restrictions and offers ease of transactions in terms of speed and cost. It also significantly reduces the costs of physical resources and staff. However the principal challenge in designing such systems is trust. Traditionally trust was built on human face-to-face interaction and the building of relationships based on reliable experiences. The real challenge for design is how to build trust into the experience. Long (2004) developed a hierarchy of customer (online) experience based on Maslow's hierarchy of needs and argues that online trust needs to be continually reinforced. He explains the four levels in the hierarchy of online experience as:

- **Level 1: *Trust*** – *Does this company/web site look like something I can trust?* Think of an online presence, e.g. web site or Facebook page, as a person. We first judge a person by the way he/she looks. If he/she looks fine, then we are willing to hear what he/she has to say. If what he/she says makes sense, then we are prepared to continue our dialogues with this person. Little by little, we begin to have trust with the person. We apply the same logic to judge a web presence, if it looks trustworthy, then we are willing to spend time on it. Thus, appearance is very important. Small companies can look like global brands on the internet. Clever strategic design could help create a professional image without big investments. However, once people are prepared to spend time with any online touchpoint, it must not let users down. To create trust, the whole experience must be intuitive, functional and enjoyable. Hence, another key consideration for design is functionality. Planning for trust requires Big-D thinking and integrated business and design strategy, then small-d design can be used to help a company build trust and reinforce it.

- **Level 2:** *Competence – Do I feel competent? Does a company look competent?* Everything that we love doing tends to make us feel comfortable. If we do not feel like we know what we are doing, we might as well stop doing it! Therefore, it is crucial that every online touchpoint is designed in the way that users can interact with it and achieve what they want without investing too much time learning about the site, functions, systems, etc. Again good use of small-d design can help create logical information architecture and enhance the usability. At this level, extrinsic motivation is the key. This kind of motivation comes from the "results" of the interaction, e.g. transferring money safely and easily. A good example is Amazon.com which offers a logical purchasing process starting from browsing products and comparing prices, right through to tracing when the order will arrive. The whole process is transparent and easy to use.

- **Level 3:** *Autonomous – Do I feel in control?* (*Freedom, control and mastery.*) The next step toward building deeper relationships is to make the users feel in control. Many online flight booking sites provide good examples in terms of allowing customers to take charge. Nowadays, when you buy plane tickets online, most sites not only show available dates and times but also displaying price differences, duration and the number of changes. In this way, customers can choose the offer that suits them best – depending on their criteria: best prices, direct flights, fastest routes, etc. Both Big-D and small-d designs are required. Giving customers too much information and options could be too overwhelming. The right balance is required. Another good example is Nike's iD range where customers are able to personalize their sport shoes, e.g. choosing colours, materials and patterns, without feeling overwhelmed by available options.

- **Level 4:** *Creativity/relatedness – Am I part of this brand? (Co-creator.)* At the highest level, customers should feel part of the brand and have a strong sense of ownership. This can be achieved by involving users in the value creating system. In other words, allowing users to co-create with a company. With the advance of online collaborative platforms nowadays (for an example see Open IDEO: www.openideo.com) and emerging practices (like crowdsourcing), working with customers has been made easier. A rapid increase in the number of web sites allowing users to create contents and encouraging active participation (e.g. YouTube, Facebook and Twitter) demonstrate that people are keen to play the role of co-creator. One of key success factors is in interface design. For example, YouTube and Facebook are not the first of their kinds. However, they outperform pioneers, such as Myspace, through user-friendly interface design.

Table 6.6   Building trust in e-business through design

Designing for trust	Associated design risks
Product/service features must be accurately presented	Misrepresentation of features, exaggerated claims, repetitive data, communication "noise" (the superfluous content which hides the key offerings.)
Ease of use of ordering system	System failures, complexity, long response times, complicated features and instructions, necessity to start from beginning if something goes wrong.
Correct information regarding delivery mode and times	Delays in delivery, over optimistic promises.
Good quality of products and packaging	Damages and goods returned often resulting from product weaknesses and inadequate packaging and lack of understanding of handling methods.
Transparent order tracking system	Poor information design, difficult to access/interpret.
Presenting legal compliance, rights and guarantees	Suggesting reluctance to comply by using "small print" and excessively complex wording.
Active user community linked with positive company feedback	"Over hype" of products/services leading to unrealistic expectations and possible impatience for next product/service.
Delivering the brand promise and (preferably) added value	Lack of consistency and quality throughout the brand experience (one weak feature may destroy all the strong features).
Relationships and links to other trusted sites	Poor technology performance, need for compatible software and applications.

Long (2004) also addressed trust dimensions and showed that appearance relies on graphic design, information architecture and information design, behaviour is directly influenced by interface design and reputation is connected to past experience, sharing of experiences and the expression of the brand. However improper use of design in business, which Long calls "trust-busters," can damage trust as shown in Table 6.6. The table incorporates some of the dimensions identified by Long but is extensively adapted to address the implications for design strategy.

Even companies that do not do business online cannot ignore the importance of web presence. A study carried out by Google in 2011 demonstrated consumers' complicated online paths to purchase. The process a person takes to find out information about products/services and evaluate one product/service against the others has become increasingly complex. For example, before buying a washing machine, a customer may visit retail sites, price comparison sites, peer review sites and product comparing sites (e.g. www.which.co.uk). One of the most complex journeys identified by Google relates to the travel industry. People visit a variety of web sites, e.g. tourist authority sites, TripAdvisor and tour operators' sites, before deciding on the places, dates, durations and service providers.

Interestingly, in some product categories, people prefer to search with generic terms, e.g. property in Central London. Nevertheless, in certain categories, people prefer to search with brand names, e.g. Samsung Galaxy Tablet. According to the study, the majority of people who start the search with the brand name tend to stay with that particular brand. Thus, it is in all companies' interest to encourage people to start by thinking of their brands when they begin looking for products/services. Good use of Big-D and small-d designs can really help create a strong brand and enhance brand recall as mentioned in Chapter 3. The longer a company can keep customers engaged with their online touchpoints while they search for information and evaluate all available options, the better the chance of getting them to purchase their products/services. Hence, online touchpoints (e.g. web sites) must be carefully designed.

Example: Polyvore

Polyvore (www.polyvore.com) was ranked number 28 in Fast Company's The World's 50 Most Innovative Companies 2012. It has recently become the most popular fashion site on the Internet. In 2012, Polyvore had more than 17 million visitors per month. This was achieved through one underlining principle: democratizing fashion. Polyvore enables people who love fashion, not fashion editors, to define what is "hot" for the season. Fashion lovers can choose from more than 40 million product images to create "sets," collages that look like fashion magazine pages with every item available for purchase. Basically, people can create their own fashion magazines, which they can share with others. Allowing people to co-create values not only helps build strong relationships, but also leads to the creation of an online community.

6.3.5 Ageing Population

The World Health Organization (WHO, 2007) reports that the world population is rapidly ageing and the proportion of the global population aged 60 and over will double to 22% by 2050. By then there will be more old people than children for the first time in human history. The increase in the older population is much faster in the developing countries. The UK Design Council reported that by 2020 more than half the adults in the UK will be aged 50 or over.

Despite the evidence of the fast increasing older sector, business and brand managers have been slow to recognize the implications, identifying and addressing the changing needs and targeting their products and services accordingly. Stroud (2005) suggested that the reluctance to develop brands and products for older consumers might be caused by poor marketing assumptions, and posed questions as shown and extended in Table 6.7. He urged business managers not to miss this good opportunity, since the number of older consumers continues to grow, while that of younger people gradually shrinks. Moreover, the older generation market is not as saturated as that of younger groups. Currently most brands are focusing on young consumers and neglecting older groups. Hence, there is a strong

Table 6.7 Designing for older consumers

Questions for designers	Design opportunities
1. Does designing for the old alienate the young and vice-versa?	• Appealing to the old can alienate the young, but appealing to the young can alienate the old. • There are still many brands and products that do not take older consumers' needs and preferences into consideration and are unlikely to appeal to them. • Use inclusive design to reconcile needs.
2. Are older people less willing to try new brands than younger people?	• Experts suggest that brand promiscuity declines with age, but at a later stage in a consumer's life. As people age and have the opportunity to experience more brands, they will naturally decide their preferences. • Older people are willing to try new brands if they are relevant to them. Design brands which are relevant.
3. Is it important to design appropriately for them when they are young and try to retain their lifelong loyalty?	• This assumption is true but in some categories only, e.g. food and drink. If consumers did not experience these products as a child, it is difficult to persuade them to try when they are older. This is why some people find it difficult to try food products from other cultures. • There are many other product/service categories for designers to address.
4. Do older people want to regard themselves as young and therefore designers need not address them specifically?	• Older people are able to screen marketing campaigns that are not relevant to them. They are experienced and discerning, therefore, they tend not buy into something that is not designed for them.
5. To what extent are older people stuck in their ways and reluctant to try new things?	• In some countries, older people are reluctant to try something new. But there is strong evidence that in other cultures they are looking for new adventurous experiences and often have higher economic resources.

chance of becoming a dominant brand in this emerging market. In addition, older people are likely to have more disposable income than those of younger groups, since their mortgages are already paid off, their children have already graduated, they are in a higher position in their careers and they have more spare time to spend on hobbies and leisure activities. The opportunities arising for design strategists are shown in column two.

Company managers may think that targeting older people means they have to completely change the ways they design products/services.

Traditionally, it was believed that there were big differences in terms of preference between younger and older consumers. Nowadays, most experts realize that the ageing process is varied from one person to another, but research reveals that lifestyles and leisure patterns of people in their 50s are rather similar to those in their 30s and 40s (Scales and Scase, 2000). However, there are some differences in terms of practical requirements due to the decline in sensitivity of all senses among older consumers, see some examples below.

- *Vision*: Increased sensitivity to glare; decreased ability to see objects clearly; need for greater illumination; difficulty adapting to changes between darkness and brightness.
- *Hearing*: Decreased hearing acuity (volume); loss of pitch discrimination; reduced speech discrimination and comprehension; altered directional hearing.
- *Touch*: Decreased tactile sensitivity; pressure sensitivity; and thermal sensitivity

Table 6.8 shows that in some activities, the levels of engagement vary little over many decades whilst others show more significant change.

Where the level of activity is relatively constant, product and service functions should be designed so that consumers from all age groups could use them without any difficulty. Pirkl (1994) observed that "many designs intended to address the physical limitations of the elderly, instead present and reinforce a stereotype image." In fact, not many older people want to buy products/services designed specifically for "senior" consumers. Furthermore, Dann (2007) pointed out that "few people on reaching 50 are happy to be branded a 'senior'. Baby boomers want to 'reinvent retirement' in the same way they reinvented the teenagers in the sixties." This does not

Table 6.8 Patterns of lifestyle consumption by age decade and gender

	Men				Women			
Activities	30–39	40–49	50–59	60–69	30–39	40–49	50–59	60–69
Watch TV	98.6	98.5	99.8	99.0	98.7	98.4	99.1	99.1
Listen to radio	93.6	92.7	89.8	85.4	91.3	87.8	84.9	80.8
Listen to records/tapes	89.5	83.0	72.1	67.2	91.7	84.2	72.2	62.3
Read books	60.0	60.4	57.3	60.0	70.0	72.9	72.2	62.3
Visit friends/relatives	97.4	94.2	95.1	93.8	98.1	97.8	97.0	95.5
Gardening	51.5	55.8	62.1	68.1	49.7	54.7	57.9	54.0
House repairs/DIY	68.1	64.1	64.4	57.4	40.9	36.9	31.8	20.9
At least one outing (including a walk)	70.5	63.7	61.5	54.9	53.4	50.1	50.6	44.5
At least one outing (excluding a walk)	48.6	37.7	29.2	19.6	21.7	16.6	14.0	9.7
Played sport	82.1	73.3	66.8	60.6	68.5	61.3	57.4	50.6
Belonged to any club	32.8	29.8	28.0	26.8	18.4	15.9	14.8	16.7
Belonged to social club	6.5	6.4	5.5	7.0	2.4	1.3	1.2	2.6
Belonged to sports club	19.0	16.4	17.0	15.0	6.8	7.3	6.2	6.4

Source: General Household Survey, 1997 (cited in Scales and Scase, 2000).

mean that they see themselves as people in their 20s. Szmigin and Carrigan (2000) suggested that "older people want to see images which are aspirational in their terms; healthy, fit looking people in their age group." In this case, the term *baby boomers* refers to people born from 1946 to 1964.

To accommodate both young and older groups, strategic thinking is required. Take the film industry as an example. Over the last decade, cinemagoers aged 45–65 have increased significantly. In the UK, between 1997 and 2007, the number of cinema tickets sold to audiences aged over 45 has doubled, from 19 million to 38 million. Baby boomers are roughly 25% of all cinemagoers, up from 15% in 1997. It was observed that despite the growing demand, it is still difficult to find films that explicitly engage with older people's lives. Experts pointed out that, in America, most executives are "youth-obsessed." Hence, films that address ageing are perceived as "box-office passion-killers." These executives want "speedy" profits. That is why they prefer young audiences who will turn out in big numbers for opening weekends. Older people cannot always go on the opening weekend as they may have more complicated lives; they have other things to do. Moreover, many of them want to hear the reviews before making decisions. To accommodate older cinemagoers, the current practices have to change. Moreover, many older groups find cinema designs off-putting, as they were not created with older people in mind. Significant incomes could be generated with good use of Big-D and small-d designs to make the whole cinema experience more attractive to older customers as well as younger groups.

Example: OXO

A good example of brand that uses design to appeal to both younger and older consumers is OXO (www.oxo.com). Its mission is simple – providing innovative consumer products that make everyday living easier. This value proposition appeals to all groups – young and old, male and female, left- and right-handed, etc. Its simplistic-design products with practical functionality are created based on Ron Mace's *Universal Design* principles, outlined below:

---

1. *Equitable use:* The design is useful and marketable to people with diverse abilities.
2. *Flexibility in use:* The design accommodates a wide range of individual preferences and abilities.
3. *Simple and intuitive use:* Use of the design is easy to understand, regardless of the user's experience, knowledge, language skills, or current concentration level.
4. *Perceptible information:* The design communicates necessary information effectively to the user, regardless of ambient conditions or the user's sensory abilities.
5. *Tolerance for error:* The design minimizes hazards and the adverse consequences of accidental or unintended actions.
6. *Low physical effort:* The design can be used efficiently and comfortably and with a minimum of fatigue.
7. *Size and space for approach and use:* Appropriate size and space is provided for approach, reach, manipulation and use regardless of user's body size, posture or mobility.

Source: Center for Universal Design.

Example: Nintendo Wii

Nintendo Wii is a good example of a product which capitalized on both the financial crisis and ageing population. Less disposable income tends to keep people at home more. Offering an interactive game with health and wellbeing benefits is thus an appealing proposition. Good use of inclusive design (design for all ages and abilities) engages the whole family, shares the cost and promotes social inclusion.

Management can use strategic design thinking to address the issues of the changing demographics of the human population by encouraging designers, particularly young designers, to research and develop concepts for the real world around them, instead of perpetuating the idea that all new design is aimed at their peer group. Design strategy has the inherent power to challenge the status quo and generate new methods and ideas to help management through this major challenge.

6.3.6 Open Design

Open design is essentially free sharing of ideas and is defined as "design whose makers allowed its free distribution and documentation and permitted modifications and derivations of it" (Van Abel, Evers and Klaassen, 2011). In other words, creators share design documents, which normally are treated as trade secrets (such as CAD models and editable graphic files), and allow people to distribute and modify their designs freely. Imagine that a designer designs a coffee cup. The design owner decides to share the design with other people by not only uploading sketches and photorealistic-rendering pictures on to the Internet, but also sharing all the technical drawings created using CAD software. Anyone who has these files can modify and manufacture this cup in quick time without any problem.

Many people may deem this idea crazy – why would anyone share their intellectual property rather than finding the way to protect it? Recent trends suggest that many creative communities are now willing to share ideas in order to come up with better solutions to certain problems. In fact, the idea is not new. Think about Wikipedia which shows exactly how open design works. A person writes an article and shares it with other people. Anyone can distribute and modify it freely. Through collaboration, this article has evolved and is continually updated. Thus, working with other people has helped to achieve potentially better results than working alone.

To see how this concept works in the design context visit online platforms, such as Thingiverse (www.thingiverse.com) where people can share their designs freely. With emerging technologies, like 3D printing, anyone can produce their own products. If for example, someone sees a design of a lampshade that they like on the Internet, the technical drawing of it can be downloaded and modified (e.g. adding some patterns), sent to a 3D printer and which produces the personalized lampshade. A 3D printer works in a similar way as to a 2D printer. However, by replacing ink in a printer with other materials (e.g. ceramic powders, plastic powders, metal powders or even melted chocolate) a 3D printer can print three-dimension objects instead of 2D graphics. It requires heat, adhesive or other methods to make sure that powders stick together permanently.

Some experts perceive open design as a natural progression from previous movements towards *open innovation* and *open source*. Avital (2011) observed that the new product development process has become more and more open and transparent. In the first movement, open innovation, organizations realized that they could no longer rely on knowledge generated in house. Some of their intellectual property (e.g. patents) has never been exploited, since it does not fit the companies' missions, visions and strategic directions. Open innovation encourages organizations to exchange knowledge in order to innovate more effectively. As a result, knowledge exchange becomes more open. Since these businesses concentrate on acquiring and brokering knowledge, the openness is limited to "viewing", so people can see what has been developed.

In the second movement, open source, the key players are developers, especially software developers. Upon realizing that collaboration could lead to better outcomes, developers make blueprints of their designs (in most cases, source code of computer programs) available to users and other developers for use or modification. In this way, programs can be improved and shared with other developers and users. Through this practice, the development of a product is distributed among members of developer communities. Since open source encourages people to use and improve the product, the level of openness and collaboration has increased. People are involved in the development by helping to modify the outcome.

Open design goes beyond companies and developer communities. The key players are consumers, as they are the ones who make the design their own: acquire it, modify it and materialize it. This practice reflects changes in consumers' behaviours. People become more and more interested in playing a creator role. They want to design something for themselves. This is why platforms for user-generated content, e.g. YouTube, have become very popular. Polyvore, which was mentioned in the previous section, also capitalized on this emerging trend. IKEA Hackers (www.ikea-hackers.net) provides a good example of demonstrating changes in people's preferences. This blog features interesting designs created by parts and components obtained from IKEA. Nevertheless, people do not follow IKEA's original designs. They modify, customize and repurpose IKEA's products to suit their needs. For example, they create beautiful shelves out of parts designed for a table and chairs!

The implications of open design for strategic design management are major. It is clear that design disciplines need to adapt themselves to these trends rapidly. Management need to reconsider their protective, sometimes over protective, stance in locking away intellectual property, in order to prevent others using or exploiting it. Rather than focusing on designing finished products, designers learn to act as agents, facilitators or enablers who help people design what they want. This means systems design will become even more important, as designers are likely to design platforms to help people create products/services by themselves. This requires a significant change in terms of mindset among both managers and designers. Big-D is likely to play an increasing role in helping management come up with new value creation processes and different ways of serving customers.

Examples: Nokia, Motorola and Phonebloks

Nokia is one of the very first companies to embrace the open design concept. The company has published a number of CAD files of the Nokia Lumia 820's case on Thingiverse web site where people can download, modify/customize and print out 3D models of their own versions. For more information visit: http://www.thingiverse.com/thing:43157

More customizable phone ideas will be introduced in the near future, as Motorola collaborates with Phonebloks to introduce the first modular smartphone to the market. Each part of the modular smartphone will work like a LEGO brick so that consumers can "pick and mix" different hardware to create a perfect phone that matches their personal requirements. For more information visit: https://phonebloks.com/en/goals

6.3.7 Collaborative Consumption

The term *collaborative consumption* was coined by Botsman and Roger (2010a). The concept challenges the conventional economy model that organizations must own assets, e.g. knowledge, people, machines or spaces, and that they need to produce products or deliver services (Brodwin, 2012). The collaborative consumption concept argues that you do not need to "own" these assets. Value can be created by sharing and making better use of underutilized assets.

In considering most office spaces, most companies only need/use them from 9 am to 5 pm. So what about the 6 pm to 8 am period? These spaces are empty, underutilized. So such questions arise as, "Would it be better to rent them out to companies that work nightshift?" In this way, rental costs can be shared. This is a win-win situation. Now by looking around your personal work and living space ask the question, "Is there anything underutilized in this room, house or office?" Perhaps the lawnmower is used only once a month. Would it be better to rent it out to neighbours who need to mow the lawn, but do not have a lawnmower?

Online platforms where people can share underutilized things are increasing, e.g. Ecomodo (http://ecomodo.com) which allows people to lend and borrow equipment, skills or spaces, and shows a growing demand in terms of collaborative consumption and a developing higher level of trust people have with others. The idea of sharing rather than owning promotes many innovative practices. For example, time banking is a service exchange concept which uses units of time as currency (see http://community.timebanks.org for an example). Users register to become part of a service exchange community. A web site designer, for example, may share his/her skills by spending 12 hours designing a web site for one member of a community. This means the designer may earn 12 hours of service(s) from other member(s). The credit may be spent by asking another member of this community with accountancy skills to help to complete the designer's tax return (eight hours) and another person with cooking skills (four hours) to teach the designer how to bake sourdough bread.

Because of the sharing nature, some experts call this emerging concept *sharing economy* or *peer-to-peer economy*. Several experts suggest that collaborative consumption can be considered a cornerstone of the new economy. Economic downturn and climate change make people and businesses rethink the ways they consume and create values. The collaborative consumption economy supports sustainable development, e.g. sharing products helps reduce materials and energy consumed during production and distribution. The idea also promotes social capital or benefits derived from social relations (e.g. networks and social groups). This concept has strong link with open design. Thus around the concepts of open innovation, open source and open design a new collaborative consumption economy is emerging.

Botsman and Roger (2010b) grouped the variety of collaborative consumption practices into three broad categories, which can help business managers rethink their offers:

1. *Product service systems:* Companies could exploit this opportunity (people want to use products, but do not want to own them) by offering products as a service rather than sell them as products. The success of services, such as Zipcar, shows that there are plenty of people who need a car, but do not want to deal with all issues that come with owning a car, e.g. road tax, maintenance and insurance. Most car producers have been slow to respond to this trend. Their collaboration with companies like Zipcar could provide better offers.
2. *Redistribution markets:* Companies should explore how used/pre-owned goods can be redistributed: move them from people who do not need them to those who do. Currently, the redistribution is done by communities mostly via online platforms, e.g. Freecycle (see http://uk.freecycle.org), which help people redistribute everyday products they no longer need in their local areas. For example, when people decide to move house and there are many pieces of furniture that they do not want to take with them, but which are still in good condition. The items could be given for free to people in the neighbourhood who want them. Businesses can capitalize on this trend by helping people deal with logistics of redistributing goods.
3. *Collaborative lifestyle:* Recently, people with similar needs or interests, like growing their own foods, have come together to share resources and skills to achieve what they want. People who want to grow vegetables, but do not have land are now working with those who do (see Landshare www.landshare.net). Collaborative lifestyle covers all aspects of life ranging from sharing parking spaces, e.g. www.parkatmyhouse.com and living spaces, see www.cohousing.org.uk, to peer-to-peer lending (www.zopa.com). Businesses, and especially design disciplines, can exploit and enhance this movement by helping with systems design, interaction design and experience design.

What are the implications of collaborative consumption on strategic design management? It is apparent that business managers need to rethink their offers and explore ways they could support people in achieving collaborative consumption practices. Big-D design can help with the change of business and management thinking and the transition to new business models in particular by identifying opportunities to respond to and capitalize on this movement. The role of small-d design expands too, by helping to address practical issues such as designing interactions and experiences for new systems and new services. Small-d designs could also make online platforms created to support collaborative consumption practices more intuitive, practical and engaging. This emerging concept offers great opportunities for design disciplines to go beyond designing products/services and tackle the entire ecosystem of value creation.

Example: Airbnb

Airbnb (www.airbnb.co.uk) was ranked number six in Fast Company's The World's 50 Most Innovative Companies 2014. The company is described as a "trusted community marketplace" that allows people to rent out their spare rooms or vacant homes to complete strangers. According to the company's records in April 2014, it has more than 350,000 hosts in 34,000 cities in 192 countries and already has more than 11,000,000 guests. Good use of design thinking is evident in its straightforward system, user-friendly web site and carefully-planned safety policies. It was observed that, by summer 2014, Airbnb could become the world's largest hotel chain without owning a single hotel.

6.3.8 Emerging Markets

Many respected commentators agree that emerging markets, especially the BRIC countries (Brazil, Russia, India, South Africa and China, recently joined by South Africa to form an International development bank), will be key players in terms of production and consumption in the future. Senior management in many big corporations, e.g. Coca-Cola believe expanding into these emerging markets is the key to their survival.

According to Ramzy (2009), in 1930 Coca-Cola had profits of $13 million and operated in more than 24 countries. In recent years (2008), Coca-Cola had profits of $5.8 billion and operated in more than 200 countries. The growth rate in emerging markets is very lucrative. For instance, in 2009 Coca-Cola had 33% sales growth in India and 14% in China. The average American drinks 412 bottles of Coca-Cola products a year – it is just 28 in China and seven in India. Evidently, there is large space to grow. Nevertheless, entering emerging markets means big challenges. *Time Magazine* (2009) observed that two of the biggest emerging markets are not the biggest spenders when they reported:

> although America accounts for only about 4.5% of the world's population, its consumers spent about $10 trillion in 2008. By contrast, although China and India collectively account for nearly 40% of the world's population, their combined consumption was only about

$2.5 trillion in 2008. For a region steeped in a culture of saving, this will not be an easy transformation.

To enter these emerging markets successfully, company managers have to rethink the ways they create and deliver values. While people in developed countries do most research online, e.g. checking price comparison web sites and peer reviews, in emerging markets, most purchasing decisions are made inside stores. For example, in China, 45% of consumers make purchasing decisions inside stores, compared with 24% in the US. Hence, D'Andrea, Marcotte and Morrison (2010) suggested that a store should display the broadest possible range of products. Since salespersons play an important role in helping customers making decisions, they must be knowledgeable about products/services and they should be seen as frontline educators rather than shop assistants. Therefore the entire store experience must be carefully designed to provide in an engaging manner all information required to make decision.

In developed markets, products/services are divided into different segments according to buyers' incomes, e.g. premium ranges for the highest earners, mid-range products for the middle-class consumers and affordable ones for people with low incomes. However, the strategy of creating products for all income segments does not work in the same way in emerging markets. Most consumers buy either the cheapest or the best. For commodity products, e.g. foods, or those without emotional connections, e.g. hair dryers, they choose the lowest-price items that offer acceptable quality. People tend to save up to indulge in more aspirational categories, such as home entertainment, mobile communication and luxury fashion goods. Evidently, they buy a lot of the cheapest and a little of the best. Thus, for essential product categories, good use of design can help a company provide low-price but decent quality products. For potential self-indulgent categories, design could help create more relevant and appropriate aspirational choices.

Managers and designers should not only address practical issues, such as how people shop, but also they must consider how to establish meaningful emotional connections. Take British tea brands as an example. The UK has many high-quality tea brands, e.g. Twinings, PG Tips, Yorkshire Tea and Tetley. However, none of them dominates the world market. In fact, Lipton (Unilever), a brand without a rich tea heritage has managed to become the leader of the tea market worldwide. It has number one market share in China and the US. The reason is that most British brands praise themselves on the quality of the products and focus on communicating quality of the taste. This approach works for the UK market, since the tea culture is already well established. However, for consumers who do not know much about the British tea culture, this approach is not very effective. Lipton's success was the result of its strategy of selling the culture, not the product. It targets high-end female office workers and makes Lipton tea a fashionable lifestyle choice.

However, emerging markets are not only places for big companies to make money but also they are likely to play a key role in creating and delivering products/services. According to Schuman (2010), one of the key trends reshaping global business is the rise of non-Japanese Asian brands, e.g. Chinese, Taiwanese and South Korean. For the past 60 years, Asian producers produced consumer products with great efficiency, but were not good at designing and branding. Now they have developed expertise in innovation, design and marketing and their cultures favour excellent packaging design. Samsung is now a top mobile phone brand in the US. Acer is the world's number two PC brand, ahead of Dell.

A decision to enter a new market needs a careful consideration. Will the business managers apply the same strategy to all markets? Or will they tailor the strategy to match individual markets? Kurtz and Boone (2006) suggested a company could adopt a *global strategy* where all offers are standardized with minimal modifications required, such as IKEA does. IKEA products are more or less the same in all markets. Small modifications are applied, such as offering larger furniture for the North American market and providing smaller items for Japanese market where the living spaces are limited.

By contrast a company can apply a *multi-domestic strategy* by tailoring its offerings to match specific targets in each nation. Levitt, 1986 (cited in McGrath, 2000) observed that:

> the multicultural corporation knows a lot about a great many countries, and continually adapts itself to their supposed differences. The global corporation knows one great thing about all countries, lures them to its custom by capitalising on the one thing they all have in common. The global corporation looks to the nations of the world not for how they are different, but how they are alike.

Most successful global brands manage to identify the needs, wants and dreams that people around the world have in common, like owning a beautiful, high-performance car (BMW) and having affordable meals in friendly environments (McDonalds). Design research can help managers to understand common needs through a series of ethnographic and creative experiments, while small-d design can help to make sure all offerings and touchpoints have universal appeal.

The next questions are: Will management emphasize the original value regardless of where the company goes to? Or will managers choose to go to great lengths to study and react to local cultural requirements? If the business chooses the first option, it is termed a value exporter. By choosing the second option, the business is termed a *value collector*. Grinyer (2001) used the term *value exporter* to describe brands with their values strongly related to national characteristics and which use their design strategy to differentiate them from others, such as Harley-Davidson, Volvo and Braun. According to the author, value collectors are brands which heavily invest in market research in order to provide value that local consumers want, for example Samsung, Unilever and Panasonic. Organizations that choose this option usually establish country-based design studios practising cross-cultural teamwork.

Based on the two value options, Grinyer pointed out that, broadly speaking, there are three strategic design directions available for global brands: (1) speak your own language relentlessly and never waver, stay true to your brand value and identity and do not change design language wherever you go (e.g. B&O); (2) turn local values into global virtue, use your national characteristics as unique selling point and present them in the way that appeals to people from other cultures (e.g. Muji); or (3) speak your own language with a local accent, adapt original characteristics to suit different markets/tastes (e.g. Mandarin Oriental hotels). The Mandarin Oriental group uses different fans to symbolize different cultures. For example, Mandarin Oriental, Hong Kong's fan is a Canton fan, while Mandarin Oriental, Bangkok's fan uses a traditional Thai artistic style to depict the life by the river dating back to 1810.

So what are the implications of emerging markets on strategic design management? Business managers need to explore how to collaborate with them in creating and delivering values, as well as to investigate how to fulfil their needs and wants in the ways that suit their lifestyle and preferences. Design thinking and design research can help identify opportunities and come up with innovative products/services to serve emerging markets more effectively. It can also be used to critically evaluate the threats from these fast-learning and often aggressive competitors. BRICs brings entirely new dimensions to global business and makes the need for designing and delivering better products services and experiences more and more urgent.

Big-D strategic thinking should be open and holistic, ready to think what was hitherto unthinkable and encouraging talented creative designers to constantly review global trends and changes.

Example: P&G

P&G initially entered emerging markets with two types of products – premium products for affluent targets and cheaper versions for less affluent consumers. The company quickly found out that this strategy did not work. Even people with low incomes expect more than practical products, they care about "beauty" just like the rest of the market. As a result, P&G changed its strategy and decided to work with local consumers to find out their specific needs in order to develop products accordingly. The *$2 a Day* project was created to identify innovative ways to serve low-income consumers in developing countries that had to live on just $2 per day. Design and ethnographic research was put into good use, as P&G sent thousands of employees to live with and observe potential customers.

This resulted in many new ideas for innovation. For example, the company identified that, in certain rural areas of China, people have difficulties cleaning their bodies – not because of water concerns, but because of privacy issues. They have no bathroom and there are several generations under one roof. This insight helped P&G coming up with a new body cleansing product which works like a hand sanitizer that can be wiped away easily in any private space. This means users can clean themselves while having their clothes on –P&G already uses this kind of technology in its existing hair colour products. Hence, it was able to apply this technology to create new products quickly. This example shows how design research and collaborative design could help multinational companies understand and develop products/services that truly match consumers' requirements in the emerging market.

6.4 DESIGN-DRIVEN BUSINESS MODEL

A design-driven company should enhance management through design (Borja de Mozota, 2003). This means using design thinking to focus on producing/supplying creative solutions to the market. Borja de Mozota explains the effects of using the managerial approach to enhance design and using strategic design to enhance management. The managerial approach to design management seeks to enhance design using managerial methods, whereas the strategic design approach uses design knowledge to improve management.

Whilst the first approach develops methods and measures for design applications to such areas as quality control, the second approach promotes creativity, ideas management and develops a shared vision. The second approach is both more challenging and potentially more relevant to contemporary business management and more rewarding.

Moving towards a design-driven business model requires an understanding of the potential of design to deliver strategic directions, positioning and creative solutions. In a design-driven organization design will have a major role and responsibility at all levels and strategic design management will require suitably skilled staff. Table 6.9 identifies what types of management staff are required and outlines their responsibilities.

Table 6.9 Design and design management responsibilities

Level	Job titles	Outline duties
Strategic	Design Director, Head of Design, Chief Design Officer	• Contributing to the organization's strategic direction and developing design strategy to drive/support it.
Tactical	Design Manager, Creative Director, Studio Manager	• Interpreting design strategy for creative briefs. • Forming appropriate design teams for each project. • Managing design staff and cross-functional team-working. • Allocating resources and monitoring development, progress.
Operational	Design Project Manager, Designer	• Managing design projects to meet time, budget and quality standards set. • Creating concepts and developing designs to add value to the organization.

Hands (2009) makes a case that design should be invited into the board-room. He argues that design can make significant impacts in culture, com-mitment, organization, process and strategy and gives seven key reasons:

1. *Empirical:* Design disciplines excel at gaining first-hand experience in order to identify "real" problems and create a holistic context of the problems.
2. *Empathic:* Design disciplines are champions in user-centred approach and always take users' requirements and expectations into consideration.
3. *Political:* Persuasive design can drive all stakeholders toward desired directions.
4. *Perfectionist:* Being critical of final results means designers will "strive for perfection" – they will develop, test and refine their designs until they achieve a high standard.
5. *Free thinking:* Designers are good at lateral and blue-sky thinking. They also master both divergent and convergent thinking, which are required for innovation developments.
6. *Flexible:* Being responsive to the fast-changing world, design disciplines can help a company address emerging challenges and opportunities positively.
7. *Communicators:* Strong visualization skills help a company engage all stakeholders and wide audiences in new ideas, projects or activities.

One of the most debated issues is whether to establish an in-house design team or outsource from design consultancies. There is no con-sensus on this with many successful design-led organizations building in-house teams (e.g. Samsung, Apple and BMW) while others outsource (e.g. Swatch, Alessi and B&O). The advantages and disadvantages are explored below by building on the work of Von Stamm (1993, cited in Borja de Mozota, 2003).

Advantages of an *in-house design team*:

- Design reflects more closely the true company culture and character.
- May be less expensive than contracting design firm/consultants.
- Affords easier meetings, co-ordination activities and control.

Disadvantages of an *in-house design team*:

- Can become blinkered by company norms and expectations.
- Too inward focussed on existing portfolio and expectations.
- Lack of creativity resulting from more systematic than systemic thinking.
- May be more expensive in terms of remuneration and overheads if projects are not continuous.

Advantages of using an *external design service*:

- May bring more new creative ideas from wider vision.
- Not constrained by company culture and characteristics.
- May offer special expertise and skills not available in-house.
- More potential design options/proposals/visions.
- Savings on training and employment overheads as only paid by project.

Enhance partnership by design	Enhance key activities by design	Enhance value proposition by design	Enhance customer relationship by design	Enhance the segmentation and targeting by design
• Create trust • Establish transparent collaboration processes • Maintain good relationship and profossional work experience	• Improve the quality • Support other key functions • Motivate staff	• Create visionary directions • Explore new possibilities • Identify emerging or latent needs	• Eliminate negative experience • Enrich memorable experience • Create two-way communication	• Conduct design research to identify the most valuable target markets • Gain first-hand experience of people's problems
	Enhance competencies by design		Enhance value delivery by design	
	• Optimise resources • Make the most of tangible/intangible resources • Create new assets (e.g. IPR)		• Simplify value delivery process • Provide notable customer journey • Offer holistic solutions	

Enhance cost effectiveness by design	Enhance revenue streams by design
• Explore new ways of achieving same results at lower costs • Find new ways of increasing values at the same costs • Identify new ways of overcoming financial obstacles	• Investigate new ways of growing customer base • Find new ways of generating revenue streams • Improve the efficiency of current practices

Figure 6.1 The Design-driven business model
Source: Adapted from Osterwalder and Pigneur, 2010.

Disadvantages of using an *external design service*:

- Lack of understanding of company culture and issues which may lead to misunderstanding and inappropriate design solutions.
- Difficulties of accessibility to key people, coordination and possibly confidentiality of information and intellectual property.
- Organization may lack skills to evaluate the design work.
- Lack of ownership and pride if design is bought in.
- Potential problems with manufacture of the externally developed design.
- Difficulty of control and continuity in the relationship.
- Potential high costs especially where the design firm's reputation is high.

A design management model presented by Bruce and Copper (1997) shows design contributing, and potentially driving, business through a well-established business planning and control cycle, identifying problems/opportunities, refining ideas, implementing solutions and evaluating outcomes. A design-driven business model framework based on the canvas provided by Osterwalder and Pigneur (2010) shows the power of design to enhance all business outcomes as shown in Figure 6.1.

The framework developed by Johnson, Christensen and Kagermann (2008) also demonstrates how design can be the catalyst for developing a successful business model:

- *Value proposition:* Design-led value creation to develop sustainable compelling values.
- *Key resources*: Design-led value chain to exploit existing assets and create new resources.
- *Key processes:* Design-led process to motivate staff and enhance performance.
- *Profit formula*: Design-led business to come up with holistic solutions to grow the market base.

The design-led business model is the current most advanced case for using design throughout every aspect of the business, from seeking and evaluating new directions to implementing innovative solutions. It needs visionary leadership to embrace the principles and develop the confidence and know how. Managers need to become design thinkers and designers must encompass management and commercial acumen into their mindset.

6.5   CASE STUDY 4 – DESIGN-DRIVEN COMPANY: LG ELECTRONICS

LG Electronics in South Korea has adopted design strategy faster than most global corporations. Their strategy for growth and rapid expansion is to secure their competitive edge through design and innovation.

The current CEO (cited in Schuman 2010) says "going forth, we really have to come up with breakthrough solutions. We're going in Apple's direction – coming up with the solution rather than just the device." Their corporate vision, to be among the global top three, is underpinned by their growth strategy based on design and innovation. LG state their belief that "only great people can make a great company." They pursue fast innovation and fast growth through product leadership of creative, top quality products, and market leadership to achieve top ranking in global markets by employing the best people. Their culture aims to be totally positive with "no excuses," trying harder, building teams, encouraging group pride and promoting individual's creativity and freedom.

They claim that every member of the management team, including the CEO, predicts that design could be combined with cutting-edge technologies in order to drastically change the way we live and play a pivotal role in creating new cultural pathways. This demonstrates a strong positive belief that design leadership can find future directions.

LG began their design-driven approach by establishing the Life Soft Research Lab at their corporate design headquarters in Seoul. The leader was a visionary design engineer and the staff were chosen from different disciplines, including anthropology and psychology who engaged with designers to predict social futures. Unlike many research units, they did not spend much time in the office, but went out into the field to immerse themselves deeply in the world of their audience. This design-led futures focus gives them confidence in establishing new directions and results in designs that integrate physical and cognitive ergonomics with technology and meet the emotional needs of their customers.

The corporation has invested heavily in design. In Seoul alone, they have several hundred designers working on developing and implementing their design strategy. In addition they currently have five international corporate design centres in Italy, China, USA, India and Japan and a newly established design studio in London. Their in-house teams are multidisciplinary and multinational. In addition they feed the flow of ideas through cooperation with leading university design schools. Arguably the most important element of their success in using design to drive business is the way they empower designers. They show a belief in the ability of designers lead the organization through their passion and enthusiasm, which turns innovative designs into business opportunities.

Some questions for discussion:

- Is it possible for all organizations to first identify the required solution (be it economic, social, environmental or political) then use design to drive the strategy to meet the need?
- How can design strategists balance the time spent in the field observing real world trends/change with the time spent in the organization exchanging ideas/experiences?

6.6   SUMMARY OF KEY POINTS

- Design has the potential to drive business and change business models.
- Conventional business models omit design but show core elements which can be directly linked to design.
- Emergent models slowly recognize the growing influence of design to drive value creation.
- The current conceptual economy era demands new ideas beyond basic products and services : design can drive this imperative new thinking.

- Corporate social responsibility (CSR) is not an option; legal compliance is not enough, businesses are now required to be "good."
- Design can address many of our global economic and social problems and change attitudes and lifestyles.
- Design can lead sustainability by offering new choices and reducing environmental impacts.
- E-business redefines the way business is conducted worldwide; design is needed to build trust.
- Improper use of design can undermine business success.
- Designers can "make a difference" in terms of wealth and wellbeing.
- Social problems like the ageing population can be tackled through inclusive design.
- A design-driven business model enhances management through design.
- Managers need to become design thinkers.
- Designers need business and management thinking.

6.7   FURTHER CONSIDERATIONS

Amidst all the complexity and pressures of the modern business environment, managers understand that performance and survival still depends upon generating profits. The entire purposes of business are under review and more than ever they are accountable for their actions. Where the "old" model of business continues to be practiced, there is a natural tendency to adopt the adage "if it ain't broke, don't fix it." But progressive managers know it has to change and are increasing looking to unlock the power of creative thinking, as epitomized by designers, and infuse it into the business. This is relatively new territory and the degree of confidence varies greatly. Managers in the old mindset may still regard design with suspicion, perhaps fearful of the competence in handling the explosion of new ideas and openness, and possibily suspicious that incorporating design is expensive. The integration of management and design thinking will nevertheless gain momentum because consumer demand for new and better products/services/experiences continues unabated.

6.7.1   Exercise the Mind....

1. The changing expectations of consumers (in any chosen industry)
2. The different perceptions of what constitutes a "luxury experience" and how design strategy can respond to changes.
3. New products and services which communicate a commitment to sustainable futures through their brand promise.
4. The influence of social networking on lifestyles and wellbeing.
5. New products/services/experiences for the ageing population.
6. The risks and benefits of integrating creative design thinking into the business model.

6.8 GLOSSARY

CAD model: CAD is short for computer-aid design. In this case, CAD models are referred to as three-dimensional models created by design software packages. A CAD model accurately represents the geometry of the design (e.g. dimensions and details) and, in most cases, the look and feel of the final outcomes.

3D printing is an additive manufacturing process, which creates three-dimensional solid objects based on digital files (e.g. CAD models). The technique can create both prototypes and actual products, e.g. jewellery and medical products.

Crowdsourcing is "the practice of obtaining needed services, ideas, or content by soliciting contributions from a large group of people and especially from the online community rather than from traditional employees or suppliers" (Merriam-Webster Dictionary, 2013). For example, a charity needs new ideas on how to provide better services at lower costs. It may obtain ideas/solutions through crowdsourcing practices by posting request for ideas online and collect suggestions from the public.

Take back programme: Nowadays, companies, especially those in the electronic sector voluntarily take back their products after the end of life. Retrievable components may be reused, repaired, reconditioned or recycled to create new parts/products.

6.9 REFERENCES AND ADDITIONAL READING

Avital, M. (2011) The Generative Bedrock of Open Design. In B. Van Abel, L. Evers, R. Klaassen and P. Troxler (eds), *Open Design Now: Why Design Cannot Remain Exclusive*. Amsterdam: BIS Publishers, 10–13.

Bill and Melinda Gates Foundation (2008) *Transcript of Bill Gates – 2008 World Economic Forum – Creative Capitalism*. [WWW] Bill and Melinda Gates Foundation. Available from: http://www.gatesfoundation.org/speeches-commentary/Pages/bill-gates-2008-world-economic-forum-creative-capitalism.aspx [Accessed 26 July 2011].

Borja de Mozota, B. (2003) *Design Management: Using Design to Build Brand Value and Corporate Innovation*. New York: Allworth.

Botsman, R. and Roger, R. (2010a), *What's Mine Is Yours: The Rise of Collaborative Consumption*. New York: HarperCollins.

Botsman, R. and Roger, R. (2010b) Beyond Zipcar: Collaborative Consumption. *Harvard Business Review*, October 2010, 30.

Brodwin, D. (2012) *The Rise of Collaborative Consumption Economy* [WWW]. Available from: http://www.usnews.com/opinion/blogs/economic-intelligence/2012/08/09/how-collaborative-consumption-reinvigorates-our-economy [Accessed 2 May 2013].

Bruce, M. and Cooper, R. (1997) Using Design Effectively. In M. Bruce and R. Cooper (eds), *Marketing and Design Management*. London: International Thomson.

Casadesus-Masanell, R. and Ricart, J. E. (2011) How to Design a Winning Business Model. *Harvard Business Review*, 89 (1/2), 100–107.

Clinton, B. (2009) Creating Value in an Economic Crisis. *Harvard Business Review*, September, 70–71.

Collings, R. (2010) *Corporate Social Responsibility*. [WWW] Design Council. Available from: www.creative-net.co.uk/Documents/About%20design/Business%20 essentials/Corporate%20social%20responsibility/Corporate%20social%20 responsibility.pdf [Accessed 29 August 2011].

Coleman, R., Clarkson, J., Dong, H. and Cassim, J. (2007) *Design for Inclusivity: A Practical Guide to Accessible, Innovative and User-centred Design*. Aldershot: Gower. Crainer, S. (2000) *The Management Century*. New York: Booz-Allen & Hamilton

D'Andrea, G., Marcotte, D. and Morrison, G. D. (2010) Let Emerging Market Customers Be Your Teachers. *Harvard Business Review*, December, 115–120.

Dann, S. (2007) Branded Generations: Baby Boomers Moving into the Senior Market. *Journal of Product & Brand Management*, 16 (6), 429–431.

Design Council. (2001) *Living Longer*. London: Design Council.

Doane, D. (2003) An Alternative Perspective on Brands: Markets and Morals. In R. Clifton and J. Simmons (eds), *Brands and Branding*. London: The Economist.

Ghemawat, P. (2010) Finding Your Strategy in the New Landscape. *Harvard Business Review*, March, 54–60.

Google (2011) *Beyond Last Click: Understanding your Customers' Online Path to Purchase* [WWW]. Available from: http://www.thinkwithgoogle.com/insights/ emea/library/studies/beyond-last-click/ [Accessed 28 April 2013].

Grinyer, C. (2001) Design Differentiation for Global Companies: Value Exporters and Value Importers. *Design Management Review*, 12 (4), 10–14.

Hands, D. (2009) *Vision and Values in Design Management*. Lausanne: AVA Academia.

Hilton, S. (2003) The Social Value of Brand. In R. Clifton and J. Simmons (eds), *Brands and Branding*. London: The Economist.

Johnson, M. W., Christensen, C. M. and Kagermann, H. (2008) Reinventing Your Business Model. *Harvard Business Review*, 86 (12), 51–59.

Kurtz, D. and Boone, L. (2006) *Principles of Marketing*. Mason: Thomson Southwest.

LG (2011) Vision. [WWW]. Available from http://www.lg.com/uk/about-lg/corporate-information/overview/vision.jsp [Accessed 25 May 2011].

Long, K. (2004) Customer Loyalty and Experience Design in E-business. *Design Management Review*, 15 (2), 60–67.

Merriam-Webster Dictionary (2013) Crowdsourcing. [WWW] *Merriam-Webster Dictionary*. Available from: http://www.merriam-webster.com/dictionary/crowd-sourcing [Accessed 15 May 2013].

Negroponte, N. (1995) *Being Digital*. New York: Vintage Books.

Olins, W. (2001) Brand: Who's Wearing the Trousers [WWW] *Economist*. Available from: www.economist.com/node/770992?story_id=770992 [Accessed 7 May 2011].

Osterwalder, A. and Pigneur, Y. (2010) *Business Model Generation*. Hoboken: John Wiley & Sons.

P2P Foundation (2012) *Synthetic Overview of the Collaborative Economy* [WWW]. Available from: http://p2p.coop/files/reports/collaborative-economy-2012.pdf [Accessed 3 May 2012].

Pink, D. H. (2006) *A Whole New Mind: Why Right-Brainers Will Rule the Future*. London: Marshall Cavendish.

Pirkl, J. J. (1994) *Trangenerational Design: Design Products for an Ageing Population*. New York: Van Nostrand Reinhod.

Ramzy, A. (2009) Coke's Recession Boomlet: "New" Markets in India and China and an Old Playbook are Offsetting Sluggish U.S. Sales. *Time Magazine*, 174 (11), 41–43.

Rare Corporate (2011) *A Short Guide to Corporate Responsibility Reporting*. [WWW] Rare Corporate Design. Available from: http://rarecorporate.co.uk/ UserFiles/File/short_guide_to_CRR.pdf [Accessed 28 June 2011].

Rigby, D. K., Gruver, K. and Allen, J. (2009) Innovation in Turbulent Times. *Harvard Business Review*, June, 79–86.

Roy, R. (2006) *Products: New Product Development and Sustainable Design*. Milton Keynes: Open University.

Schuman, M. (2010) Defying Gravity: Aggressive LG Gained on Rivals in the Recession – It's Leading a New Wave of Rising Asian Brands. *Time Magazine*, 176 (5), 41–43.

Scales, J. and Scase, R. (2000) *Fit and Fifty?: A Report Prepared for the Economic and Social Research Council*. Colchester: Institute for Social and Economic Research.

Stanford University (2010) *Our Vision*. [WWW] Institute of Design at Stanford. Available from: http://dschool.stanford.edu/big_picture/our_vision.php [Accessed 6 May 2011].

Stroud, D. (2005) *The 50-Plus Market*. London: Kogan Page.

Szmigin, I. and Carrigan, M. (2000) Does Advertising in the UK Need Older Models? *Journal of Product & Brand Management*, 9 (2), 128–143.

The Times (2008) Shopping to Change Lives. *The Times: Law*, 8 January 2008, 3.

Usunier, J. C. and Lee, J. A. (2009) *Marketing Across Cultures* (5th edn). Harlow: Prentice Hall-Financial Times.

Van Abel, B., Evers, L. and Klaassen, R. (2011) Preface. In B. Van Abel, L. Evers, R. Klaassen and P. Troxler (eds), *Open Design Now: Why Design Cannot Remain Exclusive*. Amsterdam: BIS Publishers, 10–13.

Van Abel, B., Evers, L., Klaassen, R. and Troxler, P. (2011) *Open Design Now: Why Design Cannot Remain Exclusive*. Amsterdam: BIS Publishers.

Verganti, R. (2008) Design, Meaning, and Radical Innovation: A Metamodel and a Research Agenda. *Journal of Product Innovation Management*, 25, 436–456.

White, P., Belletire, S. and St. Pierre, L. (2007) *Okala: Learning Ecological Design*. Phoenix: Industrial Design Society of America (IDSA).

World Health Organization (2007) *Global Age Friendly Cities: A Guide*. Geneva: World Health Organization.

6.10 ONLINE RESOURCES

1. Center for Universal Design: www.ncsu.edu/project/design-projects/udi/
2. Collaborative Service: www.sustainable-everyday.net
3. Design Council – CABE: www.designcouncil.org.uk
4. Design Management Institute:www.dmi.org
5. Designing with People: http://designingwithpeople.rca.ac.uk

Chapter 7

CORPORATE RESPONSIBILITY AND DESIGN

A new form of enterprise is emerging. This new organization seeks to embrace the triple bottom line (TBL). Instead of pursuing profit and economic wealth only, the organization seeks to be competitive by also generating social value and environmental benefits. Indeed the principal objective of this new type organization may be social innovation and social enterprise. Managers have new responsibilities to identify and set social and environmental goals aligned to organizational goals. These goals must be realistic and measurable despite their often intangible nature.

New ideas from designers and new design strategies are needed to support and drive social innovation and to address environmental challenges, such as the reduction/elimination of waste. There has never been a time when it was more important to review the business model using design thinking. The TBL carries with it the promise of more complexity but also greater opportunities to achieve competitiveness and differentiation through effective use of creative design.

The 4Ds model of design management can drive the development of design strategy towards the achievement of social and environmental goals and help to achieve the optimum balance for the delivery of the brand experience.

Objectives for this chapter:

- To explain the emergence of the new triple bottom line (TBL) enterprise model.
- To discuss the implications of TBL for management and design strategy.
- To identify the driving forces of competition leading to the need to create social wealth and protect the environment responsibly.
- To explore how managers should set economic, social and environmental goals.
- To examine new forms of enterprise based on social innovation and social enterprise.
- To show why social innovation requires ideas and leadership from designers.
- To consider the alignment of social and environmental goals and organizational goals.

- To compare the cradle-to-grave model for design, which seeks to miti- gate impacts on the environment throughout the product life cycle, with the cradle-to-cradle approach, which aims to eliminate waste through a closed loop system.
- To explain why innovation at the bottom of the economic pyramid can be profitable.
- To evaluate the use of co-design and co-production to increase the effec- tiveness of design solutions, promote ownership and increase acceptance of the outcomes.
- To show how the 4Ds model of design management may be used to progress towards social enterprise status.
- To suggest methods for reviewing and measuring social and environmen- tal goals/targets.
- To explain how design thinking can be applied to ascertain the current use of TBL principles, define suitable but challenging goals, formulate a pragmatic strategy and evaluate performance.

7.1 DESIGN RESPONSIBILITY

In general, being responsible is being accountable for your actions. When discussing managing design responsibility, it means responsibility at both individual and organizational levels.

At the individual level, design disciplines should act responsibly – *but who should design disciplines be responsible to?* Sethia (2005) suggested that design practitioners, including designers, design thinkers, design strategists and design managers, should be responsible to their clients, their custom- ers, themselves and society. Obviously, design practitioners must do their best to satisfy customers' needs, wants and dreams, while making sure that their work fulfils their clients' or their organizations' missions, visions and business objectives. For example, designing a safe and practical product that fulfils customers' needs as well as generating profits for their client or their organization. However, it is important that design disciplines main- tain their integrity – stay true to themselves and follow the code of conduct in their fields. They should also be responsible to society by taking poten- tial environmental, social, cultural and ethical impacts into consideration when carrying out their work.

The next key question raised by Sethia is: *What should design disciplines be responsible for?* He suggested that design practitioners should be respon- sible for design outcomes (e.g. products, services or systems), their choice of technology (e.g. does this technology exclude anyone? Does this manu- facturing process have negative impacts on the environment?), their users (e.g. how could design empower people and help them achieve their aspira- tions?) and the environment (e.g. how could design promote eco-efficiency and sustainable development). Madsen (2005) proposed another but com- plementary way of looking at design responsibility as he suggested that we should make sure that the outcome (ends), how it is done (means), and the circumstance influencing how it is done (constraints), comply with the code of ethical conduct.

Being responsible at the corporate level is often referred to an act of giving something back to society. The concept of corporate social responsibility (CSR) has evolved from simply passively responding to social and ethical demands to being proactive and seeking innovative ways of making profits while serving people responsibly. The evidence of large corporations embracing the CSR concept can be seen everywhere. For instance, the FTSE4Good Index Series has been developed to "objectively measure the performance of companies that meet globally recognised corporate responsibility standards," for more information visit: http://www.ftse.co.uk/Indices/FTSE4Good_Index_Series/index.jsp.

Design has the potential to help an organization incorporate CSR principles into all key activities, for example by delivering socially responsible products/services, communicating social and ethical values to wider audiences, and reducing environmental impacts in the workplace. Koo and Cooper (2011) defined design management for CSR as "effective management of (1) designing a business and organisational process for CSR and (2) creating design outcomes that include: (a) socially responsible products and services; (b) socially responsible operating environments; and (c) CSR-informed communication strategies." Many experts argued that design can contribute beyond helping businesses to do well by doing good. Good use of design could address the whole "triple bottom line."

The term *triple bottom line* (TBL), was developed by John Elkington in 1994, who presented it as a win-win-win business strategy. He suggested corporations to go beyond generating economic value and add two additional features, social and environmental value (Elkington, 2004). This chapter will explore how design strategy can contribute to the TBL and other emerging concepts, like social innovation.

7.2 REVIEW OF EMERGING CONCEPTS

7.2.1 Triple Bottom Line: People, Planet, Profit

Triple bottom line starts with responsibility towards fellow human beings, continues with taking responsibility for the survival and sustainability of our planet Earth, and ends with the generation of profit. It is thus a reversal of the business concept of profit first practised by organizations for many decades.

This can only be achieved by creating economic, social and environmental values and is thus similar to the principles of sustainable development, which aim to meet the needs of the present without compromising the ability of future generations to meet their own needs; thus making life better for everyone (United Nations Commission on Environment and Development, 1987; cited in White, Belletire and St Pierre, 2007).

Elkington (2004) identified seven key drivers behind the widespread adoption of the new principle, as shown below:

1. **Market:** Gone are the days of simply complying with ethical and social demands. Businesses now perceive the TBL as a means to compete in a

highly competitive market. In order to win customers' hearts and minds, it is important to deliver desirable products/services that make people feel good about themselves, e.g. creating jobs for people in developing countries and reducing environmental impacts by choosing an energy-efficient product. Good use of the TBL approach and effective design has helped brands/companies (such as Innocent, Ben & Jerry's and Green & Black) differentiate themselves in the saturated market and stay away from commodity products.

2. **Values:** People are now more interested in human and societal values, such as the sense of belonging and the sense of community. This change influences their purchasing criteria and behaviour. An increase of web sites such as www.betterworldshopper.org, which provide comprehensive information regarding social and environmental practices of brands/companies, clearly demonstrates that CSR has become a key purchasing criterion.

3. **Transparency:** Due to the revolution of the Internet and social networks, it has become harder to hide bad practices: think about the impacts of web sites such as WikiLeaks and TripAdvisor. The only way to survive is by being honest and well-behaved. Patagonia, an outdoor clothing business, take honesty to the next level by creating the footprint chronicles web site (http://www.patagonia.com/eu/enGB/footprint) which allows customers and the general public to trace the carbon footprint of their products. This practice helps the firm differentiate itself from other competitors and position itself as an ethical brand.

4. **Lifecycle technology:** The focus of companies began to shift from producing products to delivering values (or functions that the products offer). Rather than thinking that people buy a car from a company and then concentrating all the effort on designing, manufacturing and distributing the car, it is better to step back to see the big picture that people actually buy an ability to safely, conveniently and comfortably travel from A to B. Dos Santos, Krämer and Vezzoli (2009) described this shift of focus from selling product to delivering values as satisfaction-based economy. The term *satisfaction-based* suggests that the user may not have the ownership of a product, but his/her needs are fulfilled through the use of the product and value-added services. Once companies understand what values they actually offer (rather than what products they produce and sell), they can explore other ways of satisfying people needs in a less material-intensive manner.

5. **Partners:** Companies increasingly work with other firms (including their competitors) in order to deliver a holistic solution to customers. The most significant changes, such as electric cars, cannot be realized by one company. It requires collaboration of various parties, for example automotive companies, energy suppliers, infrastructure providers (e.g. charging station) and the government. By involving all parties and exploring problems/opportunities from various perspectives, the outcomes are more likely to address all important aspects.

6. **Time:** To achieve social and environmental agendas, a company needs long-term visions, and strategies. Design thinking can really help businesses explore and imagine possible futures, and plan strategies accordingly, see www.forumforthefuture.org for an example.

7. **Corporate governance:** Good governance has become an essential factor that helps a company attract consumers and talented employees. There is no single authoritative definition of the term *good governance*. However, the word "governance" is often associated with "ruling and managing." Hence, good governance could be simply described as an approach to management that encompasses and encourages transparency, democracy and accountability. Design, especially Big-D design, can help companies create the climate/organizational cultures that promote equality, involvement, sharing and openness.

The TBL concept can be used as a design management tool. It can help an organization frame its strategic plans to ensure that the value creation process and the outcomes address economic, social and environmental needs in a holistic manner.

Planet: Environmental Bottom Line

Creating environmental values to sustain our planet is about reducing environmental impacts and making the best use of natural resources/energy. Bhamra and Lofthouse proposed *"Six Rules of Thumb"* to help organizations design and deliver their offers in an environmentally friendly way. They are:

1. *Re-think:* Rethink the product and its functions.
2. *Re-duce:* Reduce the energy and resource consumption in the whole life cycle
3. *Re-place:* Replace hazardous substances with environmentally sound alternatives.
4. *Re-cycle:* Use those materials which can be reused or recycled.
5. *Re-use:* Design in such a way that the product or part of it can be reused.
6. *Re-pair:* Design a product that is easy to repair.

People: Social Bottom Line

Creating societal values is about promoting social inclusion and social interaction across different generations and cultural backgrounds. This means designers must build social capital and adopt an inclusive design approach. The idea of social capital suggests that social connections and networks (e.g. friendships and partnerships) have economic values and could promote economic growth. Hence, relationships between individuals and/or organizations should be nurtured by making sure that their offers (e.g. services) include everyone and encourage people to interact with those from other social groups. The Ageing Population Panel (2000) suggested that *"Designing for Social Inclusion"* has four cornerstones:

- *Stimulation:* Design should keep mind and body active and healthy.
- *Flexibility:* Design should be able to adapt to suit different users.
- *Independence:* Design should prevent or delay dependency.
- *Social interaction:* Design should promote a sense of identity as a full member of society.

Profit: Economic Bottom Line

The survival and sustainability of organizations requires managers to give continued attention to the economic bottom line as it is about creating wealth and this means constantly improving and innovating by fostering collective creativity internally and externally. Dos Santos, Krämer and Vezzoli (2009) provided an interesting case study of Masisa, a solid wood product producer operating in many countries, such as Chile, Argentina, Brazil and Venezuela. Recognizing that many people in these countries could not afford to buy household furniture, the company came up with the strategy that generates profits and improves the quality of life of local people.

The conventional business model of manufacturing furniture at the plants and then distributing products to customers incurs a lot of costs, which makes the final offers unaffordable for many potential customers. By rethinking the business model and involving customers in the value creation process, the company managed to overcome previous problems and expand their market. How did they do it? The firm set up small plants in the areas that they would like to sell their products and employed local people to work in the plants and distribute products to customers in their neighbourhoods. Getting local people to sell products in their neighbourhoods has proven to be very effective – this echoes the idea that social networks do have economic values! By creating jobs for local people, the company managed to expand their market and generate more profits. This case study showed that the symbiosis of relationships between organizations and society can be very beneficial.

7.2.2   Social Innovation and Social Enterprise

Definition of Social Innovation

One of the simplest and clearest definitions of social innovation was given by Mulgan *et al.* (2007). The authors defined innovation as "new ideas that work" and, therefore, the term *social innovation* was described as "new ideas that work in meeting social goals." Social goals, in this case, range from creating opportunities for disadvantaged people to strengthening the sense of community across different groups of people.

Key Drivers of Social Innovation

Murray, Caulier-Grice and Mulgan (2010) observed that the concept of social innovation emerged as a means to address complex social issues which could not be solved by either the public or private sectors. The bureaucratic structure and "old-school policies" impede the government's ability to tackle social problems efficiently, while the lack of economic incentives make most private companies reluctant to respond to social challenges. As a result, many progressive thinkers decided to take charge and take control of the situation. They noted that there are several factors that contribute to the emergence of the concept.

Firstly, the digital revolution, – i.e. online communication, high-speed broadband, smartphones, web tools and social network sites, has helped people with common interests find and collaborate with each other.

Secondly, boundaries between consumption and production have become blurred. People no longer wait for someone to come up with a solution that answers their needs. They want to be part of creating that solution. Moreover, collaborations and iterative developments have become increasingly important – see emerging practices, such as open sources and open design discussed in Chapter 6 for examples. Further, people are becoming more and more socially and environmentally conscious, as they pay more attention to such developments as the Fairtrade certified mark and so forth. Putting all these factors together, groups of socially and environmentally conscious people, who are keen to take charge of these undesirable situations, have emerged. They use social networking tools to collaborate and seek innovative means to solve problems. Since this social innovation concept is truly bottom-up, it promotes user-centred practices, starting with people, and democratizes the development process by involving everyone.

Social Innovation Model

Murray, Caulier-Grice and Mulgan (2010) proposed a social innovation model which consists of six key stages: (1) prompts, inspires and diagnoses, (2) generates proposals and ideas, (3) prototypes and pilots, (4) sustains, (5) scales and diffuses, and (6) promotes systemic changes. Design, especially design thinking, has the power to contribute or even drive social innovation and social enterprise development through these steps. Brown and Wyatt (2010) argue that design thinking is essential to the success of social innovation projects. They gave a very compelling case study of a young Indian women who cannot get safe water from the community treatment plant and has to fetch unclean water from a local borehole 300 feet away because she cannot carry the 5-gallon jerry can that the facility requires her to use. Good use of design research and participatory design can prevent this kind of problem from happening in the first place. Table 7.1 demonstrates how design could support social innovation from the beginning right through to the end, matching potential roles of strategic design and design tools against main activities and requirements of all six key stages described above.

Example: OpenIDEO

One good example of how design could support and drive social innovation is OpenIDEO (www.openideo.com). This open innovation platform encourages people from various backgrounds to "design together for social good." It sets out clear principles, encouraging design that is: (1) inclusive, (2) community-centred, (3) collaborative, (4) optimistic and aims for (5) continuous improvement.

OpenIDEO works with various organizations to come up with "challenges" addressing diverse social issues. Every challenge starts with a big question, such as how might we create healthy communities within and beyond the workplace? After the challenge is posted, members of the OpenIDEO community go through three main phases of the design process – inspiration, ideation and evaluation. People can contribute in many different ways, e.g. sharing insights/photographs during the inspiration phase, submitting sketches/ideas/business models during the ideation phase and

Table 7.1 Strategic design for social innovation

Six stages	Purpose	Strategic design roles/tools
Prompts, inspires and diagnoses.	Identifying real problems and/or needs for innovation through proper ethnographic and action research.	Design research tools for: problem identification, engaging communities, extracting insights and key themes.
Generates proposals and ideas.	Co-creating "with" people not "for" people using creative tools, such as forum theatre and participatory workshop.	Ideation, inclusive design and co-creation, creative tools, co-design, human-centred design, visualization.
Prototypes and pilots.	Carry out an iterative process of prototyping and testing and refining ideas with all key stakeholders.	Prototyping products/services/ experiences, testing and refining.
Sustains	Ensuring long-term financial sustainability – business models developed concurrently with innovation developments and user trials.	Long-term design strategy, sustaining creative environment, integration into business model.
Scales and diffuses	Spreading and focussing ideas or expanding practices – clear strategies, such as licensing and franchising.	Developing policies, engaging stakeholders, communication design, auditing and impact assessment tools.
Promotes systemic changes	An ultimate goal – changing the concept/mindset.	Systems thinking tools, change management frameworks, implementation planning.

assessing/revising other people's ideas during the evaluation phase. Finally, the winning concepts are selected. These concepts are made available for anyone to use, build upon and share legally – in a similar way to Creative Commons (see http://creativecommons.org for further information).

Definition of Social Enterprise

The burgeoning of collaborative networks and increasing emphasis on human values is leading to more democratizing and transparent practices. This situation also leads to a new breed of organizations, a *social enterprise,* which is defined as "a business with primarily social objectives whose surpluses are principally reinvested for that purpose in the business or in the community, rather than being driven by the need to maximise profit for shareholders and owners" (DTI, 2002). The study carried out by the Department of Trade and Industry observed that successful social enterprises share the following characteristics:

- gaining independence and autonomy through trading;
- entrepreneurial, innovative, risk-taking behaviour;
- flexible and adaptable practices;
- customers and community focus;
- stakeholder engagement;

- democratic and participative management;
- delivering socially and/or environmentally as well as financially; and
- financially viable, gaining their income from selling goods and services.

Social Enterprise Model

A social enterprise is a business. Hence, it carries out some form of trading, which is mainly for a social or environmental purpose. The Charities Aid Foundation (2008) pointed out that there are three ways that social impacts can be created through trading activities:

1. **"Profit generator"** model: Engage in a trading activity that has no direct social impact, make a profit, and then transfer some or all of that profit to another activity that does have direct social impact. One Water (www.onewater.org.uk) is an example. As a company it produces and sells products that have nothing to do with the communities that it aims to help. However, it donates 100% of the profit to social projects.
2. **"Trade-off"** model: Engage in a trading activity that does have direct social impact, but manage a trade-off between producing financial return and social impact, see the Ethical Property Company (www.ethicalproperty.co.uk) for an example. This property agency shares its office spaces (15 centres altogether across the UK) with charities, social enterprises, voluntary and campaign groups. Similar to the first model, its business has nothing to do with people that it supports (e.g. not-for-profit organizations), but the way it does business helps people achieve what they would like to achieve.
3. **"Lock-step"** model: Engage in a trading activity that not only has direct social impact, but also generates a financial return in direct correlation to the social impact created. Abel & Cole (www.abelandcole.co.uk) provides an example. The company works directly with food producers (e.g. farmers and butchers) to deliver high-quality seasonal food products to customers in an environmentally-friendly manner (e.g. reusing delivery boxes). What it trades and the way it trades creates economic, environmental and social values. The firm also received many awards for its outstanding customer services.

Design can contribute to all three models. Good use of small-d design can help create desirable products/services that help support good causes. Big-D design can help a company manager to integrate ethical practices into their business activities, e.g. designing workplaces and job descriptions in the way that does not exclude disadvantaged people. In addition, Big-D and small-d designs could be help a company design a business and its offers in a way that directly supports its social missions, e.g. creating jobs for people whom they want to help.

7.2.3 Cradle-to-Grave versus Cradle-to-Cradle

Cradle-to-Grave

The cradle-to-grave model is currently the most frequently encountered approach to show how design is used to mitigate impacts on the environment throughout the product life cycle. The objective is to create more value for less environmental impacts by using such principles as green design, eco-design and eco-efficiency. An example of how the environmental aspects are factored in to the design process can be seen in the World Business Council for Sustainable Development's "Seven Elements for Eco-Efficiency Improvement":

- Reduce material intensity
- Reduce energy intensity
- Reduce dispersion of toxic substances
- Enhance recyclability
- Maximize use of renewables
- Extend product durability
- Increase service intensity

In order to reduce environment impacts, it is important to measure the current impacts – what causes the impact and how it impacts on the environment. *Life cycle assessment* (LCA) is the methodology commonly used by managers to measure the environment impacts throughout the whole product life cycle. This methodology is also known as life cycle analysis and cradle-to-grave analysis. The approach is considered scientific and comprehensive (but very time-consuming), since it analyzes every single stage of the product life cycle in detail. LCA sees each stage of the product life cycle as a transformation process – input(s) have been transformed into output(s). Some experts describe this transformation process a "black box" system. You do not need to fully understand what happens inside the black box (e.g. how a particular technology works). However, you must be able to quantify all inputs (e.g. materials and energy) and outputs (e.g. by-products, wastes and emission). These accumulated inputs and outputs determine environment impacts of the product over its entire life cycle.

Lewis *et al.* (2001) explained that the LCA methodology is divided into four stages. Firstly, the goal and scope must be defined. It is important to establish what you want to know and clarify the boundaries of the systems that will be included in the assessment. Secondly, the life cycle inventory analysis must be carried out. This stage is about establishing the flows of materials and energy through the product system. This analysis results in a long list of resources used and emissions to the environments (e.g. solid wastes and airborne wastes). The next stage is the life cycle impact assessment, which determines environmental impacts of all resources and emissions identified through the previous stage. This is probably the most difficult part, since environmental impacts of some substances are not available or unreliable. Finally, the results are interpreted and checked for their validity. Since the final conclusions are based on a lot of calculations and assumptions, it is crucial that everything is done thoroughly. The LCA results could highlight key areas that require serious attention, which could help designers and developers to improve the design to make it more environmentally friendly.

Example: ZEDfactory

ZEDfactory is a good example of how companies focus on carbon footprint reduction. The firm is a leader in the field of low carbon architecture. It provides various creative solutions ranging from a sustainable home to large-scale urban planning. ZEDfactory collaborated with BioRegional to create Beddington Zero Energy Development (BedZED), the UK's largest mixed use sustainable community. Residents are encouraged to reduce their carbon footprint through numerous initiatives, such as onsite car club and waste management. (For more information: www.zedfactory.com).

Cradle-to-Cradle

The ultimate objective of the cradle-to-cradle model is to create a closed loop ecosystem where wastes and by-products are used to create new value, thus eliminating waste. McDonough and Braungart (2002) called this "upcycling," a process for redesigning wastes into new products. They argued that the current recycling process, which they called "downcycling," means the quality and value of the materials drops every time it is recycled. Moreover the recycling process consumes much energy and requires (potentially harmful) additives to compensate for the reducing quality. The authors promoted the idea of the "upcycling" process, which requires creativity and design thinking instead of energy and resources to breathe new life into wastes or products at the end of their life cycles.

From Waste to Want

From Somewhere is a creative sustainable fashion brand founded by Orsola de Castro and Filipo Ricci since 1997. Their collections are made with pre-consumer wastes, such as swatches, off-cuts and end of rolls. Each garment is unique and individually cut from high-quality reclaimed fabrics. To demonstrate that this concept is suitable for both niche and mainstream markets, the company worked with Tesco's F&F line to develop a six-piece collection from obsolete jersey stock, end of rolls and pre-consumer textile waste. Tesco claims that this practice helps slow down the unnecessary virgin textile production and reduce wastes within its supply chains. The recent collaboration between From Somewhere and Speedo to create a capsule design collection from unsold stock and surplus pieces of Speedo LZR Racer suit shows that the upcycling process has a wide range of application.

7.2.4 Co-design and Co-production

In a world where stakeholders, particularly consumers, are increasingly demanding to be consulted and/or involved in the development of products and/or services which impact upon their daily lives, the trend towards co-operative creation is gaining momentum. The boundaries around organizations are rapidly disappearing in favour of flexible, responsive organisms which interact with the wider world around them. Managers need new tools for this cooperative and sharing paradigm.

Co-design

One such valuable tool is *co-design*, a distinctive approach to design that emphasizes the creative contribution that can be made by potential users, clients and other stakeholders in a product or system. Co-design is defined as collective creativity of designers and people who are not trained in design through the whole design process (Sanders and Stappers, 2008). It is widely used in the private sector for both products and services, to accelerate user acceptance and reduce potential failure. Also co-design is gaining momentum in the public sector as a way of engaging citizens in design exploration. The co-design approach reflects a shift from user-centred design, which treats the user as the subject, to participatory design wherein the user becomes a partner, which aligns well with the concerns of the voluntary sector. The concept of co-design fits well with TBL principles, as it empowers people and helps develop social capital further.

What makes co-design different from other forms of collaboration is the role of users who are expected to be involved in all stages of the design process: problem definition and opportunity developments, research and analyses, ideation and design development, commercialization, including marketing, manufacturing and distribution, and after-sales when products or services reach target audiences (Sanders and Simons, 2009). Thus, co-design goes beyond a traditional user consultation and/or qualitative user research.

Co-design has become more important in the past few years due to three main reasons. Firstly, the collaborative approach helps democratize the design/innovation development process. It is only right that people who will be (directly or indirectly) affected by outcome(s) should be involved in creating and making key decisions during the development process. Secondly, involving all key stakeholders in the design process could help (1) identify and tackle potential problems early in the process, (2) make sure that the outcomes match requirements and expectations of all parties and (3) accelerate the buy-in among all key stakeholders. In addition, many experts perceive co-design as a transformation process. Engaging non-designers in the design process could help these people develop new skills, new ways of thinking and confidence to use their creativity to tackle everyday issues.

Although all stakeholders should normally be involved in the co-design process, it is important to note that not everyone is interested in "creating" products or services. Involving people who are not trained in design can be problematic. Sanders and Westerlund (2011) pointed out that novices may spend too much time on one early idea rather than exploring many possibilities. Besides, they may find it difficult to create ideas if they do not think that they are creative or have sufficient knowledge to contribute. By contrast there is also the danger that untrained designers see themselves as designers and insist upon pursuing ideas which have fundamental flaws.

Good use of design and design thinking are needed to take all key stakeholders on the co-design journey successfully. This must include good design management leadership to promote communication and mutual respect.

Co-production

Many experts see *co-production* as a natural progression of co-design – after getting people involved in designing products/services, it makes sense to continue working with them to deliver the outcomes as well. The term/practice is rooted in public service delivery. For example, Boyle and Harris

(2009) suggested that "co-production means delivering public services in an equal and reciprocal relationship between professionals, people using services, their families and their neighbours. Where activities are co-produced in this way both services and neighbourhood become far more effective agents of change." Nowadays, the practices are widely adopted in other sectors.

An example of the application may be getting parents to help to design "stay & play" services for their toddlers. They could become involved in delivering services as well, e.g. getting them to help run certain games/play activities or involving them in preparing healthy snacks for their children. The question arises "will people be willing to help your organization delivering services for free?" If this service means something to them and they are keen to be involved in designing it, then there is a strong chance that they will be happy to help with delivering services – providing that they do not feel exploited!

Example: Open Door Project, Grimsby

This health and social care project (Bontoft, 2006) provides a good example of how co-design and co-production can be used to tackle serious social issues in a collaborative and sustainable manner. It is complex and goes to the heart of human needs. It shows how the use of the co-design and co-production tools can bring real benefits through the integration of Big-D thinking and small-d design.

Bontoft's study found that people in certain areas of Grimsby have experienced many serious social and economic problems, such as low income, low employment, a high crime rate, high health deprivation, poor education, barriers to good housing and a poor living environment. As an example, a girl in Grimsby's South ward aged 15–17 is three times more likely to get pregnant than a girl in a neighbouring ward. A man living in an area of high multiple deprivations will die seven years earlier than the regional average. Clearly, people in these areas needed help to improve their health and their quality of life

Rather carrying out user research in a conventional manner, the team employed the co-design and co-production approach. They got people to help them conduct the research by, for example, giving young people disposable cameras to take photographs of what they saw as "central" to life in their town so that the project team could see Grimsby through local people's eyes. Over 200 printed cards asking people for their "gripes" (complaints) about their past experience of health care were left at strategic places like doctor's waiting rooms and the Grimsby library. Through this collaborative research, the team managed to engage with hard-to-reach people, such as problematic drug users, homeless people, offenders and sex workers. The co-design approach yielded many insightful results. One of the major findings was that many individuals who seriously need help come from backgrounds where "aggressive" behaviour is the norm (to be heard, you have to shout). This kind of behaviour intimidates doctors, nurses and other health professionals. Thus, they want to "get rid of them" by dealing with them as quickly as possible and trying to distance themselves from these problematic groups. This is why many groups of people were seen to have poor relationships with health practitioners and only seek professional help when their health gets really bad rather than getting advice before their health conditions become serious.

The co-design and co-production approach helped the team to identify priority areas. In order to prevent health problems of people living in the deprived areas (based on the principle that prevention is always better than cure), people must have good relationships with and trust health practitioners, that is to say they need to believe that service providers do care about them and will listen to them. It is important to create a friendly atmosphere – using both tangible and intangible design – with a strong sense of professionalism, and give these people reasons to engage with health professionals before it is too late, for example by providing childcare support. By involving people in delivering some of the services (e.g. Tukes Café in Grimsby is run by and for people with mental illnesses), people feel empowered and have ownership of the services, which in turn builds stronger relationships between users and service providers. (For more information visit: www. thebiglifegroup.com/open-door.)

7.2.5   Innovation at the Bottom on the Pyramid

If the world is represented as a pyramid and the population divided into different groups according to their annual incomes, at the top of the pyramid, there would be a relatively small number of people (75–100 million). These are the people who earn more than $20,000 per year. They are the people whom most brands and companies target, since they have relatively high disposable incomes and can afford to buy luxury products/services. At the middle of the pyramid, will be the people with annual incomes between $1,500 and $20,000. This group is larger than the previous group (1,500–1,750 million). They are the main targets of value-range and mid-range products/services.

At the bottom of the pyramid lies the majority of the world's population (4,000 million). Despite the large size, 65% of the world's population, most brands and companies overlook this group, since each individual in this group earns less than $1,500 per year. In some areas, people earn less than $200 per year.

According to Prahalad and Hammond (2002), this group is an untapped market with strong potential. Rather than competing with other brands and companies in the highly saturated upper market, innovative ideas and clever use of design could help a company improve the quality of life of people at the bottom of the pyramid whilst making considerable profits. The authors pointed out that most companies have incorrect assumptions about this group, believing for example that poor people will not "waste" money on premium products. In fact, they often buy luxury items. While people at the middle of the pyramid tend to save up money in pursuit of better futures (e.g. buying a car), those at the bottom accept their reality, such as the fact that they will not be able to afford a house. Thus, they would rather buy something that could improve their quality of life right now like premium kitchen gadgets and mobile phones.

The authors also observed that people at the bottom of the pyramid pay much higher prices for most things than middle-class consumers do. For example, they cannot get a loan from a bank and, thus, have to borrow money from local lenders who charge them much higher interest rates than high street banks. Since they may have no access to bulk discount stores (often located further away), they pay much higher prices for food and commodity products at smaller local outlets. As individuals, their purchasing power may be rather low. However, as a group, people at the bottom of the pyramid have great purchasing power. Instead of selling a product to each individual, it makes more sense to sell a community a product/service. For example, each family may not be able to afford a broadband internet service. Nevertheless, the whole community can afford the service. So accepting and allowing them to share makes good business sense. Evidently, managers need innovative business models and a new way of designing and delivering their services.

Prahalad and Hart (2002) suggested that there are several commercial infrastructures that should be put in place in order to serve people at the bottom of the pyramid profitably. For example, an organization management should explore how to create buying power, e.g. generating incomes. The Masisa case study mentioned earlier in this chapter demonstrated how a business could create jobs for people so that they can afford to buy its products. By good use of Big-D design thinking a company can come up with a win-win business model and clever small-d design could ensure that products and production processes match local skills and local resources. Moreover, a company should investigate how to tailor their products and services to suit target audiences. Good use of co-design and co-production can ensure that the products/services fulfil user requirements and suit their budgets. Robust products are recommended, since they are likely to be operated in harsh environments where, for example, it is excessively hot or dusty.

Example: Tata Nano

The small car Tata Nano is a good example of how good design can create economic, social and environmental values. Everything is designed to be efficient. All unnecessary parts are removed to reduce the cost and make it more energy-efficient. Obviously, heavy vehicles, like a truck, require more fuel than light ones, such as a Smart car. Nevertheless, the car's road safety is not compromised. Its price tag makes it affordable for wide range of people, especially those at the bottom of the pyramid. The whole car actually costs less than a MacBook. This product helps improve the quality of life of many people – for example, a family with low income can afford to travel by car rather than trying to fit everyone on a motorcycle, a common dangerous practice. Although it does not generate a big profit margin, it makes profit and helps management to position the "Tata" brand favourably on the innovation map.

7.3   4Ds OF DESIGN-DRIVEN TRIPLE-BOTTOM-LINE ORGANIZATION

All businesses/brands have the potential to achieve the triple bottom line (TBL). Williams (2008) identified three categories: those which demonstrate a modern "Ideal" of the new style enterprise, those which "Adapt" to the new environment and those which "Adopt" the TBL standards from the start, see Figure 7.1. She argues that clarity of direction and creative design thinking are required to address sustainability and ethical issues.

Hence the 4Ds design management model should enhance direction, identify opportunities, drive change and evaluate progress toward social enterprise status as follows:

1. Determining the current use of design – finding out how design is used to address social and environmental opportunities/challenges.
2. Defining and aligning environmental and social goals with organizational goals – identifying opportunities for design and establishing realistic goals regarding sustainable development and social innovation.
3. Designing activities, environment and cultures to achieve goals – using Big-D and small-d design to enhance positive social and environmental impacts.
4. Deciding whether a company achieves its goals – objectively assessing sustainable development and social innovation performance.

The key elements of the 4Ds approach to social enterprise are shown in Table 7.2. The interrelationships of four key elements can be illustrated as shown in Figure 7.2.

7.3.1   Determining the Current Use of Design

Determining the current use of design is particularly challenging for management because it involves the ability to audit and review the environmental and social impacts across a very broad spectrum of organizational activities. There are many powerful tools used by management for environmental analysis with much of the emphasis on technology-based impacts but few follow through to closely examine the influence of design. However,

Figure 7.1   Three categories of brands
Source: Williams (2008).

Table 7.2 Key elements of the 4Ds of design contributions in CSR

Strategic level	Tactical level	Operational level
Determining		
• Current use of strategic design for TBL	• Current design TBL performance	• Quality of designs against CSR standards
Defining		
• Ethical brand values • Social innovation goals • Sustainable development goals	• Ethical brand strategy • Sustainable strategies • Social innovation strategies	• Plans for ethical product/service development • Ethical brand message
Designing		
• Design strategy for sustainability and social innovation • Ethical design policy	• Plans for ethical product development • Co-creation process	• Ethical products • Sustainable processes • Social engagement initiatives/schemes
Deciding		
• The appropriateness of the strategy and policy	• The quality of social and sustainable plans	• The performance of products/services

measuring the influence of the organization's design policies, processes and practices can provide the platform for building a reputation for responsible business practice. The extent to which an organization is prepared to be self-critical will also greatly affect the rigour with which this step is pursued. It may be a measure of the maturity and self-confidence of the management to encourage the open dialogue and searching questions for an honest evaluation.

Measuring Design Responsibility at the Strategic Level

The extent to which design may influence a company to develop a TBL approach at strategic level will first depend on the organizational character. Elkington (2004) divided organizations into four categories of TBL-related awareness and this provides a useful platform on which to assess the degree to which strategic design is employed, see Table 7.3.

Example: LUSH

LUSH is a good example of the "corporate butterfly" that respects people and the environment. Originating as a supplier of the Body Shop, Lush has always shared the same belief and values with Body Shop founder Anita Roddick. Their handmade cosmetics use little or no packaging. Evidently, the firm is working towards becoming a social enterprise, as it continues to invest in communities that produce their products and protect animals.

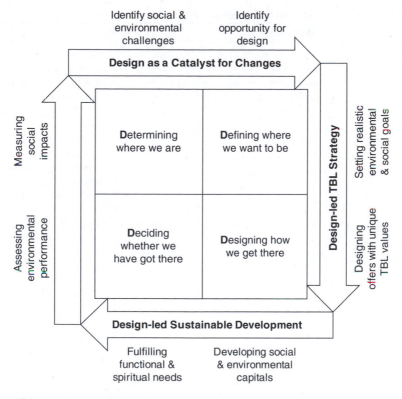

Figure 7.2   Design contributions to triple bottom line

Measuring Design Responsibility at the Tactical and Operational Level

This may begin with an assessment of the level of social responsibility as a platform for planning actions, using such frameworks as the seven social wins of brand in Chapter 6. Frameworks for sustainability, e.g. eco-efficiency (see Chapter 6) and WBCSD's seven elements for eco-efficiency, may be used to assess and plan design responsibility tactics.

The Ecodesign Web developed by Loughborough University provides a good framework to measure the current use of sustainable design at operational level. It comprises seven key categories to be rated on a scale 1–5 (1= very bad; 5= very good).

1. **Materials selection** – type/number of materials (e.g. renewable and recyclable materials).
2. **Materials usage** – appropriate amount for function; number of parts.
3. **Distribution** – type and amount of packaging; type of transport; distance transported.
4. **Product use** – type and amount of energy usage; use of refills and/or consumables.

Table 7.3 Relationships between design and corporate characteristics

Category	Characteristics	Design
Corporate locusts (cannibals)	These are the "bad guys" who care only for economic profit and growth with no concern for the global social, environmental and human damage they cause.	• No long-term goals and policy regarding social responsibility and design for sustainability. • No strategic design used for TBL.
Corporate caterpillars (slugs)	Only marginally more responsible as they damage only their more local or regional environment.	• No long-term goals and policy regarding social responsibility and design for sustainability. • Minimal strategic design for TBL.
Corporate butterflies (birds)	Show their acceptance of corporate social responsibility and TBL sustainable business models and gain recognition for their policies.	• Set long-term TBL goals and design responsibility policies. • Good use of strategic design to establish/enhance ethical brand image and influence others.
Corporate honeybees (bees)	The "good guys" who give positive benefits at local, regional, even global level through strong sustainable business model and clear ethical stance.	• Set long-term TBL goals and design responsibility policies. • Good use of strategic design.

Source: Based on Elkington (2004).

5. **Optimal life** – reliability; durability; easy to maintain; easy to repair; upgradable.
6. **End of life** – reuse of product/components; refurbishment; recycling materials.
7. **New way of doing it** – shared use; multifunction products; services; renting.

Example: DePloy

DePloy (http://deployworkshop.com) is a pioneering company designing and making high-end sustainable womenswear. Their aim is "to make the fashion process less wasteful, more sustainable, and more interactive with the consumer." They design and make multipurpose garments, sourcing their fabrics ethically and using responsible manufacturing methods. Garments are designed with up-to-date construction methods and fine tailoring, and they use hidden poppers to connect modular garments. Each modular item can be connected to create new outfits, thus allowing women to customize/transform their clothes into something new, or wear as separates. They display sensitivity to changing user needs and a social awareness of changing lifestyles. This enables their customers to customize their clothes according to their needs whilst reducing material consumption and waste by prolonging the product life. Their business shows that clever use of modular design, material selection and material usage, can be successful in differentiating the brand while fulfilling the emotional needs expected by customers of demi-couture garments.

7.3.2 Defining and Aligning Environmental and Social Goals with Organizational Goals

The second "D" of the design management model, is "defining" and begins with the degree to which management are ready to accept that designing for environmental and social goals will help them deliver "success." If they remain locked into the mindset that economic performance remains the only legitimate measure of success, they will not move forward to embrace the new opportunities and may well lose out to their more progressive rivals.

Adopting the TBL means establishing goals for economic, social and environmental capital. The process should start by identifying all stakeholder needs. White, Belletire, and St Pierre (2007) suggested that the needs of four key stakeholders should be looked at: the user, the environment, the society and the client/organization.

Jennings (2004) saw the TBL approach as a means to create the three different types of capital – economic, social and environmental capital. In this case, the financial capital refers to the financial gains from the products/services that an organization offers. Since generating social capital is about developing and nurturing social connections and networks (which have potential economic value), an organization must build and maintain good relationships with their employees, partners (suppliers), key stakeholders (investors and customers) and the general public. Going beyond reducing the negative approach by considering environmental impacts only, organizations can create environmental capital by growing natural resources and promoting biodiversity. Jennings' ideas can be used to identify opportunities for strategic design in creating and utilizing the TBL capitals, see Table 7.4.

Elkington (2004) recommends that TBL principles must be integrated into:

1. **Balance sheets** – making a financial plan more transparent and accountable.
2. **Boards** – making top management take full accountability and using the principles to guide the corporate governance and its strategy.
3. **Brands** – using the power of brands to engage investors, customers and consumers directly in social and sustainability issues.
4. **Business models** – placing the principles at the very DNA of business.

The strategic challenges and complexity of using design to create, nurture and utilize all three capitals further strengthens the argument for a new type of design strategist.

Table 7.4 Relationships between strategic design and different capital

Generating capital	Capital type	Opportunities for Design	
		Creating capital	Utilizing capital
Economic	Financial	• Increase financial capital by cutting down unethical and unsustainable practices	• Reinvest in the TBL balanced ventures
	Goods and services	• Build ethical and sustainable design competencies	• Provide ethical and sustainable offerings
Social	Employees	• Recruit and nurture people who share similar values • Provide the right climate and proper training programmes	• Make employees active citizens of communities and committed brand ambassadors
	Stakeholders and society	• Collaborate with local people to deliver offerings with real social impacts	• Nurture relationships to strengthen brand image and innovation capabilities
Environmental	Raw materials	• Develop sustainable design competencies and make ethical choices of materials	• Turn the capabilities into competitive advantages and key differentiation
	Biodiversity	• Embrace biodiversity by injecting flexibility into the design process and choose reliable sources/suppliers	• Use materials that fit local requirements and reduce the carbon footprint by adopting local sourcing

Source: Based on Jennings (2004)

Example: Toyota

Toyota is an example of a company with long-term social and environmental visions.

They seek to "offer the safest and most responsible ways of moving people." Although they encountered recent setbacks owing to certain safety concerns they maintain their commitment to the guiding principles they established in 1992 to respect people and their differences and to contribute to the economic and social development of countries where they operate. Their social targets focus on exceeding customer expectations and human resource development, whilst their environmental targets concentrate on developing sustainable technologies, design for recycling and reducing CO_2 emissions.

7.3.3   Designing Activities, Environment and Cultures to Achieve Goals

The design of appropriate activities requires much breadth of vision. Management must support Big-D design thinking to engender an open ongoing dialogue about the changing world around the organization, and everyone should contribute, not only the managers and design strategists.

This collective "intelligence" must be coordinated and captured and the debate kept vibrant at all times. This culminates in the creation of a design strategy to set appropriate goals and plan the required design activities/ projects to achieve the organization's economic, social and environmental goals. Frameworks and tools for economic and sustainable development have been discussed in previous chapters. Thus one framework incorporating culture for designing for social innovation is presented here.

Strategic Framework for Social Innovation

A valuable strategic framework for social innovation was provided by Ted Matthews from Urban Idea Bakery (2011). He proposed a holistic co-creation framework which goes beyond the TBL and incorporates also cultural values. His idea encompasses four core values: economic, social, environmental and cultural. He suggested that social innovation should begin with capturing user requirements (including those of direct users, indirect users and third parties), then identifying existing barriers which prevent users from fulfilling their needs, then immediate effects, consequent impacts (including social, environmental, economic and cultural impacts) and stakeholders who would be affected by this change should be made explicit, before commencing design and development. It is important to stress that "effects" are not the same as "impacts." All actions lead to some form of results which are often referred to as effects. For example, changes in design curriculum obviously affect staff and students. Impacts are described as what differences certain effects make. Hence, changes in design curriculum could impact on the design industry, design professionals and the creative economy. In order to deliver solutions to fulfil economic, social, environmental and cultural requirements, it is important to take available resources, as well as pros and cons into consideration, e.g. looking at all potential barriers (e.g. possible negative effects, possible negative impacts and persons who might be negatively affected by the solution) and positive outcomes (e.g. positive effects, positive impacts and key beneficiaries).

Example: Marks & Spencer (M&S)

M&S is a good example of a company with clear sense of strategic direction towards achieving the TBL. Their "Plan A," which was established in 2007, focuses on five key issues:

1. **Climate change:** become carbon neutral, e.g. improve energy efficiency in stores.
2. **Waste:** send no waste to landfill, e.g. use sustainable materials for packaging.
3. **Natural resources:** extend sustainable sourcing, e.g. select ethically certified suppliers.
4. **Fair partner:** help improve the lives of people in the supply chain, e.g. help suppliers set up ethical factories and actively support community projects.

5. **Health and wellbeing:** help customers and employees lives healthier lifestyles, e.g. remove artificial colours and flavouring and provide traffic light nutritional food labelling.

They established a consultation process and set clear targets and measurement of performance methods expressing them as open commitments.

Using Co-creative Strategy to Engage all Stakeholders

Another practical way of planning design management strategies to achieve TBL goals is proposed by Ramaswamy and Gouillart (2010). The authors recommended the co-creative strategy as a means to help businesses address the needs of wider audiences beyond their investors, shareholders, customers and business partners and start embracing their employees, suppliers, surrounding communities and the society. For them, the best way to serve the interests of all stakeholders is by involving them in the strategic planning and design development processes. The co-creative strategy focuses on stakeholders' experiences and their interactions with each other and the organization. The co-creation process typically includes:

- Identify all stakeholders touched by the process (employees, customers, suppliers, distributors, communities).
- Understand and map out current interactions among stakeholders.
- Organize workshops in which stakeholders share experiences and imagine ways to improve them.
- Build platforms to implement ideas for new interactions and to continue the dialogue among stakeholders to generate further ideas.

By adopting the co-creation approach all aspects of strategy, such as value, goals, key focus and competitive advantages reflect the needs of all key stakeholders.

The traditional strategy approach creates value by first defining customer experience to deliver to targeted customer set whereas the co-creative strategy creates value by continually improving experiences for all stakeholders. In establishing goals the traditional strategy approach establishes the goals from the start and makes no major changes but co-creative strategy starts with a clear strategic goal but allows the full strategy to emerge responsively over time. Traditional strategists focus on trying to maximize the business share of the created value and beat competitors. The focus of co-creation strategy is on the interests of all stakeholders and uses systems thinking to increase the overall market: the share of value becomes secondary. Finally the traditional strategists seek competitive advantage through reducing production/distribution costs and engaging in acquisitions and investments to drive down costs. The co-creation strategists gain advantage by increasingly engaging stakeholders and by co-creating new interactions and experiences, which increases productivity and creativity and lowers costs and risks.

7.3.4   Deciding Whether a Company Achieves Its Goals

Self-assessment is challenging. Much will depend on how high the bar is set by the senior management and this is turn reflects their vision and personal ethics. The setting of moderate goals may not be enough and design thinking is needed to explore the opportunities, assess their potential to add value and formulate a pragmatic strategy. But to evaluate whether an organization achieves its TBL goals, it is necessary to assess its social and environmental impacts. Tools, such as the Ecodesign Web (Bharmra and Lofthouse, 2007), are useful for evaluating the environmental impacts of the business offers. However, to measure business performance in relation to both environmental and social impacts, it is important to set clear goals so that a company can self-assess whether they have achieved their targets or not. M&S and Toyota provide examples of good practice in assessing and reporting progress. They make regular checks to monitor their progress, set realistic but challenging goals for the next stage towards their quest to become truly sustainable and socially responsible organizations – see http://plana.marksandspencer.com and www.toyota-global.com/sustainability.

Measuring social impacts are considered more "tricky." It is difficult to precisely evaluate what differences a company makes to society and thus more subjective. In a report submitted to the Bill & Melinda Gates Foundation, Tuan (2008) analyzed the pros and cons of eight different methods currently used to measure social impacts of organizations, especially those in the not-for-profit sector. Most of these methods were based on the two ideas of *cost-benefit analysis* and *cost-effectiveness analysis*.

The differences between the two approaches are best explained through examples. Consider the case of giving £100 to Charity A in India. Using the cost-benefit analysis approach, the charity will be able to report that this donation has helped provide malaria vaccines to 10 children, which in turn, has saved potential treatment costs by X and freed up doctors' time to treat other patients by Y. If the charity uses the cost-effectiveness approach, it can report the cost per child cured of malaria and how the results are more effective than other schemes.

Richardson (2004) proposed a cost-benefit analysis (CBA) for a TBL organization by generating questions about the external costs and benefits which the organization generates.

The key question for such external influences may be "What are the external environmental, social and human costs and benefits?" Table 7.5 suggests how design strategy may be used to maximize the external benefits whilst minimizing negative impacts for a TBL-aware organization. It provides a platform for addressing complex choices with which management are faced and a basis for evaluating their effectiveness.

Another social impact measurement which has become widely adopted in past few years is *social return on investment* (SROI). The concept was developed based on the cost-benefit analysis, social accounting and social auditing (New Economic Foundation, 2008). The formula can be simply described as:

SROI = Net present value of benefits/Net present value of investment

The approach was designed based on the TBL principles, since it put stakeholders at the centre to make sure that the needs and interests of

Table 7.5 Maximizing external benefits through design

Impact on costs/benefits for:	Role of design strategy
Consumers	• Adding value – perceived value of product/service over the price paid. • Integrating added environmental benefits. • Reducing/eliminating harmful effects.
Investors	• Maintaining a strong responsible ethical and environmental reputation. • Contributing to profitability.
Staff	• Promoting responsible practices, staff development and wellbeing. • Minimizing stress and health problems.
Work environment	• Improving the work environment and harmonizing it with the external environment.
Suppliers	• Using sustainable design to increase supplier responsibility, economic growth and efficiency.
Local community	• Engaging with the external community to identify opportunities to contribute to economic growth and regeneration. • Actively seeking ways to support sustainable local and government initiatives. • Identifying and mitigating negative impacts on local community
Wider society	• Eliminating all harmful emissions/effects on the environment. • Seeking appropriate opportunities to support social projects.

all parties are taken into consideration. The New Economic Foundation explained that the SROI analysis includes four main stages:

Stage 1: Boundary setting and impact mapping:
1.1. Establish the parameter for the SROI analysis. It is about drawing a scope through proper consultations with all parties. Which outcomes should be included or excluded?
1.2. Identify, prioritize and engage stakeholders. Who are your stakeholders? What are your goals and objectives? What are your main focuses or priorities?
1.3. Develop a theory of change. What are your inputs, outputs, outcomes and impacts?

Stage 2: Collecting data:
2.1. Select indicators. Indicator is a piece of information could help you determine whether positive change has taken place or not, e.g. the number of unemployment is reduced.
2.2. Identify financial values and proxies. Expressing the indicators in financial terms, e.g. reducing the employment rate means more people can

pay tax (how much money would the government gain through additional tax payment?), less people requiring financial support from the
government (how much money does the government save in total?)
2.3. Data collection. How are you going to collect evidence? (Interview,
focus group, etc.)

Stage 3: Modelling and calculating:
3.1. Analyze inputs. Checking all the costs and investments (e.g. time and
staff).
3.2. Add up the benefits. Identifying all benefits (e.g. the net saving of
local governments).
3.3. Project value into the future. Assess the longevity of the programme.
Consider a company which invests money in youth training programmes. What will happen after this company stops providing financial support? Is the programme self-sufficient to continue providing
high-quality training without financial support from the company?
3.4. Calculate the SROI. Comparing the benefits against the costs and
investments.
3.5. Conduct a sensitivity analysis. To what extent would your results
change if your assumptions change? If the best scenario cannot be
achieved, how does it affect the result?

Stage 4: Reporting and embedding:
1.1. Prepare the SROI report. Making sure that the report makes sense to all
parties.
1.2. Communicate and embed. Treating it as an on-going process (similar
to financial audit).

By conducting such a rigorous analysis, social impacts of organizations can
be determined. Good use of tools, such as CBA and SROI, can help a company ensure that their targets are met and build up valuable knowledge for
informing future strategy. However, the key to successful TBL design strategy lies in the balance between the objective measurements and the subjective judgements. If the balance is too biased to the objective/quantitative
measures, it may be too rigid to allow for insightful evaluation and new
thinking. Indeed there is a danger that the management may be measuring the wrong factors. On the other hand, if it is too subjective, it may lack
features of accountability and cause disharmony among the managers and
designers through widely varying interpretations of the strategy.

7.4 CASE STUDY 5 – TRIPLE-BOTTOM-LINE ORGANIZATION: THE BODY SHOP

The Body Shop is arguably the most important pioneering business in the
field of environmental and social responsibility. It was founded by Anita
Roddick in 1976 and presently has 2,400+ retail outlets in 61 countries.
Anita Roddick (nee Perilli) found her inspiration in Berkeley, California
when she visited a shop selling natural soaps and cosmetics and sold by

immigrant women shop assistants. The products were environmentally friendly and the employment policy a contribution to the social and economic wellbeing of the immigrant community. Roddick purchased the naming rights from this origin Body Shop and opened her own shop in Brighton, UK. The new shop quickly captured the imagination of consumers and further outlets were opened. The success of The Body Shop is firmly based on the character and vision of Anita Roddick. It was founded on her personal values which she strove to maintain as the business grew. Radical new principles were introduced changing the thinking about business models forever.

The platform for the business model was a caring face: caring about people and the environment. Indeed the caring extends to all living creatures as they claimed to be the first brand to prohibit the selling of cosmetics tested on animals. Protection of animal rights goes deep into the hearts and minds of many people and thus buying from The Body Shop was immediately perceived as "doing good." It quickly became more of a movement, a major shift in social values, than a conventional business.

The brand developed into a world leader in social and environmental responsibility. This complicated the operation of the business but yielded benefits. It seemed consumers worldwide were ready to engage with a responsible brand. As consumers they liked to regard themselves as responsible (although much research shows they did not always choose more expensive environmentally friendly products) and feel ownership of a brand which reflected their inner values.

Design played a major role in this first to become famous TBL business. The Body Shop became a consistent added-value experience, and the human senses of sight, touch and particularly smell were engaged well. Right from the recognition of the brand identity, through the logo and the store fronts, consumers gained a sense of belonging to a community, "their" community, waiting to welcome and embrace them. The design remained "down to earth," reflecting the brand's firm roots in nature, in sharp contrast to other cosmetic brands which offered glamour and fantasy, a dream of fame and celebrity status.

Roddick showed the way but remained clear about the three main responsibilities of a company. She recognized that a company must be profitable, but declared that this should not be achieved through exploitation such as human rights abuses (such as child labour) and environmental damage (such as the destruction of the rainforest). It was also important to her that the employees should feel a sense of pride in their work. This employee engagement also contributed to the concept of internal branding, whereby employees become the frontline ambassadors for the brand.

The Body Shop maintained profitability but Anita Roddick sold the brand to the cosmetics giant L'Oreal in 2006 and died the next year. This move caused controversy as L'Oreal is part owned by Nestle –itself no stranger to controversy about ethical business practices – and still uses animals to test new cosmetics ingredients. Roddick claimed The Body Shop would act like a "trojan horse" and change the L'Oreal brand from the inside. The extent to which that may happen is yet to be revealed, but L'Oreal have maintained their sub-brand The Body Shop's brand values and revitalized the brand for a new younger generation of ethically minded consumers. They appointed their first "brand ambassador" Lily Cole as the new face of the "Beauty with A Heart" campaign. Improved online retailing has received much design attention and integration into social networks and new concept stores, based on storytelling, launched. As a confirmation of the success of the refreshed branding, the business made an additional 9.1% profit in the year 2012, much of the extra coming from the Middle East and South East Asia.

Any business which sets out to be essentially "good" will attract close scrutiny and The Body Shop has been much criticized for alleged short-comings in its delivery of the brand promise. One of the main criticisms became known as "greenwashing," which is broadly a tendency to claim environmentally friendly practices without sufficient care to ensure that they do indeed improve the environment. Thus the challenges for success-ful TBL businesses are arguably much greater than for the former economic-only driven businesses. But businesses no longer have a choice, as failure to encompass responsible behaviour is no longer acceptable.

Business managers can use Big-D design to generate a wider understand and vision of the changing expectations, for example in the beauty indus-try there is an explosion of interest in cosmetic surgery for both men and women. They must involve and integrate the practices of small-d creative designers to deliver experiences which fully reflect their "face" to the world.

A summary of some of the design strategy challenges which may face The Body Shop in maintaining its reputation as the leading socially and environmentally responsible brand experience may be seen below:

Big-D design strategy	Brand experience for TBL	Small-d delivery
Animal rights	Caring for all living creatures.	Continual search for "pure" natural ingredients.
Environmental protection	Taking a lead in the responsibility for the survival of our planet.	Vigilance in using only environmentally friendly materials and processes and generating creating ideas to improve the environment.
		Appropriate responses to negative publicity.
Young people's brand	Reflecting youth culture.	Energizing experiences – reflecting shifting social concerns and values.
Against ageism	Emergent images of "new" meanings of beauty.	Inclusive design whilst avoiding alienation.
Ethical stance on explosion of interest in cosmetic surgery.	Promoting natural or enhanced beauty.	Entire range of designed products and services.

Some questions for discussion:

- Can The Body Shop change/influence the reputation of its owner L'Oreal as a responsible, caring corporation?
- How can design strategy interpret/reflect shifting social values?
- Is it possible to eliminate every harmful effect which an organization may have on its environment?

7.5   SUMMARY OF KEY POINTS

- The new triple-bottom-line (TBL) enterprise requires much strategic design management thinking.
- TBL is driven by competition and the need to create social wealth and protect the environment responsibly.
- Economic, social and environment goals must be set by organizational management.
- New forms of enterprise based on social innovation and social enterprise are emerging.
- Social innovation requires ideas and leadership from designers.
- Managers must align social and environmental goals to organizational goals.
- The cradle-to-grave model for design seeks to mitigate impacts on the environment throughout the product life cycle.
- The cradle-to-cradle approach aims to eliminate waste through a closed loop system.
- Innovation at the bottom of the economic pyramid can be profitable.
- Co-design and co-production can be used to increase the effectiveness of design solutions, promote ownership and increase acceptance of the outcomes.
- The 4Ds model of design management may be used to progress towards social enterprise status.
- Social and environmental goals must be reviewed and measured.
- By ascertaining the current use, defining suitable but challenging goals, formulating a pragmatic strategy and evaluating performance, design strategy can drive the achievement of TBL.

7.6   FURTHER CONSIDERATIONS

Exercise the Mind...

- Can an organization survive by giving attention only to economic objectives?
- In the TBL model how can management ensure the design strategy balances the economic, social and environmental goals and creates synergy? What happens if one of the goals becomes dominant?
- Is the cradle-to-cradle approach desirable? Is it truly achievable?
- Are there potential pitfalls in environmental design given the limitations of scientific knowledge?

- How can brand experiences be designed and managed to deliver all the TBL values and incorporate cultural awareness?
- What design strategy can managers use to reach the "bottom of the pyramid" economic sector?
- How best can management measure intangible benefits of social and environmental achievements?
- Can design thinking help managers to explore the changing world and select the important impacts upon the organization and the brand(s)?

7.7 GLOSSARY

Co-design: Design Council, UK defined this design practice as "a way to design a solution for a community with that community."

Corporate social responsibility was defined by the European Commission as "the responsibility of enterprises for their impacts on society."

Social enterprise: Social Enterprise UK defined the term as "a social enterprise is a business that trades for a social and/or environmental purpose." It will have a clear sense of its "social mission": which means it will know what difference it is trying to make, who it aims to help, and how it plans to do it. It will bring in most or all of its income through selling goods or services. And it will also have clear rules about what it does with its profits, reinvesting these to further the "social mission."

Social innovation: The Center for Social Innovation at the Stanford Graduate School of Business defined the term as "the process of inventing, securing support for, and implementing novel solutions to social needs and problems."

The triple bottom line (TBL) "focuses corporations not just on the economic value they add, but also on the environmental and social value they add – and destroy. At its narrowest, the term 'triple bottom line' is used as a framework for measuring and reporting corporate performance against economic, social and environmental parameters" (SustainAbility, 2003 cited in Vanclay, 2004). SustainAbility is a consultancy founded by John Elkington, who coined the term.

7.8 REFERENCES AND ADDITIONAL READING

Ageing Population Panel. (2000) *The Age Shift: A Consultation Document*. London: Department of Trade and Industry

Bharmra, T. and Lofthouse, V. (2007) *Design for Sustainability*. Aldershot: Gower.

Bontoft, M. (2006) *The Design of a Co-produced Health & Social Care Service in Grimsby*. [WWW] The Big Life Group. Available from: http://www.thebiglifegroup.com/userfiles/file/Openment%20Door/open%20door%20report%20(ebook).pdf [Accessed 12 June 2013].

Boyle, D. and Harris, M. (2009) *The Challenge of Co-production: How Equal Partnerships between Professionals and the Public are Crucial to Improving Public Services*. London: NESTA.

Brown, T. and Wyatt, J. (2010) Design Thinking for Social Innovation. *Stanford Social Innovation Review*, Winter 2010, 31–34.

Charities Aid Foundation. (2008) *The Three Models of Social Enterprises: Creating Social Impact through Trading Activities: Part 1*. London: Charities Aid Foundation.

DTI (Department of Trade and Industry). (2002) *Social Enterprise: A Strategy for Success*. London: Department of Trade and Industry

Dos Santos, A., Krämer, A. and Vezzoli, C. (2009) Design Brings Innovation to the Base of the Pyramid. *Design Management Review*, 20 (2), 78–85.

Elkington, J. (2004) Enter the Triple Bottom Line. In A. Henriques and J. Richardson (eds), *The Triple Bottom Line: Does it All Add Up?* London: Earthscan, 1–16.

Jennings, V. (2004) Addressing the Economic Bottom Line. In A. Henriques and J. Richardson (eds), *The Triple Bottom Line: Does it All Add Up?* London: Earthscan, 155–166.

Koo, Y. and Cooper, R. (2011) Managing Corporate Social Responsibility through Design. *Design Management Review*, 22 (1), 68–79.

Lewis, H., Gertsakis, J., Grant, T., Morelli, N. and Sweatman, A. (2001) *Design + Environment: A Global Guide to Designing Greener Goods*. Sheffield: Greenleaf Publishing.

Madsen, P. (2005) Responsible Design and the Management of Ethics. *Design Management Review*, 16 (3), 37–41.

Matthew, T. (2011) *Designing Social Innovation: The Urban Ideas Bakery*. Designer-led Workshop at the 6th International Conference on Inclusive Design: Include 2011, London: 18th–20th April 2011.

McDonough, W. and Braungart, M. (2002) *Cradle to Cradle: Remaking the Way we Make Things*. New York: North Point Press.

Mulgan, G., Tucker, S., Ali, S. and Sanders, B. (2007) *Social Innovation: What it is, Why it Matters and How it can be Accelerated*. Oxford: SAID Business School.

Murray, R., Caulier-Grice, J. and Mulgan, G. (2010) *The Open Book of Social Innovation*. London: NESTA and The Young Foundation.

Prahalad, C. K. (2010) *The Fortune at the Bottom of the Pyramid: Eradicating Poverty Through Profits*. Upper Saddle River: Pearson Education.

Prahalad, C.K. and Hammond, A. (2002) Serving the World's Poor, Profitably. *Harvard Business Review*, September, 48–57.

Prahalad, C.K. and Hart, S. (2002) Fortune at the Bottom of the Pyramid. *Strategy + Business*, First Quarter, Issue 26, (26), 1–14.

Ramaswamy, V. and Gouillart, F. (2010) Building the Co-creating Enterprise. *Harvard Business Review*, October, 100–109.

Richardson, J. (2004) Accounting for Sustainability: Measuring Quantities or Enhancing Qualities. In A. Henriques and J. Richardson (eds), *The Triple Bottom Line: Does it All Add Up?* London: Earthscan, 34–44.

Sanders, E. and Simon, G. (2009) *A Social Vision for Value Co-creation in Design*. [WWW] Open Source Business Resource. Available from: http://www.osbr.ca/ojs/index.php/osbr/article/ view/1012/973 [Accessed 9 July 2012].

Sanders, E. and Stappers, P.J. (2008) Co-creation and the New Landscapes of Design. *CoDesign*, 4 (1), 5–18.

Sanders, E. and Westerlund, B. (2011) *Experience, Exploring and Experimenting in and with Co-design Spaces*. [WWW] MakeTools. Available from: http://

www.maketools.com/articles-papers/SandersWesterlundNordes2011.pdf (Accessed: 26 June 2014)

Sethia, N. (2005) At the Bottom of the Pyramid: Responsble Design for Responsible Business. *Design Management Review*, 16 (3), 42–49.

The New Economic Foundation. (2008) *Measuring Value: A Guide to Social Return on Investment,* (2nd edn) [WWW] The New Economic Foundation. Available from: http://www.neweconomics.org/publications/entry/a-guide-to-social-return-on-investment [Accessed 12 June 2013].

Thorpe, A. (2007) *The Designer's Atlas of Sustainability*. London: Island Press.

Tuan, M.T. (2008) *Measuring and/or Estimating Social Value Creation*. [WWW] Bill and Melinda Gates Foundation, Available from: www.gatesfoundation.org/learning/documents/wwl-report-measuring-estimating-social-value-creation.pdf [Accessed 28 June 2011].

UNDP (2008) *Creating Value for All: Strategies for Doing Business with the Poor*. New York: UNDP.

Vanclay, F.M. (2004) Impact Assessment and the Triple Bottom Line: Competing Pathways to Sustainability? Sustainability and Social Science Round Table Proceedings, 12 December 2003, University of Technology, Sydney.

White, P., Belletire, S. and St. Pierre, L. (2007) *Okala: Learning Ecological Design*. Phoenix: Industrial Design Society of America (IDSA).

Whitney, P. (2004) Designing for the Base of the Pyramid. *Design Management Review*, 15 (4), 41–47.

WBCSD (World Business Council for Sustainable Development) (2000) *Eco-efficiency: Creating More Value with Less Impact*. Geneva: World Business Council for Sustainable Development.

Williams, C. N. (2008) *Conscience Brand*. Master Dissertation, Brunel University.

7.9   ONLINE RESOURCES

1. NESTA: www.nesta.org.uk
2. New Economic Foundation: www.neweconomics.org
3. Social Enterprise UK: www.socialenterprise.org.uk
4. Make Tools (Co-design/co-creation): www.maketools.com
5. Social Innovator: www.socialinnovator.info

Chapter 8
STRATEGIC DESIGN MODEL FOR E-BUSINESS

Managing design strategy has a new set of challenges in responding to changes created by the digital age. The rapid changes thrust upon businesses, organizations and individuals in the past two decades have been unprecedented. These changes have changed forever the way we work, live and communicate. Whilst the speed of communications has increased beyond what humans imagined possible, the consequences are not well understood. Indeed the digital age has created as many complex questions as it has opportunities. It has rendered many businesses, economic and social models obsolete. It has generated many difficult questions like the degree to which businesses and government should be open to scrutiny, and certainly driven the demands of consumers and public for greater transparency.

Designers and managers need to contextualize their thinking and skills to support and drive new forms of e-business enterprise and the need for more a human centred, community building and networking society. The evolution of the Web from version 1.0 to the anticipated Web 3.0 continues to radically change the way people communicate and interact. Design strategists must be aware of the new models of consumer journeys and choice and the power of the digital world to make or break businesses, other organizations or governments in a short time. They must also build new models to help bring the clarity of design solutions to the changing world.

Using the 4Ds model of design management can provide a framework for meeting these challenges and achieving superiority in e-service design and branding.

Objectives for this chapter:

- To introduce the challenges for design strategy in the digital age.
- To explore the implications for management and design resulting from the digital economy.
- To review the emergence of e-business models.
- To identify the key drivers of e-business.
- To explain how the 4Ds model can be used to respond to the drivers.
- To determine how well design is used in the online environment.
- To establish strategic design directions for the digital economy.

- To explore the design activities, environment and cultures required for the digital economy.
- To demonstrate how managers can assess the design performance.
- To evaluate a case study of a successful design-driven e-business.

8.1 STRATEGY FOR THE DIGITAL AGE

The speed and manner in which we communicate has changed dramatically and continues to change exponentially. Information designers, web site designers and graphic design were at the forefront of the World Wide Web. Nowadays the design challenge has greatly extended to include interaction designers, interface designers and designers who can integrate the multiple communication channels into service design and branding.

While the first generation of the World Wide Web (Web 1.0) is a collection of web pages, images, videos or other digital assets that is hosted on one or several web servers, the second generation (Web 2.0 or Social Web) is about web-based communities and hosted services, such as social-networking web sites, which aim to facilitate creativity, collaboration and knowledge/ideas/information sharing between users. Web 2.0 has witnessed a big shift from corporate-generated content to user-generated content (see web sites such as YouTube and Facebook, for examples). Businesses and brands now take comments and suggestions from peer-to-peer review sites seriously. The worldwide emergence of e-government (e-Gov) shows that nowadays governments genuinely investigate new ways of engaging people, providing more efficient services to citizens and becoming more transparent. The timeline (or a quick scan of web-based developments over two decades) demonstrates the shift from using the Internet as a distribution channel to building an entirely new business model.

1993	Mosaic	The first web browser that supported pictures
1994	Amazon	Online retailer
1995	eBay	Auction site
1996	Hotmail	Web-based email service
1997	Netflix	Online video rental service
1998	Google	Search engine
1999	MySpace	Online social network site
2000	TripAdvisor	Peer-to-peer review services regarding travelling information
2001	Wikipedia	Online open encyclopaedia
2002	Confused.com	The first UK car insurance comparison site
2003	Skype	Online peer-to-peer communication services
2004	Facebook	Online social network service
2005	YouTube	Video sharing and rating site
2006	Twitter	Online social networking and micro-blogging services
2007	iPlayer	Internet television and radio
2008	App Store	Virtual store for digital applications

2009	Kickstarter	Crowd funding site
2010	Instagram	Online photo and video sharing
2011	iCloud	Cloud storage and cloud computing services
2012	Spacehive	The world's first crowdfunding platform for civic projects

It is hard to believe that around 20 years ago (1993) there were very few web sites on the World Wide Web. Now most people and organizations occupy certain spaces/content online – think about your Facebook, LinkedIn and Twitter accounts! Corporates used to see the Internet as another channel to sell products/services – some may remember the boom and bust of the first dot-com generation. Amazon.com was first set up to sell books online. Nowadays, it has evolved into a digital marketplace where anyone can trade easily and safely.

Whilst social networking sites are still regarded as quite a new concept to many businesses and organizations, they have been around since 1999, more than a decade ago. Individuals were quicker to realize the potential of the Internet and start to make a good use of it – examples can be seen in the emergence of user-generated platforms, e.g. MySpace and TripAdvisor. Also, the practice of searching information online in order to find the best deal has been around since 2002. Growing peer-to-peer review has made it much more difficult for brands and companies to hide anything negative about their performance. Nowadays, "brand promise" is not what a company tells their consumers, but what most people say about that particular organization and collectively agree upon. Even classified information is not so easy to hide these days. WikiLeaks, an online publication of private and classified materials, has been around since 2006 and has achieved notoriety. An increasing level of public scrutiny of brands and companies makes the concept of triple bottom line become even more important in the current marketplace.

In just a few years, we can see significant changes of perception that people and companies have of the Internet, from a new retail channel to a new way of working together for better results, see Wikipedia for an example. Presently, the idea of working together to achieve better outcomes goes to the next level. Crowdfunding platforms such as Kickstarter (www.kickstarter.com) help people with good ideas, but not enough financial resources, to raise sufficient funds to support their new ideas and new business ventures. New kinds of business models have been spawned. There is no need to have physical spaces or tangible products anymore. Apple's App Store is a good example of a pure digital business, a virtual shop plus digital products. This kind of platform gives birth to new businesses, see Instagram for an example. It is interesting to see that now not-for-profit organizations and social enterprises are starting to make good use of the Internet and digital technologies. An emergence of collaborative platforms, such as Quirky (http://www.quirky.com), help people invent and materialize products more easily.

There are various predictions for the third generation Web 3.0. Most experts agree that the World Wide Web will be more personalized, immersive and intuitive. For example, a 3-dimension virtual environment may become more common. In this way, users could "walk, run or even fly" around a virtual store instead of "navigating" from one page to another. So, for example, the user can shop in a virtual store instead of the tedium of navigating screens like the pages of a book. Both Big-D and small-d designs are needed to make the most of new opportunities. Big-D design is needed to cope with the wider complex organizational and social changes and a new type of small-d designer is needed to design and develop integrated applications which improve our lives. This situation leads to new breeds of design disciplines. Traditionally, graphic design, information design and web site design dominated the Internet. Nowadays, interaction design, interface design and service design are the most sought-after disciplines. In the future, other design professions may have more roles to play in this field.

8.2 IMPLICATIONS OF THE DIGITAL ECONOMY

8.2.1 Implications at the Macro Level

In his book *The World is Flat*, Friedman (2006) provided compelling evidence on how the Internet and digital technologies have helped create a level playing field for everyone. An ability to connect and collaborate with everyone gives all competitors an equal opportunity. Thus, seemingly, the evolution of digital technologies has shrunk the world by making people, organizations and countries more connected. Digital technologies also play a key role in promoting globalization.

Friedman (2006) divided the globalization into three waves. The first wave (Globalization 1.0) dated back to 1492 when Christopher Columbus started the connections between the "Old World" and the "New World." The author pointed out that the key questions in Globalization 1.0 era were: "Where does *my country* fit into global competition and opportunities? How can I go global and collaborate with others through my country?"

Globalization 2.0 started in roughly 1800 with the Industrial Revolution and ended in 2000. The authors argued that the key players during this period are international companies. Hence, the key questions were: "Where does *my company* fit into the global economy? How does it take advantage of the opportunities? How can I go global and collaborate with others through my company?"

According to Friedman, at the moment we are in the third era (Globalization 3.0), which is probably the most exciting, since the main driving forces are individuals. In the past, you needed a big company to help you turn your innovative idea into reality. Nowadays, you do not need big companies to back you up. You can raise funds through a crowdfunding platform, outsource the production to other companies across the world and sell your products through the digital market place. This means everyone now can ask themselves: "Where do *I* as an individual fit into the global competition and opportunities of the day, and how can I, on my own, collaborate with others globally?"

New opportunities for design have arisen from the transaction alternatives between businesses/organizations and consumers/citizens. Chaffey (2011) summarized how the digital platform facilitates these transactions and Figure 8.1 summarizes a range of implications for new management thinking and design strategies.

In the UK alone, the Internet contributed around £100 billion or 7.2% of GDP in 2009 (Kalapesi, Willersdolf and Zwillenberg, 2010). This contribution was considerably larger than that of many big industries, such as construction, transportation and utilities. Interestingly, for every £1 of e-commerce goods and services that the UK imports, it exports £2.80. Thus, it is predicted that the UK Internet economy is likely to grow by 10% per year, probably reaching 10% of GDP by 2015. The key driver behind this growth is consumption. According to the report UK residents are active online shoppers – 62% of adults, approximately 31 million people, purchased goods or services online in 2010. A study conducted by Google (2011) also pointed out that, in the UK market, £1 in every £4 of marketing budgets is spent online. New Zealand provides a further fine case study example of a country quick to grasp opportunities offered by the digital age.

		From: Supplier of content/service		
		Consumer or citizen	**Business (organization)**	**Government**
To: Consumer of content/service	Consumer or citizen	• Product/service/ brand intelligence • Social networks • Personal online face-to-face talking • Blogs and much spam	• Marketing of products, e.g. Amazon • Building and protecting corporate reputation, e.g. BP • News media, e.g. News Corporation • Deals comparator/broker, e.g. Money Shop	• Inland Revenue tax and national insurance collection • Government public information • Political debates
	Business	• Product services offers • Consumer individual collective feedback, pressure groups and campaigns	• Business deals and opportunities, e.g. Euroffice • Business relationship-building, e.g. BP • Media tools, e.g. Emap business publication • Market for B2B, e.g. EC21	• Tax collection, e.g. corporation tax and VAT, and governmental support, services and transactions • Statutory regulations and compliance
	Government	• Complaints and suggestions to government from groups or individuals • Collective opinion on government performance and popularity	• Government policies and programmes for economic growth • Feedback to government through businesses and non-governmental organizations	• Inter-departmental governmental development and execution of programmes • International government co-operation and diplomacy

Figure 8.1   Implications for new digital age relationships

The digital technologies and the Internet bring changes to every part of human lives – healthcare, entertainment, transportation, education, etc. The concept of *telehealth*, where telecommunication technologies are utilized to support the delivery of health-related services, has helped health professionals across the world collaborate and exchange ideas more effectively as well as bringing patients closer to healthcare practitioners. This concept led to many opportunities for design, e.g. designing products that allow people to monitor their health at home while regularly keeping their doctors informed, or creating an online community where people with common health problems can share tips and advice.

Digital technologies and the Internet have dramatically changed the way music and films are consumed, shared and reviewed. Digital platforms give people more choices and flexibility – consumers are no longer forced to buy a whole album if they like only one song! Moreover, more and more people listen to their peers rather than professional critics when it comes to newly released films and books. People might not so commonly sit in front of a television to watch the same programme, but they still want to share experiences with others. Again this creates new opportunities for design, as well as new products/services – see the Zeebox (http://zeebox.com) for an example. Even the way people watch TV programmes or films may be changed in the future. Projects such as Finnish TV series *Sydän kierroksella* (*AccidentalLovers*, http://crucible.mlog.taik.fi/productions/accidental-lovers) have already explored new ways of interacting with audiences by allowing people to decide how the story should evolve, e.g. whether they want a happy ending or a tragic one. Imagine the new opportunities for design this possibility could bring – what if we can direct the film the way we like? TV programmes and films will become more like games where our contributions are significant to how the story unfolds.

Many leading universities, research institutes and those in the cultural sector, e.g. museums and galleries, have already started exploring how digital technologies and the Internet could help them educate and inspire people in new ways. Big names such as NASA, Harvard University and the Smithsonian Latino Virtual Museum have created virtual spaces in the SecondLife platform. Virtual museums or classes allow people from around the globe to be "there" no matter where they actually are in real time. This leads to new ways of learning, archiving artwork, experiencing art and sharing cultural experiences. This development generates seemingly endless design opportunities, e.g. designing virtual experiences for museums that complement the physical ones and displaying artwork in new setting. Artwork can be hung in (virtual) space rather than a white blank wall! This changes interactions significantly as in the current predominantly physical world people cannot touch most exhibits, whereas in the virtual world, they can "touch" anything with causing any damage.

Technologies allow design thinkers to explore new possibilities in new meaningful ways. Inevitably the design development process has changed. Members of a product development team from across the globe can create and modify design in real time. Products can be prototyped quickly and accurately with help from digital fabrication technologies, e.g. 3D printing and laser cutting. Concepts, such as Fab Lab (http://fab.cba.mit.edu/about/faq) introduced by MIT Media Lab, help start-up entrepreneurs and inventors produce "practically everything" without worrying about the high costs often associated with tooling and mass production. The digital economy is having a major influence on the way design is used and managed.

The way of involving people in design development has also changed. People were used to consulting, giving feedback about existing products and testing new products/prototypes. Nowadays people take a more proactive role in the design development. Emerging practices, such as crowdsourcing (the idea of sourcing/obtaining ideas, information, content, etc., from the general public or the "crowd") help developers, policy makers and key decision makers gain more ideas and better outcomes than the traditional approach. *Britain in a Day*, a crowdsourced film project led by Ridley Scott and Morgan Matthews, got people around the UK to capture their everyday lives (http://www.bbc.co.uk/programmes/p00kqz5p). More than 11,500 clips were submitted and the involvement resulted in a rich self-portrait documentary of modern lives in the UK. The idea of *crowdfunding*, or raising funds from the general public to support development projects, normally through an online platform, e.g. Kickstarter (www.kickstarter.com), has changed the way developers, inventors and creative entrepreneurs think, work and bid for money. Pitching the bids through a crowdfunding site is not the same as asking bank managers for money. People may not be excited by the ROI plan, but they are interested in finding out why this project is such a good idea that makes it worthy of their financial support. It is about making innovative ideas attractive in the human-centred perspective rather than financial senses.

8.2.2 Implications at the Micro Level

Consumers and Citizens

The digital platform significantly changes the way consumers consume. It changes what they buy, how they buy it and how they are involved in creating what they want to buy. For example, Edelman (2010) observed that consumers traditionally start with a large number of potential brands and eventually narrow their choices until they select a specific brand to buy. This process is sometimes described as a "funnel" model. After purchase, their relationships with brands are formed based on their experience with the products/services.

Edelman points out that nowadays consumers do not necessarily narrow down their choices systematically. They "add and subtract brands from a group under consideration during an extended evaluation phase." After purchase, they have an "open-ended" relationship with brands and often share their experience online. Hence, there is a need to reconsider how to attract/maintain relationships with customers. A study conducted by Google (2011) confirmed Edelman's claims, as it observed that consumers no longer neatly follow the funnel model. The results showed that consumers spend rather longer time researching about products/services online and, in some categories, the research and evaluation process could last a month or even longer.

According to Edelman, the new customer decision journey comprises of four main stages:

1. *Consider*: Begin the journeys by identifying potential brands from various sources.
2. *Evaluate*: Seek inputs from peers, reviewers, retailers brands and competitors.
3. *Buy*: Decide based on acquired information and the design at the point of purchase.
4. *Enjoy-Advocate-Bond*: Build relationships with brands based on their experience.

Research conducted by McKinsey & Company revealed that a large number of consumers conduct online research about the products "after" purchase and voice their opinions about products/brands experience online. The research also shows that if brands create strong bonds with consumers, they may skip the "consider" and "evaluate" stages entirely, indicating they have built the highest level of trust

It is observed that most businesses concentrate their communication effort during the "consider" stage instead of "evaluate" and "enjoy-advocate-bond" which have a stronger influence on customers' decisions. It is interesting to note that most offline channels, e.g. TV commercials and store displays, can only influence consumers during the "consider" stage. Most shoppers tend to search for information from product comparison sites and peer/expert rating sites during the "evaluate" stage. This shows that businesses would be wise to pay more attention to online communities and find ways to engage with them positively. Customer relationship management (CRM) and brand communication need redesigning to address these changes of behaviour.

Businesses/Organizations

So whilst digital technologies are clearly changing the way all organizations operate, Jutla, Craig and Bodorik (2001) noted that certain traditional competencies, e.g. R&D, manufacturing and distribution, remain important for e-businesses. They observed that managing relationships with all stakeholders, such as customers, suppliers and distributors, in the value creation/delivery process has become more crucial to the success. Hence, effective knowledge management is required in order to develop in-depth understanding of their requirements and satisfy these needs properly.

Patrick (2003) warns businesses that there are several issues that needed to solved or taken into consideration. As people are empowered and have more control and can, for example, buy what they want, when they want it, they expect interactions like the buying processes to be more streamlined and straightforward. The usual limitation of physical sites like restricted opening times should not apply to virtual stores. The author notes that the most important issue is changing the companies' mindset that e-business is more than a channel and that it requires a new business model. Design thinking can help businesses make the most of their online presence, especially when constraints, such as small physical space and limited staff resources are no longer applicable.

Governments

e-Government (short for electronic government) has become widespread in a short period of time. The aim is to utilize digital/ICT technologies to enhance interactions between governments and citizens, businesses and other governmental organizations. Design has been playing an active role in making these connections cost-effective, transparent and engaging. Good examples include the *Apps for Democracy* competition (www.appsfor-democracy.org) which aims to enhance civic engagement and exchange of ideas/information. Citizens welcome opportunities to suggest ideas to local/national governments – see an online petition site (http://epetitions. direct.gov.uk/) for an example. There have also been recent examples of anti-government protests fomenting rapidly through fast communications among disaffected citizens. The paradox is now that no government can operate effectively without these channels but the risk of protest becomes much higher if the electorate feel they are getting it wrong.

Changes in the Ways that Corporates Serve People – Facebook

The success of social networking sites like Facebook signifies significant changes of consumer behaviours on a global scale. The concept of online security, privacy and anonymity needs to be redefined, since many people nowadays are willing to share personal, and sometimes very private, information in public, when the sharing of such information would have been unthinkable a decade ago. Social networking sites, such as Facebook, fit well with the trends suggesting that people will rely less and less on verbal communication, and increasingly use other means of communications (e.g. short messages and images).

Facebook was not the first social networking site. MySpace was the pioneer and also the leader in terms of social networking back in the early 2000s. Hartung (2011) pointed out that one of the key factors behind the success of Facebook is "white space" management. The concept of white space management was coined back in the early 1990s. White space is basically described as an area in between business functions. Imagine you have a fantastic new idea but it does not fit neatly into any existing department, business activities or current product lines. Consider where it would go. The idea would almost certainly fall in between departments and nobody would take it forward, thus it would be soon forgotten. Actually, some ideas that fall in the white space are perhaps the most exciting ones. The fact that these ideas do not belong to any existing functions/strategies/offers suggests that they step into a new territory that nobody occupies or has noticed before.

Hartung believed that Mark Zuckerberg's willingness "to allow Facebook to go wherever the market wanted it" is the key to success. User requirements which do not fit into existing offers do not "fall between the cracks." The company listens and pushes itself to accommodate these needs. By having no fixed rules and no fixed plans, the company managed to defeat MySpace and become a leader in the social media field. This clearly displays a good use of Big-D design thinking. Facebook provides a good example of how online business should be both responsive and personalized. Small-d designs also play an important role in ensuring good experience and ease of use. Most influential are the simple designs that are easy to understand and do not restrict too much or interfere with user-generated content.

Changes in the Ways that Corporates Work with People – Quirky

Quirky (www.quirky.com) is an interesting example of how online communities could support and enhance the product development process. The process starts with an inventor submitting a product idea – there is a small charge for this. Next, the idea will be reviewed and refined by the "community." In this case, the community is a group of people who are interested in design and development: anyone can sign up to be part of the community. The key role of the community is to help evaluate and develop product ideas further. Each idea is reviewed and screened by two groups of people: the community and the Quirky team. The selected idea will be refined further by its inventor, Quirky staff and the community. By the end of this co-creation process, all aspects of the product (e.g. design, branding and pricing) will be fully developed ready for the final market research. If everything goes well, the product will be manufactured and sold through two main channels: direct sales via quirky.com and retailers. Everyone who is involved in this process will get paid.

Quirky shares 30% of all revenue brought in by direct sales from quirky. com and 10% of indirect retail sales revenue with all contributors. At least 42% of that shared revenue goes to the inventor. According to the web site, since it launched in 2009, it has brought 362 products to the market, built up the network of 188 retail partners and has 436,000 community members. Although the idea of online collaboration is not new, Quirky is one of the very first that makes the process easy to be involved, as well as sharing benefits with all contributors. The use of Big-D design thinking is evident in the innovative business model and the way it operates. The small-d designs are effectively employed in all touchpoints, e.g. the review and voting system. For more information, visit: http://www.quirky.com/learn.

8.3 REVIEW OF E-BUSINESS MODELS

Kotler and Armstrong (2004) define *e-business* as "the use of electronic platform – intranets, extranets, and the Internet – to conduct a company's business." Perception of e-business has changed over the years. More than ten years ago, Timmers (1998) came up with 11 types of e-business as follows:

1. *E-shop*: An additional outlet for promote a company and its products at lower costs.
2. *E-procurement*: An additional inlet for seeking suppliers of goods/services.
3. *E-auction*: An electronic bidding mechanism – no need for prior movement of goods.
4. *E-mall*: A collection of e-shops, aggregators and industry sector marketplace.

5. *Third party marketplace*: An online marketplace for various brands.
6. *Virtual community*: A social networking site focusing on added value of communication between members.
7. *Value chain service provider*: A provider who supports part of value chain, e.g. logistics.
8. *Value chain integrator*: A provider who focuses on integrating multiple steps of the value chain.
9. *Collaboration platform*: A 'space' that provides a set of tools and information environment for collaboration between two parties, e.g. collaborative design.
10. *Information broker*: An information service provider, e.g. Google and Yahoo!
11. Trust and other services: Services who add value to e-businesses, e.g. consultancies, market research companies and credit checking/rating services.

A more recent study simplifies the classification. Weill and Vitale (2001, cited in Janssen, Kuk and Wagnaar, 2008) offer eight atomic business models for classifying e-commerce web sites as follows:

1. *Content provider*: Provides content (information, digital products and services).
2. *Direct-to-consumer*: Provides goods or services directly to the customer, often bypassing traditional channel members.
3. *Full service provider*: Provides a full range of services in one domain (e.g., financial, health, industrial chemicals) directly and via allies, attempting to own the primary customer relationship.
4. *Value-net-integrator*: Coordinates activities across the value net by gathering, synthesizing, and distributing information.
5. *Shared infrastructure*: Brings together multiple competitors to cooperate by sharing common IT infrastructure.
6. *Intermediary*: Brings together buyers and sellers by concentrating information.
7. *Virtual community*: Creates and facilitates an online community of people with a common interest, enabling interaction and service provision.
8. *Whole-of-enterprise*: Provides a firm-wide single point of contact, consolidating all services provided by a large multi-unit organization.

Example: Netflix

Netflix is a good example of how digital technologies can change the way business operate entirely. The idea of Netflix came out of the frustration of the co-founder of the company who was fined $40 when he was late returning the movie *Apollo 13* to his local video store. With that amount of money he could have bought the video and still had some change! The firm was founded in 1997 and its original business model was a DVD rental by mail service. Customers paid a flat-rate monthly subscription rather than a per-disc rental fee. There were no late penalties. Customers could keep a movie as long as they wanted. However, in order to make their monthly subscription worthwhile, it was better to return a movie as soon as they finished. Customers chose videos that they wanted via Netflix.

com. They would then receive their orders by post. To return the videos, customers simply put them back into and resealed the protective Netflix mailer envelopes. Moreover, they were not charged for mailing expenses. It can be seen that at the beginning, digital technologies and the Internet were perceived as an enabler that allowed the company to connect and provide a service to customers. At this stage, the use of Big-D design thinking was evident in the way the company reinvented the video renting service, while small-d designs were used to make sure that all touchpoints are user-friendly.

Customers made their videos choices in their "requested queue" at Netflix.com. Available DVDs from the customer's request list are mailed out. In order to make sure that customers would continue to require their services, it was in the company's best interest to encourage customers to keep adding new videos to their request list. As a result, the company began to use digital technologies as a means to understanding customers' profiles and preferences. The personalized video recommendation system, peer review and video rating helped the company tailor their offers to suit individual users and build good relationships with customers. Subsequently, Netflix was often ranked top in terms of customer satisfaction and had a large number of loyal customers. This heralded a major change in the role of digital technologies and the Internet. They were used as a means to build relationships and personalize services to suit different users in a cost-effective way. At this stage, the use of Big-D design thinking was evident in the way the company built upon their strengths, while small-d designs were employed to create a good brand experience, ensuring that every aspect of the operation was straightforward and enjoyable.

Ten years later (2007), the company utilized digital technologies to reinvent its business model again, as it started to provide streaming videos on demand. Using their expertise and knowledge of customer preferences, the company continues to offer high-quality services and good experience. Big-D design thinking is evident in the way the company redesigned its business to take advantage of digital technologies and address customer demands, while small-d designs are used to create and maintain an added value brand experience across all channels. It is important to point out that while big video rental companies, such as Blockbuster, face financial difficulty at this time, Netflix continues to expand to new markets. It shows their creative and strategic thinking in taking advantages of digital technologies ahead of their competitors.

8.4 4Ds OF DESIGN-DRIVEN E-BUSINESS

8.4.1 Key Drivers of e-Business Adoption

Key drivers of e-business adoption could be divided into two groups (DIT, 2000, cited in Chaffey, 2011). Firstly, a good use of e-business could improve *cost efficiency* by increasing the speed with which supplies can be obtained, increasing the speed with which goods can be dispatched, reducing sales and purchasing costs and reducing operating costs. Moreover, it can improve the competitiveness of the business by improving the range and quality of services offered; avoiding losing market share to businesses already using e-commerce, and improving an ability to deal with customer demand. According to Chaffey (2011), from his survey with 275 managers, the main benefits of e-business were revealed as follows:

1. Improved information sharing (customer service), 97%
2. Enhanced communications and information sharing (communication), 95%
3. Increased consistency of information (customer service), 94%
4. Increased accuracy of information (customer service), 93%
5. Reduced or eliminated processing, 93%
6. Easier organizational publishing, 92%

Strategic design can respond to the drivers of e-business and accelerate adoption. The 4Ds model can be used to maintain and enhance these identified benefits by:

1. *Determining the current use of design* – finding out how design is used to address key requirements of the online business environment;
2. *Defining strategic directions to take a full advantage of the digital economy* – identifying opportunities for design and establishing realistic design goals;
3. *Designing activities, environment and cultures to exploit the digital economy* – planning how design should be used to address user requirements, utilize online technologies and differentiate the brand/company from its competitors;
4. *Deciding whether a company achieves its strategic directions* – objectively assessing design performance in key strategic areas.

Table 8.1 shows the key elements of the 4Ds model application to design-driven e-business and the conceptual model is presented as Figure 8.2.

8.4.2   Determining the Current Use of Design

In order to find out how design is used to address key requirements of the online business environment, it is important to identify the key aspects of e-business to which design can contribute. Schoenfeldinger, Bangerl, Nusser and Pachauri (2002) proposed a framework called "FOCAL" which summarizes all key aspects into five categories as follows:

1 *Focus*: Capabilities of an organization. This aspect has a strong link with the unique selling points (USPs) of the company – a firm should only promise what it can (or has capabilities to) deliver. The company should know what its prime business activity is: Is it a service/product provider? (e.g., Salesforce, www.salesforce.com), a gateway provider? (e.g., eBay) or infrastructure provider? (e.g., VeriSign, www.verisign.co.uk).

Key questions for design are:

• Has design been used to support the main business activity?
• How effective is the use of design?
• How can design be used to support the key business activity further?

Table 8.1 Key elements of the 4Ds of design-driven e-business

Strategic level	Tactical level	Operational level
Determining		
Current design strategies • Brand identity • Brand personality • Trust/reliability	**Current design plans** • Design coherence • Differentiation • Experience	**Current design projects** • Usability • Communication design • Brand touchpoints
Defining		
Goals • Online value proposition • Design competencies	**Approaches** • Optimum operations • Selected media	**Implementations** • Appearance (graphics) • Behaviours (interaction)
Designing		
Strategies • Targets and position • Competitive advantages • Design policies • Management process	**Methods** • User engagement • Stakeholder involvement • Design language	**Projects/activities** • System design • Registration process • Navigation system • Transaction process
Deciding		
Strategic performance • Security • Transparency • Trust/reliability • Robustness	**Tactical performance** • Brand loyalty • Community • Network building • Service design	**Operational performance** • Information design • Interface design • Pleasurable products/ service design

2 *Opportunity*: This component links all capabilities to create the USPs of the organization. Should a company concentrate all its capabilities to provide a commerce platform for its partners? (e.g., Alibaba Group, http://www.alibaba.com), or should a firm use its capabilities to add values to products/services while acting as a middleman between businesses and consumers? (e.g., Polyvore, www.polyvore.com). Should a company use its capabilities to create a community hub? (e.g., LinkedIn)

Key questions for design are:

• Has design been used to investigate and evaluate opportunities available for the company?
• How can design be used continually to identify emerging opportunities that the firm could leverage its' capabilities into?

3 *Channel:* This aspect deals with infrastructures required to connect what a company offers to its audiences, e.g. e-portal (such as Amazon.com), web sites, mobile apps, etc. Nowadays each company uses multiple channels to attract, engage and serve its consumers. Many firms choose to have

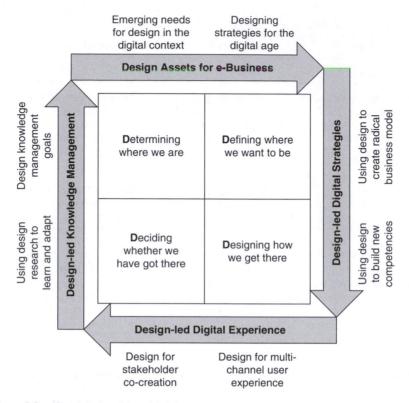

Figure 8.2 4Ds of design-driven business model

both physical and online shops, as well as physical and virtual products/services. Consider high street banks which have physical branches, a web site, tangible products (e.g. mortgage) and online services (e.g. online credit checking).

Key questions for design are:

- Has design been used to support the value delivery process through multichannels?
- If so how effectively?
- How should design be used to ensure positive and coherent experience across all channels?

4 *Audience:* Currently, a company has to consider those beyond its direct target customers. It is important to take online communities into consideration when planning business activities. These communities may directly/indirectly influence the main target group. Since e-businesses often rely on numerous partners, such as suppliers, retailers and distributors, it is crucial to build good relationships with all of them.

Key questions for design are:

- Has design been used to engage and build strong relationships with all potential audiences?
- How should design be used to facilitate collaborations?

5 *Leverage:* The final component is about exploring how certain areas could be improved further. The authors suggested that there are many ways that a company could leverage the business, e.g. reducing costs, improving quality of service, increasing revenues and exploring opportunities to create a win-win situation with current competitors or other businesses. In the automotive industry many car companies share parts/components in order to reduce costs. In the e-business context, several online game companies and social network providers collaborate since they are good at building communities. These joint forces make the communities that they create even stronger, see for example the partnership between Facebook and Zynga (https://zynga.com).

Key questions for design are:

- Has design been used to help a company leverage its business to create new possibilities?
- How can design improve the business further?

Phillips (2003) provides another framework for auditing the current situation and usage of strategic design. The key aspects for auditing involve:

1. *Scale:* How many sites a company has? How many countries does it operate in?
2. *Consistency:* How coherent are all web sites? Such aspects as corporate identity, page layouts, graphic styles and information architecture.
3. *Reach:* Has a company managed to reach all potential target audiences? Are key messages communicated clearly to target markets?
4. *Personality:* Is brand personality correctly portrayed through web sites? Through choice of words and images, manners, behaviours and interactions. What is the tone of voice? Is it formal or informal; active or passive; dry or friendly?
5. *Content:* How the content is described? How the content is organized? It may be technical or jargon-free; comprehensive or simplified.
6. *Usability:* Is the web site easy to use? The transaction and navigation processes.
7. *Visibility:* Are targets aware of the brand? Can users find the web sites?
8. *Technology:* Does a company have all technical expertise/competencies required?
9. *Management:* Who is responsible for managing the design of all web sites? How is the design managed? Is there any management process in place?

To illustrate how this framework could be applied, ASOS, the UK's largest online fashion and beauty store, is used as an example, see Table 8.2.

Table 8.2 The design audit for ASOS

Key areas	Examples of key considerations	Design elements	
		Appearance	Behaviour
Scale	• One web site for the global market	Global	Standardized
Consistency	• Consistency of all key elements: product search, navigation process, checking out system	Coherent	Coherent
Reach	• Visitors: Over 13 million visitors a month • Users: 5.3 million registered users • Reach: 3.0 million customers from 160 countries	Attractive	Approachable
Personality	• Targets: "fashion forward 16–34 year olds" • Brand identity: Look and feel, touchpoints	Young, stylish	Experimental, friendly
Content	• Product: Sizes, colours, materials • Designers: Celebrities, "Your Designers" • Brand: Own brands, independent brands • Fashion: Street style, style guides • Community: Blogs, fan page	Comprehensive	Personal
Usability	• Navigation: Product search • Purchase: Check out, returns and refunds	Simple	Easy to use
Visibility	• Brand presence: Brand awareness	Trend-following	
Technology	• Transaction: Registration, security • Logistics: Tracking system, delivery	Trustworthy	Practical
Management	• Direct marketing: Email alert	Reliable	Professional

8.4.3 Defining Strategic Directions to Take Full Advantage of the Digital Economy

Online Value Proposition

In order to set challenging and realistic goals, the online value proposition (OVP) should be considered to identify the benefits to be gained through e-business/online services. According to Chaffey (2011), the OVP is expressed as six Cs as follows:

1. *Content*: Rich information can influence the customer decision processes, strengthen customer relationships and enhance brand experiences.
2. *Customization*: Products, services and content can be tailored to suit individual customers, e.g. recommended items and email alert.

3. *Community*: Social networking services (e.g. forums, chat-rooms, blogs and fan pages) can establish strong community and facilitate networking among users.
4. *Convenience*: Products, services and content can be accessed 24/7.
5. *Choice*: The online platform provides wider choice of products and suppliers. Online marketplaces, such as Kelkoo (www.kelkoo.com), allow customers to shop and compare prices. Several brands see the online platform as opportunities to widen their offering, e.g. Tesco offers financial, insurance and travelling services.
6. *Cost reduction*: In general, products, services and content can be purchased at relatively lower prices online. Low-cost airlines make a good use of the online platform to reduce their operating costs and which contributes to keeping their prices competitive.

Figure 8.2 shows the application of the six Cs of OVP to three well-known online brands. LinkedIn requires design focussed on trust, networking and community building, while Money Supermarket requires trust, transparency, ease of use and personalization.

Goals for Design

OVP choices affect design goals and provide a platform for (a) making the best use of the online platform to deliver design-led added value and brand promises and (b) what kind of design competencies an organization should invest in. Table 8.3 shows how the value proposition leads to the design of enhanced experiences.

Since the values/promises will be created and delivered through a number of stakeholders, it is important to identify all key stakeholders and their roles in the value delivering process, as well as explore how design could be used to support them. Jutla, Craig and Bodorik (2001) identified and summarized e-business stakeholders as follows:

- *Strategic Partners*. This group of stakeholders includes current and new alliances. They play an important role in helping a company grow and enhance its business – reach new markets, open new channels, increase brand awareness of certain groups, deliver new products/services, improve the speed to market, increase market shares and share resources. Since they contribute at the strategic level, it is crucial to embrace them as part of the ecosystem. Holistic design thinking, system design, communication design and information design are needed to help facilitate all the collaborations.
- *Operational Partners*. This group of stakeholders helps a company add value at the operational level, for example by reducing supply costs, shortening lead times, improving product/service quality during the manufacturing process and supporting product customization/personalization. Although they contribute at the operational level, it is also important to involve them in the value proposition planning. As with the strategic group, holistic design thinking, system design, communication design and information design are needed to support the collaborations of all parties involved.

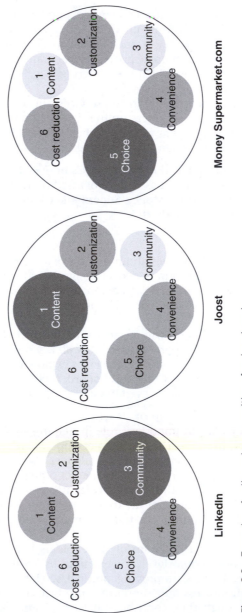

Figure 8.3 Examples of online value proposition of various brands

Table 8.3 Relationships between design and value proposition

Value proposition	Emotional experience	Key design competencies required
1. Content	Accurate/precise and entertaining	Communication design, interface design
2. Customization	Personal identity, empowerment	Experience design, interaction design
3. Community	Belonging and engaging	Experience design, interaction design
4. Convenience	Easy and straightforward	System design, service design
5. Choice	Feeling in control and transparent	System design, information design
6. Cost reductions	Satisfaction and freedom	System design, service design

- *Governance*, in this case, is defined as "the system of ruling by an act, manner or function of a government whether it is a nation, province, district, organisation, or institution." This group of stakeholders is considered very important, since e-businesses are created and sustained according to the rules emanating from this group of stakeholders. They also play an essential role of providing legality, trust and perhaps safety to the e-business activities. Design can help companies understand and address these rules positively and make sure that all products/service comply with the regulations and industrial agreements.
- *(Online) Community* offers values in various ways, such as helping a company gain better understanding of its' customers and providing useful reviews. Online communities also add spiritual/emotional values to the brand/company, as well as providing support to other customers, such as answering questions regarding certain features of products, services and systems. Good use of system design and communication could help build a strong community and encourage co-creation between the company and its community.
- *Customer*: This group of stakeholders provide direct/indirect revenues for a company. They offer a number of values, such as providing useful feedback about the products and/or services, giving inputs into the product development process through appropriate co-creation activities. System design, experience design, communication/interface design and interaction design are crucial to the success of these collaborations with users, while product/service design is vital to maintain good relationships with customers.

Not every company starts an online business. Many organizations which currently carry out some forms of e-business activities started offline. Making sure that online and offline strategies and activities complement, rather than compete with, each other is considered challenging. According to Gulati and Garino (2000), strategic options available to a company range from having offline and online divisions within a company to separating an online entity from an existing offline company and setting up a new brand/company.

Tesco is an example of a company that uses an online platform to complement an original business offline. The company started off as a grocery company. Nowadays, it offers a wide range of products and services, including mobile network services, banking products, insurance, apparel and travel packages. Most of the extended products are available online only from Tesco Direct (www.tesco.com/direct). In this way, online offers do not compete with offline products. Moreover, it does not make any sense to store all these extended lines in physical stores. The company takes advantage of an online platform to effectively increase the "share of wallet." Tesco may have more or less the same number of customers, but because there are more things that they could buy from the company, it makes more money by increasing customers' spending at Tesco. Nevertheless, managing customer expectation is very tricky. Although Tesco tries to separate online businesses from the offline ones, since they still operate under the same brand, customers may believe that they could make an enquiry about online products and get support from staff in physical stores. Holistic design thinking and a careful system design are vital therefore, to support customers effectively as well as provide positive experiences through all channels.

Barnes and Noble Inc. is a further example of a company that chooses a strategic option at the other end of the spectrum by setting up a spin-off for its online business. Barnes and Noble Inc. is a leading retailer of content, digital media and educational products in the US. Their spin-off online company, BN.com (www.barnesandnoble.com), is the Internet's largest bookstore. This USP is made possible by leveraging key strengths of Barnes and Noble Inc., such as a large number of warehouses across the US. This allows BN.com to stock over one million book titles for immediate delivery; the company claims that the site has more titles than any other online bookseller. Strategic leverage also helps the company to become a leader to the eBook market by offering over one million eBooks in its online store. Interestingly, despite creating a spin-off business, the same brand name is still applied. Hence, it is likely to face similar challenges to those mentioned earlier, e.g. online customers seeking help from staff in physical stores and expecting the same kind of experience from both online and offline stores. A recent dramatic fall in their online book retail business profits has opened up opportunities for design thinking to revisit the relationship between online and physical bookstores and seek new ways to integrate the experience.

The critical strategic question for management may be whether to integrate or separate online and offline business activities. Gulati and Gardino (2000) recommended that there were four key areas that should be taken into consideration: brand, management, operation and equity, generating further key questions:

- Will online and offline businesses share the same brand name?
- Or should a company create a new brand for its online business?
- Should both businesses be managed by the same management teams?
- Or should they be managed by completely different groups of people?
- Should/could online and offline businesses share some operational infrastructures and resources (e.g. distribution systems)?

- Should the new business be fully owned by the parent company?
- Or should it be partially owned by the parent company and the rest is owned by strategic partners?

In terms of branding, the authors pointed out that the decision is a trade-off between *trust* and *flexibility*. Using the same brand name as the parent company could help building trust. However, it may reduce flexibility, since the new business is expected to deliver similar products/services or conform to certain values/principles. Good use of design thinking and communication design could help a company plan a sub-brand/new brand or extend the current brand to accommodate new business activities. Regarding the management, while using the same management teams could lead to well-aligned objectives/strategies and synergies between the two businesses, having separate team could lead to a more sharp and focused objectives/strategies. The authors emphasized that "companies do not have to make an all-or-nothing decision – they can integrate certain functions and leave others separate." Good use of system design and communication design could help a company plan and maintain good flow of information across the teams and encourage cross-pollination of ideas.

Leveraging operational infrastructures is generally more effective. However, in some cases, it could prevent online divisions from exploring innovative means of doing business, which may be more effective and desirable from customers' point of view. Good use of system design can help a company make effective use of existing operational resources and infrastructures. Having 100% ownership (equity) of its online business allows a parent company to gain all the benefits and have full control. However, sharing the costs and the risks of the new online venture through joint partnership is also advantageous. Good use of design thinking can help attract suitable partners or plan an innovative business model.

8.4.4 Designing Activities, Environment and Cultures to Exploit the Digital Economy

This pragmatic planning stage is about using design to differentiate offers, attracting customers and building brand equity. To get to know consumers, Rollins (2009) segments consumers of the social web (Web 2.0) into four groups according to their expected online experiences. The first category is the user who is motivated by the "I can (do it)" motivation. He/she is seeking an on-demand experience and has no time to waste and thus requires ease of navigation, control and instant delivery – an example is the iPlayer. The users who look for personal experiences express their motivation as "I matter" and consider themselves something of a celebrity. Thus they seek dialogue, acknowledgement of their status, customization to meet their personal needs, privilege to make them feel special and popularity among their peers. An example of this category is YouTube. Some users say "I connect" and are motivated by engaging experiences. They want to go beyond observing and acquiring what they need and seek participation, immersion and inspiration from the engagement. Twitter is an example of this segment. Finally there is the group which aspires to drive socio/cultural changes through networking which is termed "I am." They seek self-expression and influential interactions in their desires to change our world. WWF One Planet Challenge is an example of this category.

Based principally on understanding consumer expectations, further design research can be carried out to identify opportunities for new and/or improved products and services and strategic directions can be planned to deliver and enhance them. The design strategist may wish to further divide into sub-categories, for example by age groups and interests. For example more teenagers may be found in the "I matter" segment and there could also be gender differences. Table 8.4 uses Rollins' (2009) experience segments as a platform and shows some design implications and priorities which can help to ensure that design activities are suitably resourced and planned.

The reference to "responsible safeguards" highlights the serious global concerns about the high level of online fraud. While this is frequently regarded by designers as outside their sphere of responsibility, it is important that design strategy for online systems involves the advice of security experts and technologists and provides valuable creative thinking, particularly concerning human behaviour, to support the development of safeguards. Designers should also be engaged in developing contingency plans for the effects of cyber-attack.

Example: NIKEiD

NIKEiD (http://nikeid.nike.com) is an example of a successful service made possible by a good combination of design (e.g. product design, interaction design, system design and service design) and digital technologies. The service allows users to personalize Nike's clothing products, such as colour

Table 8.4 Relationships between expected experience and design directions

User experience	Corporate goals	Design priorities	Examples of design activities
24/7 service available on-demand	• Foster debate and discussion • Create "buzz" to make sales	• Simplicity • Intuitiveness • Usability	• Intuitive navigation • Secure transaction • Simplified comparison process
Customized and personal	• Retain customers • Build loyalty	• Expressiveness • Personalization • Identification	• Personalization options • Constant feedback (e.g. ranking) • Customization
Engender engagement	• Heighten awareness • Stimulate through trial	• Fun/Playfulness • Pleasurable • Absorbing	• Games and playful graphics • Real-time update (e.g. newsfeed) • Animation
Reaching out/ networking	• Attract collaborators • Acquire new opportunities	• Open innovation • Co-design process • Content management	• Channels for idea exchange • Effective collaboration methods • Responsible safeguards

schemes and fabrics. This service provides both personal and engaging experience, as users are involved in co-creating the final products. The good use of design is evident throughout, e.g. an intuitive navigation, an easy-to-use system and a simple layout. Due to its success, the service has been expanded to integrate new technologies and mobile applications, e.g. Nike PHOTOiD (https://photoid.nike.com). This new service allows users to submit their Instagram photographs and select the sport shoes that they want. Then the software will automatically create and send a design based on the colour scheme of the submitted photographs to users. Users can choose to save the designs, share them or purchase them.

Anderson (2009) proposed the *User Experience Hierarchy of Needs* model which explains the six stages that most technology products go through as they become more mature.

1. *Functional (Useful)*. At the most basic level, a digital product/service is often designed from a task-focused point of view. The most important thing is to ensure that the product/service works as intended. Think about the first generation of online shops.
2. *Reliable*. After discovering a new digital product/service and finding it actually works, the user requires the reassurance that this product/service will be available when it is needed and offer accurate and trustworthy information. Think about when eBay and Amazon.com first started. People know that they worked, but they also wanted to make sure that the sites provided accurate information about products advertised on the web sites.
3. *Useful*. The next milestone is about using user-friendly and intuitive design to ensure that products/services are easy to use and will not cause any problems. For products/services where users are driven by the end results (extrinsic motivations), e.g. using the Internet banking, comparing grocery prices or buying train tickets online, making sure the experience is painless, transparent and straightforward is the key.
4. *Convenient*. An old sage once said "convenience can be more important than free." This is because many people dislike hassle. Some coffee shops offer a "free" Wi-Fi connection at a cost of filling out a registration form. Some people will not respond to such an offer since their time and personal information is more valuable than a free Wi-Fi service. Good products/services should be very convenient and easy to use – everything seems to make a perfect sense from customers' perspectives.
5. *Pleasurable*. Once all technical issues have been resolved and all practical aspects have been addressed, the key to differentiate the product/service from those of competitors' is providing a memorable experience that is worth sharing with other people. The author pointed out that it is rather difficult for many companies to go beyond providing "convenient" products/services and offering "pleasurable" experiences to users. Google is convenient and easy to use, but it is questionable whether many people would describe the experience as memorable.
6. *Meaningful*. At the highest level, the focus has shifted to "experience." The key factors are people, activities and context. Hence, it is about

providing experiences that have personal significance – giving people a sense of fulfilment. Consider the feeling of enjoyment that people gain when they contribute to online forums – they may feel that their opinions are listened to; that people follow their advice; that they help solve others' problems, etc. Good digital products/services/experiences are designed to be enjoyable and purposeful.

Example: Zopa

Zopa (www.zopa.com) is an example of an organization that uses design thinking to exploit the digital economy. It is the UK's largest peer-to-peer lending site and also considered one of the most trusted personal loan providers. The organization created an online platform that brings together people who want to borrow money and those who want to invest. By bypassing the banks, both parties benefit – borrowers pay less interest for their loans and investors gain more money for their investments. The design of processes/systems is reliable and straightforward. The design of all touchpoints is simple and intuitive. It is not a kind of task that users "enjoy" doing. However, it offers alternative ways of lending and borrowing which provide better experiences for both parties, especially those who would not be able to borrow money through the banks due to their poor credit ratings in the past.

Example: Foursquare

Foursquare (https://foursquare.com) is a location-based social networking application for mobile devices, such as smartphones and tablet computers, that encourages people to explore and share information about places that they discover/visit with friends. Users can simply "check in" to a place (e.g. a coffee shop, a train station or a gallery) to earn some points or collect badges. The more users interact with certain places or give comments, the sooner they could become regarded as experts in particular subjects (e.g. restaurants) and places.

Businesses have begun to realize that they could use Foursquare as a means to engage with existing and potential customers. By providing incentives for people who visit their store, companies can connect with their customers in an interesting way. The History Channel is often used as a good example of how to use Foursquare in a meaningful manner. The channel encourages audiences to explore local history hidden in their neighbourhood, which creates a lot of interest among audiences and increases the popularity of the channel. This example shows that as businesses start exploring how to exploit digital technologies in creative ways. Design thinking is required to explore new concepts.

8.4.5   Deciding Whether a Company Achieves Its Strategic Directions

Assessing Basic Performance

Neilsen *et al.* (2001) pointed out that e-business is about empowering customers. People must feel in control, they can buy what they want, when they want it. When customers feel powerless they will leave the web site and disconnect with the brand. It can be concluded that the most important factors are usability, trust and adaptability and this generates a number of key questions for design as shown in Table 8.5.

Assessing Strategic Performance

Strategic performance is ultimately about the design of the brand. Upshaw (2001) recommends that the organization should build a masterbrand platform that creates superiority online, not just differentiation. He suggests this brand platform should comprise position, personality and attitude.

Table 8.5 Basic performance assessment

Key elements		Key questions
Usability	Navigation	• Is the navigation process intuitive and practical? • Can a user find the required content, product or service? • Is it tolerant of mistakes?
	Registration	• Is the registration process simple and clearly explained? • Does a user have a full control over confidential information?
	Transaction	• Is each step of the transaction clearly explained and reassuring? • Is a user allowed to change his/her mind and cancel the order?
Trust	Security	• Does a user feel safe when using the web site? • Can a user trust the transaction process?
	Transparency	• Are all terms and conditions clearly described? • Is there any hidden information? (e.g. small print)
	Feedback	• Is the current status confirmed and the next stage indicated? • Does a user feel reassured in the "journey"?
Adaptability	Choice	• Does a web site provide a wide range of choices? • Is comparison made easy? • Is relevant information (e.g. product specs) clearly presented?
	Differences	• Does design address cultural differences? • Does design address local preferences and requirements?
	Personalization	• Does a store recognize a user and recommend suitable items? • Is a user allowed to personalize the online environment or transaction choices?

This generates such key questions for evaluation of performance as:

1. *Position*: Do our customers perceive us the leader of the category? Is our brand the first one that comes to their minds? What makes customers choose us instead of other online and offline brands? Does design establish and reinforce our position?
2. *Personality*: How do customers perceive us? Is this the correct brand image? Does design communicate our brand personality accurately? Does design bring our brand identity to life? Do all design elements support brand personality?
3. *Attitude*: Is our brand attitude (e.g. belief and core values) relevant to customers? Does it inspire customers? Does design clearly communicate our brand attitude? Is our belief and core values embedded in all products and services?

Kearney (1999) suggested that digital customer experience includes four different stages:

1. *Attract and Re-attract*. In the highly competitive environment like the digital marketplace, a company must develop distinctive value proposition that can catch customers' eyes. This process starts by building awareness of its site. Next, it has to communicate its value propositions in a compelling manner. To sustain and grow the business, the company must make sure that customers "revisit" its site(s). The revisit is influenced largely by the initial experience. Hence, the company should make sure first-time visitors have a good experience, all touchpoints are aesthetically pleasing, all functions are practical and intuitive and all promises are delivered. The experience can be continually improved as the company learns more about the customers (through the personal information that customers provide, and the ways they navigate and interact with the site) and can tailor its offers to suit individual customers.
2. *Retain and Engage*. The next stage is about keeping customers interested in the sites and its offers. Design can help to make sure that the site and offer always look attractive, contents are well presented and all touchpoints create/reinforce emotional engagements.
3. *Expand*. This step takes the company beyond retaining and engaging with existing customers. It is about developing an in-depth understanding about them in order to expand the share of their wallets. Think about recommended books or other products on Amazon.com or elsewhere. This practice aims to get people to buy more or find out more about other products/services that the company currently offers. Good use of customers' information and effective tracking systems certainly helps. Effective use of design can also help, by making sure that recommended products/services are presented in ways that are relevant, exciting and meaningful to customers.
4. *Delivery and Service*. The final aspect is about making sure that the company lives up to its' promises, delivering goods/services that match (or, if possible, exceed) customers' expectations. Logistics and stakeholder management play a big role in ensuring that customers receive what they want when they want it. Design, especially systems design and

communication design, can help to make the process more efficient and transparent in customers' eyes, e.g. allowing orders to be traced or showing the best deal available.

Kearney (1999) also proposed the "7Cs" framework that could help a business plan and implement digital customer experiences. Additionally this framework has the potential to be used as an assessment framework, as a means to check whether the company has taken all important factors into consideration and if it has achieved its targets in certain areas. The 7Cs framework includes:

1. *Content*: Does the site have compelling content? Is it relevant and useful for customers?
2. *Convenient*: Is it easy to use and navigate? Are all functions and features quick to load?
3. *Communication*: Does the site encourage/support two-way communication between the company and its customers? Is the site well designed and beautifully presented?
4. *Customer Care*: Is the entire customer journey process well planned and managed? Are customers properly supported and informed every step of the way? Is customer care integrated as part of the service delivery process?
5. *Connectivity*: Is it easy to find the company? Does the company select suitable alliance sites that could direct potential customers to its site?
6. *Community*: Does the company facilitate/support the development of an online community? (An online community of loyal customers brings many benefits to the firm. People could support each other, e.g. sharing tips on how to make the most of the products and update each other on up-coming products/services in which they are interested.)
7. *Customization*: Can the company customize its interfaces (e.g. content and features) and offers to suit individual customers?

By combining Kearney's four stages with the 7Cs, a matrix for measuring design performance in key areas directly influencing digital experiences can be created, see Table 8.6.

Table 8.6 Framework for checking design performance

	Attract & re-attract	Retain & engage	Expand	Delivery & service
Content	How well was design used to make content attractive for existing and new customers?	How well was design used to make content engaging for long-term customer relationships?	How well was design used to make content (recommended features) relevant and meaningful?	How well was design used to keep users informed throughout the whole process?

Continued

Table 8.6 Continued

	Attract & re-attract	Retain & engage	Expand	Delivery & service
Convenient	How well was design used to ensure the ease of navigation and ease of use for first-time visitors?	How well was design used to improve experiences and make the process more convenient?	How well was design used to make sure that other products and services are promoted?	How well was design used to streamline the delivery process and make it as simple as possible?
Communication	How well was design used to communicate the firm's value proposition and USPs in a compelling manner?	How well was design used to facilitate two-way dialogues between the company and customers (e.g. forums)?	How well was design used to engage users in new product developments to ensure that new offers suit their needs/wants?	How well was design used to maintain regular dialogues with customers throughout the service delivery process?
Customer care	How well was design used to inform new customers about customer care policy and practices?	How well was design used to support new and existing customers and help solve their problems?	How well was design used to expand customer care practices beyond industrial standards?	How well was design used to support customers at all touchpoints of the delivery process?
Connectivity	How well was design used to grasp potential customers' attention to the company links and encourage them to visit the web site?	How well was design used to ensure that customers can find and contact with appropriate staff when they need help and support?	How well was design used to enrich dialogues with the firm and customers to enhance the connectivity and emotional engagements?	How well was design used to ensure that customers can connect with the firm anytime they want during the delivery process?
Community	How well was design used to inform new customers about its community and encourage them to join?	How well was design used to support its online community and reward loyal customers?	How well was design used to empower its community and get users more involved in key business activities	How well was design used to assist the peer-to-peer support provided by the community of customers?
Customization	How well was design used to communicate that customers are empowered and given full control?	How well was design used to customize interfaces to suit customers' needs and interests?	How well was design used to customize products/services to suit individual customers' needs and interests?	How well was design used to customize the delivery process to match customers' lifestyles?

8.5   CASE STUDY 6 – DESIGN-DRIVEN E-BUSINESS: AMAZON

Amazon.com is the largest online retailer in the US. The corporate mission is to be "Earth's most customer-centric company for four primary customer sets: consumers, sellers, enterprises, and content creators." While failure rate of e-businesses is relatively high, Amazon goes from strength to strength.

According to Amazon (2012), some major achievements are:

- Sales grew from $15.7 million in 1996 to $147.8 million – an 838% increase.
- Cumulative customer accounts grew from 180,000 to 1,510,000 – a 738% increase.
- The percentage of orders from repeat customers grew from over 46% in the fourth quarter of 1996 to over 58% in the same period in 1997.

Amazon is always at the forefront of the e-business revolution. Its progress bears a resemblance to Kalakota and Robinson's (2001) *"e-business evolution"* model. The company was founded in 1994 and in 1995 it started an online book store. The business model could be described as *e-channel*, as it used the Internet as a distribution channel of physical products. The success was attributed to user-friendly interaction design, i.e. a simple navigation process and secure transaction system. In 1997, the experience design was taken to the next level, as the web site started recommending other books that may interest users. The company really made good use of the online platform by expanding product offerings (such as CDs and DVDs). In 2001, the firm made a significant move, as it turned into an *e-portal* or an online marketplace which connects disparate buyers and sellers from various industries. In 2006, the company expanded its services to cover both physical products and electronic products, e.g. music and video files for downloading. All these strategic decisions ensure that Amazon has always maintained the edge over its competitors. Although nowadays all book shops offer online options, consumers choose Amazon due to the variety of choices, the ability to compare prices and the fast delivery service.

A recent interview with Jeff Bezos, the founder and CEO of Amazon.com, revealed that the company excels at white space management (see Section 8.2.2 above; Kirby and Stewart, 2007). The company looks for unexplored ideas and untapped opportunities that can improve customer experiences, and ask themselves, "Why not?" The organizational culture encourages risk taking. The key concern is not about fully justifying why the company should take bold strategic moves. It is about having a vision: "If we can get this to work, it will be big." The company also support long-term investments, as the CEO pointed out that some ideas might take five to seven years before they have positive impacts on the economics of the company. The Big-D open thinking is clearly evident in the way the company is managed and operated in that nothing is regarded as static or beyond challenging.

The company is very *customer-centric* – the key message is that: "Be afraid of our customers, because those are the folks who have the money. Our competitors are never going to send us money." Hence, the company is more interested in finding what customers want rather than what competitors are doing. In order to keep everyone in touch with customers and their needs all staff, both junior and senior, including the CEO himself, have to spend time in the fulfilment centres, warehouses for storing and distributing products to customers. Everyone must be able to work in a call centre! These customer-centric practices help the top management to truly understand their customers. When Bozos was questioned about why he allowed negative comments of products on its site, he simply replied: "We don't make money when we sell things; we make money when we help customers make purchase decisions." The strong user empathy does fit well with strategic design thinking and designers understand they are designing systems to support the business ethos. Anders (2012) observed that Amazon does not rely on segmentation personas commonly employed in marketing research, since they are too imprecise for its customer-centric developments.

Interestingly, although a company is operating in the fast-moving digital market, it is *not* always chasing these changes. The company often asks itself what would not change in the next five or ten years. This kind of question encourages long-term investments, especially radical ideas that need a few years to develop and test. The company focuses on fundamental values that would not change over time, such as the variety of selection, low prices and fast delivery. It is unlikely that customers would want higher prices, slow delivery and small selection of products/services in the next few years. Even though Amazon focuses on fundamental requirements, the company constantly reinvents itself and often comes up with new innovations that improve customer experiences. By way of examples, the company was an early entrant into the ebook industry with its proprietary ebook format and reader, the Kindle. The design of Kindle's hardware and software has been a key factor of the success. The first generation of Kindle was not well received, but the company listened to customer feedback and improved their products accordingly. As a result, it is now able to expand into the tablet computer market. Kindle Fire's success is related to its strategic directions and good use of product and interface design.

Small-d design is an important factor of Amazon's success since 1995. Its web site set the standard in terms of ease of navigation and check out, intuitive interaction, transparent and secure transaction process and standardized product descriptions. The major redesign of its site often involved customers' inputs. This practice shows that the company is able and willing to adapt and evolve in order to address customers' needs effectively.

Some questions for discussion:

- How does Amazon use design to build trust in the service/user experience?
- How can Amazon use design thinking to evolve the user experience from traditional book reading to digital formats?

8.6   SUMMARY OF KEY POINTS

- The digital age continues to transform the way business, governments and people communicate.
- Web 1.0 was about disseminating information, much of it poorly designed and confusing.
- Web 2.0 supports community building and social interaction.

- Web 3.0 is expected to facilitate more personalization and new forms of interaction.
- Designers need to make online transactions more transparent and human centred, primarily to build trust.
- The digital platform changes the customer journey and decision-making process.
- Designers need to develop awareness of the opportunities and challenges afforded by new e-business models.
- Design management strategists need new models to establish strategic design directions in the digital economy.
- Management need open design thinking to use design effective development of products, services, environment and cultures.
- The 4Ds design management model can determine how well e-enterprises use design, set directions based on generating online value, design for differentiation, brand building and online environments, and evaluate performance in the quest for superiority.

8.7 FURTHER CONSIDERATIONS

8.7.1 Exercise the Mind....

- Are some businesses more inherently suited to online forms than others?
- Is trusting a web-based business the same as trusting a friend?
- Will retail business become totally online?
- How can designers combat the growing trend of cyber-attack on well-known brands?
- Will social networks reduce the vocabulary of languages?
- How can designers help organizations to protect their reputation in an age of transparency?
- Will virtual experiences become more highly regarded than real human experiences?
- How can designers use digital technology to enhance human life?

8.8 GLOSSARY

Digital economy: Although there is no single authoritative definition of this term, the Department of Broadband, Communications and the Digital Economy, Australian Government, defined the digital economy as "the global network of economic and social activities that are enabled by information and communications technologies, such as the internet, mobile and sensor networks."

Digital fabrication is the process that utilizes digital technologies to join the design process with the manufacturing process, which helps shorten the development process. The principle is that by creating designs in digital formats (e.g. CAD models), they can be analysed and materialized through an additive manufacturing process – a process that creates prototypes or products by adding materials, e.g. 3D printers, or a subtractive manufacturing process – a process that creates prototypes or products by removing materials, e.g. CNC machines.

E-Health: The World Health Organization (WHO) defined the term as "the transfer of health resources and health care by electronic means." It encompasses three main areas: (1) the delivery of health information, for health professionals and health consumers, through the Internet and telecommunications; (2) using the power of IT and e-commerce to improve public health services, e.g. through the education and training of health workers; and (3) the use of e-commerce and e-business practices in health systems management. **Telehealth** and **Telecare** are part of e-health services.

Fab Lab is short for Fabrication Laboratory which originated from MIT Media Lab. The idea is to provide a small-scale workshop using digital fabrication technologies to help inventors, start-up entrepreneurs, creative professionals and those in the educational sector realize their ideas and learn about digital fabrication technologies. The concept has been implemented worldwide, e.g. Afghanistan, Chile, Ghana and Indonesia.

Telecare allows people to monitor and manage their health with support from health professionals in order to maintain their independent living.

Telehealth focuses on remote monitoring of physiological data (e.g. blood pressure) that can be used by health professionals for diagnosis or disease management.

8.9   REFERENCES AND ADDITIONAL READING

Amazon (2012) *Annual Report.* [WWW] Amazon. Available from: http://phx.corporate-ir.net/phoenix.zhtml?c=97664&p=irol-reportsannual [Accessed 14 July 2013].

Anders, G. (2012) Inside Amazon's Idea Machine: How Bezos Decodes The Customer. [WWW] Forbes. Available from: http://www.forbes.com/sites/georgeanders/2012/04/04/ inside-amazon/ [Accessed 14 July 2013].

Anderson, S. P. (2009) The Future of Search: A Different Perspective. *Design Management Review*, 20 (1), 23–30.

Chaffey, D. (2011) *E-business and E-commerce Management: Strategy, Implementation and Practice* (5th edn). Harlow: Prentice Hall Financial Times.

Edelman, D. C. (2010) Branding in the Digital Age: You're Spending Your Money in All Wrong Places. *Harvard Business Review*, December 2010, 62–69.

Faust, W. and Householder, L. (2009) Get Real and Prosper: Why Social Media Demands Authentic Brands. *Design Management Review*, 20 (1), 45–51.

Friedmand, T. (2006) *The World is Flat: The Globalised World in the Twenty-first Century.* London: Penguin.

Google. (2011) *Beyond Last Click: Understanding your Customers' Online Path to Purchase* [WWW] Google. Available from: http://www.thinkwithgoogle.com/insights/emea/library/studies/beyond-last-click/ [Accessed 28 April 2013].

Gulati, R. and Garino, J. (2000) Get the Right Mix of Bricks and Clicks. *Harvard Business Review*, May–June, 107–114.

Hartung, A. (2011) *How Facebook Beat MySpace.* [WWW] Forbes. Available from: http://www.forbes.com/sites/adamhartung/2011/01/14/why-facebook-beat-myspace/2/ [Accessed 4 July 2013].

Janssen, M., Kuk, G. and Wagnaar, R.W. (2008) A Survey of Web-based Business Models for E-government in the Netherlands. *Government Information Quarterly*, 25 (2), 202–220.

Jutla, D. N., Craig, J. and Bodorik, P. (2001) *A Methodology for Creating e-Business Strategy.* In Proceedings of the 34th Hawaii International Conference of System Science. [WWW] IEEE Xplore. Available from: http://ieeexplore.ieee.org/xpl/articleDetails. jsp?reload=true&arnumber=927073 [Accessed 5 July 2013].

Kalakota, R. and Robinson, M. (2001) *e-Business 2.0: Roadmap for Success* (2nd edn). Addison Wesley.

Kalapesi, C., Willersdolf, S. and Zwillenberg, P. (2010) *The Connected Kingdom: How the Internet Is Transforming the UK Economy*. London: The Boston Consulting Group.

Kearney, A. T. (1999) Creating a High-Impact Digital Customer Experience (White Paper). [WWW] Laboratório de EficiênciaEnergéticaemEdificações. Available from: http://www.labeee.ufsc.br/~luis/egcec/artigos/atk-digital%20customer.pdf [Accessed 14 July 2013].

Kearney Korea LLC, A.T. (2012) The Internet Economy in the United Kingdom [WWW] Vodafone. Available from: http://www.vodafone.com/content/dam/vodafone/about/public_policy/articles/internet_economy_uk.pdf [Accessed 14 July 2013].

Kirby, J. and Stewart, T. A. (2007) The Institutional YES: How Amazon's CEO Leads Strategic Change in a Culture Obsessed With Today'S customer. *Harvard Business Review*, October 2007, 74–82.

Kotler, P. and Armstrong, G. (2004) *Principles of Marketing (10th Edn.)*. Upper Saddle River: Pearson Prentice Hall.

Neilsen, J. Molich, R., Snyder, C. and Farrell, S. (2001) *E-commerce User Experience*. Fremont: Nielsen Norman Group.

Phillips, E. (2003) From Chaos to Constellation: Creating Better Brand Alignment on the Web. *Design Management Review*, 14 (2), 42–49.

Rigby, D. (20101) The Future of Shopping. *Harvard Business Review*, December 2011, 64–76.

Rollins, N. (2009) OPEN Digital Experience Design: Strategic Trends-based Approach. *Design Management Review*, 20 (1), 31–38.

Rudd, N. (1999) Going Direct: Design and Digital Commerce. *Design Management Journal*, 10 (1), 17–22.

Schoenfeldinger, W., Bangerl, H., Nusser, H. and Pachauri, M. (2002) FOCAL Point: A Framework for Deriving Business Models in e-Business. In Proceedings of the 28th Euromicro Conference [WWW] IEEE Xplore. Available from: http://ieeexplore.ieee.org/xpl/articleDetails.jsp?reload=true&arnumber=1046179&contentType=Conference+Publications [Accessed 5 July 2013].

Timmers, P. (1998) Business Models for *Electronic Markets. Electronic Markets*, 8, 2, 3–8.

Upshaw, L. B. (2001) Building a Brand.com. *Design Management Review*, 12 (1), 34–39.

Vernuccio, M., Barbarossa, C., Giraldi, A. and Ceccotti, S. (2011) Determinants of E-brand Attitude: A Structural Modelling Approach. *Journal of Brand Management*, 19 (6), 500–512.

8.10   ONLINE RESOURCES

1. MIT Media Lab: www.media.mit.edu
2. Connected Digital Economy: https://cde.catapult.org.uk
3. RCUK Digital Economy: www.rcuk.ac.uk
4. Technology Strategy Board: www.innovateuk.org
5. The Connected Kingdom: www.connectedkingdom.co.uk

Chapter 9

STRATEGIC DESIGN FOR THE PUBLIC AND VOLUNTARY SECTORS

Strategies for design can be formulated for many problems and for the promotion of better futures. Every social, economic and environmental problem lends itself to the potential application of design thinking to design better systems, services and products to improve human life. This chapter discusses how managing design strategy can be employed for public transport, health, education, crime reduction, poverty, ecology and reduction of conflict. It explains how managers of major global brands charities can use design to communicate powerful messages but can also go further by using emotional design to engage and motivate. A common feature of all the good practice identified is participation, allowing all of the stakeholders to contribute and take pride and ownership in the outcomes. The relative importance of design strategy for this sector is growing, arguably faster than the commercial sector, as more and more organizations are formed to address perceived threats to human life and urgent needs for reform.

The 4Ds model of design management can be used to determine social and environmental goals and perceived reliability, define directions to inspire and get people engaged, design powerful communications through storytelling and emotional design and decide on what level of social and/or environmental value is added.

Objectives for this chapter:

- To introduce the concept of design for caring;
- To show how design strategy can address transportation needs;
- To explain how design can contribute to and drive healthcare needs;
- To discuss the potential of design strategy to create better places to live, work and play;
- To explain the growing influence of design thinking and practice in city design and branding;
- To discuss the ways in which design improves education;
- To evaluate the role of design in charity branding and performance improvement with case study examples;
- To explain the application of the 4Ds model to not-for-profit organizations.

9.1 DESIGN FOR CARING

The concept of design for caring is not new but has gained much momentum in recent years. Since the 1950s there have been major movements which influence design, e.g. the Barrier Free Movement and the Disability Civil Rights Movement. The first accessibility standard entitled *A-117 - Making Buildings Accessible by the Physically Handicapped* was issued in 1961 by the American Standards Association. Publications in the field date back to 1970s when Papanek (1971) published a seminal book called *Design for the Real World: Ecology and Social Change* in which he urged the design community to address social and environmental issues and the requirements of non-mainstream users, e.g. disabled people. In the early 1990s Ron Mace proposed *universal design* (UD), which was defined as "the design of products and environments which are usable by all people, to the greatest extent possible, without the need for adaptation or specialized design" (The RL Mace *Universal Design* Institute, 2011) The concept is now frequently referred to as inclusive design. The term *inclusive design* is defined as "design of mainstream products and/or services that are accessible to and usable by, people with the widest range of abilities within the widest range of situations without the need for special adaptation or design" (BSI, 2008).The Cambridge Engineering Design Centre (EDC, 2010) proposed the "waterfall" model to describe the inclusive design process (http://www-edc.eng.cam.ac.uk/betterdesign/process).

The process contains four main stages:

- *Discover*: The systematic exploration of the perceived need to ensure the right design challenge is addressed, with due consideration of all stakeholders; leading to the first output, an understanding of the real need.
- *Translate*: The conversion of this understanding into a categorized, complete and well-defined description of the design intent; leading to the second output, a requirements specification.
- *Create*: The creation of preliminary concepts that are evaluated against the requirements; leading to the third output, concepts.
- *Develop*: The detailed design of the final product or service, ready to be manufactured or implemented; leading to the final output, solutions.

It can be seen that the process is similar to other design processes. The main difference is in the mindset – making sure that the designs can be used by a wide range of people: children, older people and people with disabilities. In 2004 the concept of *Design for All* (DfA) was proposed for design which promotes "human diversity, social inclusion and equality" (The EIDD Stockholm Declaration, EIDD Design for All Europe, 2004). Nowadays design goes beyond usability and physical requirements and tackles complex difficult to define problems like safety and crime reduction. For example, the Design Against Crime Research Centre, University of the Arts London (www.designagainstcrime.com) explores how social design can be applied to reduce and prevent crime. Their projects cover a wide range of issues such as bicycle theft, pickpocketing and graffiti. Another interesting work investigating how design could reduce and prevent crime is the Design Council's

Think Thief (http://www.designcouncil.org.uk/Documents/Documents/ Publications/Think%20Thief_Design_Council.pdf). Experts pointed out that people commit crimes because they feel "safe" to do so – they remain anonymous and unnoticeable when committing the crime; they can get away easily, etc. Clever use of design can help deter crimes. For example, good store layout that does not have any dark corner and makes sure every part of the store is in full view of staff and other shoppers can reduce the number of shoplifting incidents. The same principles may also prevent school bullying, but many bullies like an audience and may thus favour the open space. Good design can reduce crimes without compromising on important aspects of products/services/experiences. For instance, one project explored how to prevent a pint glass and a beer bottle from being used in a "glass attack" which often causes serious injury to victims. While using "plastic" cups and bottles seems like a sensible option, it affects user experience and the pleasure of drinking. So both Big-D and small-d designs were used to come up with two practical solutions: a tougher glass that cannot be broken easily and a glass that shatters into small pieces when broken without any sharp edges that can be used as a weapon. Thus, people can still enjoy their drinks and the injuries from glass attacks can be reduced.

9.2   DESIGN AS A DRIVER OF TRANSPORTATION

9.2.1   Need for Design Contributions

Public transport has numerous design components such as vehicle design, graphic design for signage, information design for timetables, environmental design for stations/stops, interface design for kiosks, service design at the human interface, systems design of the network and product design of, for example, seats. In order for such complex systems to work well, holistic design thinking is required to deliver the best experience.

In the quest to make countries/cities attractive to visitors and investors, politicians are giving high priority to designing and developing good public transport. Because of the inherent complexity, it is suggested that holistic thinking should begin with Soft Systems Methodology (SSM) proposed by Checkland and Scholes (1999) as a means of identifying the key stakeholders, understanding their relationships and defining the problem(s). Investing time and effort with such a methodology can help to reconcile the needs of the stakeholders and strive to design a system which satisfies all of them. A tool for the achievement of a *"root definition"* can be applied using the mnemonic CATWOE:

1. *Clients* – Who would be benefited or affected by the system?
2. *Actors* – Who would be responsible for making the system work?
3. *Transformation* – What are the inputs and outputs of the system?
4. *Weltanschauung (Worldview)* – What viewpoint makes this system meaningful?
5. *Owner* – Who has the authority to stop or change the system?
6. *Environmental constraints* – Which external constraints does this system take as a given?

A further potentially valuable tool is the "rich picture." It is simply a drawing usually on an A3 size sheet of paper, of all the stakeholders with (brief) comments to show their principal interests and potential conflicts. No special drawing skills are required as "stick" figures can be used and symbols to represent resources and relationships.

Whilst the methodology is beneficial for modelling the differing, and often conflicting needs inherent in public transport, it can also be used for any complex human activity system as a precursor to formulating a new or revised strategy. Originally devised for the careful definition and reconciliation of complex information systems' needs, it has the potential to bring clarity and increased confidence in defining needs across a wide range of design and branding problems. A root definition implies that the design is firmly founded on an insightful understanding of the needs of all stakeholders. The tools are arguably more powerful than brainstorming as they are more structured and purposeful and invariably stimulate new thinking.

9.2.2 Design as a Driver for Improvements

Good use of design can drive innovation in transportation, e.g. reducing energy consumption and improving fuel efficiency, enhancing drivers' and passengers' experiences as well as saving time and money, for example reducing queuing time. Transport for London (TfL) uses design strategy as a key driver. Their product design guideline (see Table 9.1) addresses user requirements for legibility of signage, accessibility of bus stops and station furniture, through a fusion of aesthetics, appropriateness and economics.

Examples of design-led innovation in transportation are:

- **ULTra** (Urban Light Transport) is an example of design for caring in the public transport context. The system is a form of personal rapid transit (PRT) usually featuring automated small vehicles (for small group travel) operating on a network of specially built guide ways. User experience is at the centre of the ULTra system. The vehicle is accessible for all groups of users. Various user trials were conducted to ensure usability. The automatic system allows users to use the vehicles on demand 24/7. Moreover, it offers privacy and non-stop travel to the destination with no transfer. The operating process is straightforward and easy to operate. For more information: www.ultraglobalprt.com
- **The Taiwan High Speed Rail** (HSR) is an example of design for caring in the public transport context. User accessibility and usability are major considerations of the design. For example, every train is equipped with handicapped accessible seats and washrooms. HSR has fulfilled unmet needs and enables people of Taiwan to access to all parts of the country easily. All touch-points are well designed to ensure a pleasant experience. Recent figures show that the majority of people chose HSR over domestic flights and personal vehicles. For more information: www.thsrc.com.tw/en
- **Incheon International Airport** is the largest airport in South Korea. It was named the Best Airport Worldwide by Airports Council International for seven consecutive years (2005–2012). One of the major factors contributing to its success is good design. The beautiful, yet practical and

Table 9.1 Transport for London's product design guideline

Aesthetics	Appropriateness	Economics
Consistent approach Uses consistent design language and details	**Installation** Reduces pre-site works and avoids unauthorized removal	**Tooling** Reduces costs of tooling and protects IPR of TfL
Interfaces Fit the surroundings and do not compromise customers' and staff safety and security	**Removal** Minimizes damages, on-site labour costs and end-of-life environmental impacts	**Parts** Makes good use of existing resources, shares experience and ensure the compatibility
Colours, materials and finishes Follow corporate identity and use "self-finish" materials	**Inspections** Ensure clear sight lines and ease of use for users/staff	**Context** Products can be fixed on floors, ceilings and walls
Ergonomics Addresses physical and cognitive ergonomics (e.g. perception)	**Security** No hidden place and areas that may attract litter	**Simple and flexible** Products are adaptable to all sites with minimal adjustments
Project drivers Meet user needs and aspirations in terms of technology and style	**Understanding** Ensure the clarity of any words and pictograms	**Spare parts** Keep costs of spare parts down and ensure the availability
Disability issues Ensure visibility and choose appropriate colour contrast	**Operation** Mechanism is robust and gives sufficient feedback	**Ease of access** Products are easy to access for service and removal
LBA and heritage issues Take London heritages (e.g. listed buildings) into consideration	**Cleaning** Avoids fussy details and uses "self-cleaning" materials	**Added value** Do more for less – satisfy users while keeping maintenance low
Commercial opportunities Identify opportunities for sponsorships, co-branding and advertising and their added values	**Vandalism** Ensure durability and reduce the potential and probability of damages	**Economic** Think about added values first, then ensure low impacts of financial resources

Source: Transport for London (2009).

environmentally friendly architecture helps differentiate the airport from other competitors. The airport maximizes user experience by providing a wide range of services, such as golf course, spa, casino, ice skating rink and nursery. It plays an important role in promoting Korean culture by including attractions such as Korean Culture Street and Korean Culture Museum, inside the airport. Incheon International Airport provides a good example of design for caring, as it pushes the boundaries in terms of customer experience and emotional connections in many different levels. It also shows that good design can help to turn a terminal into an attractive destination for worldwide travellers. For more information: http://www.airport.kr/eng

Many cities and countries realized that public transport is an important touchpoint of their brands. People form opinions about cities and countries based on facilities that the places offer. Poor public transport can lead to negative experiences and poor impressions. By contrast, well-designed public transport can create positive images of cities and countries, and help persuade visitors, investors, students and high-skill workers to visit, invest, study and work. Many cities go beyond delivering practical issues (e.g. punctuality, efficiency, convenience and user-friendliness) and use public transport as a means to inspire residents and people from outside. A number of Moscow's underground stations showcase beautiful designs and offer cultural experiences. Stockholm's Metro stations are described as the "world longest art exhibition." This emotional design approach adopted by many cities and countries demonstrates the caring beyond physical wellbeing and goes further to embrace emotional needs.

9.3   DESIGN AS A DRIVER OF HEALTHCARE

9.3.1   Need for Design Contributions

Increased application of design strategy in the healthcare sector has resulted from recognition by healthcare providers that they must raise standards and enhance patient satisfaction. Recent research shows that better patient experience means faster recovery whereas a bad experience could delay the patient's recovery speed. According to Baxter, Mugglestone and Maher (2009), the National Health Service (NHS) identified three core focus areas as follows:

- *Patient safety* – the environment and processes are in place to ensure that no harm comes to patients.
- *Patient experience* – understanding patients' satisfaction with their experience of care; the compassion, dignity and respect with which they are treated.
- *Effectiveness of care* – understanding how successful the service is in delivering the expected results, through a variety of measures; clinical and patient reported.

In order to achieve these target areas, the NHS recognized that the co-design approach and patient involvement were required. Evidently, getting patients involved in designing services that they will receive could lead to higher satisfaction. Moreover, involving patients in the co-design process provides many benefits, such as increased patients' confidence, reduced anxiety, improved relationships and trust between patients and healthcare professionals.

From a human-centred design perspective, involving patients in the co-design process could lead to better patient choices. Cottam and Leadbeater (2004) suggested that "the biggest untapped resources in the health system are not doctors, but users." Baxter, Mugglestone and Maher (2009) argued that users or patients have experiential knowledge (knowledge derived from first-hand experiences) that could help healthcare providers develop more appropriate, effective, cost-effective and sustainable services. This practice helps empower people, which leads to higher self-esteem and self-efficacy. These positive characteristics are very important, since they encourage a person to take charge of his/her own situation and solve problems himself/herself rather than asking for help or waiting for support. As a result, the Institute for Innovation and Improvement, NHS, introduced the Experience Based Design (EBD) approach and produced EBD guidance, including case study materials and tools, to assist health providers in adopting the new practices and co-design services with their patients and staff. For more information: http://www.institute.nhs.uk/quality_and_value/ experienced_ based_design/the_ebd_approach_(experience_based_design).html

Waitemata District Health Board (DHB), New Zealand, also introduced the co-design approach to health practitioners as a means to improve their services. In their guidance, *Health Service Co-design* (Boyd, McKernon and Old, 2010), the co-design process was divided into six stages:

1. *Engage* – Establishing and maintaining meaningful relationships with patients to understand and improve healthcare services. This critical element underpins all improvement work and is continuous throughout.
2. *Plan* – Working with patients and staff to establish the goals of the practitioners improvement work and how you might go about achieving them.
3. *Explore* – Learning about and understanding patient experiences of services and identifying improvement ideas.
4. *Develop* – Working with patients to turn ideas into improvements that will lead to better patient experiences.
5. *Decide* – Choosing what improvements to make and how to make them. Its success depends on an understanding of the patient journey and the insights about service improvement this offers.
6. *Change* – Turning the practitioner's improvement ideas into action. Remembering that the practitioner does not need to make all the changes by himself/herself, and can make as many improvements in partnership with other stakeholders as possible.

A number of design research tools and techniques were recommended as a means to capture in-depth information from patients, such as shadowing, user journey mapping, emotional mapping, story boarding, personas and scenarios, and service blue printing. Further explanation and examples of these design research tools are given below:

- *Shadowing.* As the name suggested, this technique recommends that researchers follow users around, basically acting like their shadows, so that they can observe how users interact with the world around them and understand how people live their normal lives.
- *User journey mapping.* This technique allows researchers to map out the entire user journey: *How do they interact with all touchpoints of the product/service? How do they navigate from one touchpoint to another? What*

happens during the process? In this case, the tool can help health providers understand patients and other stakeholders' (e.g. carers and families) experiences. The outcomes can help them identify problems and areas for improvement in order to make the journey more pleasant and effective. The example of the user journey map is shown in Figure 9.1.

- *Emotional mapping.* This technique allows researchers to map out thoughts and feelings that occur to a user during the entire journey. In some cases, the user journey map and the emotional map are combined together in order to provide a more holistic view. Both tools are parts of the user journey analysis. Users are asked to accurately record their feelings and thoughts throughout the whole process. A reflective interview at the end of the process may be used to gain further insights and get users to explain what they actually thought and felt at particular stages. The outcomes can help health providers identify problems and areas for improvement beyond practical issues – for example, stress caused by poor visiting experiences and anxiety caused by lack of communication. An example of the user journey map is shown in Figure 9.2.

- *Storyboarding.* This technique can be used to capture or represent research results, as well as to visualize how people may interact with a new product or service. Researchers can use cartoon-style or photographic storyboards to capture the experiences that individual users currently go through. Researchers can also turn all user experiences that they recorded into one story and then draw a storyboard to visualize it. Moreover, after developers come up with new ideas for a product/

Scenario: Your friend is unwell. You look up the contact details of his doctor and make an appointment on his behalf. You take him to see a doctor who prescribes medicine for him. You also help get the medicine.

Touchpoints	User Needs			
	Find the contact details	Make an appointment	Take him to see the doctor	Get the prescribed medicine
Phone		2. Call the reception. Cannot find the slot until the evening		
Internet	1. Look up the detail online. It is not easy to find the number			7. Check the internet to find the nearest pharmacy that still opens
Public Transports			3. Take him on the bus. Have to compete with other commuters during rush hours	8. Take the bus to the pharmacy
Reception			4. Inform the reception that the patient has arrived	6. Collect details about prescribed medicine from the reception
Doctor			5. See the doctor	
Pharmacy				9. Get the medicine

Figure 9.1 An example of the user journey map

Thoughts	Why it is so difficult to find the contact details on the website?	Why can't we have an earlier appointment? Don't want to travel at 5 pm.	Should we call the reception that we are 10 minutes away? Don't want to be late.	Glad to hear that he is ok. It's worth all the hassle...	Why did they give us a late appointment? we may not able to get medicine today!	Why can't the doctor provide medicine as well? It is difficult to run around.

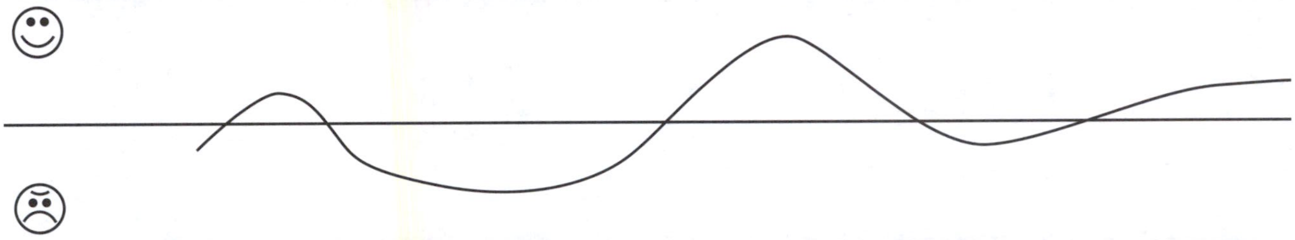

Stage	Find the contact details	Make an appointment	Inform the reception	See the doctor	Get the prescription	Get the medicine
Feeling	Worried, Anxious, Concerned	Disappointed that he cannot see the doctor until evening	Relieved that you made it in time despite the traffic	Relieved that your friend is ok and will get well soon	Worried, not sure which pharmacy would still open	Relieved that you found the pharmacy and got the drug
Opportunities	Better website design	A system to notify patients if earlier appointments are cancelled	A system that allow patients to notify the doctor that they are on the way		A list of local pharmacies including their addresses and opening times	

Figure 9.2 An example of the emotional map using the same scenario

service, they can use a storyboard to visualize how people may find out, acquire and use their product/service. In this case, storyboarding can be used to explore and capture patients and other stakeholders' stories. The outcomes can help health providers come up with new innovation that eliminate negative experience in the story, as well as enhance the positive ones.

For more information about tools and techniques for co-design, visit: www. healthcodesign.org.nz and www.servicedesigntools.org

9.3.2   Design as a Driver of Healthcare Improvements

Good use of design can drive innovation in the healthcare sector – ranging from better environments to more efficient services. The Design Council successfully commissioned several projects exploring how good design can be used to improve the healthcare services.

- *Design Bugs Out*: The project provided evidence that good design can help address problems in healthcare infections, especially MRSA. They demonstrated that by designing hospital equipment and furniture that is easy to clean and easy to use, it will stay cleaner – and this in turn helps to reduce the risk of infection. Four teams of designers and British manufacturers were formed to develop new pieces of hospital furniture, such as bedside cabinet, commode and patient chair. They shared their research and expertise and designed functional products that make cleaning quicker and easier and eliminate dirt traps. Each design was tested and evaluated using eight "showcase" hospitals and the furniture proved to be easier to clean. The rigorous assessments replicated routine hospital cleaning procedures of typically contaminated hospital furniture. Full details of the evaluation can be downloaded from: https:// www.gov.uk/government/publications/ design-bugs-out-product-evaluation-report. For more information: http://www.designcouncil.org.uk/ our-work/challenges/health/design-bugs-out/
- *Design for Patient Dignity*. This project explored how to use design to enhance privacy and reduce stress caused by patients sharing accommodation and bathrooms with the opposite sex. The solutions were simple yet creative and included patient gowns and capsule bathroom facilities, see: http://www.designcouncil.org.uk/our-work/challenges/ Health/ Design-for-Patient-Dignity. A similar strategy was proposed by Gotah (2007) who defined "dignity" as "being respected." Patient privacy was revealed as the highest priority. Small incidents, e.g. opening the door without knocking, can negatively influence the patient experience, whereas taking patients to the toilet can make the experience positive. Service design and training were shown to build trust and relationships.

The Design Council (2006) also showed how co-design can be used to address complex problems like diabetes management. A set of example cards covering diabetes needs and concerns (such lifestyle habits and self-medicating fears) was designed in collaboration with patients at Bolton Diabetes Centre to facilitate dialogue between patients and medical experts. These cards can help personalize each consultation to reflect individual needs. For more information: http://www.designcouncil.org.uk/Case-studies/Diabetes-management/

The NHS's *Design for Patient Safety* series addresses how better design can reduce risk, improve the working environment and ensure better, patient-centred care. The thinking behind this series is founded on the assumption that human beings make mistakes because the systems, tasks and processes they work within are poorly designed. Thus effective design can be used to deliver products, services, processes and environments that are intuitive, simple to understand, simple to use, convenient and comfortable. This results in the reduction of errors, for example by designing drug packaging so that it is easy to distinguish one drug from another, the chance of administering the wrong medicine can be reduced. The series seeks to explore the wealth of knowledge and methods from the design world that can be applied to improve healthcare products and processes. This *Design for Patient Safety* series won "best management of design in a public or non-profit organisation" category at the Design Management Europe Awards 2008, thereby demonstrating the power of design thinking to deliver improvements. For more information see: http://www.nrls.npsa.nhs.uk/resources/collections/design-for-patient-safety/

9.4 DESIGN AS A DRIVER FOR BETTER PLACES TO LIVE, WORK & PLAY

9.4.1 Need for Design Contributions

Needs for Design as the Community Level

Recent research suggested that people experience more stress from the fear of crime than from any direct experience of it (Cooper *et al.*, 2009) and poorly designed/maintained public spaces, e.g. poorly lit alleyways, contribute to this fear (Butterworth, 2000). Lam *et al.* (2011) reported that public space designs have strong influences on both safety and perception of safety. A principal factor that affects the perception of safety is the way things are kept and cared for. For example, when people walk on a street where everything is boarded up, they become more vigilant or wary. Poorly designed public spaces can decrease the perception of safety, which results in a lower level of human activity in the area that finally makes the area become unsafe. However well-designed public spaces can enhance the perception of safety and increase the level of human activities in the area, which helps attract more people/businesses to the area and eventually makes the area safer. At present, most public spaces are designed to keep the maintenance costs low and withstand vandalism. Although these designs make streets safe, they do not make people *feel* safe, e.g. street furniture made from steel bars reminds people of a prison. Moreover, many public designs are driven by highway engineering which concentrates on practical purposes only. For instance, lighting was designed to provide sufficient light for roads but does not go on to consider how safe people might feel during night.

It is apparent that there is a need to make the public spaces "look safe" as well as be safe. Good use of design approaches, such as user-centred design, inclusive design and co-design, can help key decision makers, e.g. urban planners, to ensure that the public spaces they design match people's practical requirements and emotional expectations.

Needs for Design as the Strategic Level

Some experts have urged key decision makers to go even further and start seeing a place, such as a neighbourhood, district, town or city, as a brand. Place branding is not a new subject but not yet widely employed. The concept is rooted in place marketing where marketing tools and techniques were applied to help cities and countries compete for investment and tourism, see Ward (1998) and Kotler *et al.* (1999) for examples. Due to these marketing driven origins, city branding is often perceived as a way to boost the economy rather than fulfilling the aspirations of citizens. For instance, Van Gelder and Allan (2006) defined a city brand as the promise of value that has capability to retain city businesses, residents and institutions, as well as attract new investors, visitors and talent. Anholt (2004), a renowned place branding expert, suggested that a city brand comprises of six core components as follows:

1. *Presence* – the city's international status and standing.
2. *Place* – people's perceptions about the physical aspect of the city.
3. *Potential* – the economic and educational opportunities of the city.
4. *Pulse* – people's perceptions about the appeal of the city in a short and long term.
5. *People* – people's perceptions about the habitants of the city.
6. *Prerequisites* – people's perceptions about the basic quality of the city.

Although city inhabitants play an important role in shaping perceptions of outsiders toward their areas and should be given more opportunities to co-create the brand of their cities, city branding is often carried out in a top-down fashion by local authorities in close consultation with powerful business leaders, and inputs from residents are limited. This lack of contributions from the local community can lead to a "disconnection" between people and the place (Kavaratizis and Ashworth, 2008). Good use of design approaches, such as user-centred design, inclusive design and co-design, can help to overcome this problem. These design practices should be applied at both the strategic and operational levels.

9.4.2 Design as a Driver of Participatory City Design and City Branding

Big-D Design Thinking

Gilmore (2002) stressed that successful place branding must be "an amplification of what it is already there and not a fabrication." The author pointed out that a brand of a place should be not artificial creation that imposed from the outside. She proposed a brand positioning diamond containing four elements: macro trends, stakeholders, core competencies and competitors. According to this model, a city brand should be created based on core competencies of the city with regard to requirements and aspirations of all key stakeholders, e.g. local businesses and residents, macro trends and the brand positions of their competitors. Aitken and Campelo (2011) argued that a bottom-up process and a participatory approach should be integral parts of place branding. They believed that if the local community is given an opportunity to co-create the brand of the city, the result will be more authentic and sustainable. Moreover, the sense of belonging and ownership will be increased.

Aitken and Campelo (2011) advanced the idea of stakeholder engagement further, as they proposed a bottom-up approach for place branding based on co-creation principles. Their four Rs model for the social ownership of a place brand comprises of four fundamental elements, namely *rights, roles, responsibilities* and *relationships* (senses of place). According to their model, the city branding process should start with an in-depth understanding of people's relationships and connections with each other and a place. In this way, people are properly engaged and have a strong sense of ownership. Charles Landry proposed the ideas of the "creative city" in the late 1980s, which has become a new city planning paradigm. The idea is rooted on the belief that every city has potential to be creative – creativity, in this case, goes beyond the artistic sense. Cities could be seen as "creative" in the way that it addresses sustainable issues or promotes social inclusion. By getting people more engaged and taking ownership as well as responsibility, more ideas on how cities, places and regions can become more creative will be generated.

Small-d Experience Design

Experience design should be used to create positive experiences throughout the whole customer journey. It is important to start even before visitors arrive at the place/city with such questions as: *How best to communicate accurate information about the town/city in an inspiring way? How best to capture people's attention?* Which medium (e.g. web sites) is suitable for which target group? Once the people arrive, everything counts. All the tangible and intangible touchpoints, such as public transportation, signage and public spaces, contribute to the experience and, hence, must be carefully designed and managed. Even when people leave the city, design can still be used to remind people of their good experience and firmly occupy spaces in their minds/memories. They may purchase souvenirs and, more importantly, retain vivid positive memories which can encourage them to revisit, spread the brand virally or invest in the future.

9.5   DESIGN AS A DRIVER OF EDUCATION

9.5.1   Needs for Design Contributions

Educational approaches from primary schools to universities have changed rapidly in recent years towards a new student-centred approach to promote curiosity and lifelong learning. According to Cannon and Newble (2000), characteristics of the student-centred learning are:

- Students have responsible and active role (in planning their learning, interacting with teachers and other students, researching, assessing)

- Students required to make choices about what and how to learn
- Emphasis on integrating learning across the curriculum
- Emphasis on enquiry-type activities
- Teacher as guide, mentor and facilitator of learning
- Intrinsic motivation (interest, curiosity, responsibility)
- Focus on cooperative learning
- Learning can occur anywhere
- Greater flexibility in learning and teaching
- Greater flexibility in assessment with self and peer assessment becoming more common
- Long-term perspective: emphasis of lifelong learning

This has implications for the design of systems, products, services, and environments. The new approach to education emphasizes realistic problem solving, collecting, analyzing and synthesizing information, then working in groups to generate solutions. According to Kolb's Experiential Learning Theory (ELT), the learning cycle can be divided into four stages:

- *Concrete experience (CE)*: Learners are given an opportunity to experience a new situation and/or reinterpret their existing knowledge/understanding (feel).
- *Reflective observation (RO)*: Learners are encouraged to reflect upon that experience or reinterpretation and extract the main lessons learned (think).
- *Abstract conceptualization (AC)*: Learners turn their experiences and new insights into new knowledge or modify their existing understanding (conceptualize).
- *Active experimentation (AE)*: Learners test the new knowledge by applying it and see whether it works as intended/expected (test).

Based on Kolb's ELT model, four learning styles were proposed:

1. *Diverging for CE & RO*. This type of learner is considered a divergent thinker and is good at reviewing things from different perspectives. He/she is more of an observer than an active participant and looks to gather information and use imagination in order to solve problems. Their style of thinking/learning makes them good at idea generation and they like to work in groups where they listen with an open mind and receive personal feedback on their ideas. Design can be used to encourage imagination and idea exploration, e.g. taking people to new environments and asking them to observe, reflect and come up with new ideas.
2. *Assimilating for RO & AC*. This type of learner prefers a concise, logical approach. They are keen on new ideas and concepts but like good clear well-founded explanations rather than practical opportunities. They can organize broad-based complex information into a clear logical format to enhance understanding. The style shows them to be less focused on people and more interested in ideas and abstract concepts. Such people are more attracted to logically sound theories than approaches based on practical value. People with this style prefer readings, lectures and exploring analytical models. Design can be used to create engaging learning materials and lecture notes to meet their needs.

3. *Converging for AC & AE*. This type of learner likes to solve problems and enjoys using his/her learning to find solutions to practical issues. They favour technical tasks and applications as against involvement and/or concern with people and interpersonal aspects and are good at finding practical uses for ideas and theories through experimentation and simulation. Design can be used to create challenging tasks, engaging activities and workbooks.
4. *Accommodating for AE & CE*. This type of learner is a "hands-on" person and likes to use his/her intuition. People with this learning style tend to rely on others for information, then they conduct their own analysis using a practical, experiential approach. They favour new challenges and experiences, and put their plans into action. Their learning style is team and target based and they use initiative and experimentation to achieve objectives and complete jobs. Design can be used to create interactive activities and experimental spaces where they can try ideas freely, e.g. online platforms.

Regardless of learning styles, it is important to encourage learners to adopt a deep approach where learners are more interested in long-term benefits rather than short-term gains (e.g. passing exams). New ways of teaching and learning, such as problem-based learning, game-based learning and integrative learning, require design thinking to create interactive learning experiences so that learners play active roles in acquiring knowledge rather than listening to lectures.

9.5.2 Design as a Driver for Improvements

Design strategy can be applied to promote active learning in classes, as well as address many educational problems such as bullying and alcohol/drugs in schools, and to enhance the entire learning experience for teachers, students, parents and the wider community. *Design Out Crime* initiative uses design thinking to tackle crimes in many areas including violence and petty crime in schools. Through participatory research key challenges were identified and potential design solutions generated – see Table 9.2. For the full report see www.designcouncil.org.uk/Documents/Documents/OurWork/Crime/DOC_schools.pdf

In terms of environment, there is much evidence that design can be used to enhance the environment for learning, giving students more opportunity to learn in an active, self-directed manner with support. The campaign for new learning environment conducted by the UK Design Council (2005) showed that current school environments, e.g. classrooms, were designed for the "one size fits all" approach which is no longer suitable for the education model in the 21st century. More bottom-up practices and personalized learning experiences are required. This situation provides interesting challenges and opportunities for design. The experiments carried out as parts of this campaign showed that changes in classroom layouts and furniture could improve student engagement and communications. It demonstrated that design has an important role to play in enhancing the effectiveness of teaching and learning by creating right climates for learning.

Table 9.2 Designing out crime in the school context

Problems	Challenges	Potential design solutions
At school	1. Reducing the opportunity for bullying, violence and vandalism in school's unmonitored areas 2. Reducing theft and vandalism of personal property brought into school 3. Providing in-school security measures that help people feel protected and secure 4. Improving security and safety at the school gates and school car park	• Using new and innovative lighting design to remove the sense of threat associated with out-of-the-way spaces and dark corners • Instilling young people with a sense of pride and respect for the school environment
On journeys to and from school	5. Improving safety, trust and respect when travelling by bus 6. Reducing crime, bullying and intimidation when walking to and from school	• Redesigning the bus journey system to reduce fear • Improving visibility and lines of sight along existing routes
Beyond school	7. Reducing cyber-bullying on mobile phones and the Internet 8. Tackling boredom by providing access to information and engaging activities 9. Improving relationships and trust between young people and adults	• Reinventing the youth club for today's young people • Using relevant communication channels to provide access to local information and activities

Another example in terms of design in education is the work of the Sorrell Foundation. The foundation is a champion of design in schools and seeks to "inspire creativity in young people and improve the quality of life through good design." Through their Saturday Club, students aged 14–16 are given a chance to explore their design talent and the *Joined Up Design for Schools* project puts students in the role of clients for a school design project. Working in teams they create a design brief for designers and/or architects (www.the-sorrellfoundation.com). The *Our New School* project has similar principles, promoting collaboration between design disciplines and key stakeholders to improve experiences (www.ournewschool.org). Some experts are new arguing the design should go beyond addressing effective learning environments and design thinking should become part of the school curriculum.

9.6   DESIGN AS A DRIVER OF CHARITIES

9.6.1   Need for Design Contributions: Branding

Charities are not the most prominent users of design, yet according to Saxton (2002) they are amongst the strongest brands of any organization with images often powerfully and universally known. He notes that the need for charities to have a coherent brand is disputed by some charity practitioners. Further he argues that charity brands are different from commercial brands and should not adopt their practices because:

• As they "desire to change the world" their personalities are much deeper than most commercial brands and thus they need design to communicate their core values and beliefs in a compelling manner;
• Because they have smaller budgets design is needed to make cost-effective practices, e.g. direct marketing, go further;
• A national or global rebranding exercise will be too costly and time consuming for most charities to cope. Thus, design thinking is required to make the most of all their assets, in particular their identity and networks.

However, charities are currently urged to rethink their approaches in response to changing economic circumstances. Donating and volunteering cannot be so much relied upon. Main barriers to volunteering are work commitments and childcare obligations, (Communities and Local Government, 2010). The situation is amplified in developing countries, for example just 24.3% of Thai people donate money (Give to All Project, 2009). Hence design thinking may be needed to find new ways of giving.

9.6.2 Design as a Driver of Improvements

Improving the Brand

A strong image can enhance trust and credibility for charities (Saxton, 2002). His five motivations for charity brand communication demonstrate how design can make a positive contribution as shown in Table 9.3. Going up the levels of core elements increases loyalty, commitment and tolerance of mistakes, whereas going down the levels increases the need for personal benefit and rewards.

Table 9.3 How design can influence five motivations

Core elements	Design contributions
1. Vision	Design thinking can be used to create a powerful vision which is a basis for strong and loyal following.
2. Values and beliefs	Compelling communication design can deliver values and beliefs explicitly.
3. Capability	Communication design can send a clear message about the charity's capability, e.g. previous achievements, which help build trust and credibility.
4. Specific action/ behaviour	Communication design can create a powerful offer with specific outcomes, such as: "£1 will for feed a child for a month." It clearly describes what the charity is about and initiates relationships between people and the brand.
5. Local/environment	Good use strategic design can build peer pressure which is one of strongest motivations for people to take part.

9.6.3   Need for Design Contributions: Offerings

One definition suggested for design is "making things better for people" (Richard Seymour quoted in Design Council, 2008). Such a definition aligns well with the concerns of the charity sector. As charitable organizations increasingly find themselves competing to attract funding and resources to support their missions and deliver services (Charity Commission, 2007), their ability to innovate and design new ways of delivering services will be crucial to their success. A recent study conducted by Dearden, Lam, William-Powlett and Brodie (2012) suggested that design practices, especially co-design, could help charities deliver better offerings at lower costs.

Good use of co-design has potential to improve products/services, while saving time and money. Firstly it can be achieved by involving users in designing products/services that they will use to help ensure that the outcomes fulfil their requirements. In this way, charities can reduce unnecessary costs and focus on what users really want. The second step to improvement is treating users as equal partners rather than recipients, which assists the charities to gain a valuable taskforce. This can be particularly helpful to small charities to overcome problems caused by the lack of staff. Further, good use of co-design also leads to several social benefits, such as encouraging self-help and positive behaviour change, as well as growing social networks to support resilience (Boyle and Harris, 2009). Co-design has proved to be useful for the third sector, as it excels at increasing stakeholder engagement, which can lead to higher productivity, higher creativity and lower costs and risks (Ramaswamy and Gouillart, 2010). For example, Aid to Artisans (www.aidtoartisans.org) uses co-design between trained designers and a small community of artisans as a means to create values for the community beyond immediate economic opportunities.

Case Study 1:   MERU http://meru.org.uk

MERU (http://meru.org.uk) is a medium-sized charity based in Surrey, UK that designs and manufactures specialized equipment for children and young people under 25 with disabilities living in London or South East England. They have presently 12 permanent staff and around 40 volunteers. The staff includes in-house design engineers working in design studios and workshops for producing prototypes and manufacturing custom-made devices. Their main sources of income are annual grants and fund-raising activities. MERU's main activities are:

- *Custom-made products*: MERU's custom made service benefits disabled young people who cannot find the product(s) they need anywhere else on the market. Meru's design engineers custom-design and manufacture new and complex products which address wide ranging needs, from communication and leisure to bathing and safety. Some examples of the many custom-made products include a foot-free device to activate the sustain pedal on a piano and an alternative remote control for a remote-controlled car.

- *Ready-made products*: Initially all the products were custom made but repeat requests for similar products lead to the introduction of ready-made products. These products include devices to provide stability and support, such as an attachment providing stability for children using school chairs, a travel chair, a powered indoor wheelchair for one- to five-year-olds, power chair accessories and holding and positioning products, e.g. a detachable pull for fiddly zips.
- *Advice service*: Given the limited financial, physical and human resources MERU has to custom-make products, they need to be sure that a solution does not already exist on the market. Thus they have acquired an advanced knowledge base on the products available and the needs of clients and employ an in-house physiotherapist and provide an advice phone line to advise anyone who is finding it difficult to locate a product supplier to meet a child or young person's needs.

MERU's custom-made products are all developed using a co-design process between a design engineers and beneficiaries. It begins with the matching of a suitable design engineer with a client need through a project referral committee. A design engineer who has the requisite skills and expertise is responsible for assessing the referral. Following approval of the referral, the design engineer starts working with the beneficiary on the design of the product. This co-creation of the design brief is considered crucial to the quality of the product. Brainstorming and props are used for problem definition and ideation stages, though most often it is done by discussions between the designer and the client beneficiary and or their parent/carer about the requirements of the product. Except in cases where the beneficiary has severe cognitive impairment, all beneficiaries are involved in all the key stages in the co-design process: defining problems, creating the brief, developing design concepts, selecting concepts, finalizing details and testing the product. Adopting the co-design practice has become a central pillar for the charity to fulfil user requirements and in turns help children and young people with disabilities to build their confidence to communicate their needs and wants clearly and their confidence in daily life.

Case Study 2:   The Blackwood Foundation www.mbha.org.uk/blackwood-foundation

The Blackwood Foundation (www.mbha.org.uk/blackwood-foundation) is a medium-sized charity established by its parent charity, non-profit company Blackwood, four years ago. The organization promotes independent living and provides support for people with a disability or other support needs. The foundation presently employs just two members of staff, the managing director and his assistant, although it has access to a wider range of experts in the parent company Blackwood. The principal aim of the charity is to be "a catalyst for innovation, development and improvement." It currently provides two services: one which connects people with disabilities or support needs with designers, and the second which connects people with an interest in independent living to enable them to share problems, ideas and recommendations.

Eleven consultation workshops were held by the Blackwood Foundation in 2009 involving people interested in independent living across Scotland. They included activities that invited the participants to identify designs that they liked most and those they disliked primarily through frustration in using them, and used the outcomes to ensure maximum participation and discussion. The findings of the workshops revealed that many participants have strong potential to play co-creating roles in the design and development of new products since many of them knew what they wanted and some had already designed/modified products or built environments to suit their personal needs. The workshops also identified that the users were given limited opportunities to input in the design process, despite their interest and willingness to participate. A further valuable finding of the workshops was that participants were not aware of existing products and services on offer to support their independent living. As a result of these findings, the Blackwood Foundation developed two new services, one to connect users with each other, and the other to connect users with designers.

- *Connecting users with each other*: The Foundation developed the online service bespoken (www.bespoken.me), a social media site that "brings together anyone with an interest in independent living." This site offers a forum for people to exchange ideas, tips, problems and recommendations on independent living. It includes examples of good designs so that members are made more aware of existing solutions in the market and recent developments.
- *Connecting users with designers*: This service connects users with designers through a university engagement scheme. The Blackwood Foundation conducted the pilot work for this new service with the School of Engineering and Design at Brunel University. The Foundation bespoken forum members presented problems and/or new design opportunities for a student to work on and set a design challenge for a final-year design student by asking them to co-create a design. In this way a trained designer is encouraged to co-design a product with real users.

Through careful management of the co-design practice the charity found that users really wanted a space to exchange ideas, and they can work with users to achieve the desirable results. The co-design practice also helps the charity connect users with young designers. This offers useful learning experiences for the young designers concurrent with educating users about the design process, which can help them develop more meaningful and effective independent living solutions.

9.7   4Ds OF DESIGN-LED NOT-FOR-PROFIT ORGANIZATION

A caring and sharing philosophy is becoming increasingly important, and is likely to go even beyond the public sector and not-for-profit organizations. Evidence to support this includes:

- The shift from "fast capital" to "slow capital," characterized as no rush to conclusions, flows into company based on company (not investor) needs, starts small and grows with the company, no set timetable to get liquid, and takes time to understand the company and its people (Wilson, featured in Gupta, 2010).
- Generosity is crucial to the survival of the "connected economy " in which all parties are physically/virtually scrutinized by the public (Godin, featured in Gupta, 2010).

- The concept of "collaborative consumption" by Botsman and Roger (2010) is considered one of the ten ideas that will change the world (Walsh, 2011). It proposes changing the mindset from the pleasure of owning things to the pleasure of sharing things. Examples are sharing sites, such as Ecomodo (www.ecomodo.com).

The 4Ds Design Management model can capitalize on the trends and embrace design for caring by:

1. Determining the current use of design – finding the key values/require-ments of the not-for-profit sector;
2. Defining strategic directions to inspire the public – identifying oppor-tunities for design strategy, setting realistic goals that align with core beliefs;
3. Designing activities, environment and cultures to engage society – planning how design can engage public audiences, create new brands, deliver added-value services and continually build trust and loyalty;
4. Deciding whether it is effective – objective open review of design perfor-mance (Table 9.4) (Figure 9.3).

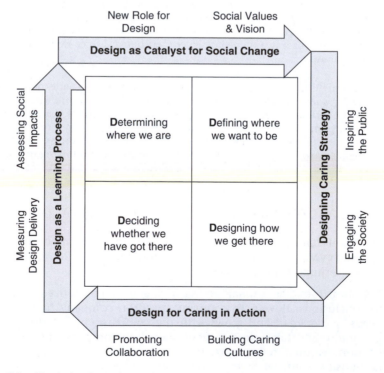

Figure 9.3   4Ds design for caring model

Table 9.4 Key elements of the 4Ds of not-for-profit organizations

Strategic level	Tactical level	Operational level
Determining		
Public perception on: • Values and beliefs • Visions	Public perception on: • Past achievements • Capabilities	Public perception on: • Actions/activities • Outcomes
Defining		
Strategic goals for design • Brand image • Brand loyalty • Brand trust	Tactical goals for design • Public engagement • Network development • Capacity development	Operational goals for design • Cost reduction • Communication design • System design
Designing		
Design strategy • Brand communication • Brand association	Design methods • Participatory design • Design empathy	Design projects • Product design • Service design
Deciding		
Public perception on: • Trust and credibility • Loyalty	Public perception on: • Overall performance • Progress toward goals	Public perception on: • Overall delivery • Overall experience

9.7.1 Determining the Current Use of Design

Press and Cooper's (2003) design audit provides a useful framework for determining the current use of design. Table 9.5 shows how Cancer Research UK make good use of design in all key strategic areas identified.

Determining Current Design Strategies

Clarity of the brand message and emotional connections are vital and therefore it is important to find out the public perception. Motivations to support any charities and voluntary organizations are very personal as shown by Communities and Local Government *Citizenship* Survey (2010), thus the design of the brand plays a crucial role in gaining people's support.

Determining Current Design Performance

Consider how well design is used to deliver the brand promise, communicate previous achievements and make the giving process easy and transparent. This will increase "reliability" which is the top criterion when making donation decisions (Phatanarajata, 2010).

Table 9.5 Areas for a design audit and an example

Areas	Design elements	Cancer Research UK
Physical manifestations of design	• Visual identity • Corporate design standards • Products • Work environment	It has strong corporate identity with a powerful strapline. All materials are well designed.
Design management	• Design resources: human, physical, internal, external • Design skills • Design training • Design management: process, procedures, guidelines • Design funding: investment and return • Design department: location, service, aim and objectives • Project management	Although overall brand experience is not strictly controlled, all touchpoints and key messages are coherent, uplifting and positive. Activities, e.g. events, are engaging.
Corporate culture	• Corporate design strategies • Design awareness/understanding • Design champions • Integration of design and other functions • Design activities undertaken	The design culture is evident. Many promotional materials were designed by the internal design studio.
Environmental factors	• Market trends (which could affect design decisions) • Design trends • Legislation • Standards • Technology trends	The charity is at the forefront of the research and development in the related fields.

9.7.2 Defining Strategic Design Directions to Inspire and Engage

A well-designed brand strategy is the first requirement for successful not-for-profit organizations. Therefore, this section discusses the use of emotional branding and strategic directions for inspiring people to get involved.

Defining Current Situations

Greenstein, development director of the Arts and Business Council, observes that many not-for-profit organizations are reluctant to think of themselves as brands, since they see brands as marketing tools rather than an organizational principle which directs their strategic plans (Tan, 2003). She notes that numerous such organizations use design and branding in an "ad hoc" manner. If they are to survive and grow they must establish clear goals and strategy for branding and design. Many charities rely on overused words (Tan, 2003). Words like trustworthiness, dignity and professionalism cannot help to differentiate brands. To maintain motivation, not-for-profit organizations should ensure their values are still relevant, meaningful and inspiring. Saxton (2002) offered a more comprehensive list of values often associated with charity as shown below:

Accountable	Conservative	*Friendly*	Passionate
Ambitious	*Determined*	Focused	Practical
Approachable	Dedicated	Generous	*Professional*
Authoritative	Direct	Greedy	Reputable
Bold	Dynamic	*Helpful*	Responsive
Boring	*Effective*	Heroic	Rich
Caring	Engaging	Inclusive	Supportive
Cautious	Established	Independent	Sympathetic
Challenging	Exciting	*Informative*	Traditional
Complacent	Exclusive	Innovative	*Trustworthy*
Compassionate	Fair	Inspiring	Visionary
		Outspoken	Welcoming

Those highlighted are the top ten qualities the public would like in their ideal charity. Since these values are overused to describe charities' philosophy, design thinking is needed to make the brand stand out from the crowd. Saxton (2002) also stresses that not-for-profit brands require the same elements as commercial brands, e.g. name, logo, house design style and strapline to capture the brand essence succinctly and differentiate and reinforce messages.

Example: Cancer Research UK and Macmillan Cancer Support

Cancer Research UK and Macmillan Cancer Support are leading charities in the UK. The former focuses on research and the latter on helping people to live with cancer conditions. Both charities make effective use of design and branding to differentiate from each other, as well as project inspiring images. They strategically use different corporate colours – Macmillan Cancer Support uses green and Cancer Research UK uses pink. Although both organizations use storytelling to communicate their work and achievements, Cancer Research UK focuses on how advanced research saves lives while Macmillan Cancer Support demonstrates how good support makes differences to patients' quality of life.

Defining Strategic Directions: Design-led Branding

Success factors for the formulation of a design strategy for not-for-profit branding were identified by Hales (2011) and suggestions made to overcome the resistance to design and branding and to make the brand relevant and inspiring. Table 9.6 shows the success factors, their descriptions and practical suggestions for design.

Example: Unicef

Because brand and design must be carefully managed, leading organizations such as Unicef have developed guidelines to ensure that their brands are used correctly and coherently. They recognize that good design management

Table 9.6 Formulating strategic directions for not-for-profit design-led branding

Success factors	Descriptions	Practical suggestions	Examples/methods
Anticipate and manage resistance.	As design and brand are perceived as costs rather than investments, revising/refreshing the brand and investing in design can lead to both internal and external resistance.	**Have a compelling story:** Develop a clear and consistent logic behind branding activities incorporating all stakeholders and carefully disseminate it.	Design can help bring the story to life for all groups.
		Tailor your message: Whilst maintaining clear central values, adjust your story/messages to suit all key stakeholders based on their motivations – e.g., explaining to donors how much money will be used in design and branding.	Design research can obtain insight about each group and thus messages can be modified appropriately.
		Be flexible and available: Choose a good mix of appropriate communication channels that ensure that the story is effectively communicated.	Design can help connect to each group effectively.
		Listen and respond: Prepare to answer and respond to various questions both prior to launch and post-launch of the brand	Design can help a brand positively respond to comments/ suggestions from all stakeholders.
Keep loyalists on your side.	Ensure that the design and branding activities do not disengage any stakeholders.	**Build on existing trust:** Gain in-depth understanding of what stakeholders value and show how these aspects will continue in the future.	Design research can gain in-depth understanding of key stakeholders and identify their values and motivations.
		Keep an open dialogue: Shape visions and strategic directions with stakeholders rather than impose goals and objectives on them.	Co-design process can ensure stakeholder engagement and reconcile their differences.
Maintain momentum post-launch.	The real changes come after the (re-)launch of the brand. It is vital to maintain momentum.	**Develop hallmarks:** Create a hallmark which, in this case, is a proof-point that captures the essence of the brand idea.	E.g. Design has been used to transform Oxfam's second-hand shops into the brand hallmark that displays products from around the world. This helps reinforce the message about Fairtrade and global poverty.
		Engage and empower: Invite employees, volunteers and the public to continually co-create with the brand in order to strengthen emotional bonds.	Participatory design process can help connect with internal and external stakeholders.

requires flexibility. Unicef therefore uses keywords, such as simple, optimistic, bold and contemporary, to describe its design language rather than providing a rigid framework. To ensure that people understand rationales behind the design choices and the messages that the charity wants to disseminate, all visual elements are fully explained. For instance, the lowercase font was chosen for the logo in order to give a friendly and approachable image. Examples of how the brand should be applied, as well as "Do's and Don'ts" are given. This shows that the organization takes design and brand seriously and sees them as important factors representing who they are and what they stand for. For more information see http://www.unicef.org/tfyr-macedonia/Brand_ToolKit_EN_Jan2011(1).pdf

9.7.3   Designing Activities, Environments and Cultures to Engage the Public

People volunteer because the cause is very important to them and they want to improve things (Communities and Local Government, 2010). Thus, the design strategy must support the clear and positive communication of tangible results and brand values that are relevant to people. Core components of the brand strategy – vision, action and expression – must be aligned, (Wheeler, 2009). Wheeler's framework to achieve this is shown in Table 9.7 can be used to generate many pragmatic components of the design strategy.

Designing Engagement Activities

Design can go beyond identity, campaigns and events and use powerful storytelling and emotional design principles to engage people. Programmes such as Comic Relief (www.comicrelief.com) and Sport Relief (www.sportrelief.com), demonstrate how fun, enjoyment and humour can engage people to volunteer, donate money and/or carry out good deeds. Another example of how to use design effectively to link "having fun" with "doing good" is GoodGym (www.goodgym.org) which pairs people who would like to get fit with isolated older persons in their local areas. GoodGym members get to do exercises while running errands for older people who take the role of coach to keep them motivated. This way, the exercise becomes more purposeful and fulfilling and is considered much better than mechanically running alone on a treadmill. The prospect of losing weight and getting fit whilst helping others has proved a captivating idea.

Table 9.7   Designing activities, environments and cultures to engage the public

Brands	Vision	Actions	Expression	Experience
Greenpeace	Campaigning for a green and peaceful world	Designing compelling campaigns to raise awareness and attract supporters	Designing visuals: Powerful name • Plain and simple logo/ typeface	Using creative ideas and sometimes shocking tactics to convey messages

Doing good while having fun has been taken further by some organizations which use digital games as a catalyst to bring about social change. A leading example is Games for Change (www.gamesforchange.org) a not-for-profit organization established to create and distribute digital games for humanitarian and educational purposes, which offers 143 non-commercial games covering a wide range of issues, such as poverty, human rights and health. The games include strategic planning and role playing. Contemporary digital games are regarded as powerful tools to raise awareness of social and environmental issues, such as climate change and world food shortages. They are also used to enhance civic engagement and encourage desirable behaviours, such as sensible alcohol drinking. The use and benefits of such games is supported by the director of game research and development at the Institute for the Future (TED, 2010), who pointed out that the design of games addressing real world problems which are challenging but winnable, can invite and attract people who are not currently engaged with social and environmental issues to become more involved.

Zynga, a social game leader, successfully supported the Save the Children charity in 2009 to raise money for its Japan Earthquake Tsunami Children Emergency Fund by enabling in-game donations through virtual goods purchases in Zynga games like *FarmVille*. All of the income from the sale of the virtual goods was donated to Tsunami relief. According to reports more than one million US dollars were donated by gamers within 36 hours.

Using digital games as a means to enhance civic engagement has strong potential. Fogg (2003) proposed that technologies can be used to influence people's attitude and behaviour changes. He explained that technologies can be used first as a tool to making the targeted behaviour easier to do, second as a medium to allow people to see consequences of certain behaviours and third as a social actor by rewarding people with positive feedback. Experts stress that "the goal of successful game design is the creation of meaningful play" (Salen and Zimmerman, 2004), and this creates an opportunity for designers to link the meaning through cause-and-consequence relationships that can promote desirable attitudes and behaviours.

Freerice.com (http://freerice.com/) is a not-for-profit organization owned and supported by the United Nations World Food Programme. The organization aims to "provide education to everyone for free and help end world hunger by providing rice to hungry people for free." To achieve this aim the organization designed and set up online quiz games, whereby for every answer that the player gets right, the organization promises to donate ten grains of rice through the World Food Programme. At the core is a clear explanation of cause-and-consequence relationships and this helps the organization to successfully engage a wide-ranging audience to provide free education to people on various subjects, such as English, maths, science, geography and humanities. Consequently the participants learn through playing and doing the good deed of donating the rice at the same time.

However, not all games are so successful at changing attitudes and behaviours. *Darfur is Dying* (www.darfurisdying.com) is a survival game simulating the brutality of genocide in the Darfur region of Sudan. The objective of the game is for players to negotiate their way to forage for water urgently needed for the refugee camp while making sure that they will not be captured by the Janjaweed militia and face a horrific death. Despite the fact that the game was well received by players worldwide, and its success in raising awareness globally, the real crisis remains unaffected. Thus, the challenge of connecting the game with actual activities remains, and as yet it cannot deliver the desired behavioural changes. Big-D design thinking is required to making the act of playing meaningful and to avoid accusations of exploiting, or even glorifying, human suffering.

Designing Environments and Cultures

Design strategies should be developed which go beyond creating campaigning materials and address the right environment and climate for collaboration and sharing. The Glass-House Community Led Design (www.theglasshouse.org.uk) offers good practices on how design can be used to create appropriate environment and culture for such.

The Glass-House Community Led Design is an independent UK national charity supporting and promoting public participation and leadership in the design of the built environment and collaborative design processes. The charity was founded on the principle that the quality of surrounding environments directly affects people's quality of life and, thus, local people have the right to be at the heart of decision making about their places. Built environments principally fulfil functional needs, but The Glass-House encourages design to go beyond tangible objects and deliver solutions to emotional needs. They focus on the design process and give much attention to the activities before the construction takes place by creating an insightful understanding of a place, and activities after the construction is completed which reveal the changes in people's behaviours and relationship with place.

The organization sees itself as an independent enabler which offers a wide range of support for communities and the professionals with whom they collaborate by, for example, providing a bespoke training programme or by injecting innovation into professional practice.

Discussion, understanding and respect for all parties to the design process are central to the delivering of solutions which satisfy all stakeholders. One of the ways in which The Glass-House promotes this is by organizing a debate series every year that brings together communities, local authority officers, builders and developers, housing associations, design practitioners, universities and students in plenary sessions and "asks them difficult questions" about wide ranging issues concerning relationships of people, place and practice. These vibrant debates can help to remove or ameliorate stereotypes and misconceptions and promote open honest conversations and a better understanding of others reality. During one of the debates, a park manager explained that:

> I don't like skateboarders. It's not because of the reason you think it is. I don't like them because of the wax on the bottom of their skateboards. When they glide across the steps or benches, it leaves a wax surface that I've got no cleaning agent in the world to get rid of it.

The debates also focus people's minds on the big picture of how places are shaped. "Imagine you are building for someone you love" was the plea from another audience member, responding to the question of how we can make better places that are valued by a community and respond to their needs.

Design strategy is used to find new and attractive ways to engage people and encourage them to visualize and generate ideas about their spaces. For example, in order to help people to think and share ideas collectively about a playground, the organization put art and craft materials in a park and invited families to design models of play equipment. The Glass-House has also used interesting props, such as straw bales, to help people visualize spatial relationships, like where the walls and doors would be in a space. Replicating the designers' use of mock-ups, the straw bales were left in an open space and people were encouraged to experiment with them. Through good use of design thinking, community members became more engaged and were happy to participate in playful, yet meaningful activities. Further, by applying the techniques of designers the people began to think outside the box. Accepting the right of a broad representation from the community to play an active role in designing their own environment is an important tenet for human rights and good use of design approaches, e.g. co-design, can help create the inductive climate for collaboration.

To get all stakeholders together to create a shared vision for change, it is necessary to find a "neutral space" where everybody feels comfortable and valued, and is treated as equal. Designers and public artists who continue to believe they are the only people capable of creating the new environment can find this transition to sharing uncomfortable. The Glass-House works to create an environment in which all those collaborating in a design process feel valued and respected and which draws on the spectrum of experience and skills to come up with more informed and creative design solutions.

Table 9.8 Methods for assessing social impacts

Tools	Purposes	Methodology
Cost-effectiveness analysis	Combining identified measures of impacts with costs so that programmes, policies and projects can be ranked based on this effectiveness.	Comparing cost to non-financial benefits or impacts (e.g. cost per high school graduate).
Cost-benefit analysis	Quantifying the benefits and costs associated with an intervention and comparing them to see which one is greater.	Identifying results and costs and then comparing net present value of costs and benefits (e.g. which sector gained most benefit).
Social return on investment	Helping practitioners and investors measure success/ achievements and make decisions regarding the on-going use of resources.	Using a set of matrices to quantify the social returns, e.g. individuals' wellbeing.

Continued

Table 9.8   Continued

Tools	Purposes	Methodology
Robin Hood Foundation's benefit-cost ratio	Translating outputs (immediate results of a programme) and outcomes (impacts on wider audiences) into tangible value, e.g. the boost of incomes, living standards and general wellbeing.	Comparing the estimated earning boost with "Robin Hood" factors – the grant and contributions made by the organization. (Principally associated with the fair distribution of wealth.)
Acumen Fund BACO ratio	Quantifying an estimated social output and comparing it with alternative charitable options designed for that particular social issue.	Calculating net cost per unit of social output and comparing results with similar schemes as a measure of effective use of resources.
Hewlett Foundation expected return	Asking appropriate questions for every investment portfolio: *What is the goal? How much good can it do? Is it a good bet? How much difference will we make? What is the price tag?*	Identifying targets, ideal outputs, the likelihood of success, and associated contributions/costs and then establishing the returns.
Cost per impact	Providing tools to help philanthropists understand potential of their contributions.	Multiplying "cost per beneficiary" with "success rate."
Foundation investment bubble chart	Using bubble charts to represent number of people/beneficiaries reached by the organization and its programmes.	Using size of bubble and colour coding (e.g. yellow = mature organization) to visualize results.

9.7.4   Deciding Whether an Organization Achieves Its Strategic Goals

Tools have been developed to help not-for-profit organizations to check their performance, especially to assess the social values of their activities. A report by Tuan (2008) for the Bill and Melinda Gates Foundation identified eight approaches to the measurement of social impacts. Some approaches have already been discussed in Chapter 7. However, further methods for measuring social impacts are presented in Table 9.8. Further information on these methods can be found at https://docs.gatesfoundation.org/Documents/wwl-report-measuring-estimating-social-value-creation.pdf

9.8   CASE STUDY 7 – DESIGN-LED NOT-FOR-PROFIT ORGANIZATION: WWF

The World Wildlife Fund (WWF), now 50 years old, is the world's leading independent environmental organization. WWF addresses global threats to people and nature, working in 100 countries. The charity employs an experienced full-time design manager to manage their design activities across a broad spectrum of activities. The recognition of their aesthetically pleasing logo is almost universal. Their strategy is to generate great creative ideas and use design to maximize their impact. Good use of visual design is evident in many of their campaigning materials, using powerful images and compelling messages.

One example of a recent high impact idea was the WWF Earth Hour which reminded people that we have only one planet on which we live and encouraged millions of people around the world to switch off their lights at the same hour, at 8.30 pm on 23 March 2013.

To address these mega issues WWF works closely with partners like Coca-Cola and Avon Cosmetics and collaborated with Sony and IDEO to launch the *Open Planet Ideas* platform (www.openplanetideas.com) which gives people the opportunity to explore and exchange ideas on how today's technology could be repurposed for environmental or social good, thus putting human needs first. The final outcome (+U) is an application that matches local people with local projects. Its use of the latest geolocation and gaming technology can help make volunteering quicker, easier and more social. It has a potential to attract more people to volunteering and bring changes and improvements to their communities/environments.

Working in partnership with BioRegional (www.bioregional.co.uk), WWF declared "if everyone in the world lived like an average European we would need three planets to live on" and "If everyone in the world lived like an average North American we would need five planets to live on" (World Wildlife Fund, 2006) and established ten principles for sustainability:

1. *Zero carbon*: Reduce and ultimately eliminate carbon emissions caused by fossil fuel use in heating, cooling and providing power and heat to buildings.
2. *Zero waste*: All materials should be valued as potential resources, through reusing, reprocessing or energy from waste.
3. *Sustainable transport*: Reduce carbon emissions relating to travel.
4. *Local and sustainable materials*: Choose materials to deliver high performance in use with minimized impact in manufacture and delivery.
5. *Local and sustainable food*: Promote local, seasonal and organic produce resulting in reduced emissions from food production, packaging and transportation.
6. *Sustainable water use*: Reduce energy used in water supply and waste water management; reduce local flooding risks.
7. *Natural habitats and wildlife*: Conserve and enhance biodiversity.
8. *Culture and heritage*: Engender a sense of community through enhancing or reviving valuable aspects of local culture and heritage.
9. *Equity and fair trade*: Promote social justice through local economic development and fair trade internationally.
10. *Health and happiness*: Increase health and overall wellbeing of all involved in the project through design, facilities and operation.

As a further measure to help people adopt these principles, WWF provides an ebook and other publications showcasing their selected good examples of sustainable products, buildings and services which successfully adopted this approach. Mata de Sesimbra, Portugal, is one of the examples. The Mata de Sesimbra is an eco-tourism project combining ecological buildings, non-polluting transport means, reforestation and nature protection.

For more information: www.oneplanetcommunities.org/communities/endorsed-communities/mata-de-sesimbra/

The use of design is embedded in all WWF operations, from effective communication (channels, networks and graphics) aimed at high-involvement audiences, through to merchandising of products such as stationery and books for lower-involvement consumers. Wally, Wendy and Fang merchandise are examples of well-designed, simple and playful products with inclusive appeal. The products are also tagged with bite-sized information regarding wildlife and environment, raising awareness and reinforcing brand values in a subtle manner.

WWF's recent programme of "adopting" wildlife animals, demonstrates great understanding of the general public. Donors are motivated by good causes and strong results. Details of adopted animals will be regularly updated and sent to donors. The donation methods are simple, straightforward and flexible and the amount of donated payment can be easily changed.

Some questions for discussion:

- How can WWF use design to communicate the benefits of protecting wildlife to human beings?
- To what extent does the manager of design strategy need to be aware of debates and controversy surrounding environmental issues e.g. global warming?

9.9   SUMMARY OF KEY POINTS

- Design strategy is now a powerful tool for addressing concerns across the entire spectrum of caring for human life.
- Many benefits can be derived from using design thinking to address and solve complex transportation systems.
- Design thinking is successfully applied in contributing to and driving healthcare improvements.
- Better places to work, live and play can be achieved using design strategy.
- Design strategy plays a major role in participatory city design and branding.
- Education systems and practice can be improved by design.
- Charities need design strategy for successful branding and maintaining/improving their performance.
- The 4Ds design management model can be applied to support not-for-profit organizations by identifying opportunities, engaging and inspiring people, delivering consistent added value and continuous review of performance.

9.10   FURTHER CONSIDERATIONS

9.10.1   Exercise the Mind…

- How can design increase people's trust in charities?
- Which charities offer the most compelling brand messages?

- Can communities design their own solutions without professional designers?
- Should design thinking be included in the school curriculum?
- What examples of good design thinking can you identify in the public environment in which you live?
- What further improvements in your healthcare and education systems could be addressed by design thinking?

9.11 GLOSSARY

Not-for-profit organizations (or nonprofit organizations: NPOs) are organizations that were set goals other than making and distributing profits. Their purposes often relate to societal or environmental issues. This group covers a wide range of organizations, e.g. charities, voluntary groups, local sport clubs (aiming to support grassroots-level sport rather than earning money) and faith groups. Although, these organizations may generate profits, they use incomes to support their main purposes, e.g. humanitarian activities.

Place branding is an umbrella term covering subjects, such as city branding and nation branding. The idea is rooted in the fact that, nowadays, counties/cities are competing with each other for attention from investors, tourists, talented professionals, students, etc. In order to compete effectively, cities and countries have to (re)discover their core values so that they can differentiate themselves from other competitors.

Soft systems methodology is a systematic approach proposed by Checkland and Scholes to help solve complex ill-defined (or soft) problems. In this case "the sum is greater than the parts." In order to tackle a complex problem, it is crucial to see the big picture – see how everything is interconnected and interrelated. By clearly visualizing the situation that needs addressing (or the system), the problem can be properly defined and tackled.

The third sector is sometimes called the voluntary sector, civic sector or the not-for-profit sector. It is referred as the "third" in relation to the public and private sectors. This sector comprises of various not-for-profit nongovernmental organizations, e.g. charities, voluntary groups, universities, political parties, social clubs, community interest companies (CICs) and social enterprises. For more information see: www.ncvo-vol.org.uk/sites/default/files/uk_civil_society_almanac_2012_section.pdf.

9.12 REFERENCES AND ADDITIONAL READING

Aitken, R. and Campelo, A. (2011) The Four R's of Place Brandin. *Journal of Marketing Management, 27* (9–10), 913–933.

Anholt, S. (2004) Branding Places and Nations. In R. Clifton and J. Simmons (eds) *Brands and Branding: The Economist Series*. London: Profile Books, 213–226.

Baxter, H., Mugglestone, M. and Maher, L. (2009), *The EBD Approach: Experience Based Design: Using Patient and Staff Experience to Design Better Healthcare*

Services. Adridge: Institute for Innovation and Improvement, National Health Service.

Botsman, R. and Roger, R. (2010), *What's Mine is Yours: The Rise of Collaborative Consumer.* New York: HarperCollins Publishers.

Boyd, H., Mckernon, S. and Old, A. (2010), *Health Service Co-design: Working with Patients to Improve Healthcare Services.* Auckland: Waitemata District Health Board.

Boyle, D. and Harris, MI. (2009), *The Challenge of Co-production.* London: NESTA.

BSI (British Standards Institute) (2008) *BS 7000-10:2008: Design Management Systems – Part 10: Vocabulary of Terms Used in Design Management.* London: British Standards Institute.

Butterworth, I. (2000) *The Relationship Between the Built Environment and Well-Being: A Literature Review.* Melbourne: Victorian Health Promotion Foundation.

Cannon, R. and Newble, D. (2000). *A Handbook for Teaching in Universities and Colleges* (4th edn). London: Kogan Page.

Charity Commission. (2007), *Stand and Deliver – The Future for Charity Providing Public Services.* Liverpool: Charity Commission.

Checkland, P. and Scholes, J. (1999) *Soft System Methodology in Action.* Chichester: John Wiley and Sons.

Communities and Local Government. (2010) *2008–09 Citizenship Survey: Volunteering and Charitable Giving Topic Report.* London: Department for Communities and Local Government.

Cooper, R., Evans, G. and Boyko, C. (2009). *Designing Sustainable Cities: Decision Making Tools and Resources for Design.* Chichester: John Wiley and Sons.

Cooper, R., Wootton, A. B., Davey, C. L. and Press, M. (2005) Breaking the Cycle: Fundamentals of Crime-Proofing Design. In R.V. Clarke and G.R. Newman (eds) *Designing out Crime from Products and Systems (Crime Prevention Studies Vol. 18).* Criminal Justice Press, 179–201.

Cottam, H. and Leadbeater, C. (2004) *Red Paper 1: HEALTH: Co-creating Service.* [WWW] Design Council. Available from: http://www.designcouncil. info/mt/RED/health/REDPaper01.pdf (Accessed: 27 June 2014)

Dearden, A., Lam, B., William-Powlett, K. and Brodie, E. (2012) Exploring Co-design in the Voluntary Sector. 18th *NCVO/VSSN Researching the Voluntary Sector Conference 2012*, 10–11 September 2012, University of Birmingham, UK.

Design Council. (2003), *Design for Patient Safety.* London: Design Council.

Design Council (2003), *Think Thief: A Designer's Guide to Design out Crime.* [WWW] Design Council. Available from: http://www.designcouncil.org.uk/ Documents/Documents/Publications/Think%20Thief_Design_Council.pdf

Design Council. (2005) Learning Environment Campaign Prospectus: From the Inside Looking Out. [WWW] Design Council. Available from: http://www. designcouncil.org.uk/Documents/Documents/Publications/Learning%20 Environments%20Campaign_Design_Council.pdf [Accessed 25 July 2013].

Design Council (2006) RED HEALTH Report: Design Notes 01: The Diabetes Agenda. [WWW] Design Council. Available from: http://www.designcouncil. info/RED/health/REDDESIGNNOTES01Bolton.pdf (Accessed: 27 June 2014)

Design Council (2008) *Designing Demand: Richard Seymour.* [WWW] Design Council. Available from: http://www.designcouncil.org.uk/our-work/leadership/

designing-demand/what-is-designing-demand/audio-about-designing-demand/ richard-seymour/ (Accessed: 9 July 2012).

Design for All Europe: EIDD (2004) The EIDD Stockholm Declaration 2004. [WWW] Design for All Europe. Available from: http://www.designforalleurope. org/Design-for-All/EIDD-Documents/Stockholm-Declaration/ [Accessed 27 June 2014].

EDC (Cambridge Engineering Design Centre). (2010) *Inclusive Design Process* [WWW] Inclusive design toolkit. Available from: http://www-edc.eng.cam. ac.uk/betterdesign/process/ [Accessed 17 July 2013].

Florida, R. (2002), *The Rise of the Creative Class – and how it is Transforming Leisure, Community and Everyday Life*. New York: Basic Books.

Fogg, B. J. (2003) *Persuasive Technology: Using Computers to Change What We Think and Do*. London: Morgan Kaufmann Publishers.

Gilmore, F. (2002) A Country – can it be Repositioned? Spain – the Success Story of Country Branding. *Brand Management*, 9 (4–5), 281–293.

Gotah, W. (2007) *Patient Dignity*. Master Dissertation. School of Engineering and Design. Brunel University.

Gupta, I. (2010) *What Matters Now*. [WWW] Available from: http://sethgodin. typepad.com/files/what-matters-now-1.pdf [Accessed 25 June 2011].

Hales, G. (2011) *Not-for-profit Branding: Maximizing Chances for Success*. [WWW] Interbrand. Available from: http://www.interbrand.com/Libraries/ Branding_Studies/Interbrand_Not-for-profit_Branding.sflb.ashx [Accessed 26 June 2011].

Kavaratzis, M. and Ashworth, G. J. (2008) Place Marketing: How Did We Get Here and Where Are We Going? *Journal of Place Management and Development*, 1 (2), 150–165.

Kotler, P., Asplund, C., Rein, I. and Heider, D. (1999), *Marketing Places Europe: Attracting Investments, Industries, Residents and Visitors to European Cities, Communities, Regions, and Nations*. London: Pearson Education.

Lam, B., Chan, Y. K., Whittle, J., Binner, J., Frankova, K. and Garton, L. (2011) Voice Your View: An Inclusive Approach to Civic Engagement. *Proceedings of 6th International Conference on Inclusive Design (Include 2011)*. London, April 2011, http://www.hhc.rca.ac.uk/2968/all/1/include-2011.aspx.

Landry, C. (2000), *The Creative City: A Toolkit for Urban Innovators*. London: Earthscan.

Papanek, Victor (1971), *Design for the Real World: Human Ecology and Social Change*. New York: Pantheon Books.

Phatanarajata, L. (2010) *Design and Branding Model for Children Charity in Thailand*. Master Dissertation. School of Engineering and Design. Brunel University.

Press, M. and Cooper, R. (2003) *The design experience: The role of design and designers in the twenty-first century*. Aldershot: Ashgate Publishing.

Ramaswamy, V. and Gouillart, F. (2010) Building the Co-creating Enterprise. *Harvard Business Review*, October, 100–109.

Salen, K. and Zimmerman, E. (2004) *Rules of Play: Game Design Fundamentals*. Cambridge, Massachusetts: The MIT Press.

Saxton, J. (2002), *Polishing the Diamond: Values, Image and Brand as a Source of Strength for Charities*. [WWW] Available from: http://www.nfpsyn-ergy.net/includes/documents/cm_docs/2008/p/3_polishing_the_diamond.pdf [Accessed 25 June 2011].

Tan, P. (2003) *Down to the Core: Branding Not-for-Profits.* [WWW] Brand Channel. Available from: http://www.brandchannel.com/features_effect.asp?pf_id=140 [Accessed 26 June 2011].

TED. (2010) Jane McGonigal: Gaming can Make a Better World [online video]. Available from: http://www.ted.com/talks/jane_mcgonigal_gaming_can_make_a_better_world.html [Accessed 29 August 2012].

The RL Mace Universal Design Institute. (2011) *Principles of Universal Design.* [WWW] The RL Mace Universal Design Institute. Available from: http://www.udinstitute.org/principles.php [Accessed 17 June 2011].

Transport for London. (2009) *Product Design Guidelines.* [WWW] Transport for London. Available from: http://www.tfl.gov.uk/assets/downloads/corporate/tfl-product-design-guidelines-issue02.pdf [Accessed 22 July 2013].

Tuan, M. T. (2008) *Profiles of Eight Integrated Cost Approaches to Measuring and/or Estimating Social Value Creation.* [WWW] The Bill and Miranda Gates Foundation. Available from: http://www.gatesfoundation.org/learning/Documents/WWL-profiles-eight-integrated-cost-approaches.pdf [Accessed 6 July 2011]

Van Gelder, S. and Allan, M. (2006) *City Branding: How Cities Compete in the 21st Century.* London/Amsterdam: Placebrands.

Walsh, B. (2011) 10 Ideas That Will Change the World. *TIME Magazine*, March 17, 2011.

Ward, S. V. (1998) *Selling Places: The Marketing and Promotion of Town and Cities 1850–2000* [WWW] E & FN Spon. Available from: http://journals.cambridge.org/action/displayIssue?iid=64584 [Accessed 27 July 2012].

Wheeler, A. (2009) *Designing Brand Identity: An Essential Guide for the Entire Branding Team* (3rd edn). New Jersey: John Wiley & Sons.

World Wildlife Fund (2006) *Living Planet Report 2006.* [WWW] World Wildlife Fund. Available from: http://wwf.panda.org/about_our_earth/all_publications/living_planet_report/living_planet_report_timeline/lp_2006/ [Accessed 24 July 2013].

9.13   ONLINE RESOURCES

1. Design Council: www.designcouncil.org.uk
2. The Glass-House Community Led Design: www.theglasshouse.org.uk
3. NHS's Experience Based Design: www.institute.nhs.uk/quality_and_value/experienced_based_design/the_ebd_approach_(experience_based_design).html
4. Designs of the time 2007 (Dott 07):www.designcouncil.org.uk/our-work/challenges/Communities/Dott-07/
5. One Planet Living: www.oneplanetliving.org

Index